Cohabitants and the law

Cohabitants and the law

Anne Barlow, BA, Solicitor and Lecturer in Law
at the University of Wales, Aberystwyth

with contributions from
David Josiah-Lake, LLB, Solicitor,
Fisher Meredith Solicitors, London

2001
Butterworths
London

Members of the LexisNexis Group worldwide

United Kingdom	Butterworths Tolley, a Division of Reed Elsevier (UK) Ltd, Halsbury House, 35 Chancery Lane, LONDON, WC2A 1EL, and 4 Hill Street, EDINBURGH EH2 3JZ
Argentina	Abeledo Perrot, Jurisprudencia Argentina and Depalma, BUENOS AIRES
Australia	Butterworths, a Division of Reed International Books Australia Pty Ltd, CHATSWOOD, New South Wales
Austria	ARD Betriebsdienst and Verlag Orac, VIENNA
Canada	Butterworths Canada Ltd, MARKHAM, Ontario
Chile	Publitecsa and Conosur Ltda, SANTIAGO DE CHILE
Czech Republic	Orac sro, PRAGUE
France	Editions du Juris-Classeur SA, PARIS
Hong Kong	Butterworths Asia (Hong Kong), HONG KONG
Hungary	Hvg Orac, BUDAPEST
India	Butterworths India, NEW DELHI
Ireland	Butterworths (Ireland) Ltd, DUBLIN
Italy	Giuffré, MILAN
Malaysia	Malayan Law Journal Sdn Bhd, KUALA LUMPUR
New Zealand	Butterworths of New Zealand, WELLINGTON
Poland	Wydawnictwa Prawnicze PWN, WARSAW
Singapore	Butterworths Asia, SINGAPORE
South Africa	Butterworths Publishers (Pty) Ltd, DURBAN
Switzerland	Stämpfli Verlag AG, BERNE
USA	LexisNexis, DAYTON, Ohio

A CIP Catalogue for this book is available from the British Library.

[Publishing history if required]

ISBN 0 406 94151 3

Typeset by Kerrypress Ltd, Luton, Bedfordshire.
Printed and bound in Great Britain by William Clowes Ltd, Beccles and London.

Visit Butterworths LexisNexis *direct* at www.butterworths.com

Preface

Since the last edition of this book in 1997, we have witnessed some interesting developments in the law as it affects both opposite-sex and perhaps in particular same-sex cohabitants. This is an area of law where the implementation of the Human Rights Act 1998 in October 2000 was also awaited with interest and has perhaps had more indirect than direct influence as to how Parliament and the courts have developed and will continue to develop the law relating to cohabitants. One turning point for same-sex cohabitants came at the end of 1999 in *Fitzpatrick v Sterling Housing Association Ltd* [2000] 1 FCR 21. Here, the House of Lords accepted for the first time that in the context of Rent Act tenancy succession at least, same-sex partners, whilst not able to live together as "husband and wife" could constitute members of each other's families (see Chapter 10). The new Criminal Injuries Compensation Scheme for fatal injuries goes further, recognising same-sex cohabitants of two years standing as well as opposite cohabitants as eligible claimants under the scheme (see Chapter 5). Similarly, the Law Commission in its report *Claims for Wrongful Death,* 1999, Law Com. No 263, has also recommended that the Fatal Accident Act 1975 should be amended to permit claims by same-sex partners, who alongside opposite-sex cohabitants should become eligible to claim bereavement damages, currently a preserve of the married (see Chapter 5).

Nonetheless, despite demographic trends in family restructuring away from marriage becoming even more firmly established during this period, with opposite-sex cohabitation predicted to double by 2021 (Shaw and Haskey (1999), *Population Trends 95*, p. 13), the response of the law has remained very piecemeal. Thus there is still no cohesive body of law which constitutes a 'divorce law equivalent' for cohabitants in England and Wales, whether same- or opposite-sex, and the law affecting them still ranges over many areas of expertise. This is in contrast not only now to Sweden, Australia and Canada, who continue to lead the field and promote equality between all families, whether centred on married or cohabiting, same or opposite-sex partnerships, but also to many of our European neighbours. Denmark and Germany have introduced partnership laws enabling same-sex couples to register their relationships and achieve a status equivalent to marriage in legal terms. France and the Netherlands now have such partnership registers available to both same- and opposite-sex cohabitants, creating a new form of legally recongnised relationship giving marriage-like rights but determinable by either party on notice on agreed terms. Whilst the Law Commission's consultation paper on homesharing is still awaited, both the Law Society (in 1999) and the Solicitors' Family Law Association in 2000 have put forward proposals for a cohesive reform of cohabitation law, which would include both same and opposite-sex cohabitants and extend family law remedies to them on relationship breakdown (see Chapter 1). In Scotland, the Scottish Executive has finally adopted the Scottish Law Commission's 1992 proposals on reform of cohabitation law in its White Paper on *Parents and Children* (2000) and, in addition to updating their more marriage-centric law to acknowledge the existence of cohabiting relationships, also intends to permit claims by cohabitants who have suffered "economic disadvantage" as a consequence of a cohabitation relationship (see Chapters 1, 10 & 11). In Northern Ireland, the Law Reform Advisory Committee has made radical recommendations which include the automatic sharing of beneficial interests of the family home purchased or transferred after a cohabitation period of two years (*Matrimonial Property*, 2000, Belfast: the Stationery Office). For the moment in England and Wales, however, in the absence of a successful Private Members' Bill, there is no prospect of speedy reform.

The purpose of the third edition therefore remains to draw together the disparate areas of law affecting cohabitants; but in updated form. In order to ensure that full justice was done to the many procedural and legal aid reforms which have taken place since the last edition, I have been greatly assisted by contributions from solicitor and author David Josiah-Lake who, unlike myself, has not forsaken private practice, and thus has been able to bring his more recent practical experience to the book. This edition again concentrates on the position of cohabitants, whether heterosexual or same-sex, who are living or have lived together in fairly long-term relationships and the term "unmarried family" used in the book should be construed in this context.

The original structure of the book has been retained in this third edition, with the first part (Chapters 1–6) examining the law which affects the unmarried family when living together as a unit. In particular, the proposed changes to give unmarried fathers parental responsibility on joint birth registration are considered in Chapter 2; the Homelessness Bill currently before Parliament and the implications of the House of Lords decision in *Fitzpatrick* is looked at in Chapter 3. The implications for cohabitants of Children's Tax Credit and Working Families Tax Credit are set out in Chapter 4, with Chapter 5 looking at developments in the law where a cohabitant dies and Chapter 6 marking the fall out of the approach to financial provision on divorce post-*White v White* where a cohabitant or their partner is involved in on-going divorce proceedings with a former spouse. Part II picks up some of the same themes but with the focus on relationship breakdown. Developments in the law relating to domestic violence contained in Part IV Family Law Act 1996 and the Protection from Harassment Act 1997 are discussed in Chapter 7, alongside reforms to the homelessness legislation specifically directed at better protecting victims of domestic violence. The advent of CAFCASS is noted in Chapter 8 with developments in the Children Act case law meriting much discussion. The Child Support Act 1991 has been substantially amended by the Child Support, Pensions and Social Security Act 2000 and has again made radical reforms which come fully into force in April 2002 and this is discussed in Chapter 9. The provisions in Part IV of the 1996 Act permitting transfer of tenancies between cohabitants on relationship breakdown have thrown up some practical difficulties which are considered in Chapter 10. The continuing unsatisfactory state of the law following recent cases relating to resulting and constructive trusts is explored in Chapter 11 and confirms the very real need for at the very least a clearer framework for the ground rules establishing such trusts in the family home context. Unfortunately, the long awaited Law Commission Consultation Paper on Homesharers (referred to in Chapter 11) which is considering reform of the law relating to the property rights of homesharers, has yet to see the light of day.

It is to be hoped that in the next five years the benefits of a more cohesive approach which acknowledges the benefits of treating all family law issues consistently, regardless of the chosen family structure, will commend themselves to the policy makers and legislators.

Once again the breadth of the subject matter has meant that it has not been possible to deal with all relevant topics in this edition. Both child abduction and the position of children of unmarried families in care are omitted as they are well documented in specialist texts.

Although it is felt the book will be a useful resource for those teaching family law, it is aimed primarily at the practitioner. This edition again includes (with the usual caveats!) suggested framework precedents for cohabitation agreements and declarations of trust in respect of the family home, which it is hoped will be of some practical use. The law referred to is that as of 1 October 2001.

I have once again been fortunate in the support and encouragement I have received in writing this book. Whilst taking full responsibility for all its imperfections, I would like to thank David Josiah-Lake for his valuable input to this edition and those of my colleagues at the University of Wales, Aberystwyth who have and assisted its progress through their comments and discussions on many issues.

Last but not least, I would like to thank my family – Mark, Rosa and Sylvie – for having once again accepted the disruptions to our family life during the writing process.

Anne Barlow
October 2001

Contents

Table of Statutes

Table of Statutory Instruments

Table of cases

D

I

J

K

Part I

Living together

Chapter 1

The cohabitation relationship

1 Introduction

1.01 One of the most difficult aspects of attempting to write a book about the 'unmarried family' is the lack of satisfactory terms to describe both the family arrangement itself and the adult members of such a family unit. Despite the increasing social acceptance of these relationships, this task becomes more difficult where it is attempted, as here, to encompass the legal position of both opposite-sex or heterosexual couples who are living together in a form of 'quasi-marriage', and same-sex or 'gay' couples living together as a joint unit in one household because of their relationship with each other.

1.02 The word 'cohabitation' has come to denote the situation where two people live together as husband and wife in a family framework analogous to marriage, without actually having gone through a ceremony of marriage. The parties involved in such an arrangement are often described as 'cohabitees', although the words mistress, common law husband/wife, *de facto* spouse and spouse equivalent are amongst a wealth of alternatives, none of which is completely satisfactory. Despite its common usage, it has often been pointed out that the word 'cohabitee' is grammatically incorrect and as in the last edition the term 'cohabitant', first used in Part IV Family Law Act 1996 (FLA 1996) is adopted here.

1.03 There is no formal definition of 'living together as husband and wife' but the phrase, or variations of it, is often used in a legal context (see for example s 62(1) FLA 1996). It is now clear that this phrase is, at least for the moment, limited to opposite-sex couples as confirmed in the House of Lords decision of *Fitzpatrick v Sterling Housing Association Ltd* [1999] 4 All GR 705. The Law Commission in its Fourteenth Annual Report acknowledged that there were inconsistencies in legal definition, but has not as yet addressed the problem:

> 'There is a growing tendency for the law to attach specific legal consequences to relationships outside marriage, but there is not as yet a wholly consistent approach in the different statutory provisions . . . It may well be that there are valid policy reasons which dictate the use of different language in different statutes; nevertheless there is clearly a risk that difficulties of interpretation will occur.' (Law Commission No. 97, para. 2.32).

It seems to be assumed, at least by Parliamentary draftsmen, that where a phrase such as 'living together as husband and wife' is used in statutes, such a situation is easily recognisable and thus not worthy of detailed definition. Whether or not such an assumption is justified is debatable, particularly as the definitions do vary from statute to statute. The Law Commission is still reviewing what it has described as the 'unfair, uncertain and illogical' law relating to the property rights of unmarried couples and other home-sharers, and it is hoped that a clear definition of cohabitation will emerge from this. Indeed, as noted below, both the Law Society and the Solicitors Family Law Association have proffered definitions which may eventually be adopted in statutory form. From a practitioner's point of view, however, for the moment each case has to be examined on its own facts in the context of the situation in which advice is sought. Thus for present purposes, attention is merely drawn to the fact that statutory definitions do vary and will be examined where appropriate in the ensuing chapters

1.04 It is worthy of note here that the European Court of Justice has held that the definition of the term 'spouse' does not include heterosexual cohabitants for the purposes of European Community Law (see *Netherlands v Reed*: 59/85 [1986] ECR 1283). However, and significantly, given the implementation in October 2000 of the Human Rights Act 1998 (HRA 1998), there has been an increasing recognition in Strasbourg of the unmarried cohabiting family. Thus in *X, Y and Z v United Kingdom* 20 EHRR CDG, a case involving the relationship between children born by AID to a mother whose cohabitant and the children's 'social father' was a female to male transsexual, the European Court of Human Rights held that whether or not a relationship amounting to 'family life' protected by Article 8 of the European Convention existed was a question of fact. Relevant factors to consider included whether the couple live together, the length of their relationship and whether they have demonstrated their commitment to each other by having children together or by any other means. Nonetheless, the position of same-sex cohabitants is not currently assisted by Strasbourg case law. Thus, the decision of the European Commission on Human Rights that where same-sex couples cohabit in a stable relationship, this does not fall within the scope of Article 8 of the Convention remains good law (see *X and Y v United Kingdom*, (Application 9369/81), 32 Decisions and Reports 220), although this of itself did not prevent the House of Lords finding that a surviving partner of a long-standing same-sex relationship was a member of his deceased partner's family for Rent Act tenancy succession purposes (*Fitzpatrick v Sterling Housing Association* [2000] 1 FLR 271). Furthermore, a decision that such a couple are not 'living together as husband and wife' which in turn means that one is not able to succeed to the council tenancy of the other on death, is not unjustifiably discriminatory within the meaning of Article 14 (*S v United Kingdom*, (Application 11716/85), 47 Decisions and Reports 275, and see further Chapter 3). Indeed the Law Commission's definition of cohabitants in s 62(1)(a) FLA 1996 states clearly that they are 'a man and a woman . . . living together as husband and wife' and a similarly heterosexual definition of cohabitants in both the Housing Act 1985 and the Housing Act 1988 prevents a surviving partner of a same-sex couple from succeeding to the tenancy of the rented family home as a cohabitant (see Chapter 3 below).

1.05 Whilst the term 'cohabitation' is usually applied in the context of couples comprising one man and one woman, it is a term equally appropriate to homosexual (or gay) couples who live together as a result of their relationship with each other. This raises the question of whether their respective situations display any common factors or problems which affect legal status. In both cases, each member of the couple, during the currency of the relationship, would normally regard the other member of the couple as their 'next of kin' – the person whom they would wish to succeed to their estate or part of it if they were to die without leaving a Will, and the person to be notified in case of an accident or other emergency. Such couples organise themselves and live as one unit in society, which often involves purchasing or renting accommodation together and jointly purchasing household goods. It may be that no provision for contingencies such as the death of one of the parties or breakdown of the relationship is made. In addition, there are common misconceptions about the legal consequences of cohabiting or joint ownership, upon which couples may erroneously rely.

1.06 As is often the case, popular expectation and the true legal position of cohabitants may not coincide. For example, unless specific provision is made, the law does not as a rule allow people to appoint a person of their choosing as their next of kin for any purpose, whereas upon marriage a spouse automatically assumes this role.

1.07 This state of affairs means that unmarried cohabiting couples, be they heterosexual or not, are in much greater need than their married counterparts of legal advice on the consequences of joint enterprises undertaken or proposed by them. Certainly, where advice is sought on breakdown of the relationship or on death, the emotional effects and social consequences as well as the legal implications may be far more complex where the relationship involved cohabitation than otherwise would be the case. It is therefore crucial that advisors are aware of this, not only when instructed to advise at a time of crisis, but also when advising during the currency of the relationship, for example in the joint purchase of a house. If clear advice as to the legal implications is given at that stage, and a record kept or a document drawn up setting out the parties' respective shares, or at least the stated intentions as to their beneficial interests, this may avoid a dispute in the future. It may also be a good time to mention the possibility of making Wills and the unsatisfactory nature of the law on intestacy with regard to cohabitants, who are in effect the chosen next of kin of the other.

1.08 In an increasing number of situations, legal rights or restrictions similar to those applicable to married couples have been extended to members of heterosexual cohabiting couples. This has principally been done by statute. Examples include the right to succeed to an assured tenancy under s 17 Housing Act 1988, the right to claim financial provision against a deceased partner's estate (s 1(1)(ba) and 1(1A) Inheritance (Provision for Family and Dependants) Act 1975); and the right to apply for the transfer of the family home on relationship breakdown (Sch 7 FLA 1996). In other situations, the law totally ignores the cohabitation relationship, as is nearly always the case with gay couples. Even though, as discussed below, it is now possible for gay cohabitants to obtain non-molestation orders and in some cases an occupation order under domestic violence legislation due to their living in the same household, they are not classed as 'cohabitants' and the relationship itself is not recognised as being in any way akin to marriage. Again in *Fitzpatrick*, the majority in the House of Lords were willing to accept that a same-sex cohabitant of 18 years' standing who had nursed his tetraplegic partner for eight years, clearly showed marriage-like commitment, and on the strength of this could be classed as 'a member of his partner's family' for Rent Act succession purposes. However, ironically they felt unable to accept the relationship as one falling within the definition of 'living as husband and wife'.

1.09 During the 1990s, the trend had been for legislation to extend rights of heterosexual cohabitants whilst continuing to privilege marriage by giving lesser rights to cohabitants than are enjoyed by married couples. Same-sex couples, on the other hand, were ignored. Interestingly, the Law Commission's current examination of cohabitants' property rights extends to gay couples and friends and relatives living together as well as those living together as husband and wife and thus if and when reform comes, it may extend beyond same and opposite-sex cohabitants. Despite the new political climate following the 1997 general election, the Law Commission's work on these matters remains unpublished but is apparently on-going. Thus, whilst there has been some reform of the immigration rules in favour of same-sex partners, there has been no noticeable change of approach in the new millennium towards issues raised by cohabiting relationships in the property context.

1.10 There are nonetheless many similarities in both the emotional and practical approaches taken by these two different types of cohabiting couple, and in their legal status. In addition, the legal response to same-sex cohabitation seems to be following the same pattern as that previously experienced in the heterosexual context, as vividly illustrated in *Fitzpatrick* (discussed further below in Chapter 3). For these reasons, the legal position of all cohabiting couples, with or without children, heterosexual or same-sex, is the subject of this book. It is therefore intended to use the words 'cohabitation' and 'cohabitant' in both the more common and the wider context where appropriate; although the reader can assume that unless otherwise indicated, reference will be to cohabitation between a man and a woman. In addition, the term 'partner' will be employed to describe the relationship of one of the parties to the other.

2 Social background and the impetus for reform

1.11 Marriage has always been society's preferred method of structuring family life and the rhetoric of the present and former governments has been keen to reassert its importance (see for example Chapter 4 of *Supporting Families*, 1998,). There is also a great deal of social pressure to marry yet cohabitation is continuing to increase.

1.12 In the case of same-sex couples, the reason to cohabit is simple. They are unable to enter into a legal marriage in this country and any 'marriage' is void (see s 11(c) Matrimonial Causes Act 1973). In an increasing number of jurisdictions, including Sweden and The Netherlands, this is no longer the case and marriages between homosexual couples are now recognised. In addition, Domestic Partnership Agreements, whereby same-sex couples enter into cohabitation agreements which are then registered by the state and give rise to rights akin to those attributed to married couples, are now legislated for in Denmark, France, Belgium, the Netherlands the Spanish provinces of Catalonia and Aragon, and most recently in Germany. Any comparable reform in this jurisdiction still seems to be someway off, although there are signs of encouragement. Both the Law Society and the Solicitors' Family Law Association have now published proposals for reform (discussed below) encouragement*. For the moment, even where one member of a couple has undergone a sex change operation, it is not possible for them to enter into a marriage with a partner of their original sex (see *Corbett v Corbett (otherwise Ashley)* [1971] P 83 and *Corbett v Corbett (otherwise Ashley) (No 2)* [1971] P 110 and *Bellinger v Bellinger* [2001] 2 FLR 1048) unless their sex was indeterminate at birth (see *W v W* [2001] 1 Fam III). Such a position has now on three occasions been confirmed by the European Court of Human Rights not to be a violation of Article 12 of the European Convention on Human Rights which guarantees to men and women of marriageable age the right to marry and found a family (see *Rees v United Kingdom* (1986) 9 EHRR 56; *Cossey v United Kingdom* (1990) 13 EHRR 622 and *Sheffield and Horsham v United Kingdom* (1998) 27 EHRR 163). Where children are born by AID into such a relationship a female to male transsexual cannot be the registered father of the child. This too has been confirmed not to be a breach of Article 8 of the Convention (*X, Y and Z v United Kingdom* (1997) 24 EHRR 143).

1.13 Some heterosexual couples cohabit rather than marry because one of them remains married to another person. Before the divorce law reforms in 1970, it was widely supposed that the reason for the fast increasing number of unmarried cohabiting couples was the fact that one or both partners were not free to marry, and that faster undefended divorce procedures would reduce the incidence of cohabitation. However, the statistics do not bear out these expectations. Despite the continuing increase in the divorce rate, cohabitation, in so far as it can be accurately measured, is also continuing to increase, notwithstanding the availability of easier divorce. This phenomenon requires an examination of the motives for cohabitation beyond inability to marry.

1.14 Certainly, a large proportion of people now cohabit before marriage, although the period of pre-marital cohabitation is variable. The *General Household Survey 1988* (in table 3.9) showed that 26% of women under 50 who married for the first time under the age of 35 had cohabited with their husbands before marriage. In the case of second or subsequent marriages, this rose to 70% and the percentage for all marriages exceeded 50% (*Social Trends, 21*, 1991). By 1998, these figures had risen to 64% and 87% respectively (*Population Trends 101*, 2000, p. 70). In 1979, 11% of non-married women between the ages of 18–49 were cohabiting in Great Britain and this had almost trebled to 29% in 1999 (*Social Trends 30*, 2000 p. 40). Indeed in 1999 cohabitation was predicted to double over the next 25 years (See Shaw and Haskey, *Population Trends 95*, 1999, p. 13). Conversely the percentage of women who were married decreased between 1979 and 1995 from 74 to 56% (*Social Trends, 27*, 1997) and the marriage rate is now at its lowest ebb since records began (*Social Trends 30*, 2000). Another measure is the number of births outside marriage. In 1961 only 6% of children were registered as having been born outside marriage. In 1998, this figure had risen to almost 40%. Of these, 75% were registered on the joint application of both parents, 73% of whom stated the same address, and suggest that they were cohabiting (*Social Trends, 30*, 2000).

* Furthermore, whilst of no legal effect, the London Partnerships Register does now enable same and opposite-sex couples to register their relationships and take part in a commitment ceremony (see www.london.gov.uk/mayor/partnerships). Most recently in October 2001, Jane Griffiths MP Introduced a Relationship (Civil Registration) Bill into the House of Commons as a 10 Minute Rule Bill. This would enable same and opposite-sex couples to formally register their relationship then be treated as spouses in law regards to financial provisions on realtionship borrowing, inheritance, tax, housing succession, pensions and social security, domestic violence, immigration and fatal accident compensation. This Bill is widely predicted to suffer the fate of nearly all 10 Minute Rule Bills and never become law. However, it is likely to strengthen calls for reform.

1.15 More research on cohabitation, including some commissioned by the Lord Chancellor's Department, has now been carried out and looked into the reasons why people choose to cohabit. This tends to confirm the reasons proffered by commentators or based on small scale surveys and include: an ideological objection to marriage by one or both partners; a belief that a relationship is a private matter and not something which needs to be licensed by the state; a reluctance to marry following a previous failed marriage; a desire to avoid divorce on relationship breakdown and/or to avoid the legal consequences of divorce, such as payment of maintenance to a former partner; and freedom to vary the terms of a relationship without providing grounds for divorce. Perhaps a further, more troubling, contributory factor is the so-called 'common law marriage myth' whereby there is evidence that people falsely believe that heterosexual cohabitation carries with it the same legal implications as formal marriage (see eg Barlow and Duncan, 'New Labour's Communitarianism, Supporting Families and the 'Rationality Mistake': Part II' [2000] *JSWFL*, 129 **):

1.16 For whatever reasons, there has been a marked increase in the number of couples who have decided to live together outside marriage and an increase in the number of children who live with parents who are not married. Whether or not the cohabitation is intended to endure in the short, medium or long term, such periods of cohabitation engender legal consequences about which lawyers are increasingly consulted, and in respect of which there is no neat body of law. Unless and until this situation changes, lawyers must search out disparate case law and be aware of which statutory provisions recognise the existence of cohabitants. They must, for example, distinguish those which include them in definitions as a member of their partner's family, from those which ignore the relationship and treat the partners as two unconnected individuals.

1.17 Statute in our jurisdiction has been slow to recognise cohabitation, and even where it does, it tends still to privilege marriage. This is in contrast to some of the other common law based countries such as Australia and Canada where some of the rights and obligations of married couples have been extended almost wholesale to cohabiting couples, whether same or opposite sex and even beyond to other 'domestic relationships'. Thus, the New South Wales Property (Relationships)

Legislation Amendment Act 1999 affords to same and opposite-sex couples and those persons living in a 'domestic relationship' the same rights as those enjoyed by de facto heterosexual couples.

1.18 'Domestic relationship' is defined as—

'(a) a de facto relationship, or
(b) a close personal relationship (other than a marriage or a de facto relationship between two adult persons, whether or not related by family, who are living together, one or each of whom provides the other with domestic support and personal care.'

This not only abolishes all distinctions between same and opposite sex couples in relation to rights but also makes provision for non-sexual relationships of gratuitous care. Similarly in the Australian Capital Territories, domestic relationships are recognised. Section 31 of the ACT Domestic Relationships Act 1994 defines them as:

'a personal relationship (other than a legal marriage) between two adults in which one provides personal or financial commitment and support of a domestic nature for the material benefit of the other and includes a de facto marriage.'

This again encompasses and extends beyond both same and opposite-sex cohabitants. The stated intention was to prevent anyone benefiting unfairly from the financial or non-financial sacrifice of another person who has contributed to their overall financial advantage while trusting them for some consideration for that effort. The Act enables the courts to order both maintenance and property adjustment and focuses on the contributions made by the parties.

1.19 Closer to home, the Scottish Law Commission following its discussion paper (No 86) *The Effects of Cohabitation in Private Law*, recommended in its *Report on Family Law* (Scot Law Com No 135, 1992) that some limited rights currently appertaining to married couples alone should be extended to cohabiting couples. It did not in the event recommend the extension of aliment (maintenance) or financial provision on relationship breakdown to cohabitants, but did propose a right of action for compensation for any economic disadvantage suffered by either party in the interests of their partner or any child of the family. These proposals have recently been 'relaunched' in a Scottish Executive Consultation Paper *Improving Scottish Family Law* (2000) and are likely to be enacted in the near future (see Bissett-Johnson, 'Parents and Children – A Scottish White Paper on Family Law' [2000] IFL 155). The Law Commission for England and Wales was set a similar task and it is to be hoped that its eventual recommendations, currently anticipated in Spring 2002, will go beyond those proposed for Scotland in the context of property rights of cohabitants. Indeed both the Law Society (see *Cohabitation – Proposals for Reform of the Law*, 1999) and the Solicitors Family Law Association *Fairness for Families – Proposals for Reform of the Law on Cohabitation*, 2000) advocate wholesale reform of cohabitation law as it relates to both same and opposite-sex couples to enable claims for financial provision on relationship breakdown and to redress economic disadvantage, whilst agreeing that couples should be able to opt-out. Thus there does now seem to be a more focused impetus for reform of the law in England and Wales. Nonetheless, the proposals do reveal the range of possibilities for reform (see Gouriet, 'Cohabitation Update' [2000] *Fam Law* 210).

3 Characteristics of the cohabitation relationship

1.20 The legal consequences of cohabitation can be far reaching, but unfortunately, cohabiting couples rarely seek direct legal advice about their situation until a crisis, commonly in the form of death, relationship breakdown or perhaps possession proceedings is upon them. There is a common misconception amongst cohabiting couples that rights equivalent to marriage are acquired after a certain period of cohabitation.

1.21 Although the precise legal consequences of the various aspects of cohabitation will be dealt with in detail in the following chapters, a few illustrations of the possible pitfalls of cohabitation are appropriate here. They also underline the advisability of prevention, in the form of agreements or contracts, Wills and declarations of trust in relation to property, rather than the only cure available – litigation.

1.22 It is common for people to enter into joint mortgages or other loans without realising the full implications of joint and several liability. This problem is not exclusive to cohabiting couples, but they are often faced with the consequences. There is no maintenance available to either partner of a formerly cohabiting couple, no matter how long the period of cohabitation. Maintenance is available only to any children of the relationship and this will usually now be administered through the Child Support Agency (see Chapter 9). Where a property has been bought jointly by a couple, unless, as unfortunately is often not the case, there has been an express declaration of their respective beneficial interests in the conveyance, or in the form of a declaration of trust which sets out their shares, there is ample room for expensive litigation on relationship breakdown to resolve a dispute.

1.23 A cohabitant living in a property owned or rented in the sole name of his or her partner is in a precarious position should the relationship end either through breakdown of the relationship or death of the partner, unless provision has previously been made. Similarly, if Wills are not made, then on the death of one of the couple, all his or her property, including personal belongings and savings not jointly held, and in the absence of any children, will pass to an estranged spouse not yet divorced, a parent, brother or sister, rather than the partner, although where there has been cohabitation for two years prior to death and in some other limited circumstances an application may be made to the court for some provision to be made out of the estate (see Chapters 3 and 4).

1.24 Before looking at the possibility of cohabitation contracts as a means of providing for at least some of the contingencies which may arise during the course of or at the end of cohabitation, it is proposed to look at certain of the consequences of cohabitation which do not fall easily into the specific subjects covered in the following chapters and in relation to which advice is often sought.

(a) Changing names

1.25 There is nothing to prevent a cohabitant from changing his or her surname so as to be known by the same name as his or her partner. Change of name by an adult can be achieved by means of a short statutory declaration, declared pursuant to the provisions of the Statutory Declarations Act 1835; or a deed setting out details of the original name and the new name which must be substituted for all purposes thereafter. It is advisable to have a deed witnessed by a solicitor to ensure acceptance by all authorities. The original declaration or deed is then sufficient proof for banks, building societies, the Passport Office and most other purposes, to ensure that official documentation is transferred into the new name.

1.26 It is possible to change one's name merely by common usage, and some argue that this is the only way names are in fact changed, but for official purposes evidence of the change is normally required and thus a simple deed or declaration is advisable to avoid unnecessary complications and delay.

1.27 Names can also be changed by enrolled deed poll. The advantage of this is that there is an official record of the change, as the change of name is enrolled at the Filing Department of the Central Office of the Supreme Court. However, the procedure is longer, including verification of the person's identity by means of a declaration from a Commonwealth citizen and householder resident in the UK who has known that person for ten years, an advert in the *London Gazette* and payment of both the advertisement costs and a fee to the Court. (For guidance of the exact steps to be taken, and for precedents of the necessary forms, see Pearce, *Name-Changing: A Practical Guide* (1990), Fourmat Publishing and Wooderal, *Cohabitation, Law Practice and Precedents* [2001] Family Law, p 492.) It is also a procedure which is open only to citizens of the UK, Commonwealth and the Republic of Ireland.

1.28 There are still some purposes for which an enrolled deed poll is the only acceptable option to effect a change of name. In particular, some professional bodies such as the General Medical Council require enrolment before the change of name will be accepted, and thus advisors should check whether the change needs to be registered with any body likely to have such a requirement.

1.29 Changing a child's name may present more difficulty and the right, or lack of right, to do so is inextricably bound up with the law relating to children. Even where the parents of a child were never married to each other, the father has not jointly registered the birth and no court order or recognised agreement has been made granting the father custody, parental rights or responsibility, it is not clear that the mother can now safely change the child's surname, or indeed any of the child's names, without reference to the father or an order of the court (see *Dawson v Wearmouth*, [1999] 2 AC 308). Where the father's identity is unknown to the mother or where his consent is forthcoming, the change can be achieved by an adapted form of statutory declaration or deed executed by the mother. Similarly, where one of the parents dies without appointing a testamentary guardian, and there has been no previous court order, a surviving parent *with parental responsibility* is free to change a child's names if he or she so wishes. Otherwise, a specific issue order under s 8 Children Act 1989 (CA 1989) or where a residence order has been made, leave of the court must be applied for to authorise any change of name (s 13(1) CA 1989). Thus, whilst on the face of the 1989 Act (where no residence order is in force) either parent with parental responsibility can in theory change a child's name, recent case law now restricts this (see Chapter 2).

(b) Making wills

1.30 The position of cohabitants on intestacy renders them particularly vulnerable on their partner's death. As there is no blood or legal relationship between cohabitants, they do not come within any of the categories of person entitled to inherit on intestacy under s 46 Administration of Estates Act 1925. Thus, even where a cohabitant dies leaving no surviving relatives whatsoever, his or her estate will pass *bona vacantia* to the Crown rather than to the surviving partner. It is worthwhile noting that the Crown may be prepared to make an *ex gratia* payment to a cohabitant in such circumstances. Section 46(1)(vi) gives a discretion to make payments for dependants and 'other persons for whom the intestate may have been expected to make provision'. It is entirely discretionary but in fact may provide for a cohabitant who cannot make any other type of claim as they had neither lived with their partner for two years prior to the death, nor were they dependent upon them. As is detailed in Chapter 5, if reasonable financial provision has not been made for a hetrosexual cohabitant of two years standing, then a claim under the Inheritance (Provision for Family and Dependants) Act 1975 as amended by the Law Reform (Succession) Act 1995 for maintenance may be made. An alternative claim exists for dependants of the deceased. Such an application is not without difficulty. It is bound to be costly and may well be resisted by those who would otherwise inherit under the terms of a Will or on intestacy. However, the 1995 reforms undoubtedly strengthen the position of a hetrasexual cohabitant where the cohabitation has lasted two years or more.

1.31 Nonetheless, cohabitants must be advised of the advantages of Mutual Wills and the hazards of not making them. Mutual Wills, however, while avoiding the laws on intestacy, will not necessarily solve all cohabitants' problems, and much will depend on any responsibilities they have towards others. The following matters should be borne in mind when advising cohabitants in relation to Wills:

(i)   Marriage always revokes a Will. Thus if Mutual Wills have been made and the cohabiting partners marry each other, new Wills must be considered.
(ii)   Wills can be revoked or changed at any time by a testator and it is not possible to bind a partner to the terms of a particular Will.
(iii)   Without a Will, a partner will not be entitled to anything belonging to the other partner on his or her death, not even personal belongings. Only jointly owned property which has not been declared to be beneficially owned in specified shares will pass to the surviving joint owner. Thus, as discussed in Chapter 3, if property is owned jointly as tenants in common, a deceased's partner's beneficial interest will pass to the joint owner only if bequeathed to him or her by Will.

(iv)   Where a partner has a former spouse and/or children who are still dependent upon him or her, they have a right to make a claim under the Inheritance (Provision for Family and Dependants) Act 1975 that provision be made for them out of the estate. This will inevitably mean that the surviving cohabiting partner who is a beneficiary under the Will, is forced to concede or compromise the claim; or become involved in expensive litigation if advised to resist the claim, which would undoubtedly deplete the estate. Thought therefore needs to be given as to how best to balance these competing claims on the estate in a Will, in a way which would be held to be fair if challenged. Life assurance may well provide the answer in a situation where there may not be enough to provide for everyone adequately.

(v)   It can be important correctly to identify a cohabitant beneficiary in a Will. A testator who refers in a Will to his or her cohabitant as their spouse, may unintentionally defeat the gift, although case law has tended to give effect to the testator's intentions where these are clear (see, for example, *Re Brown, Golding v Brady* (1910) 26 TLR 257 and *Re Lynch, Lynch v Lynch* [1943] 1 All ER 168).

(c) Life assurance

1.32 Where cohabitants enter into joint debts such as a mortgage, attention should be drawn to the implications of joint and several liability on the death of one of the partners. The financial difficulties that this causes can be circumvented by taking out a mortgage protection policy or an endowment mortgage, which would guarantee to pay off the debt in such a situation. Where one partner is financially dependent upon the other, life assurance is even more important to avoid the risk of losing the home on the death of the breadwinner. Strong advice should be given as to the consequences of failing to make appropriate provision, even where a Will has been made making the surviving dependent partner a beneficiary. Any life policy aiming to protect the surviving partner from sole or joint debts should either be assigned to the creditor such as the mortgagee or be written in trust for the other partner. The proceeds of the policy will not then form part of the estate of the deceased partner.

1.33 Similarly, where there are likely to be competing claims on an estate from other dependants, a life policy written in trust for a cohabitant, has the advantage of not forming part of the deceased's estate, and thus could not be made subject to a claim under the Inheritance (Provision for Family and Dependants) Act 1975. If, on the other hand, the benefit of any such policy is bequeathed by Will, it forms part of the estate and could be diverted to other dependants by virtue of the provisions of the 1975 Act.

1.34 It should be noted that life assurance can only benefit a person who has an insurable interest in the assured's life pursuant to s 1 Life Assurance Act 1774 and will otherwise be void. Unlike spouses and now engaged couples, cohabitants are not deemed automatically to have such a financial interest in their partner's life but it is arguable that a financially dependent partner does have such an interest, which must be valued in accordance with the loss they are likely to suffer on the insured's death. Cohabitants are already recognised by several insurance companies as possessing such an interest and on taking out life insurance it is important to clarify the position of the insurance company involved. The Scottish Law Commission recommended (see Scot Law Com No. 135 paras 16.41–16.45) and the Scottish Executive has now agreed that Statute should clarify the position in favour of cohabitants. Such a reform seems likely to prompt consideration of the position in English law as favoured by the Association of British Insurers. Where there are joint liabilities such as a mortgage, there is obviously no difficulty in proving the financial interest in any event.

Check developments***

4 Cohabitation contracts

1.35 Having examined some of the pitfalls of unmarried partnerships and families, what can be done to avoid the problems? Are cohabitation contracts detailing the agreed basis upon which the cohabitation is to operate the answer? It is popularly thought that such a contract would be binding upon the parties in the event of breakdown of the relationship, as is indeed the case in other jurisdictions. Unfortunately, in our jurisdiction, there is still no certainty that the courts would enforce such a contract. In fact, as will be illustrated, such precedents as there are point in the other direction. However, the issue has yet to be decided in a contemporary context, and it seems increasingly unlikely that a strict approach would now be adopted given the changed mores of our society.

1.36 Contractual freedom is one of the boasts of the English legal system. In 1938 Lord Atkin endorsed the following statement made by Lord Jessel in 1875:

> 'If there is one thing more than another public policy requires it is that men of full age and competent understanding shall have the utmost liberty of contracting and that their contracts when entered into freely and voluntarily shall be held sacred and shall be enforced by the Court of Justice: therefore you have this paramount public policy to consider, that you are not lightly to interfere with their freedom to contract.' (Lord Atkin in *Fender v St John-Mildmay* [1938] AC 1 citing Lord Jessel in *Printing and Numerical Registering Co v Sampson* (1875) LR 19 Eq 462 at page 465)

However, due to other public policy considerations, it is still unclear to what extent such freedom is available to cohabiting couples who, either before or during cohabitation, wish to encapsulate the terms of the cohabitation in an enforceable contract.

1.37 Whether or not a contract will be considered valid by the courts may depend on its contents as well as on a number of other factors. It is interesting to note that in 1988, the Council of Ministers of the European Community adopted the recommendation (No. R(88)3) that member states should not preclude cohabitation contracts dealing with property and money on the ground that the parties are not married to each other. Unlike the marriage contract, a cohabitation contract is a matter of a private rather than a public agreement, and thus the starting point is that the parties are free to agree the scope and nature of the terms themselves. Whether or not all or any of the terms of such a contract will be upheld by the courts may in any event not be the parties' only motive for having an agreement drawn up.

1.38 Couples are likely to want a cohabitation contract to cover their rights and obligations both during cohabitation and on breakdown of the relationship. Unlike their married counterparts who are thought to be prevented by public policy considerations from preparing for the contingency of breakdown, a cohabitation contract would not be void by reason of providing for such an eventuality. Interestingly, the Law Society's Family Law Committee has recommended that marriage contracts providing for the division of property on divorce should be enforceable where both parties have entered into them with the benefit of legal advice (see *Law Society's Gazette* 15 May 1991, page 2) and the government's 1998 consultation paper, *Supporting Families* similarly endorsed this idea (paras 4.20–4.23). Both the 1997 Law Society and 2000 SFLA recommendations for reform of cohabitation law consider that cohabitation agreement should be enforceable. As noted above, there is a Council of Ministers' recommendation that cohabitation contracts dealing with property should be recognised. The Scottish Law Commission recommended that this type of approach should be adopted in reforming Scottish law and suggested that the following clause be enacted, a proposal endorsed by the recent Scottish Executive White Paper:

'A contract between cohabitants or prospective cohabitants relating to property or financial matters should not be void or unenforceable solely because it was concluded between parties in, or about to enter, this type of relationship.'

These developments bode well for the likely enforceability of a cohabitation contract made by heterosexual couples, where it is limited to issues of property, but before discussing enforceability in detail, the range of matters which cohabiting couples may wish to include in their contracts is considered.

(a) Contents

1.39 The exact content of each cohabitation contract is obviously a matter for the couple concerned. The advantage of drawing up a contract is that it requires the partners to consider, before there is any dispute, their respective expectations, both during the relationship and, in so far as can be foreseen, on breakdown.

1.40 It is also possible to have a contract that deals only with the eventuality of breakdown, without regulating the terms of the relationship itself. Some couples may wish to commit to writing every aspect of the agreements between them, down to the minutiae of the washing up rota, whilst others may find this unnecessary yet see the value of discussing, agreeing and recording in advance their respective rights in relation to property, maintenance and any children. The more romantic may wish instead to trust their partner sufficiently to feel sure that in the event of breakdown, a satisfactory agreement would be reached. However, sadly, the bitterness that breakdown usually engenders often means that such trust is misplaced. This is as true for cohabiting same-sex couples as it is for heterosexuals.

1.41 Some argue that to ask or advise couples to agree such matters in a formal legal document may raise problems within a relationship that were not previously present, and that accordingly matters are best left undocumented. However, it is submitted that if such an exercise reveals different understandings about the implications of a couple's arrangements, then surely this is a matter which merits discussion during the currency of the relationship where possible, rather than on breakdown when compromise or re-evaluation of the position may be much more difficult.

1.42 What should be the main tenets of a cohabitation contract? As previously indicated, it is perfectly possible to include the agreed rules upon which the cohabitation is founded; these include whether or not other relationships are permitted; how the household chores should be shared; and the amount of leisure time the parties will spend together. However, no court would ever compensate a breach of any such terms with an order for specific performance, as is the general rule with contracts for personal services. It is unlikely that a court would compensate a breach of the rules of the relationship (as opposed to the terms contained in the contract relating to property division), with damages, as it may be felt that the parties did not intend to be legally bound by such rules other than to provide evidence of breakdown of the relationship. Their inclusion can never be more than a record of the parties' intentions in those areas and should only be expressed as such in the contract.

1.43 Providing the contract meets the general criteria for an enforceable contract as set out below, contract terms which detail how property which is brought into the relationship or subsequently purchased individually or jointly by the parties, is to be treated on breakdown, may well be enforceable. At the very least it will be strong evidence of the parties' intentions at the time of the contract and will be valuable in case of dispute. Similarly, if a property is bought for occupation by the couple as a family home, a clause indicating that it is property which is to be beneficially jointly owned in stated shares may negative any contrary indication on the title documents, providing the cohabitation contract is executed as a deed. Provision can also be made for giving notice under the agreement to terminate the relationship and to provide for the agreed division of property at that juncture. A clause to pay maintenance on breakdown of the relationship to a partner who would otherwise have no right to maintenance will also prove enforceable if the contract is executed as a deed. A fairly exhaustive list of relevant matters to be considered for inclusion in a cohabitation contract are set out by Barton (*Cohabitation Contracts*, Gower, 1985, pages 55–56) and reproduced here for reference:

'(a) statement of the purpose of the contract, for example to create an equal relationship;

(b) legality of the agreement, for example to be legally binding or merely a statement of expectations;

(c) the parties, for example, statement of ages, financial disclosures and health;

(d) aims of the parties, for example their collective and individual goals in the relationship;

(e) duration, for example, for lifetime, fixed period or until specified event;

(f)   careers – employment, for example, do both want/are able to work, priorities;

(g)   income and expenses, for example, how much, and how to be treated, whether or not to pool these and also savings;

(h)   property held at inception, for example how to be treated;

(i)   property acquired during cohabitation, for example whether to be treated as community property or not, who to manage. How gifts are to be treated and whether life insurance is to be taken out, how funded and who nominated as beneficiary. Similarly, whether nomination to be made to occupational pension fund;

(j)   debts, for example, statement of what each currently owes and their attitude to credit;

(k)   living arrangements, for example, who to choose location, whether town or country, policy as to guests;

(l)   household tasks, for example, how divided;

(m)   surname, for example, each to keep his or her own, one to adopt the other's, hyphenation, the position of children's surnames;

(n)   sexual relations, for example, type, monogamy, rules for disclosure if not;

(o)   personal behaviour, for example, smoking, hobbies, private area in house;

(p)   relations with family and friends, for example any responsibility for children of previous relationship;

(q)   children, whether or not to have any, how to bring them up;

(r)   religion;

(s)   health, for example private care, whether insurance to be taken out;

(t)   inheritance and Wills, for example what if anything they will leave to each other;

(u)   breaches of the agreement, for example liquidated damages, court proceedings, arbitration;

(v)   resolving disagreements, for example professional conciliation or a named mutually agreed conciliator;

(w)   variation or renewal of the contract;

(x)   dissolution, for example when, notice, support, property, custody;

(y)   conversion to marriage.'

(b) Enforceability

1.44 The problems of enforcement have already been mentioned. The issues are raised by the law of contract, and are matters which courts must consider in relation to any contract the validity of which is challenged. There are as many as five hurdles at which a cohabitation contract may fall:

(i)   it may be found illegal or void on grounds of public policy;

(ii)   an intention to create legal relations may be absent;

(iii)   it may be found void for uncertainty;

(iv)   consideration may be absent; or

(v)   it may be found voidable where there is undue influence.

(i) Illegality on grounds of public policy

1.45 Contracts for immoral purposes, which of course include sexual immorality, are illegal and consequently unenforceable. Contracts deemed to be prejudicial to the marital state are also contrary to public policy and void. Despite the changing tide towards recognition of cohabitation in some statutes, these common law principles of the law of contract remain unchanged. Thus, although current thinking is that no court today would strike down a cohabitation contract entered into by a cohabiting heterosexual couple on these grounds, this has not yet been tested in the courts. Accordingly the current legal position remains uncertain, although the recommendation by the Council of Ministers R(88)3 and its endorsement by the Scottish Law Commission discussed above, makes it highly unlikely a contract relating to property or financial matters between a cohabiting man and woman would be declared void on public policy grounds. The validity of a contract between a cohabiting gay couple may be significantly more vulnerable to an adverse finding that it promotes sexual immorality.

1.46 The case law dates back as far as the mid-seventeenth century, and the most recent case which actually expressly considered the validity of such a contract was *Diwell v Farnes* [1959] 2 All ER 379, CA. Given that no court has yet overruled them, these cases remain *prima facie* binding precedent. In *Diwell*, Ormerod LJ stated at page 384E: ' . . . such joint venture must depend on a contract express or implied between the parties which being founded on an immoral consideration, would not be enforceable.' Many of the cases do not distinguish between parties in a long stable relationship, and a contract for the services of a prostitute.

1.47 Some ground rules can be elicited from the case law, and assist in assessing how to limit the possibility that a cohabitation contract will be held unenforceable. In *Walker v Perkins* (1764) 1 Wm Bl 517, a contract entered into before commencement of the cohabitation, and which provided for financial provision for the woman both during and on termination of the cohabitation period, was held to be void as it promoted sexual immorality. Yet an agreement entered into after cohabitation had ceased, making provision for the woman, and which was under seal, was held to be valid in *Annandale v Harris* (1727) 2 P Wms 432. Again, in *Re Vallance, Vallance v Blagden* (1884) 26 Ch D 353, where the couple had lived together for more than thirty years, and six months before his death the man had given the woman a bond worth £6,000, a court refused to set aside the gift of the bond on the basis that it was bought with immoral consideration and consequently illegal, because it was past consideration and the short continued cohabitation could not be presumed to be the consideration for the gift of the bond. As this case concerned the gift of a bond, consideration was not of course needed. However, if immoral consideration was proved, it would have rendered the gift illegal.

1.48 Thus if the contract does not actually promote sexual immorality because the cohabitation has ceased or has already commenced, there is authority for saying that the contract is not void on this ground, although care needs to be taken that there is sufficient other consideration or that the agreement is executed as a deed. Therefore, advisors should always ensure, when drafting a cohabitation agreement, that any reference to the parties' agreement to cohabit is put in the past tense, and is not drafted in such a way as to imply that the consideration for the terms of the agreement is future cohabitation. Of course, if a modern test case were to find a cohabitation contract void on the sexual immorality ground, it would not be possible to sever this part of the contract and preserve the rest of the terms as severance is not available where there is an illegal contract.

1.49 Even if the prevailing view, that no court would hold a contract illegal for promoting sexual immorality given that heterosexual cohabitation is now so socially accepted and even affords parties statutory protection in some areas, is correct, would a cohabitation contract be found void on the grounds that it is prejudicial to the institution of marriage? As Barton (see para **1.43**) suggests, such a contract may be deemed by the court to fetter the ability to marry third parties where a defined period of intended cohabitation is included, or could be found to further prejudice an existing marriage if one of the parties to the contract remains married to another. Thus there is scope for a court to find a cohabitation contract void. However, this aspect of the public policy principle has not been extended to a finding that all cohabitation contracts are prejudicial to the institution of marriage, so that at least where two single people are parties to the contract, it seems extremely unlikely that a court would be persuaded to hold the contract void. An assertion that a cohabitation contract is prejudicial to the marital state would be difficult to support, where, for example, the contract makes it clear that the cohabitation is viewed as a trial marriage. Even where parties are married to others, given the existence of divorce, it seems highly unlikely that the contract itself could be deemed prejudicial, particularly where it was entered into after separation of the spouses and after cohabitation between the cohabitants had commenced.

1.50 In a cohabitation contract between same-sex partners, the argument is perhaps open that neither party would in any event ever wish to marry a person of the opposite sex, and therefore the contract of itself is not prejudicial to the state of marriage. Accordingly, it seems most unlikely that cohabitation contracts would be unenforceable on this ground alone, and in any event, unlike contracts found to be illegal for promoting sexual immorality, it would be possible to sever the offending part of the contract leaving the remainder of the terms, for example, those dealing with jointly owned property, intact and enforceable.

1.51 A more positive view regarding the enforceability of cohabitation contracts despite the lack of modern judicial authority on the point, is given weight by recent decisions which will be more fully discussed in Chapters 3 and 11 in relation to housing and property. In these cases the courts have enforced promises made to 'mistresses' by their partners. Promises to continue to provide accommodation on breakdown of the relationship have been enforced by imputing a licence for life (see *Tanner v Tanner* [1975] 1 WLR 1346 and *Chandler v Kerley* [1978] 1 WLR 693). The courts have also found resulting and constructive trusts where cohabitants have purchased a property in the sole name of one of them, but their actions showed it was clearly intended as a joint venture (see, for example, *Eves v Eves* [1975] 1 WLR 1338 and *Cooke v Head* [1972] 1 WLR 518; *Hammond v Mitchell* [1992] 2 All ER 109). In none of these cases has there been any mention that such agreements may be illegal or void on public policy grounds, although in cases relying on trusts, such a consideration is irrelevant as the courts apply the law of trusts rather than the law of contract. However, the recommendation of the Council of Ministers made in

1988 (No. R(88)3; see page 13) does specifically deal with contracts between cohabitants and recommends that member states should give effect to these where they relate to money and property.

1.52 Where there is a child of an unmarried relationship, the courts have endorsed the making of binding agreements for maintenance for mother and child. It was said in *Horrocks v Forray* [1976] 1 WLR 230, at page 239: 'when an illegitimate child has been born, there is certainly nothing contrary to public policy in the parents coming to an agreement which they intend to be binding in law, for the maintenance of mother and child.'Of course, where there are children, it is not possible to oust the jurisdiction of the Child Support Agency or the court with regard to maintenance or financial provision, but certainly a clause providing maintenance for one or other of the partners on relationship breakdown would seem to be enforceable providing the other ingredients for a valid contract are not wanting.

(ii) Absence of intention to create legal relations

1.53 There is a rebuttable presumption that parties to an agreement regarding domestic arrangements do not intend to be legally bound. The principle was set out in the case of *Balfour v Balfour* [1919] 2 KB 571 where a promise by a husband who worked abroad, to his wife who had to stay behind on medical grounds, that he would pay her £30 per month was held to be unenforceable both because she had provided no consideration and also because the domestic nature of the agreement showed that there was no intention to create legal relations. Atkin LJ at page 578 said:

> 'Those agreements, or many of them, do not result in contracts at all . . . even though there may be what as between other parties would constitute consideration for the agreement . . . They are not contracts . . . because the parties did not intend that they should be attended by legal consequences.'

However, where there is a written agreement, especially if it has been drawn up by a legal advisor, this should be enough to rebut the presumption, as parties do not have agreements drawn up unless there is an intention that they should be legally binding (see *Merritt v Merritt* [1970] 1 WLR 1211, CA).

1.54 The case of *Layton v Martin* [1986] 2 FLR 227 provides a word of warning to cohabitants who indicate that they wish to draw up their own agreements without taking legal advice. In that case, the man wrote to the woman asking her to live with him and offering her 'financial security during my life—and on my death'. A few months later she went to live with him; they stayed together for eight years, although they separated two years before his death. However, the court refused to enforce the alleged contract against his estate and Scott at page 239 underlined the difficulty faced:

> 'In family or quasi family situations there is always the question whether the parties intended to create a legal binding contract between them. The more general and less precise the language of the so-called contract, the more difficult it will be to infer that intention.'

1.55 The content of a contract may also influence the court's view. Thus the less domestic detail that is contained, and the more terms there are relating to more legalistic matters, such as a statement of respective interests in jointly owned property, the more likely a court would be to infer the requisite intention. In any event, this is a hurdle easily overcome by cohabitants who do wish to create a binding contract; an advisor drafting a contract can, to ensure the intention is unambiguous, specifically recite the intention to be bound.

(iii) Contract void for uncertainty

1.56 As with any contract, if the terms are so vague and uncertain that they are incapable of enforcement, then this will either be a term which the court ignores, or, if the uncertainty comprises terms which are fundamental to the operation of the contract, may vitiate the whole contract. Thus, a term agreeing to make financial provision without any indication of the nature or extent or the rules according to which such provision could be ascertained would be void for uncertainty. Thus, advisors drafting a cohabitation contract should have this potential problem in mind.

(iv) Absence of consideration

1.57 As with any contract, there must be consideration for a cohabitation agreement to be enforceable. In the case of cohabitation agreements, the consideration for one party's agreeing to make financial provision for the other may be the act of cohabiting with the other party; this risks being deemed immoral consideration, consequently rendering the contract illegal. There is a simple answer; if the agreement is in the form of a deed, no consideration for the bargain is necessary. Advisors should therefore recommend a deed be executed. With the introduction of the provisions of the Law of Property (Miscellaneous Provisions) Act 1989, even the mystery of the seal has been dispensed with, and, apart from the requirements that it be in writing and dated, a document merely needs to record that it is being signed as a deed in the presence of independent witnesses to the signatures.

(v) Contract voidable for undue influence

1.58 A finding of undue influence exercised by one party over the other inducing that person to enter into the contract will vitiate the contract in its entirety. If the terms of a contract are heavily weighted in favour of one of the parties, it may be susceptible to such a finding. In contracts between spouses, there is no presumption of undue influence; to defeat a contract, it must be proved. In contrast, where a contract between an engaged couple substantially favours one party, there is a rebuttable presumption of undue influence and it must be proved that no such influence induced the less favoured party to enter into the bargain (see *Zamet v Hyman* [1961] 1 WLR 1442, CA). Whether or not there is a presumption of undue influence between cohabitants is unknown. As advisors may advise only one party to a contract (to avoid potential conflict of interest), it is obviously desirable, where there is any hint of inequality of bargaining power, to ensure that the less favoured party is urged to seek independent legal advice.

(c) Cohabitation contracts in other jurisdictions

1.59 Given that the situation in our own jurisdiction is still uncertain, it is helpful to consider the position in other common law jurisdictions to which the court could be referred. In the case of *Marvin v Marvin* 134 Cal Rptr 815 (1976) involving the actor Lee Marvin and his former cohabitant, the Supreme Court of California explicitly rejected the contention that a cohabitation contract entered into by cohabitants living in a stable relationship is unenforceable on immoral purposes ground. It said, at page 669:

> 'A contract between non-marital partners is unenforceable only to the extent it explicitly rests upon the immoral and illicit consideration of meretricious sexual services.'

This has been followed in some seventeen other states in the USA, and a similar finding was reached in the Australian case of *Andrews v Parker* [1973] Qd R 93.

1.60 In *Marvin*, the court also found that the performance of household services in a relationship between cohabitants should not be presumed to be a gift, and may thus provide sufficient consideration for a share in property owned by the other partner. It is of course by no means certain that an English court would follow this line of development. Their tendency, at least in the past, to look for constructive and resulting trusts and licences for life in the absence of any written agreement between parties, is, it is submitted, a useful barometer of the likely judicial approach to such an issue, although it is admitted that more recent cases have drawn back from this approach (see *Lloyds Bank plc v Rossett* [1990] 2 FLR 155 and Chapter 11). Parliament, on the other hand, could follow some other jurisdictions and actively encourage cohabitation agreements. This, it is submitted, would be a worthy course to adopt given the increasing number of people who choose to live together outside marriage. As noted above, there is already a recommendation passed by the Council of Ministers that effect should be given to cohabitation contracts concerned with money and property, which has been endorsed by the Scottish Law Commission. Both the Law Society and the SFLA proposals for the reform of cohabitation law, countenance a right for cohabitants to enter into cohabitation contracts co-existing with new statutory provisions regulating the rights of cohabitants.

1.61 In Minnesota, USA, a statute Minn Stat 513.076 (Cum Supp 1980) excludes, as being contrary to public policy, any claim based on cohabitation unless the parties have previously executed a contract which complies with the provisions of the statute. It must be in writing, signed by the parties and enforceable only when the relationship has ceased.

1.62 In Canada, at least five Provinces have legislated on the issue and pursuant to the Federal Modernization of Benefits and Obligations Act 2000 and order the principle of equality enshrined in the Canadian Charter of Rights and Freedoms and the Canadian Human Rights Act, any rights extended to opposite-sex couples must also be extended to same-sex couples. The most comprehensive reforms are found in Ontario Family Law Act, Prince Edward Island (Family Law Reform Act 1978), New Brunswick (Marital Property Act 1980) and Newfoundland (Matrimonial

Property Act 1979). These allow cohabitants to enter into agreements governing matters both during and after their relationships in so far as they deal with property ownership, support obligations; education and moral training of their children (although custody and access can be dealt with only in a separation agreement); and any other matter. The legislation provides for severance of a void term and will not enforce terms relating to children in so far as they are not in the best interests of the child. Such agreements must be in writing, signed and witnessed. In Newfoundland, cohabitants are permitted to opt into matrimonial property legislation and once they do, are treated as if they were spouses.

1.63 With regard to cohabitation contracts between homosexual couples, the Californian approach has been to treat and enforce these in the same way as heterosexual cohabitation contracts. In the decision of *Jones v Daley* 122 Cal App 3d 500 (1981), the court refused to uphold the contract only on the narrow ground that it was unable to sever an express term about sexual services contained in their agreement and which accordingly fell foul of the rule established in *Marvin v Marvin* (above). In a subsequent Californian decision, *Whorton v Dillingham* 248 Cal Rptr 405 (1988), the Court of Appeal were able to distinguish *Jones v Daley* and severed the sexual component of the consideration in the contract relying on the provision of other separately stated services, such as being his partner's chauffeur, bodyguard, secretary and counsellor over a period of seven years as providing consideration for the financial support and property rights promised in the agreement. The agreement was therefore enforceable on this basis.

1.64 In California and Canada at least, therefore, it seems possible to draft valid cohabitation contracts for both same-sex and heterosexual couples.

1.65 The English Law Commission in its present review of the property rights of unmarried couples has an ideal opportunity to recommend clarification of the validity of cohabitation contracts for both same and opposite-sex couples. It is hoped that the experience of other jurisdictions who recognise the need to provide remedies for problems arising out of cohabitation either in a family law forum or through the means of private contractual regulation will provide useful illustrations of possible legal responses to the social trend towards increasing cohabitation which is inevitably causing problems and which the law is currently unable to deal with in any coherent fashion. The Relationships (Civil Registration) Bill currently before Parliament would permit cohabitants to lodge their agreement on registration and this would become enforceable on relationship breakdown. As noted above, this Bill is unlikely to become law.

5 Conclusion

1.66 What are the advantages and disadvantages of entering into a cohabitation agreement, and how should clients be advised? It seems clear that where there are children, subject to not ousting the jurisdiction of the court, agreements between parents are welcomed. Furthermore, as long as the provision of sexual services is not explicit consideration, the contract is executed as a deed and the other requirements for a valid contract discussed above are met, there seems a strong chance that the English courts would enforce a contract which contemplates the division of property and financial support on relationship breakdown. Not to do so would fly in the face of the recommendation of the Council of Ministers made in 1988 that member states should recognise such contracts. In any event, if there is an agreement between parties, regardless of whether or not one would in fact seek to enforce it against the other on breakdown, it must be evidence of the parties' intentions at the time of the agreement. As such, at the very least, it provides the starting point either on separation, or on death, when there is a risk of a dispute with relatives.

1.67 An agreement may confer on a party rights he or she could not otherwise acquire; from the other party's point of view, this binds them to something they did not have to concede, yet in happier times actually wanted to give to their partner. Advisors of course need to point out the possible future disadvantages. Presumably, a cohabitation contract could attempt to opt in to matrimonial legislation by virtue of a term stating the parties agree to make such financial provision for the other as they would be required to do by the court had they married each other on the date cohabitation commenced. However, such a term on its own could provoke an unfavourable decision from an English court, either on public policy grounds, or even perhaps by virtue of the uncertainty of the provisions being contemplated. Thus any such terms should be in addition and without prejudice to such definitive provision as the parties can agree at the date of the contract.

1.68 Other disadvantages of entering into a cohabitation contract include the fact that it is of course impossible to cover every eventuality – an argument for, in appropriate cases, attempting to opt in to matrimonial legislation as a provision of last resort. A comprehensive agreement with some omissions may imply that their absence means they were deliberately excluded and so are not to be implied by a court. This again underlines the need either to make the contract clear in its limitations, for example, by confining it to maintenance and without prejudice to any other claims against property; or to be as comprehensive as possible. The best result may be achieved by a series of separate agreements dealing individually with maintenance and property during the relationship and on breakdown. These could then be amended as circumstances changed.

1.69 It is important to remember that most cases concerning relationship breakdown are settled out of court. A cohabitation agreement will always provide a starting point, or provide for conciliation through a professional agency before resorting to court proceedings. In this sense, providing the potential conflict of interest between the parties is kept firmly in mind by advisors at the drafting stage, there is much to be said for encouraging cohabitants to set down their affairs in an agreement, despite the doubts surrounding its legal enforceability. As is always the case when advising a client about a Will, advisors must emphasise the need to keep the situation under review, and to vary the contract from time to time as circumstances change.

1.70 A framework cohabitation agreement has been included at Appendix I.

Chapter 2

The status of children

1 Parental status

2.01 As was illustrated in Chapter 1, there has been a steep increase over the last forty years in the number of children registered as having been born outside marriage. In 1998, almost 40% of all children born were born to parents who were not married to each ot her. There has also been a significant increase in the number of births registered by both parents. In 1971, this accounted for 45% of such births but by 1998 the figure had risen to 75% (see *Social Trends, 30*, 2000). Seventy-three per cent of these parents gave the same address, and it is reasonable to conclude from such statistics that an increasingly significant number of children begin their lives in an unmarried family

2.02 The legal disadvantages to which a child was traditionally subjected as a consequence of having been born outside marriage have largely been swept away by various reforms, culminating in the provisions of the Family Law Reform Act 1987 (FLRA 1987). Affiliation orders were abolished, and many of the distinctions between legitimate and illegitimate children made in different enactments, such as those concerning inheritance rights on intestacy, were dispensed with. The old provisions may still be significant in some increasingly rare circumstances, as where an affiliation order was made in the past, or under a Will made before the coming into force of the relevant provisions of the 1987 Act. Despite the removal of legal discrimination towards children born outside marriage, perhaps surprisingly, the Children Act 1989 (CA 1989) did nothing to alter the position of any category of unmarried father on the birth of his child. Thus the legal situation of the father of a child born in a stable relationship between cohabitants was left identical to that of the father of a child born of a more casual encounter, with neither acquiring any automatic legal parental responsibility for their children. However, public attention has recently been focused on the discriminatory effect of the legislation on unmarried fathers. Whilst the current position has been held to be 'Human Rights Act compliant' (*B v United Kingdom* [2000] 1 FLR 1), the increasing numbers of such fathers – and Eekelaar estimates there to be over a million (see [2001] *Fam Law* 426) – combined with recognition that particularly cohabiting fathers play exactly the same role as married fathers, has highlighted the need for a review of the law. Following consultation by the Lord Chancellor's Department in *The Law on Parental Responsibility for Unmarried Fathers* (LCD, March 1998, http://www.lcd.gov.uk/consult/general/pat-con.txt) the Adoption and Children Bill

2001 (ACB 2001) was introduced and proposed to radically alter the position, as discussed below. Although the original Bill was lost as a result of the general election, it has been reintroduced to Parliament.

2.03 Before the CA 1989, when a child was born to parents who were not married, by virtue of s 85(7) Children Act 1975 (CA 1975), all the legal rights relating to the child vested solely in the mother. Affiliation orders, whilst proving paternity, did not bestow any parental rights on the father, merely the obligation to pay maintenance. Although affiliation orders were abolished, the situation was not altered by the FLRA 1987, although it did, by s 4, introduce 'parental rights orders'. This enabled an unmarried father, for the first time, to obtain a court order granting him shared parental rights and duties with the mother. Section 4 of the CA 1989 replaced and assimilated parental rights orders with 'parental responsibility orders' and also enabled both parents to agree to share parental responsibility for the child. A parental responsibility agreement avoids the need for a court order, provided it is recorded in a document in the prescribed form and registered in accordance with the regulations made under the Act. Yet the unmarried father's status at the time of the child's birth remains unaffected, whatever the nature of the relationship between the parents. As things currently stand, there is not even a presumption of paternity where unmarried parents were living together at the date of a child's conception, as exists in some other jurisdictions. Thus, if both parents wish the father to have legal recognition, then various steps have to be taken so that he acquires parental responsibility and these will be considered in the following sections. It is important to note here that these steps will continue to be relevant to some unmarried fathers even if the ACB 2001 if, as expected has a successful passage through Parliament. In particular, where their child was born prior to the new provisions coming into force, or where the child's birth is registered in the mother's sole name, the father will still not gain automatic parental responsibility.

2 Registering the birth

2.04 The birth of any child must be registered within 42 days and this legal duty rests on the mother alone where the parents are unmarried (Births and Deaths Registration Act 1953, s 10) (the 1953 Act)). Unfortunately, where the parents are not married and both wish to be recorded as parents on the birth certificate, the procedure is not as simple as for married parents. Strictly, in the absence of any specific issue order concerning the child's name (s 8 CA 1989) or of an order or formal agreement granting the father joint parental rights or responsibility (s 4 CA 1989), the choice of name to be registered for the child lies with the mother. However, there is nothing to prevent her from registering the child with the father's surname if she wishes, or indeed with any other surname It should perhaps be noted here, however, that where there is a dispute as to the name in which the child is to be registered and the mother is aware of this, the House of Lords have endorsed the view that the matter should be referred to the court regardless of whether or not the father has parental responsibility (see *Dawson v Wearmouth* [1999] 1 FLR 1167, per Lord Mackay of Clashfern at p1173B).

2.05 Sections 24 and 25 FLRA 1987 amended the 1953 Act by adding new ss 10 and 10A which set out the procedure to be followed. Paragraph 6 of Sch 12 CA 1989 has made further consequential amendments. The unmarried father is under no *duty* to register the birth, but now has the status of a qualified informant which *entitles* him to register the birth. However, this right does not automatically allow him to be recorded as the child's father on the register even if his surname is being given to the child. A record of the father's identity on the register can only be achieved in one of the following ways. Firstly, and most simply, a joint request by the mother and father (who must both attend in person) that the father's name be recorded will be sufficient. If this is not possible, then the identity of the father can be recorded by either the mother or father alone if they each make and supply a statutory declaration as to the child's paternity. Otherwise, the father's name can be recorded on the written request of either the mother or the father, providing one of the following documents is produced: a parental responsibility agreement made between the parents in proper form; or a court order made in proceedings between them for affiliation, custody, financial provision, parental rights or parental responsibility. In addition a declaration that the order or agreement is still subsisting is needed. It is also possible, by virtue of s 10A of the 1953 Act, to re-register the birth at a later stage to include the father's name. The requirements and procedure remain exactly the same and thus any of the methods described will achieve this end. However, once the child has reached the age of sixteen, their consent to the re-registration is also needed. Registration of the identity of the father of a child of unmarried parents on the birth certificate, is *prima facie* evidence of paternity and shifts the burden of proof onto the father if he later wishes to dispute it. Registration of the father's identity on the birth certificate does not of itself, however, confer any rights or duties upon the father.

3 Parental rights and duties and parental responsibility

(a) The general position

2.06 With the advent of the CA 1989, the law relating to parental rights and duties underwent a radical conceptual change. The Act replaced the concept of 'parental rights and duties' with the notion of 'parental responsibility'. This is defined in s 3(1) as: '. . . all the rights, duties, powers, responsibilities and authority which by law a parent of a child has in relation to the child and his property.'

2.07 The CA 1989 repealed the whole of the Guardianship of Minors Acts 1971 and the Guardianship Act 1973, as well as, *inter alia*, the Children Act 1975. The old concepts of custody and access also disappeared and were broadly replaced with residence and contact orders on relationship breakdown. However, in the same way that custody used to vest in an unmarried mother alone, only the mother in an unmarried family automatically acquires parental responsibility on the birth of a child (s 2(2) CA 1989), leaving unchanged the unmarried father's position of initial disadvantage. Questions of residence, contact and parental responsibility following breakdown of an unmarried relationship will be explored in Part II (see Chapter 8), and will not therefore be discussed in this chapter.

2.08 Unmarried parents can now agree to share parental responsibility, but even where no order or agreement has been made, some minimum standards are imposed upon the unmarried father. Where the father (or indeed any person) lives with a child, limited duties are found in s 1 Children and Young Persons Act 1933 to ensure the child receives an education and is not neglected or maltreated. Section 3(5) CA 1989 provides that any person who does not have parental responsibility but who has care of the child may do what is reasonable in all the circumstances of the case for the purpose of safeguarding or promoting the child's welfare. This provision enhances the position under the old law of the cohabiting unmarried father with regard to, for example, consenting to emergency medical treatment for the child.

2.09 In addition, as with married parents, where one or both unmarried parents have acquired parental responsibility, all parental rights which exist only for the child's protection diminish as the child increases in age and understanding as was decided in the case of *Gillick v West Norfolk and Wisbech Area Health Authority* [1986] AC 112.

2.10 Whilst it is now possible for unmarried parents to share parental responsibility without obtaining a court order, s 4(1)(b) CA 1989 requires an agreement between parents to share parental responsibility to be in prescribed form and recorded in a prescribed way. Whilst joint registration of the birth is likely to vest parental responsibility in the unmarried father after the coming into force of the reintroduced ACB 2001, this will not, it seems, be retrospective (see clause (7)106. Thus for some time to come, parents who become aware of the possibility of sharing parental responsibility for their child are likely to need legal advice. The introduction of the parental responsibility agreement was not coupled with any publicity aimed at informing unmarried parents of the existence of such a procedure. Perhaps not surprisingly, therefore, only a tiny minority of the unmarried parents who jointly register the birth of their child have taken advantage of this means of sharing parental responsibility. Substantial increases in the numbers of agreements registered in the first three years following implementation of the procedure showed that more parents seem to be becoming aware of the procedure. However, it does appear that the vast majority of unmarried parents remain ignorant of its existence, often believing that joint birth registration already gives them parental responsibility, whilst others may not consider the effort required to obtain a formal agreement is worthwhile.

(b) The advantages and disadvantages of sharing parental responsibility

2.11 Due to some evidence of abuse of the original procedure, highlighted in the annual report 1992/93 of the Children Act Advisory Committee the parental responsibility agreement form now requires each parent's signature to be witnessed by a lay justice or officer of the court,(Family Proceedings (Amendment No. 4) Rules 1994). Whilst the introduction of the agreement procedure and its increased use since its implementation has undoubtedly added to the numbers of unmarried parents sharing parental responsibility for their children, the number of agreements made has plateaued at around 3,000 per year, amounting to less than two per cent of all jointly registered births. These statistics, together with research which proves the ignorance of unmarried fathers and mothers about the father's lack of automatic legal status (see eg McRae, 1993, Pickford, 1999 and Smart and Stevens, 2000), seem to have made a convincing case for the reform of the law. As indicated above, if the provisions in the ACB 2001 do become law, all fathers who jointly register the birth of their child will in future automatically acquire parental responsibility (see clause 106), although unlike the position of the married father this can be revoked by the court (s 12 CA 1989). Given the courts have in practice almost always granted fathers parental responsibility even on relationship breakdown or where the parents have never lived together, such a reform would be entirely logical and in keeping with the beliefs of the general population and the practice in the day-to day-life of almost all cohabitants. Certainly, the case for keeping the availability of parental responsibility agreements a well-kept secret in order to avoid unmarried mothers being pressurised into agreeing to share parental responsibility against their better judgment, has been largely undermined by the courts' attitude to granting parental responsibility orders in all but the most extreme cases.

2.12 Before considering the procedure, it must be pointed out that, as matters stand at the moment, a mother who agrees to share parental responsibility pursuant to s 4 CA 1989 is giving up her right to sole parental responsibility of the child unless and until another court order is made restoring it. Once parental responsibility is conferred on the father, it cannot be unilaterally withdrawn by the mother. Thus, a decision to share parental responsibility at an early stage in the child's life may on the face of it have important ramifications if the relationship later breaks down and the arrangements for the child or children cannot be agreed between the parents. The existence of a parental responsibility agreement or order will be a factor to be taken into account on making orders relating to the child on breakdown, and may influence how the court views the father's role in the child's life. Any mother agreeing to share parental responsibility should accordingly be advised that, in effect, she is placing herself in a position much more akin to that of a married mother *vis-à-vis* her rights over her child. In a stable relationship, she may well be happy to take such a step, but should know at the outset the possible ramifications. If the law is reformed to give parental responsibility to all unmarried fathers who jointly register the birth, the weighing of these factors will need to be done initially at the point of birth registration. These considerations also reveal a possible conflict of interest between the parents, and separate advice may be desirable where the father seeks an agreement or intends to apply for an order. Having said this, however, case law has shown the courts to be very willing indeed to grant parental responsibility orders, even on opposed applications, as discussed below.

2.13 How much real difference a parental responsibility order or agreement will make in practice to unmarried cohabiting parents who later separate is debatable. Wherever there is a dispute, the child's interests are paramount, and thus it is likely to be the degree of parental involvement and the respective circumstances of the parents which will be critical. An unmarried father who has joint parental responsibility, but who has otherwise shown little interest in the child, will not succeed in a dispute on breakdown to any greater degree than a comparable father without parental responsibility. However, it is conceivable that an unmarried father who has had the major role in bringing up a child may find it easier to obtain an order that the child reside with him on breakdown (a residence order) if the mother has legally acknowledged joint parental responsibility. The courts have tended in the past to have a certain mistrust of unmarried fathers in custody/residence and even contact disputes, and a commitment to joint parental responsibility by the father may tip the balance away from the mother and towards the father to the extent of placing him in the same position as a married father. Certainly, a mother should be advised that she is in effect giving up her sole control over the child, although as an unmarried father can in any event apply to the court for a residence order, the making of a s 4 order or agreement does not in practice prove to be that significant. Indeed, in *Re P (a minor) (parental responsibility order)* [1994] 1 FLR 578 and in *Re S (minor) (Parental Responsibility)* [1995] 2 FLR 648, the view was taken that a parental responsibility order does not give the father the right to interfere in day to day issues, nor override the mother who had a residence order. Such an order confers status, rather than power. Section 4(3) also gives the court power to discharge a parental responsibility order or agreement on the application of a person with parental responsibility for the child concerned where the court has given leave for the application to be made. However, this course of action would have to be in the child's best interests and overcome the no order presumption laid down in s 1(5) CA 1989, and it seems clear that a court would be unlikely to take a father's parental responsibility away without very good reason, once it had been given. In *Re P (termination of parental responsibility)* [1995] 1 FLR 1048, the court did revoke a parental responsibility agreement made without the mother's knowledge that the father had abused the child, stating that it would be wrong in these circumstances for the parents to have equal status in respect of the child.

2.14 Where a parental responsibility agreement is entered into, unlike the position in relation to the making of a parental responsibility order by the courts, there is no judgment made of whether giving the father parental responsibility for the child is in the child's best interests. The mother's consent is all that is needed to effect this important change in legal status. Indeed, although a court has power to refuse to make an order even if both parents consent, it has no jurisdiction to prevent parents entering into a parental responsibility agreement even where the child is in care and the Local Authority oppose the agreement (see *Re X (minor) (care proceeding: parental responsibility)* [2000] 1 FLR 517). The advantage from the mother's point of view is that a parental responsibility order, like a parental responsibility agreement, ostensibly extends parental duties, as well as rights, to the father. Whilst such duties (including the duty to maintain a child) usually exist regardless of whether or not a father has parental responsibility, the entering into a parental responsibility agreement is a public declaration of commitment to the child. Indeed in the government consultation document *Supporting Families*, a civil baby-naming ceremony was mooted at which a parental responsibility agreement could be signed as a symbol of such commitment. However, the new approach to be taken in the ACB 2001 would not necessarily draw attention to the issue of parental responsibility at all.

2.15 A parental responsibility order or an agreement under s 4 CA 1989 also means that should the mother die, the father automatically becomes the child's guardian, as happens where a child's parents are married. However, without either of these, unless the mother has appointed the father (or some other person) testamentary guardian in accordance with the provisions of s 5(3) and (5) CA 1989 (see para 2.27), the child will be left without a legal guardian. The father who wanted to be responsible for his child would have to apply to the court for a s 4 order at that stage, or for a s 8 residence order, or for an order appointing him guardian pursuant to s 5(1) CA 1989. The research of McRae, and more recently that of Pickford and Smart and Stevens (para 2.11) shows that many cohabiting mothers and fathers are completely unaware of this fact and think, for example that the child's father is placed in the same position as a married father by having jointly registered the birth.

2.16 Conversely, where a s 4 order exists, s 5(7) provides that any appointment by the mother of a testamentary guardian other than the father does not take effect until after the death of the father with parental responsibility, unless there was a residence order in favour of the mother at the date of her death. Thus, from the mother's point of view, a s 4 order or agreement will mean that the father will automatically become the child's guardian on her death even if this is against her wishes. Assuming the ACB 2001 reforms are introduced, this will become the normal position wherever unmarried parents have jointly registered the birth. Where the parents are still living together at the time of the mother's death, this would seem to be appropriate. The situation is more difficult where the parents have joint parental responsibility but the child has lost touch with the father following breakdown, as discussed in Chapter 8 below.

2.17 A s 4 agreement, or order, is also recognition by the father of paternity and of his duties towards his child, including the duty to maintain, although a parental responsibility order was not withheld by the court to force a father to meet his maintenance obligations in *Re H (minor) (parental responsibility order)* [1996] 1 FLR 867. It enables a father to consent to medical treatment and jointly take decisions about, for example, schooling, or change of surname, which are otherwise in law the sole province of the unmarried mother. It should be noted that even where there is no s 4 agreement or order, subss 2(9) and (10) CA 1989 enable a person who has parental responsibility to arrange for some or all of it to be met by one or more persons acting on his or her behalf, although parental responsibility cannot be surrendered or transferred to another person. This gives much greater flexibility than was available prior to the CA 1989 and could be of assistance to unmarried parents who wish to share the care of their child, but do not wish to share parental responsibility.

2.18 It is thought that where parents are cohabiting in a stable relationship, they may both wish to place themselves as nearly as possible in the position of married parents and this is the intention and effect of a s 4 agreement. Nonetheless, some distinctions, although not necessarily disadvantages, remain. The citizenship of a child of unmarried parents is still transmitted through the mother rather than the father, and a child will acquire his or her domicile of origin from the mother not the father. Although it is important for both parties to understand the consequences of a s 4 agreement or order, unless breakdown or irreconcilable differences relating to the child are foreseen, such an agreement or order will enable parenthood to be shared in the same way as it is by married parents and be proof that both parents are keen to share with the other the associated rights and duties. Assuming that unmarried fathers do, following implementation of the proposed reforms, come to acquire parental responsibility on joint birth registration, they will have been placed even closer to the same position as married parents.

(c) Orders and agreements for joint parental responsibility

2.19 It was not until the introduction of s 4 FLRA 1987 that unmarried parents were able to share parental rights, duties and responsibilities. The section provided that:

> 'where the father and mother of a child were not married to each other at the time of the birth, the court may on the father's application, order that he shall have all the parental rights and duties with respect to the child.'

Thus, only the father could make the application and this is still the position with the applications under s 4 CA 1989. However, the latter section also enables parental responsibility to be shared by virtue of a written agreement between the parents, which was not possible before. The magistrates' court, county court and the High Court all have jurisdiction to hear applications for parental responsibility orders under s 4 CA 1989, although the need to apply for an order seems most likely to arise upon breakdown or, perhaps, on the death of the mother, as there should be no need to issue proceedings if the parents agree, as the parties can achieve the same end by entering into an agreement as described below. Where a parental responsibility order is sought, the procedure is now the same whichever venue is chosen, since the CA 1989 has harmonised the procedure in all three courts. Applications are made by the father's completing form C1. This is then issued by the court and the applicant must serve copies on the mother and on any other person prescribed by the court rules (see below). No supporting affidavits are required. Written supporting evidence takes the form of signed statements containing a declaration that the maker believes them to be true. The application form, together with the exact procedural steps are set out in the Family Proceedings Courts (Children Act 1989) Regulations 1991 for the magistrates' courts, and in the Family Proceedings Rules 1991 for the county court and High Court. Section 4 CA 1989 repealed s 4 FLRA 1987, but any old-style parental rights orders made under the 1987 Act will be treated as if they were parental responsibility orders made pursuant to s 4 CA 1989 (para 4, Sch 14 CA 1989). Although there is great similarity between the old and new s 4 orders, there are also some important differences. The 1989 Act changed the vocabulary from rights and duties to that of parental responsibility (defined by s 3(1)—see para 2.06), although in this context the concept remains broadly the same. In addition, the starting point for the court when asked to make a s 4 order is that it must not make any order under the Act unless it considers that to do so would be better for the child than making no order at all (s 1(5)).

2.20 Section 4(1), however, also permits an alternative to a court order:

'Where a child's father and mother were not married to each other at the time of his birth—
(a) the court may, on the application of the father, order that he shall have parental responsibility for the child; or
(b) the father and mother may by agreement ('a parental responsibility agreement') provide for the father to have parental responsibility for the child.'

Thus, an unmarried father may make an application to court for a s 4 order. He will have to show that it is better to make the order than to make no order at all and the child's welfare will be the court's paramount consideration (s 1(1)).

2.21 Case law gives guidance on when parental responsibility orders under s 4 CA 89 should be granted. In *Re H (minors) (illegitimate children: father: parental rights) (No 2)* [1991] 1 FLR 214, Balcombe LJ set out some of the factors to be considered by the court when asked to make a s 4 order. These include the degree of commitment shown by the father to the children; the degree of attachment between the father and the children; and the father's reasons for applying for an order. In this case, although the children were in care and the subject of an application that they be freed for adoption, a parental rights order was made giving him *locus standi* in the application. In *Re C (minors) (minors: parental rights)* [1992] 1 FLR 1, this approach was followed and a parental rights order was made despite the fact that all the rights were not immediately enforceable. The important question was whether the association between the parties was sufficiently enduring and whether the father, by his conduct during and since the application, showed sufficient commitment to the children to justify giving him a legal status equivalent to that of a married father, due attention being paid to the fact that a number of the parental rights conferred would be unenforceable (see Mustill LJ at page 2).

2.22 In *D v Hereford and Worcester County Council* [1991] 1 FLR 205, Ward J expanded on the text in *Re H* (above) and suggested that the test should be, has the father, or will he, 'behave with parental responsibility for the child'. Here again the child was in care. In the post-Children Act decision of *S v R (parental responsibility)* [1993] 1 FCR 331, FD, it was held that on an application for a parental responsibility order, the court should expressly consider the matters in the judgment of Balcombe LJ in *Re H* (above) and in *Re H (a minor) (contact and parental responsibility)* [1993] 1 FCR 85, CA, a parental responsibility order was granted to a father, even though it was appropriate to refuse him contact, in order to give him the right to be consulted before adoption of the child. In the later decision of *Re E* [1994] 2 FCR 709, the Court of Appeal went further, stating that where a father had shown commitment to a child, there was a presumption that a parental responsibility order should be made, providing there was no evidence that it would adversely affect the child's welfare. 'Commitment' included regular contact and financial support for the child, and in this case an order was made despite the fact that the

Court of Appeal did not reverse the decision at first instance to refuse the father contact to the child. More recently in *Re H (parental responsibility)* [1998] IFLR 555, the extension of a formal presumption in favour of granting parental responsibilty was denied. The Court of Appeal in *Re C and V (minors) (parental responsibility and contact)* [1998] 1 FLR 392 emphasised that the making of an order was designed to confer a status and it would normally be in a child's best interests for an order to be granted. The court did, however, refuse to make a parental order in *Re T (a minor) (parental responsibility: contact)* [1993] 2 FLR 450, where a father had shown total disregard for a child's welfare and attacked the mother while holding the baby and then detained it for nine days after a two-hour contact period. Similarly in *Re C and V* (above) the court made clear that an order should be refused where a father's motives for seeking an order are improper as occurred in *Re P (parental responsibility)* [1998] 2 FLR 96. Here a father's aim, it was found, was to interfere inappropriately with the exercise of the mother's parental responsibility, against whom he had made unfounded allegations. The court may however take the view that such improper interference may be effectively controlled by s 8 orders in which case parental responsibility may be granted (see *Re S (a minor) (parental responsibility)* [1995] 2 FLR 648.

2.23 The 1989 Act broke new ground in that, for the first time, unmarried parents could agree to share parental responsibility without going to court, or even asking the court to approve a consent order. However, s 4(2) stipulates that a parental responsibility agreement must be made in the form prescribed by the Parental Responsibility Regulations 1991 (SI 1991/1478) as amended. The agreement must now be completed and signed by both the mother and father whose signatures are required to be witnessed by either a Justice of the Peace, justices' clerk or an officer of the court authorised to administer oaths, who must specify the evidence of identity produced by the signatory. A separate form is needed for each child, and the parental responsibility agreements (Form C (PRA)(M)) are available from the Family Proceedings Court and County Courts which are Family Hearing Centres. The agreement will not take effect until it has been filed (together with two copies) with the Principal Registry of the Family Division at the High Court, Somerset House, Strand, London WC2 1LP. In *Re X (parental responsibility agreement)* [2000] 1 FLR 517, the ability to make an agreement was considered an important aspect of the right to privacy and family life, under act 8 European Convention of Human Rights.

2.24 Where a s 4 order or agreement has been made, s 2(7) CA 1989 provides that each person who has parental responsibility may act alone without the other in meeting that responsibility. On the face of the Act, there is no right of veto where the other person with parental responsibility disagrees with an action to be taken in relation to the child, although either parent is entitled to apply for a 'specific issue order' under s 8(1) CA 1989 (see Chapter 8 below) to determine a specific question which has arisen in relation to any aspect of parental responsibility. The only limits on the independent exercise of parental responsibility provided by the Act are that nothing incompatible with any order made under the provisions of the Act must be done; and the right of independent action does not override the need to obtain the consent of another person if this is required by statute, such as for the purposes of adoption. However, despite its plain language, the courts have not always given s 2(7) its literal meaning and seem to take the view that a parent with parental responsibility has the right to be consulted even where there is no statutory duty to do so. Thus in *Re PC (change of surname)* [1997] 2 FLR 730, Holman J decided that a parent had the right to be consulted on a child's change of name even though no residence order had been made, the sole trigger under the Act for a right to be consulted. In *Re T (a minor) (change of surname)* [1998] 2 FLR 620, Thorpe LJ stated that a mother who had unilaterally changed the child's surname had acted 'unlawfully', although on what basis was not made clear. In *Re H (Parental Responsibility)* [1998] 1 FLR 855 Butler-Sloss LJ indicated that a father with responsibility had 'the right to be consulted on schooling, serious medical problems and other important occurrences in the child's life'. And in *Re J (specific issue orders: child's religious upbringing and circumcision)* [2000] 1 FLR 571d, the Court of Appeal agreed that 'circumcision must join the exceptional categories where disagreement between holders of parental responsibility must be submitted to the court for determination'. Thus despite the ostensible power to use parental responsibility jointly and severally given in s 2(7), this has been interpreted to imply a duty to consult on at least some issues (see further Eekelaar. 'Do Parents have a Duty to Consult?' (1998) *Law Quarterly Review* 337).

2.25 Only a court can bring a parental responsibility order or agreement to an end. The application may be by one of the persons who has parental responsibility; or, with leave of the court, by the child providing he or she has sufficient understanding to make the application (subss 4(3) and (4)).

2.26 The Law Commission predicted that s 4 agreements would be used mainly by unmarried parents cohabiting in a stable relationship who do not wish to marry, yet wish to share parental responsibility. Cohabitants are also the largest group affected by the proposals to give fathers parental responsibility on joint birth registration. Shared parental responsibility can be seen to be particularly helpful, providing it coincides with the mother's wishes and the welfare of the child, in the tragic event of the child's mother dying without having appointed a guardian. However, as stated above, there is nothing to prevent the father from applying for a s 4 order at that time, or indeed from applying under s 5 to be appointed by the court as the child's guardian. However, it is possible at that stage that another individual will apply to be appointed guardian, whereas if parental responsibility is already shared, then the father would automatically become the child's guardian.

2.27 The same result can be achieved if the mother appoints the child's father (who does not have parental responsibility) as testamentary guardian in accordance with s 5(5). It is possible to appoint a testamentary guardian other than by Will. This can be done by any parent who has parental responsibility, and will have effect, providing it is in writing, dated and signed by the person making the appointment. It will still be valid if it is signed at the direction of the appointor in his or her presence and in the presence of two witnesses who attest the signature. Testamentary guardians can still be appointed by Will, but the CA 1989 procedure is simpler and can be used to vary any appointment previously made by Will. As ied above, where there is a surviving parent with parental responsibility, the appointment of a testamentary guardian takes effect only on the death of the surviving parent.

2.28 To summarise, if unmarried cohabiting parents wish to share parental responsibility this can be done by means of a parental responsibility agreement which meets the requirements of s 4 CA 1989. Where there is no agreement, the father can still apply to the court for an order and must show that to make an order is better for the child than making no order at all. This has not proved difficult even where the mother does not agree but is the child's prime carer, although the attitude of courts to this issue may vary. In *Re A (minors)* [1993] Fam Law 464, FD, the judge made a parental responsibility order despite the mother's opposition. The father had been present at the birth, was registered as the father on the child's birth certificate and had lived with the mother for three months before their relationship deteriorated. Having not seen the child for a year he applied for both contact and parental responsibility orders, both of which were made, with the judge commenting that he had shown considerable commitment to the child and loved the child as a married father would have done. In practice, it is now clear that a father who has cohabited and who has been or is likely to be granted contact where the relationship breaks down would seem unlikely to be refused an order granting parental responsibility. Indeed, given the proposals for joint birth registration to give fathers automatic parental responsibility, albeit subject to the court's power to terminate it, there would seem to be a clear move towards putting cohabiting fathers on virtually equal footing with married fathers, a position which is in keeping with what unmarried parents have believed the position to be for a long time in any event.

2.29 Nonetheless, where cohabitants have children, and seek advice, consideration should be given to the question of the benefits and possible disadvantages of parental responsibility agreements and orders. Even more important, perhaps, is the need for the parent or parents with parental responsibility to appoint a testamentary guardian for their children and such appointments should be kept under review and amended if circumstances change.

(d) Children of previous relationships

2.30 Many unmarried families include children of one of the parties by another relationship. Where the adults of a new family marry each other, their children are recognised as children of the family (s 52 Matrimonial Causes Act 1973 (MCA)). Where the adults remain unmarried no duty to maintain them will arise under the Child Support Act 1991 or otherwise and their legal status will be governed solely by the position of their natural parents and any orders made in proceedings between these parents. This will not change under the reforms proposed in the ACB 2001, as only (married) step-parents will acquire a new ability to gain parental responsibility under parental responsibility agreements. Cohabitating quasi-step-parents are not included.

2.31 Section 2(9) CA 1989 provides that any person who has care of a child may do what is reasonable to safeguard or promote the child's welfare, and accordingly where a child of a previous relationship lives with cohabiting adults, this provision covers the relationship between a child and the adult who is not the child's parent. The natural parent's cohabitant will not normally be able to acquire parental responsibility under the Act, unless he or she successfully applies for a residence order, which will be discussed below, or unless he or she is appointed the child's guardian. The cohabitant may be appointed by the natural parent as the child's testamentary guardian (as outlined above); and upon the death of the natural parent, if the deceased parent had a residence order in his or her favour, the testamentary appointment of a guardian will take effect even though the other natural parent still retains parental responsibility (s 5(7)). The surviving natural parent could however apply to the court to be appointed a guardian and such an appointment would take effect jointly with the testamentary guardian. Similarly, if the child's other parent does not have parental responsibility, which will arise in the case of unmarried fathers only, then the mother could appoint her cohabitant as guardian and this will take effect on her death.

2.32 Where no testamentary guardian was appointed but there was a residence order in favour of the deceased natural parent, the cohabitant could apply to the court to be made the child's guardian whether or not the surviving parent has retained parental responsibility. The surviving natural parent can make a similar application (see s 5(1) CA 1989). Where there was no residence order, and the surviving parent has retained parental responsibility, the deceased parent's cohabitant will not be able to apply to be appointed guardian by the court, and any testamentary appointment is postponed until the death of the surviving parent with parental responsibility. If the child's father never had parental responsibility, the mother's cohabitant, as well as the child's father, could apply to the court to be appointed guardian, in the absence of an appointment by the mother before her death.

2.33 This again highlights the importance of making arrangements for children. Another change brought about by the CA 1989 which may be of assistance in relation to children of previous relationships, is found in subss 10(2) and (5). The former enables *any* person, with leave of the court, to apply for a s 8 order. Section 8 orders will be discussed in Chapter 8, but include residence and contact orders. Thus a non-parent cohabitant who has built up a good relationship with their partner's child could apply for leave on breakdown or on the death of the partner. Where the child has lived with the non-parent for three years more, or where the applicant has the consent of the parent with a residence order or both parents with parental responsibility, then s 10(5) gives them a right to apply for a s 8 order. This right can be exercised at any time, not only in the context of breakdown or death. Thus a non-parent cohabitant living with the child and one of his or her natural parents could in theory apply for a residence order jointly with the resident natural parent. Section 12(2) then provides that if a residence order is made in favour of a non-parent, the court must make an order giving that person parental responsibility for the duration of the residence order. However, s 1(5) of course provides that in addition to applying the welfare principle, the court should not make any order unless to do so is better for the child than making no order at all. If such an order is likely to make the child's relationship with their other natural parent difficult, the court may well fall back on the 'no order' presumption.

4 Change of name

2.34 The right to change the name of a child of unmarried parents ostensibly rests with the mother alone, unless a court order affecting her parental responsibility has been made or unless the father has acquired parental responsibility. Generally, though, unmarried fathers will be unable to change their child's name unless they have parental responsibility by virtue of s 4 CA 1989 or obtain a court order. Where parental responsibility is shared, either parent can exercise it independently of the other (s 2(7) CA 1989) yet the courts have been reluctant to endorse the seeming ability of one parent to change the child's name without the other's knowledge. Any dispute can only be finally settled either by a specific issue order or where there is a residence order by an application under s 13 CA 1989. A specific issue order can be sought by either parent to resolve a change of name dispute, providing no residence order to determine with whom the child should live has been made or is being applied for.

2.35 In *Re B (minors) (change of surname)* [1996] 1 FLR 791, it was stated that such an application was a freestanding application for leave rather than a specific issue application, where a custody order but no residence order had been made. The court treated it as an application under s 13(1) CA 1989, but nonetheless found the s 1(3) checklist factors (which would have applied if it were a contested s 8 specific issue application) were a useful *aide-memoire*, as the welfare of the child was paramount. However, subsequently in *Dawson v Wearmouth* [1999] 1 FLR 1167, the House of Lords confirmed the appropriateness of an application for a specific issue order in relation to change of name applications where no residence order was in force and of the consequent application of the welfare checklist (s 1(3) CA 1989) and no order presumption (s 1(5) CA 1989) in such cases.

2.36 Where a residence order has been made, then s 13 of the 1989 Act provides that a child's surname cannot be changed without the written consent of every person who has parental responsibility, or leave of the court. Thus leave will have to be sought under s 13. As we have seen, the Act generally provides that no order should be made unless it would be better for the child than making no order at all. In addition, it specifically provides, in relation to contested s 8 applications, for the child's wishes and feelings, in the light of his age and understanding, to be taken into account. This would seem to make it imperative to apply to change a child's name only if the child agrees, or is not of an age to express his or her feelings. However, in *Re B* (above) the application to change the surname of children aged 12, 14 and 15 was refused despite their clear wishes for the change and the fact that they had already informally adopted the new name. It is worthy of note that where residence orders are made as between unmarried parents, the restriction on changing a child's surname following the making of a residence order will of course apply where the parent with whom the child does not reside retains parental responsibility following breakdown.

2.37 In *Dawson v Wearmouth* (above) the mother who had separated from her cohabitant, the child's father, registered the child in her ex-husband's surname which she and her older two children used. The father's application for the child's surname to be changed to his was refused, applying the welfare principle and the no order presumption despite the fact that the child had no blood tie with the mother's ex-husband. Again in *A v Y (child's surname)* [1999] 2 FLR 5, the application of these Children Act principles led to the refusal of a married father's application to change his child's surname to his own. The mother, knowing that the marriage was in difficulties, had registered the child in her maiden name by which the child had become known at school and in the community by the time of the hearing of the father's application some four years later. Thus it is now clear that it is difficult to change the status quo in these change of surname cases. Having said that, the very recent decision of *R (change of name)* [2001] *Family Law* 360, the Court of Appeal indicated that parents and courts should be much more prepared to contemplate the use of parents' surnames.

2.38 Some children who come to form part of an unmarried family may be the children of one of the cohabitants born during a marriage, and thus cohabitants may also seek advice if they wish to change these children's surnames. On divorce, s 13 CA 1989 always applies to changing the names of children of married parents where a residence order is made, as married parents each have and will retain parental responsibility. However, the no order presumption means that few residence and contact orders are made on divorce and these are certainly not made automatically. Generally, where parents agree arrangements for the children, no s 8 orders will be made, leaving both parents with unrestricted parental responsibility. Thus in these cases, whilst there is no clear statutory impediment to either parent changing the child's surname (see s 2(7) CA 1989), *Dawson v Wearmouth* (above) has made it clear that where there is not agreement between the parents, an application must be made to the court.

5 Adoption and infertility treatment

2.39 The Adoption Act 1976 (AA 1976) does not permit adoption by cohabiting couples, whether same- or opposite-sex; only married couples or single people may apply to adopt a child (see ss 14 and 15 AA 1976). This position will not change even if the reforms contained in the ACB 2001 are implemented. Thus if a couple wishes to adopt jointly, so that they share parental responsibility, they must be married. It is possible for one of a cohabiting couple to apply to adopt but of course detailed investigations are carried out by the local authority in relation to all members of the prospective adopter's household before a child is placed for adoption. Some local authorities may not be prepared to recommend adoption by a single person who is cohabiting, although there is nothing in the Act or the

Regulations which prevent this course of action. The investigation procedure is and is likely to remain very thorough and the initial placement of a child can take place only if the local authority or approved adoption society recommends the placement. A clear aim of the proposed new adoption law contained in the ACB 2001 is to increase the number of adoptions of children in care and at the same time to set 'National Standards for Adoption' which will speed up and clarify procedure and ensure good practice. Unfortunately, the 1993 White Paper, *Adoption: The Future* (Cm 2288), containing the Conservative government's proposals for reform, specifically rejected the proposal that the right to adopt should be extended to unmarried cohabiting couples. Nothing in the Labour government's subsequent papers (see *Adoption – the Prime Minister's Review*, Performance and Innovation Unit, 2000, and *Adoption – A New Approach*, (2000) Cm 5017) sought to change this as is line with their general pro-marriage sentiments set out in their policy document *Supporting Families* (The Stationery Office, 1998). Neither does such a policy offend the Human Rights Act 1988.

2.40 Thus, the only proposal which may affect the position of cohabitants wanting to adopt is the resurrection of old-style 'custodionship' in the shape of a special guardianship order. This was originally mooted in the 1993 White Paper (see para 5.23) and is now inserted in clause 110 of the ACB 2001. This would enable relatives or others – including, cohabitants over 18 – caring for a child to obtain legal recognition of their role without going as far as adoption. It was originally envisaged that it would supplement the option of a residence order, discussed below, as it would extend beyond the age of 16 to that of 18 and enable a guardian to appoint a replacement in the event of his or her death. It would not, however, sever links with the birth parents, affect their ability to appoint testamentary guardians, or involve the same scrutiny demanded by adoption procedures. Nonetheless, applicants will have to give three months' notice and be vetted by the local authority. In return they will be able to exercise parental responsibility to the exclusion of the birth parents, save where consent of all holders of parental responsibility is required.

2.41 Under the current law, if a woman cohabitant successfully adopts a child, it is not open for her male partner to obtain parental responsibility by virtue of a s 4 agreement or order. Section 10 CA 1989 does, enable a person, with the consent of all the persons with parental responsibility or with whom the child has lived for at least three years, to apply for a residence order. As a residence order can be made in favour of more than one person, it is possible that the court would agree to the making of a joint residence order in this situation as it may be the only way a cohabiting couple could share parental responsibility. Section 12(2) CA 1989 directs the court, on making a residence order in favour of a non-parent, to make an order giving that person parental responsibility for as long as the order remains in force. This appears to be the only way unmarried cohabiting couples can share parental responsibility for a child for whom they both care, who is not a child of their relationship.

2.42 The same difficulties would arise for a cohabiting gay couple wanting to adopt, as no adoption order can be made on the application of more than one person other than a married couple. One member of the couple could apply to adopt a child, but again the adoption agency may not regard such a placement as suitable. Given the drive to increase adoptions of particularly older children in care, and the disapproval of 'blanket-banning' of categories of prospective adopters, more local authorities should be prepared to consider individuals regardless of their sexual orientation, rather than regard homosexuality as a bar in itself as used to always be the case. In the House of Lords decision in *Re D (an infant) (parent's consent)* [1977] AC 602, concerning the father's consent to adoption, it was said that a father's homosexuality would endanger the child on account of possible approaches by men visiting his father's home. However, some twenty years on, in *Re W (a minor) (adoption: homosexual adopter)* [1998] Form 58, it was confirmed that there was no reason why one of the lesbian cohabitants should be barred from being an adopter on the grounds of her sexuality.

2.43 The difficulties relating to cohabitants adopting lead some couples to consider human assisted reproduction. Unlike adoption, such treatment is, at least in theory, available to any woman, whether married, single, heterosexual or homosexual. There is no bar on who can apply and there are certainly no rigorous investigation procedures to discover the suitability of the household for the child, although some counselling is usual. However, the availability of treatment varies from health authority to health authority. The legal status of the child born as a result of human assisted reproduction, or rather the status of the father, will vary depending on the nature of the treatment. In the case of AIH treatment, where the mother is artificially inseminated with her cohabitant's sperm, the child will be the genetic child of the parties, although as the parents are unmarried only the mother will have parental responsibility at birth. The father can, however, apply for a parental responsibility order or enter into a parental responsibility agreement in the same way as any unmarried father as described above.

2.44 If the AID method is used, whereby the mother is artificially inseminated by the sperm of an anonymous donor, the mother will of course have parental responsibility from birth, and her cohabitant may apply for a parental responsibility order by virtue of s 28 Human Fertilisation and Embryology Act 1990 (HFEA 1990). Thus, if cohabitants have a child as a result of artificial insemination, which treatment was provided by a licensed body for the man and woman together, then the man is treated as the father of the child. He can then obtain parental responsibility by virtue of a s 4 agreement or order in the same way as any other unmarried father. It should be noted that if the treatment is carried out by an unlicensed body, such as a hospital abroad, the father may not apply for parental responsibility and will not be the legal father of the child for any purpose, including the Child Support Act (see *U v W (A-G intervening)* [1998] Fam 29.

2.45 Where a cohabiting couple has a child by virtue of the *in vitro* fertilisation method (IVF) and the egg is donated anonymously and fertilised by the male cohabitant's sperm, then by virtue of s 27(1) HFEA 1990, the mother in whom the egg is placed is regarded as the child's mother and if she is unmarried then she alone will have parental responsibility of the child at birth. However, her cohabitant can obtain parental responsibility by virtue of a s 4 agreement or order as if the child were conceived naturally as set out above. If the mother is married, s 28 provides that the child will be treated as a child of the marriage unless the husband is shown not to have consented. If both the egg and the sperm are donated, then the mother in whom the embryo is placed is treated as the mother of the child. Her cohabitant is in exactly the position described above in relation to AID. Providing the treatment was provided by a licensed body for the man and woman together s 28 states that he is to be treated as the father of the child. He can therefore obtain parental responsibility in accordance with s 4 CA 1989.

2.46 Gay women can also undergo infertility treatment, although for gay men surrogacy is probably the only course and is fraught with legal and probably practical difficulties. An attempt has been made to curb commercial surrogacy, yet recognise that it happens. The Surrogacy Arrangements Act 1985 governs surrogacy agreements and, interestingly, s 30 HFEA 1990 brought into force on 1 November 1994 (SI 1994/1776) now enables the court to make an order that the commissioning married couple should be treated in law as the child's parents, providing the surrogate mother and father consent. However, this provision does not apply to unmarried couples or, it seems, single commissioning parents, who would have to rely on wardship or apply for a residence order to obtain legal parental status. The child is deemed to be that of the surrogate mother even if both the egg and sperm were donated (s 27(1) HFEA 1990). This remains an area where cohabitants compared with married couples, are disadvantaged. It should also be noted that the right to found a family contained in art 12 of the European Convention on Human Rights is unlikely to be construed to imply a right to infertility treatment. Thus the implementation of the Human Rights Act 1998 would seem to be of little assistance in either obtaining treatment or in alleging discrimination under art 14. For a discussion of those issues, see Swindells et al, *Family Law and the Human Rights Act 1998*, para 11.25 ff.

Chapter 3

Housing

1 Introduction

3.01 At some point in their relationship, cohabitants have taken a conscious decision to share accommodation with one another. This could have involved one of them moving into their partner's accommodation and giving up their own; or they may have decided to rent accommodation jointly, or buy a property together.

3.02 Legal consequences flow from each of these possibilities. Yet few couples seek, or even think of seeking, legal advice before they take the critical step, unless they happen to be in contact with an advisor about another matter. Some cohabitants may feel that the arrangement is, at first, very much on trial and is not something on which legal advice need be sought. More commonly, in the early stages, each cohabitant trusts the other and does not want to be seen questioning their faith in the relationship. There may be a rather vague intention to look into the position later. Yet all too often, it is only on breakdown of the relationship, or in the context of another crisis, such as threatened possession proceedings by a landlord or mortgagee, that the legal implications of a decision to rent or buy accommodation together will become apparent. Difficult housing market conditions across the private, public and independent sectors in most parts of Britain make it vital for cohabitants to know at the outset how a decision to share accommodation will affect each party's housing and property rights if the relationship comes to an end. Anything legal advisors can do to inform cohabitants of their respective positions before they commence living together may enable each of them to safeguard his or her interests as far as possible in advance of any crisis. It may of course not be possible or appropriate for a solicitor, who should generally take instructions rather than seek out problems, to take the initiative. Yet there are situations where an indication of the effects of cohabitation on housing rights may be welcomed and may elicit a request for more comprehensive advice.

3.03 Some of the more common problems can be illustrated. For example, where cohabitants purchase a property they will make the purchase either in their joint names or in the name of just one of them; this will have important ramifications if it becomes necessary to define their respective interests, either on breakdown of the relationship or on death. A non-owner cohabitant who has given up other accommodation may have little or no beneficial interest in the accommodation which he or she regards as home. Thus, there may be no legal rights to live there once the owner withdraws consent unless action can be taken to obtain an occupation order pursuant to s 36 (Family Law Act 1996 FLA 1996), as discussed in Chapter 7. Such cohabitants often believe that the act of cohabitation over a period of time will protect them from being "turned out of their homes", but this is not of course currently the case. Where cohabitants live in rented accommodation, their positions during cohabitation will depend on the name or names in which the tenancy is vested; and on whether the accommodation is rented in the private, public or independent sector. Problems may arise on breakdown of the relationship, on the death of the partner or the granting of a possession order. Even where a property is jointly purchased, negative equity may prevent an agreed solution being put into effect, or the death of one cohabitant may jeopardise the home of the other. Cohabitants may also find themselves homeless. In some situations, they may be eligible for rehousing by the local housing authority under their much reduced but soon to be amended duties to the homeless as set out in the Housing Act 1996 Part VII.

3.04 This chapter will consider the implications for cohabitants of the various forms of tenure in all contexts other than breakdown, and consider the situations in which cohabitants may be assisted by the provisions of the homelessness legislation, which will shortly be amended by the Homelessness Bill 2001.

2 Rented accommodation

(a) Private rented accommodation

3.05 This area of law is highly complex and it is not proposed to attempt to give anything other than a broad outline of the position as it affects cohabitants, and to detail specific problems that cohabitants are most likely to encounter. At present there are two statutory schemes which govern private sector tenancies. If a tenancy was granted before 15 January 1989, it will be governed by the provisions of the Rent Act 1977 and it will be a protected tenancy (contractual or statutory). After 15 January 1989 all residential tenancies granted (with limited exceptions where the tenant was previously a Rent Act protected tenant of the landlord) fall within the provisions of the Housing Act 1988 as amended. They will be either assured or assured shorthold tenancies where the landlord may charge a market rent and, in the latter case, there is only very limited security of tenure. Indeed, tenancies created on or after 28 February 1997 will normally be assured shorthold tenancies unless the landlord expressly states otherwise. This reverses the original presumption that a tenancy would usually be assured and abolishes the notice requirement previously necessary to create an assured shorthold tenancy (see Sch 2 Housing Act 1996) and means that assured tenancies have become the almost exclusive preserve of social landlords. A cohabitant's housing rights thus depend on when the tenancy was entered into, and the type of tenancy granted under the relevant statutory provisions.

3.06 As with any rented accommodation, another important factor which will determine a cohabitant's position is whether the tenancy is in joint names, or vested in the sole name of one of them. The importance of this distinction is discussed in

(d) below. A joint tenancy is more likely to have been granted if the cohabitants jointly looked for and found the accommodation. However, even where this has happened, many private landlords insist on putting the tenancy in the sole name of one of them, probably because this may prove advantageous if possession is ever sought. Where the tenancy is in writing it is easy to establish whether or not there is a joint tenancy by looking at the tenancy agreement itself. In some cases the tenancy may have been granted orally, and whether it is a joint tenancy or not is something that will only ever be specifically determined if it becomes necessary at a later stage. The matter will be decided by the court with reference to the parties' intentions at the time they reached agreement, and any other evidence (such as correspondence, the name or names on the rent book or which person paid the rent) available.

(b) Public sector secure tenancies

3.07 Cohabitants living in local authority accommodation are secure tenants, and their tenancies are governed by the Housing Act 1985 as amended. This is also the case with housing association tenancies granted before 15 January 1989. The advantages and disadvantages of a joint tenancy are discussed below. Public sector landlords are generally fairly willing to grant or transfer tenancies into the joint names of cohabitants.

3.08 An assignment of a secure tenancy generally results in the tenancy ceasing to be a secure tenancy, but not if the assignment is to someone who is entitled to be a successor to the tenancy, and, as set out below, a cohabitant may come within this definition providing he or she has lived in the accommodation for 12 months. Thus, where these conditions are fulfilled the tenant cohabitant may assign the secure tenancy into joint names by deed.

3.09 Local authority secure tenants have a right to buy their accommodation at a discount providing they fulfil certain conditions (see Part V, Housing Act 1985), and although a non-tenant cohabitant has no right to require to be a joint proprietor, a tenant has the right to require that up to three members of his family who are not joint tenants, but who occupy the accommodation as their principal home, purchase the property jointly with the tenant. Thus, at the request of the tenant cohabitant, providing the non-tenant partner has resided in the property for the past twelve months, or providing the landlord consents, cohabitants can jointly purchase accommodation under the right to buy provisions, even if only one of them was the secure tenant. Conversely, a joint tenant has the right to buy the premises but could not do so without at least the consent of the other joint tenant. Cohabitants purchasing accommodation under the "right to buy" scheme must of course be advised of the implications of purchasing the property and the relevant considerations are set later in this chapter.

(c) Independent sector tenancies

3.10 Since the introduction of the assured tenancy by the Housing Act 1988, housing associations have been unable to grant public sector secure tenancies, but must instead grant assured tenancies governed by Part I of the Act. Where a tenancy was granted by a housing association before 15 January 1989, it is likely to be a secure tenancy and the considerations set out above apply. Any tenancy granted after this time by a housing association (with limited exceptions where the tenant was previously a secure tenant of the association) will be an assured tenancy. Housing associations are not prevented by statute from granting assured shorthold tenancies for fixed term periods with little security of tenure, as is common in the private sector. They are at first sight entitled to charge a market rent. However, as a matter of policy, housing associations have been given the role in the housing market of providers of "social housing". Despite a statutory right for landlords granting assured tenancies to charge a market rent, the Housing Corporation's Code of Guidance, which applies to all housing associations registered with it provides that rent levels should be kept within the reach of those in low-paid employment and assured shorthold tenancies should be granted only where, exceptionally, this is the only means of fulfilling the Association's housing objectives. Nonetheless, housing association tenants now generally come within the statutory provisions of the Housing Act 1988 and are granted assured tenancies. Thus, there are different rules relating to assignment and succession for those who, after 15 January 1989, became tenants of housing associations as opposed to local authorities; this is discussed below (see paras 3.35 – 3.42). It should also be noted that s 16 Housing Act 1996 (HA 1996) has given assured tenants of "registered social landlords" (which currently mainly comprise housing associations) the right to acquire the dwelling of which they are a tenant. This scheme mirrors the "right to buy" and applies wherever the dwelling was provided wholly or in part by public money.

(d) General implications of joint tenancies for cohabitants

3.11 If cohabitants enter into a joint tenancy of private rented accommodation, or indeed any residential accommodation, then they both acquire under the terms of the tenancy agreement the right to occupy the accommodation specified in that agreement. Neither is at liberty to exclude the other from the accommodation save by court order obtained, for example, under the Domestic Violence legislation (see Chapter 7). Both are jointly and severally liable to perform the obligations under the tenancy agreement. Thus if one joint tenant who normally pays the rent fails to do so, the landlord can look to the other joint tenant to pay the whole of the rent, regardless of any arrangement made between the tenants. Failure to meet the rent demands will ultimately lead to possession proceedings which, in the case of joint tenants, must be taken against each of them.

3.12 Whatever the nature of the tenancy in other respects, where a joint tenancy has been granted and one of the joint tenants dies, the other will automatically become the sole tenant by survivorship. However, if one joint tenant leaves the accommodation permanently, then the remaining joint tenant, whilst continuing to have the right to occupy the accommodation, will need to take legal action (as discussed in Chapter 10 below) to have the tenancy transferred into their sole name either under Sch 7 FLA 1996, or alternatively, where there are children of the relationship under para 1(2)(e) Sch 1 CA 1989.

3.13 Generally, a joint tenancy gives each cohabitant security. Both have equal rights to occupy the accommodation and should therefore each be notified of alleged breaches of the terms of the tenancy agreement, or other statutory grounds for possession. There can be no challenge to the right of the survivor of joint tenants to continue to occupy the accommodation on the death of the partner, as, by operation of law, the survivor becomes the sole tenant. In addition, although not of personal concern to joint tenant cohabitants themselves, a joint tenancy which is protected by the Rent Act (in contrast to an assured joint tenancy under the 1988 Act), has the effect of enhancing statutory succession rights by permitting two further successions to resident members of the tenants' family following the death of the second joint tenant (see page 46). A joint tenancy is particularly advantageous for non-heterosexual cohabitants in relation to succession. As will be shown (see para 3.20 *ff*), whilst heterosexual cohabitants do now have the statutory right to succeed to the tenancy of their deceased sole tenant partners, this is not the case for homosexual cohabitants, or indeed any people living together other than as husband and wife, unless they come within the definition of 'a member of the tenant's family'. This has been narrowly construed, although the House of Lords decision in *Fitzpatrick v Sterling Housing Association Ltd* [2001] 1 AC 27 is helpful to same-sex couples where there is a Rent Act tenancy (see below). Generally in order to succeed to the tenancy, they must also fulfil the condition of having resided with the tenant for a period of one or two years (depending on the type of tenancy concerned) immediately before the death.

3.14 Conversely, as will be seen in the context of breakdown, there are situations where a joint tenancy may work to the disadvantage of a cohabitant. Both remain jointly and severally liable to pay the rent regardless of who remains in occupation, and as will be seen in Chapter 10, a valid notice to quit the accommodation by one joint tenant will be sufficient to determine the whole tenancy even if the other cohabitant wishes to remain in occupation and such determination may not even breach an occupation order (see *Hammersmith and Fulham London Borough Council v Monk* [1992] 1 AC 478, *Harrow London Borough Council v Johnstone* [1997] 1 All ER 929 and *Newlon Housing Trust v Alsuaimen* [1999] 1 AC 313). It is also possible that, if rendered homeless where previous accommodation vested in joint names has been given up, both cohabitants may be more readily found intentionally homeless if fault can be attached to the loss of the previous accommodation (see para 3.93 *ff*).

3.15 Whether a joint tenancy will prove more or less advantageous to a cohabitant than a sole tenancy on breakdown of the relationship depends on which of them ultimately seeks to remain in the accommodation and whether or not that person is the tenant. At the outset it is not usually possible to foresee the circumstances which may arise, and of course the scenario which benefits one cohabitant is likely to disadvantage the other. Nonetheless, it seems that overall the advantages of a joint tenancy outweigh the disadvantages for cohabitants in terms of achieving security. Such disadvantages as there are usually occur on breakdown of the relationship.

Many of the disadvantages can be overcome, but security for a non-tenant cohabitant in accommodation which he or she regards as home, particularly if deserted by the tenant partner, or sometimes on death, may be more difficult, if not impossible, to achieve. Section 53 and Sch 7 to Part IV FLA 1996 enables both joint tenant cohabitants and non-tenant cohabitants whose partner is a tenant to apply for a transfer of tenancy order on relationship breakdown. Nonetheless, it is submitted that whilst cases will vary according to individual circumstances, a joint tenant is likely to generally be in a stronger position than a non-tenant cohabitant. As will be discussed further in Chapter 10, this view is reinforced by the Court of Appeal's decision in *Gay v Sheeran* [1999] 3 All ER 795 where a former cohabitant was denied the right to seek a transfer of tenancy on the grounds that her former partner had left the property and was no longer 'entitled to occupy' it as required by Sch 7 FLA 1996. It should also be noted that the transfer of tenancy provisions in the Act can only be of assistance to heterosexual cohabitants, as s 62(1)(a) clearly defines 'cohabitants' as 'a man and a woman who, although not married to each other, are living together as husband and wife'. Furthermore, as also discussed in Chapter 10, same-sex couples who have been granted a joint tenancy (recommended as good practice in the DETR 1999 Code of Guidance to Local Authorities on Allocation of Accommodation and Homelessness 'where members of a household have a long-term commitment to the home') may not even be able to agree to surrender the benefit of the joint tenancy to their joint tenant without losing security of tenure and ultimately possession (see *Burton v Camden London Borough Council* [2000] 2 WLR 427).

3.16 All legal advisors can do is outline the implications of the options. Where appropriate, a written agreement or a Will drawn up in advance of any difficulties, can be suggested.

(e) Cohabitants and sole tenancies – the general position

3.17 Where cohabitants occupy accommodation the tenancy of which is vested in the sole name of only one of them, the non-tenant cohabitant is vulnerable. This is even more so where the tenant cohabitant is in fact a joint tenant with a third party, such as a former partner, who has abandoned the home but not formally assigned the tenancy into the sole name of the remaining tenant cohabitant. In the case of a married couple, a non-tenant spouse has the right to occupy the matrimonial home of which the other spouse is the sole tenant (or indeed a joint tenant), by virtue of s 30 FLA 1996. A non-tenant cohabitant, on the other hand, is usually no more than his or her partner's licensee in law. They have no right at all to occupy the accommodation, no matter how long he or she may have lived there, once the partner revokes the licence to occupy or leaves the accommodation without an intention to return or even, in some situations, dies. Although the situation seemed to have been greatly improved by the transfer of tenancy provisions in s 53 and Sch 7 FLA 1996 in the context of relationship breakdown, the non-tenant cohabitant or former cohabitant still has no occupation rights, nor even a right to pay the rent, unless and until the court is prepared to make either an occupation order pursuant to s 36 FLA 1996 or a transfer of tenancy order in their favour. In addition, as noted above, following the decision in *Gay v Sheeran* [1999] 3 All ER 795 there are still significant difficulties in a non-tenant cohabitant obtaining a transfer of tenancy order where their tenant partner has left the home thereby relinquishing entitlement to occupy and it now seems necessary for the remaining non-tenant partner to obtain an occupation order in order to be eligible to apply for the tenancy of the home to be transferred (see further Chapter 10).

3.18 It may be possible to ameliorate this position by creating a joint tenancy, either by a grant of a new joint tenancy by the landlord, or in some cases by way of assignment by the sole tenant to the cohabitants as joint tenants. Much will depend on the nature of the tenancy and the situation may be more complicated where the tenancy of the home was originally granted to the tenant cohabitant and a third party who cannot be traced or is not willing to co-operate. Although on relationship breakdown a transfer of tenancy application can now be made pursuant to Sch 7 FLA 1996 (providing occupation by the tenant and thus security of tenure has not been relinquished or a s 36 occupation order has been made), whilst cohabitation is on-going a non-tenant cohabitant does not have any right to insist that the tenancy be transferred into joint names. So here the consent of the partner, any third party joint tenant and, where appropriate, the landlord, will be needed. Advisors should be alert to the possibility of conflict of interest between the partners and any third party joint tenant would clearly need to be advised to take independent legal advice.

3.19 Broadly, statutory tenancies governed by the Rent Act 1977 and periodic assured tenancies arising under the Housing Act 1988 cannot be assigned without the landlord's express written consent (see Chapter 10). Contractual Rent Act tenancies and fixed term assured tenancies can be assigned during the fixed term period providing the terms of the tenancy permit assignment. Secure public sector tenancies can be assigned to a person entitled to be the statutory successor to the tenancy. Thus a tenancy can be assigned as between cohabitants providing the non-tenant cohabitant has been living with the tenant at the accommodation for the previous twelve months. If such a tenancy is still in the names of the tenant cohabitant and a third party, the situation is more complex as here there would need to be an assignment by the third party to the tenant cohabitant. They in turn would be able to assign it to their cohabitant as soon as they qualified as a successor following a further 12 months' cohabitation. In the case of local authority or housing association tenancies, it is usually possible to obtain the landlord's agreement to an assignment, or to a grant of a new tenancy in joint names. In the private sector, particularly where a Rent Act tenancy is concerned, a landlord's consent to an assignment or new tenancy which would retain Rent Act protection (see s 34 Housing Act 1988) is unlikely to be forthcoming and the parties may have little choice but to retain such security as is available to the sole tenant.

(f) Succession to tenancies on death

3.20 Where cohabitants are joint tenants, the survivor of them will automatically succeed to the tenancy on the death of his or her partner. Where cohabitants have lived together for a period of time in a private sector tenancy in the sole name of one of them, it may be possible for the surviving cohabitant to succeed to the tenancy. Succession to tenancies on death is now governed by statute and the position of non-tenant cohabitants again varies according to the nature of the tenancy. The position is also very different for heterosexual and homosexual cohabitants.

(i) Rent Act tenancies

3.21 The Housing Act 1988 made some significant changes to the law relating to succession of Rent Act tenancies. Part I Sch 4 Housing Act 1988 amended Sch 1 Rent Act 1977 and the succession provisions for Rent Act tenancies are now as follows. The surviving spouse of an original tenant (which includes a person living with the tenant as the tenant's husband or wife), automatically succeeds and becomes the statutory tenant of the accommodation on the tenant's death, providing he or she was residing with the tenant in the accommodation at the time of the tenant's death. Providing it is the first succession, the statutory tenant will remain protected by the Rent Act 1977 as long as they continue to occupy the accommodation as a residence. There is now no qualifying period.

3.22 It is now clear, however, that homosexual cohabitants have to prove that they come within the definition of a member of the original tenant's family and cannot show they fall within the specifically heterosexual definition of cohabitants. This was confirmed by the House of Lords' decision in *Fitzpatrick v Sterling Housing Association Ltd* (above) who in a case concerning a Rent Act protected tenancy held that only opposite-sex couples can live as husband and wife. This approved the earlier Court of Appeal decision in the case of *Harrogate Borough Council v Simpson* [1986] 16 Fam Law 359, relating to a public sector tenancy, where it had already been held that a couple of the same sex cannot come within the definition of husband and wife, a decision endorsed in a subsequent complaint to the European Commission on Human Rights (see *S v United Kingdom (Application 11716/85)*.

3.23 However, Sch 1 to the Rent Act 1977 provides an alternative means of succession to a tenancy for anyone who can prove they are 'a member of the tenant's family' who has resided with the tenant in the accommodation for the two years prior to the tenant's death. In the Rent Act context at least, the House of Lords in *Fitzpatrick* did confirm that the survivor of a same-sex cohabiting couple of long-standing did fall within the definition of a member of their deceased tenant-partner's family. Having established this, however, unlike those who are heterosexual cohabitants, they must in addition show that they resided with the tenant in the accommodation for a period of two years before death. Furthermore, even though the original tenancy was Rent Act protected, they can only ever succeed to an assured tenancy.

3.24 Nonetheless, this does leave same-sex couples whose home is a Rent Act tenancy in a far stronger position now than those where one partner is a secure tenant. This is because succession rules for public sector tenancies, as discussed below, specify family members who are entitled to succeed, whereas the Rent Act definition is framed more broadly.

3.25 The interpretation of the phrase 'member of the tenant's family' contained in Sch 1 to the Rent Act by the House of Lords to include same-sex couples is the latest in a series of developments in which the courts have sought to adapt the law to changing social circumstances, consistent with the aims of the Rent Acts. It had long ago been extended to some non-blood relatives. Thus it was held to include a woman who had been brought up by the tenant but never formally adopted (*Brock v Wollams* [1949] 1 All ER 715), although a *quasi* aunt and nephew relationship was not considered a sufficient familial relationship even though they had shared accommodation for eighteen years and the 'nephew' had looked after the 'aunt' during her failing health (see *Carega Properties SA (formerly Joram Developments Ltd) v Sharratt* [1979] 2 All ER 1084). Before the 1988 Act amendment, which brought heterosexual couples living as husband and wife within the definition of spouse, it had been successfully argued that such couples were members of each other's families, although the authorities were not entirely consistent.

3.26 As early as 1953, the court held a cohabitant who had lived with the deceased tenant for 12 years and had two children with him was a member of his family (*Hawes v Evenden* [1953] 2 All ER 737) in contrast, though, to the 1950 decision, of *Gammans v Ekins* [1950] 2 KB 328, which had rejected the claim of a man who had lived with the female tenant for some years and were regarded as husband and wife but had no children. More than 20 years later in *Dyson Holdings v Fox* [1976] QB 503 Lord Denning rejected the *Gammans* approach claiming it was absurd to distinguish between cohabiting couples on the basis that one had children and the other did not. In *Watson v Lucas* [1980] 3 All ER 647 the court reached the same conclusion, although a claim by a male cohabitant to succeed to the tenancy of his deceased cohabitant of five years standing had been rejected in 1979. In 1987, in *Chios Property Investment v Lopez* [1988] Fam Law 384, a cohabitant was allowed to succeed to but the court stressed the importance of a 'sufficient state of permanence and stability' having been reached in the relationship in order to constitute a family. The following year, the Housing Act 1988 implemented statutory equality between spouses and heterosexual cohabitants.

3.27 Thus the barriers to accepting heterosexual cohabitation as a family form were pushed back using this Rent Act provision, which has now been employed in *Fitzpatrick* more than ten years to accept same-sex cohabitation as a family form. The facts in *Fitzpatrick* were extremely meritorious and made clear that same-sex couples organise their lives and have much the same approach to family life as married and opposite-sex couples. The case involved the claim by Martin Fitzpatrick, to succeed to the Rent Act tenancy of his deceased partner John Thompson to their family home. They had shared what was described as a 'longstanding, close, loving and faithful, monogamous, homosexual relationship.' They had lived together some 18 years and for the last eight years Fitzpatrick had given up his job in order to nurse and care for Thompson who became a tetraplaegic following an accident. To succeed, to a Rent Act protected statutory tenancy he had to show under para 2 of Sch 1 Rent Act 1997 that he was the 'spouse' of Thompson, in that he was living with him as 'his husband or wife'. This involved convincing the court that the 1988 Act amendment to include heterosexual cohabitants within the definition of spouse extended to same sex cohabitants. If he succeeded on this point, he could remain in the home as the statutory tenant. If he could not, he may be able to stay in the home if he could show that he fell within para 3 of Sch 1 in that he was ' ..a person who was a member of the original tenant's family residing with him in the dwelling house at the time of and for the period of two years immediately before his death . . .' In this case he would succeed to a (less protected) assured tenancy governed by the Housing Act 1988.

3.28 In the Court of Appeal, Mr Fitzpatrick lost on both points. However, there was a powerful dissenting judgment from Ward LJ who was prepared to concede that a same-sex couple could live as spouses and would also qualify as members of each other's families on the basis that the Rent Act should look at family function rather than form:

> 'The question is more what a family does than what a family is. A family unit is a social organisation which functions through linking its members closely together. The functions may be procreative, sexual, economic, emotional. The list is non-exhaustive.' (*Fitzpatrick v Sterling Housing Association Ltd* (CA) [1997] 4 All ER 991 per Ward LJ at 1023]

3.29 However, the majority in the Court of Appeal did not agree on either count:

> '[T]he law in England regarding the succession to statutory tenancies is firmly rooted in the concept of the family as an entity bound together by ties of kinship (including adoptive status) or marriage. The only relaxation, first by court decision and then by statute, has been a willingness to treat heterosexual cohabitants as if they were husband and wife.' [*Fitzpatrick v Sterling Housing Association Ltd* (CA) [1997] 4 All ER 991, CA per Waite LJ, 1004b.]

3.30 The House of Lords in the event found a middle road. They unanimously refuted the notion that same-sex cohabitants could live as spouses as defined by the 1988 Act amendment to the Rent Act 1977. Lord Slynn in the leading judgement, rejected the gender neutral approach implicit in the word 'spouse' in the light of its subsequent gender-specific qualification:

> '. . .the 1988 amendment extended the meaning to include as a spouse a person living with the original tenant 'as his or her wife or husband'. This was obviously intended to include persons not legally husband and wife who lived as such without being married. That prima facie means a man and a woman and the man must show that the woman was living with him as 'his wife' and the woman that he was living with her as her 'husband'. I do not think Parliament as recently as 1988 intended that these words should be read as meaning 'my same sex partner' rather than specifically my husband' or 'my wife'. If that had been the intention it would have been spelled out. The words cannot in my view be read as the appellant contends. I thus agree as to the result with the decision in *Harrogate Borought Council v Simpson*.'[per Lord Slynn [1999] 4 All ER 705 at p 710 g-h]

3.31 Thus in this context the Law Lords were unswayed by any possibility of a functionalist approach to the construction of para 2 to Sch 1 Rent Act 1997 in contrast to Ward LJ who in the court of Appeal had said:

'I would say that there is no essential difference between a homosexual and a heterosexual couple, and, accordingly I would find that the plaintiff had lived with the deceased tenant as his husband or wife.'[per Ward LJ [1997] 4 All ER 991 at 1022]

3.32 As noted above, in the absence of a spouse or cohabitant, a member of the tenant's family may succeed on the death of the original tenant providing the family member was living with the tenant in the accommodation for two years immediately before the tenant's death. Yet in deciding whether Mr Fitzpatrick was a 'member of the family' under para 3, the majority of the House of Lords did endorse a **functional** approach and concluded using the heterosexual cohabitant cases developed under the Rent Act to reason by analogy that he was a member of Mr Thompson's family. So ironically, the family relationship which this couple had, most resembled one of de facto marriage the very relationship whose 1988 statutory definition the court had ruled they could not fall within:

'the hallmarks of the relationship were essentially that there should be a degree of mutual inter-dependence of the sharing of lives, of caring and love of commitment and support. In respect of the legal relationships these are presumed. . .In de facto relationships these are capable, if proved, of creating membership of the tenants family.' [Per Lord Stann [1999] 4 Al GR 705 at p 714.]

3.33 Thus Mr Fitzpatrick was able to remain in the family home but could only succeed to an assured tenancy at a market rent. It is ironic that this landmark decision which for the first time includes same-sex cohabitants as family members is of limited practical assistance to same-sex couples given the diminishing supply of Rent Act tenancies. As noted below, successors to more modern forms of tenancy, secure and assured, specifically list and define those family members entitled to succeed to a tenancy. At the present time, same-sex couples do not appear on either list, although there is some helpful guidance to social landlords in these situations. Whilst the Human Rights Act 1988 does not directly assist same-sex cohabitants in this connection as the Strasbourg case law itself does not regard same-sex couples as having a right to family life protected by Art 8 European Convention on Human Rights, but only a protected right to private life, this did not prevent the House of Lords from finding that family membership between a same-sex couple within the Rent Act framework had been achieved in *Fitzpatrick*.

3.34 More generally, it should also be noted that where there has already been one succession of a Rent Act tenancy by the original tenant's spouse or cohabitant, that successor's spouse or cohabitant can succeed to an assured tenancy, as can someone who is a member of both the original tenant's and the first successor's family, providing that person lived in the accommodation with the first successor for two years immediately before the first successor's death. Again, the succession is to an assured tenancy.

(ii) Succession of assured tenancies

3.35 An assured tenancy held in a sole name remains an interest in property even on the tenant's death and thus, subject to the statutory provisions governing succession, will devolve according to the terms of any Will, or, in the absence of a Will, according to the intestacy rules. At first sight this appears to have a significant adverse effect upon cohabitants who are not joint tenants as the survivor of joint tenants succeeds to the tenancy by operation of law. Indeed, where a fixed term tenancy, as opposed to a periodic tenancy, is still in existence on the death of the tenant, the tenancy will indeed devolve in accordance with any Will or the rules of intestacy and will vest in the tenant's personal representatives under the Administration of Estates Act 1925. They should then vest the tenancy by a simple assent in the beneficiaries, who may or may not include a cohabitant. Where there is no Will, a cohabitant will not be a beneficiary and a claim under the Inheritance (Provision for Family and Dependants) Act 1975 may be the only means of attempting to vest the tenancy in the surviving cohabitant, notwithstanding that the accommodation is that person's home. Even then, an application is fraught with difficulties. As shall be seen in Chapter 5, the court can look only to whether 'reasonable financial provision' has been made. This phrase has been narrowly interpreted in the case of claims by non-spouse dependants; arguably it may not extend to tenancies which have no intrinsic financial value.

3.36 The situation for a surviving heterosexual cohabitant is much better where there is a periodic assured tenancy, be it a statutory periodic tenancy arising on the expiry of a fixed term or a periodic tenancy from the outset. Section 17 Housing Act 1988 provides that the spouse, including a cohabitant living with the tenant as spouse, of a sole assured periodic tenant who was not himself or herself a successor to the tenancy, is entitled to succeed to the tenancy providing he or she occupied the accommodation as their only or principal home immediately before the tenant's death, notwithstanding the terms of any Will. The definition of 'successor' includes a tenant who became a sole tenant by virtue of the Will or intestacy of the previous tenant or by the right of survivorship under a joint tenancy. This contrasts with the Rent Act position where a joint tenancy prolongs the potential succession rights. No other member of the tenant's family (including a same-sex cohabitant) is entitled to succeed to a periodic tenancy, although where the tenant does not have a spouse or cohabitant, a tenancy which was periodic from the outset can be left by Will. However, unless the implied absolute covenant against assignment has been specifically overridden by the terms of the agreement, the personal representatives will, it seems, be unable lawfully to assign the tenancy to the beneficiary and the new tenant would not obtain security of tenure.

3.37 Another problem which may arise for cohabitants is that, in order to succeed by statute to an assured periodic tenancy, the requirement is for residence in the accommodation *by the tenant's spouse*, not residence *with the tenant*. To come within the definition of spouse, the cohabitant must show that he or she was living with the tenant as his or her wife or husband. Interpretation of this phrase was found in *Fitzpatrick* to be exclusively heterosexual. It is clear from the statute that no qualifying period of cohabitation has been imposed in contrast to other recent legislation. But where, for example, a tenant has been in hospital for a long time, leaving the partner in occupation of the accommodation, a landlord could argue that they do not fulfil the spouse condition as they are no longer living together as husband and wife. There is no requirement that the cohabitation should immediately precede the death, and it is hoped that should this issue come before them, the courts will not interpret the criterion too narrowly, but look to whether the nature of the relationship was akin to that of a husband and wife without also requiring the partners to have lived together in the accommodation immediately before the tenant's death where circumstances other than breakdown of the relationship prevented this.

(iii) Succession to public sector secure tenancies

3.38 A housing association tenant will now normally be granted an assured periodic tenancy. Accordingly, succession rights for such non-tenant cohabitants are set out above in relation to private sector assured tenancies, and are significantly less favourable than those which apply to both protected and secure tenants. Where cohabitants are living in local authority accommodation they will normally be secure tenants and there tenancies are governed by Housing Act 1985. This is also the case with housing association tenancies granted before 15 January 1989. It should first be noted that s 124 HA 1996 creates new-style introductory tenancy schemes, which means that all new periodic tenancies granted by a local authority or housing action trust operating the scheme will be for a period of one year in the first instance. Thus, in this situation the tenancy will not be secure or assured, although a cohabitant who is not a joint tenant may succeed to the introductory tenancy on death providing they have resided with the tenant for the twelve months prior to the death (see s 133 and s 140).

3.39 There can be only one succession to a secure tenancy under the terms of the s 87 Housing Act 1985 and this can be to either the tenant's surviving spouse or a member of the tenant's family. Where there was originally a joint tenancy, on the death or surrender of the last surviving joint tenant, there can be no statutory succession. In order to succeed to the tenancy, the successor must have been living in the accommodation as his or her only or principal home. In the case of a spouse, there is no prior period of qualification but the spouse must have been living with the deceased tenant at the time of death. A spouse does *not* include a cohabitant under the 1985 Act, but a cohabitant can succeed as a member of the deceased tenant's family providing he or she resided in the accommodation with the deceased tenant as their husband or wife for at least twelve months before the death.

3.40 It was thought that s 87 HA 1985 required the whole of the successor's twelve-month residence period to have taken place in the in the accommodation to which succession is sought. However, in *Waltham Forest London Borough Council v Thomas* [1992] 2 AC 198, the House of Lords found that the true construction of s 87 required residence with the tenant throughout the twelve-month period, but not necessarily in the same accommodation. Thus, a move to alternative accommodation in the year prior to the tenant's death did not prevent succession to a member of his family who had resided with him throughout this time.

3.41 Cohabitants of the same sex do not come within the definition of 'living together as husband and wife', as decided by *Harrogate Borough Council v Simpson*, (above). 'Other members of a tenant's family' are defined in s 113 Housing Act 1985, and include children, parents, grandparents, siblings, aunts, uncles, nephews, nieces, step- and half relations.

3.42 Accordingly, succession and, to some extent, assignment possibilities for cohabitants depend on the nature of the tenancy granted and the law of landlord and tenant, which, across different types of tenancy, is far from consistent in its treatment of cohabitants. Advisors need therefore to establish the nature of the tenancy before attempting to advise on cohabitants' housing rights.

3 Owner occupied property

3.43 Of the various courses open to cohabitants, purchasing a property together is the most likely to lead them carefully to consider their respective positions and to seek legal advice. They will usually instruct a solicitor, who should advise both on the implications of buying a property in their joint names. This places a heavy burden on advisors as judicial warnings abound as to the careful advice needed from solicitors in this type of transaction in order to avoid negligence claims. The courts, with justification, have become increasingly critical of inadequate advice given to joint purchasers which has in turn led to costly and unnecessary litigation between cohabitants on relationship breakdown. In *Walker v Hall* [1984] FLR 126, the Court of Appeal found that a solicitor who failed to find out the beneficial interests of joint purchasers for whom he was acting and had declared a tenancy in common without declaring any shares was guilty of negligence. Such practice was further lamented in the more recent case of *Springette v Defoe* [1992] 2 FLR 388, where property had been transferred to the parties as joint tenants in law without any declaration as to their beneficial interests in the property having been made in the transfer. Clearly, the lesson for advisors here is that prevention is better than cure.

3.44 If the property is being purchased in the name of one of them alone, then the partner may not have access to advice, even if contributing to the purchase price. In this situation an advisor may still be required to take instructions from both cohabitants. Most building societies and banks who lend money secured by mortgage on residential property require, from all occupiers over the age of 18, signed consents agreeing to postpone any interest in the property they may have or acquire, to that of the mortgagee. This is so any person in occupation (in the absence of undue influence being proven) cannot prevent the mortgagee from realising its interest should the mortgagor default (see *Williams & Glyn's Bank Ltd v Boland* [1981] AC 487). An advisor who discovers that the purchaser's cohabitant will be living in the property must explain why the consent is required by the mortgagee. This provides an opportunity to indicate the legal implications of the whole transaction to both cohabitants, even though the property is to be in the sole name of one of them. Only one of the cohabitants would in fact be the advisor's client, but a duty is owed to the mortgagee to obtain consent for its charge to have priority over any interest of the other cohabitant. A letter to the non-client cohabitant should be written, outlining the consequences of the required consent and suggesting separate legal advice should they be concerned about the position. A legal advisor is clearly in a difficult professional position here, but it may be appropriate for a declaration of trust (see 3.65 ff) to be suggested.

(a) Purchase in joint names

3.45 As with rented accommodation, if a property is purchased in the joint names of cohabitants each has the right to occupy it. Neither can lawfully exclude the other without having first obtained a court order to do so. In addition, as both names are on the title deeds, one joint owner cannot sell, mortgage or charge the property without the consent of the other, whose signature will be required to effect the sale or create the legal charge. This also means that if one co-owner wished to sell and the other refuses, an application has to be made to the court for an order to resolve. The court will either order the sale or agree to a postponement of the sale in certain circumstances. This situation usually arises on breakdown of the relationship between cohabitants and is explored in more detail in Chapter 11.

3.46 All joint purchasers hold the legal estate of their property as joint tenants in law. By virtue of s 5 and Sch 2 Trusts of Land and Appointment of Trustees Act 1996 (TLATA 1996) where there is joint ownership, a statutory trust of the land is implied. Co-owners are therefore trustees, and hold on trust for themselves as either joint tenants or tenants in common in equity. As the law allows joint owners to hold their beneficial interest in the property either as joint tenants or as tenants in common, all co-owners should be advised at the time of purchase on the broad implications of both options, so they can make an informed decision as to which properly reflects their intentions. Indeed, following amendment of the Land Registration Rules in 1997 (see SI 1997/3037 rr 19 and 98) Land Registry Transfer Form TR2 now requires a statement as to whether the property is held by the purchasers as joint tenants, tenants in common in equal shares or tenants in common in other specified shares. This decision is of tremendous importance to all co-owners, and particularly to cohabitants. Failure to explain and keep a record of the legal advice given at the time of purchase is likely to amount to negligence on the part of a solicitor (see eg *Walker v Hall* and *Springette v Defoe* (discussed above)).

3.47 When purchasing a property, cohabitants may make different contributions to the purchase price. They may agree to make unequal contributions to the mortgage repayments or other outgoings. They may decide to apply one partner's income towards the mortgage repayments and the other income towards all the other outgoings. Very often, however, the agreement reached is not set out in any legal document. Many do not appreciate that these agreements may affect their beneficial interests in the property, and that these arrangements can prove critical. Some joint purchasers may not even expressly discuss with each other their understanding of the implications of the agreed arrangements they have made to contribute to the purchase price and to the mortgage repayments, as was the case in *Springette v Defoe* (above). Yet, as was decided in that case, unless there is a common intention which has been communicated as to how the parties intended to hold their respective beneficial interests, then the presumption of a resulting trust whereby the joint owners are presumed to hold beneficially in proportion to their respective contributions, may not be rebutted. This is so even if they each shared the same intention. As Steyn LJ commented at page 394, 'Our trust law does not allow property rights to be affected by telepathy'.

3.48 The effect of this decision has been significantly modified by *Midland Bank plc v Cooke* [1995] 2 FLR 915, from which it was distinguished on the facts on the basis that the former case involved middle-aged cohabitants whose purchase of their home was akin to a commercial partnership arrangement (see Chapter 11 below). Nonetheless, the uncertainties within the law make it all the more imperative that clear advice is given on purchase and that this is translated into documentation giving effect to the true intentions of the parties.

3.49 Solicitors are often criticised for failing to explain clearly to joint proprietors, at the time of purchase, the options and their implications. Where the advisor is on notice that the joint purchasers are cohabitants, the implications of purchasing in joint or sole names, and of purchasing as beneficial joint tenants or tenants in common, must be explained to both parties so that an informed and joint decision is taken. The legal documentation should be drawn up truly to reflect and record the intentions of the co-owners at the date of the purchase, and to provide an accurate starting point to determine any future dispute. It may also be appropriate at this time to ask the cohabitants to consider whether they wish to reflect arrangements relating to other property in a written agreement, or to consider a cohabitation agreement or Wills.

3.50 In any event, in order to avoid negligence claims and disputes between cohabitants at a later stage, it is important when taking instructions on a purchase to ask crucial questions about the source of the purchase money, the proposed contributions to the mortgage and intentions as to beneficial ownership. All the options and implications need to be carefully explained, including the implications of relationship breakdown and death. It is important for advisors to discover whether there are any other potential beneficiaries who would be adversely affected by the right of survivorship in the case of a beneficial joint tenancy and, if appropriate, to suggest the need for the drawing of new Wills and explain the ramifications of the Inheritance (Provision for Family and Dependants) Act 1975 if one or both cohabitants have former spouses or minor children by other relationships.

3.51 Another issue that needs to be addressed is whether the life assurance usually offered to cohabitant joint purchasers on standard terms is appropriate to their individual circumstances. So-called 'joint life, first death' endowment policies can give unexpected results where death of both cohabitants takes place within a short space of time, particularly if, as is now common practice, the mortgagee does not take an assignment or notice of deposit of the policy, as the right of survivorship applies to the proceeds, potentially not protecting the estate of the longest surviving cohabitant. Consideration needs to be given to whether a mortgage protection policy or policies taken out by each purchaser on their own life might be more appropriate. Alternatively, a declaration of trust needs to be drawn up in relation to the proceeds of the joint life policy to avoid such an anomaly, not intended by the parties. Indeed, given the general difficulties that are predicted to arise in the case of endowment mortgages, with many policies seeming likely to produce insufficient funds to pay off the capital at the end of the mortgage term, fewer purchasers will be inclined towards endowment policies in the future in any event.

3.52 The relative merits of the main considerations to which both advisors and purchasers should apply their minds will now be considered.

(b) Joint tenancy or tenancy in common?

3.53 Regardless of their actual contributions to the purchase price, joint proprietors, whilst being obliged to hold as joint tenants in law under a statutory trust of land, have the option of declaring that they hold their beneficial interests either as joint tenants or as tenants in common. One of the most important effects of this decision is seen on the death of one of the joint tenants. If the couple are beneficial joint tenants and neither has severed the joint tenancy thereby creating a beneficial tenancy in common, the survivor of them will succeed to the deceased joint tenant's legal and equitable interests by operation of law, and become the sole owner of the property, notwithstanding the terms of the deceased joint tenant's Will. However, where there is a beneficial tenancy in common, then the deceased co-owner's share will form part of that person's estate on death and devolve according to the Will, or the rules on intestacy in the absence of a Will. If there is no Will, the intestacy rules provide that the deceased cohabitant's share of the property will be inherited by his or her next of kin, and not by the partner. The surviving partner will have to rely either on the proceeds of any life policy to purchase the other share of the property from the partner's beneficiary; or apply for provision under the Inheritance (Provision for Family and Dependants) Act 1975, which would not necessarily enable the applicant to remain in the home (see Chapter 5 below).

3.54 What, therefore, should determine whether cohabitants should be joint tenants or tenants in common in equity, and how should this be reflected in the purchase documentation? Where the contributions made by each of the cohabitants are broadly equal, and it is intended that they should contribute to the mortgage in roughly equal shares, and they agree that their interests in the property are equal and expressly wish them to remain equal, even if these circumstances change, the crucial issue is whether they wish the right of survivorship to apply. If they decide that they wish the other to inherit their share of the property without having to make a Will to that effect, then a beneficial joint tenancy should be created.

3.55 However, it could be argued that, given the present inability of the courts to intervene and adjust shares of cohabitants on relationship breakdown, it might never be appropriate to recommend a beneficial joint tenancy to cohabitant joint purchasers in case the relationship breaks down, and the original desire to share the property equally becomes inappropriate from the perspective of one of the parties. From an advisor's point of view, the safest course of action is a declaration of a tenancy in common together with mutual Wills in relation to the property being purchased. Yet there is often a formidable, if not altogether logical, reluctance on the part of cohabitants to make Wills, and a beneficial joint tenancy is seen as a means of dealing with succession to the family home without having to make difficult decisions about the destination of other assets. Another potential difficulty is that a beneficial tenancy in common expressly declaring proportionate beneficial interests based on actual and intended contributions to capital and mortgage at the time of the purchase, may not provide a flexible enough assessment of the parties' true intentions about their interests in the property. Where one is providing mainly capital and the other mainly mortgage repayments, these issues may be magnified in the effects they produce. Often, parties feel that the fairest method of assessing respective interests in the home is a retrospective one at the date the property is to be sold, taking into account the actual contributions made and not just the promise of, for example, mortgage repayments made at the date of the purchase. There is judicial approval (see *Passee v Passee* [1988] 1 FLR 263, particularly at pages 270–272) for such deferred ascertainment of the beneficial interests, where it can be inferred that this was clearly intended by the parties and this approach was approved by Slade LJ in *Springette v Defoe* (above). It therefore seems that a possible solution to the practitioner's dilemma is a declaration which creates a beneficial joint tenancy until severance by either party, whereupon a beneficial tenancy in common is created, to be held in shares specified with reference to the parties' contributions. This possibility will need careful thought by both parties and their advisors and will be discussed further below.

3.56 It falls to the practitioner acting for the purchaser to record the intentions about how the beneficial interests are to be held. In unregistered land, the conveyance should as a matter of course always contain an express declaration as to whether the purchasers hold beneficially as joint tenants or tenants in common. This, in the absence of any later evidence of a different joint intention or of fraud or mistake, will be conclusive. Where the purchase involves registered land, an express declaration always could and now must be included in the transfer document (see Land Registry Form TR2, point 12 'Declaration of Trust'). Traditionally probably the majority of solicitors did no more than complete the declaration on the old standard form of transfer stating that the survivor can give a valid receipt for capital monies arising on disposition of the land and cases may still arise where this is all that is formally recorded to assist in determining the manner in which the property is held. For many years it was not clear whether this declaration would be sufficient to create an express beneficial joint tenancy. In *Bernard v Josephs* [1982] 3 All ER 162, the Court of Appeal held that where property had been transferred to two cohabitants jointly, without any express declaration as to the nature of the beneficial ownership, there was no presumption that the parties held the property in equal shares. Instead, a court should look at all the evidence, such as respective contributions, and see whether it indicates any intention to hold the property other than in equal shares. In that case, it was decided that the parties did have equal interests in the property, but much time and expense would have been saved if the transfer had indicated the parties' intentions at the time of purchase. In the more recent decision of *Huntingford v Hobbs* [1993] 1 FLR 736, a majority of the Court of Appeal rejected the contention that the standard declaration on the transfer of registered land form, that the survivor of the two cohabitant joint proprietors could give a valid receipt for capital money arising on the disposition of the land, constituted a declaration of trust that they held the property as beneficial joint tenants. They found that because such wording could equally have been employed to indicate that they were holding the beneficial interest as trustees on behalf of a third party, it did not constitute a declaration of their beneficial interests in the property. Furthermore, extrinsic evidence was not admissible in this context and thus the interests fell to be decided in accordance with the principles of resulting, implied or constructive trusts.

3.57 Thus, to create a beneficial joint tenancy, an express declaration of trust unambiguously to this effect must be entered into by the joint purchasers and will now be recorded on the Transfer Form in which the respective parties' shares must be indicated. Where the conveyance or transfer did not include a declaration of the beneficial interests but has indicated joint ownership, a separate declaration of trust document, executed by both parties, should be drawn and placed with the title deeds. Once there is an express beneficial joint tenancy, then each party will be deemed to have an equal interest in the proceeds of sale even if the joint tenancy is subsequently severed (see *Goodman v Gallant* [1986] Fam 106) unless, as suggested above, each party's beneficial interest on severance has been specified in the original declaration. Thus if it is intended to pursue this option, a beneficial joint tenancy should be indicated on the transfer or conveyance but made subject to the terms of the separate declaration of trust which becomes effective on severance of the joint tenancy. Where there is an initial joint tenancy, it can later be severed by either of the joint tenants, by service of a notice of severance on the other party or by course of dealing. As soon as a joint tenancy is severed, a tenancy in common arises and the right of survivorship no longer applies. Each co-owner's share will then devolve separately with his or her estate. If instructed to sever a joint tenancy, the client should be advised to make a new Will.

3.58 Even if the parties have contributed in unequal shares to the purchase price of the property, they may still if they wish purchase as beneficial joint tenants. However, as has been seen (*Goodman v Gallant*, above), even after the tenancy has been severed, they will normally still hold the property in equal shares, although where separation takes place some adjustment may be made to reflect varying contributions made after the separation.

3.59 Where there are unequal contributions to the purchase price and on purchase the parties wish this to be reflected in their respective interests in the property, then a beneficial tenancy in common is needed. To create a beneficial tenancy in common an express declaration should be made in the conveyance or transfer, or in a separate declaration of trust document, clearly stating the proportions in which the property is held by the co-owners. Express declarations of trust can be simple documents and must be in writing following the requirements of s 53(1) Law of Property Act 1925 (see eg Appendix II).

3.60 Where advisors are acting for joint purchasers, it should be standard practice to ask whether they wish to hold the property as joint tenants or tenants in common. It is arguable that a beneficial joint tenancy is never appropriate in the cohabitation context. Whatever the answer, an express declaration should be made at the time as it should avoid future disputes. It may well be appropriate to set out in a separate trust, not only the capital contributions to the deposit, but also any credit to be given for a 'right to buy' discount; the parties' proposed present and future contributions to the mortgage and other outgoings; and the planned use of the property as a family home. In effect, a small scale cohabitation agreement dealing specifically with the parties' intentions in relation to the home could be drawn up.

3.61 To summarise, any advisor instructed to create a tenancy in common should immediately advise on the position of each cohabitant on death. Without a Will leaving their interest in the property to the other, a partner's share will devolve according to the intestacy rules on their next of kin, which may not reflect his or her true wishes. In the case of registered land, an advisor must now indicate on the transfer, and the Land Registry application form the nature of the joint ownership. As discussed above, the relative shares of tenants in common either on purchase or following severance of a beneficial joint tenancy, must in any event be recorded on the transfer and/or in a separate declaration of trust.

3.62 Those purchasing as tenants in common, specifying fixed shares, should also be advised that the declaration of trust can be varied in the future, but only by agreement. If joint purchasers' true common intention is reflected by declaring neither a beneficial joint tenancy nor a beneficial tenancy in common in specific shares, there are two further possibilities to consider. Firstly, it may be possible to create a beneficial tenancy in common which builds in flexibility in the way in which the shares are calculated. A deferred ascertainment clause recording the common intention of the method in which the beneficial interests are to be calculated would be a way of achieving this. The advantage is that important issues like the value of contributions in kind, such as home improvements or perhaps child care, could be built into the method of assessment. A method of dealing with negative equity if this was considered in need of different treatment to the proposed division of positive equity could also be addressed. The potential difficulty with this approach is that it is open ended and risks leaving the couple with too much to argue over should the relationship break down. However, it does at least leave the couple with a clear common intention which with careful drafting could provide a couple with the flexibility to take future events into account, yet provide them with a fixed framework for determining their interests on relationship breakdown. For an attempt to achieve this effect see Appendices I and II.

3.63 Secondly, there seems to be no reason why cohabitants who are purchasing a property jointly and who wish during the currency of the relationship to be beneficial joint tenants, taking advantage of the right of survivorship – yet who, should the relationship break down, do not necessarily want to hold the property in equal shares on severance of the joint tenancy – should not be able to enter into an effective 'hybrid' declaration of trust. The declaration should make clear either the proportions in which the beneficial interest is to be held on severance, or the method of calculating them if deferred ascertainment is preferred. Again, an attempt to achieve this is set out in Appendix II.

3.64 Both of these options should only be used where they clearly coincide with the joint purchasers' intentions at the time of purchase. Thought does need to be given to these options when the parties are not satisfied that either of the two more straightforward options meet with their true intentions. They both have the advantage of flexibility and the disadvantage of lack of immediate certainty. It could be argued that, framed in the right way, they can effectively achieve for the unmarried couple a fairer method of dividing property on relationship breakdown in accordance with principles decided by the couple when they were at one, and which they may accordingly be happy to agree to abide by with the minimum of dissension on breakdown.

(c) Purchase in sole name

3.65 If for tax or other *bona fide* reasons, cohabitants who are both contributing to the purchase of a property wish it to be purchased in the sole name of one party, it is still possible to have a declaration of trust as to how the equity is held. Although this would give only an equitable, rather than a legal, interest in the property to the non-purchaser cohabitant, it would still be clear evidence of the parties' respective interests in any subsequent dispute between them. A non-owner partner who has contributed in money or money's worth is likely in any event to be able to prove a beneficial interest in the proceeds of sale and can make an application under s 14 TLATA 1996; see Chapter 11. Accordingly, although such situations are likely to be rare, where a beneficial interest is acknowledged or apparent from the outset, a declaration of trust should be drawn up, setting out the respective interests under the resulting trust and reciting the contributions made by each party.

3.66 Where an advisor is acting for a mortgagee as well as a sole purchaser, enquiries must be made in respect of others who will be occupying the property. If the existence of a cohabitant is thereby revealed, then the cohabitant will be required to sign a declaration that any interest in the property that they may have does not have priority over that of the mortgagee. Enquiries as to whether the cohabitant is contributing to the purchase price should be made of both parties, and, if a contribution is confirmed, further questions as to the basis upon which this is being done would seem to be entirely appropriate. Such a revelation would in any event provide an opportunity, if not always a duty, to discuss the possible consequences of cohabitation in a home purchased by one cohabitant, and to advise on the merits of drawing up full documentation to record the parties' intentions with regard to the property which is to be the family home. Independent advice will, following decisions on undue influence in the married context such as *Barclays Bank plc v O'Brien* [1994] 1 AC 180 and *Midland Bank v Cooke* (above), always be appropriate for the non-purchasing cohabitant. Such advice at an early stage may prevent the need for litigation later, and to that extent must be of benefit to all concerned in the proposed transaction. Enquiries may reveal that the proposed contribution takes the form of a loan or a gift, and not a contribution to the purchase price, in which case the loan agreement or deed of gift should be drawn up as appropriate, and the desirability of independent advice clearly explained.

3.67 The need for a declaration of trust may arise where parties agree to cohabit in a property already owned by one of them, and the in-coming partner pays for improvements to the property or contributes to the mortgage repayments. It is open to them to transfer the property into joint names, but this may involve obtaining a mortgagee's consent, and possibly paying stamp duty, land registration fees, legal costs and disbursements as on a new purchase. Some cohabitants may prefer to make a declaration of trust, although from the non-owner cohabitant's point of view, this would confer only an equitable rather than a legal interest and would be enforceable against their partner only. The need for Wills to be drawn up should be considered, as, if they hold the property as tenants in common, their shares will devolve with their respective estates. A later purchaser for value of the property would normally raise enquiries about the interests of any other adult occupier of the property, and where the cohabitant is in actual occupation of the property, the owner cohabitant will not be able to give vacant possession without the partner's co-operation, and a purchaser is likely to be put on notice. The partner would in any event have an overriding interest where the title is registered (s 70(1)(g) Land Registration Act 1925). At the very least, a declaration of trust gives the non-owner cohabitant documentary evidence of his or her interest in the property which will prove helpful on relationship breakdown.

3.68 Unfortunately, express declarations of trust in these circumstances are rare. Where there is no declaration of trust, and a dispute arises on the breakdown of the relationship, the onus is on the non-owner cohabitant to prove that he or she has a beneficial interest in the property. The courts have in some cases been prepared to find implied, constructive or resulting trusts in a property of which only one cohabitant is the legal owner, deeming the owner to be holding the property in trust for both cohabitants. Another possibility where only one cohabitant is the owner is to find that a licence for life has been granted to the non-owner. This is only likely to arise in special circumstances and will never be easy to prove. These issues, which usually arise in the context of breakdown of the relationship, or, possibly, on death, are dealt with in detail in Chapter 11.

3.69 It should also be borne in mind that a non-owner cohabitant, or indeed in some situations a joint owner cohabitant, may wish to assert rights of beneficial ownership or occupation as against a mortgagee. The home may be mortgaged by one partner without the other's knowledge or consent; usually the mortgagee's rights will prevail, unless, in the case of registered land, there was actual occupation of the land before the creation of the charge (*Williams and Glyn's Bank v Boland*, above). Where the land is unregistered, the mortgagee's claim will only be defeated in this way if the mortgagee is on notice of the actual occupation. A detailed discussion of the issues is outside the scope of this book, but for a concise and most helpful account of the position, see Michael Daniel's article *Spouses, Cohabitants, Their Home and Their Lenders* (Family Law, 1990, page 445).

3.70 There has been a plethora of cases considering the issues of misrepresentation and of undue influence where a spouse or cohabitant is asked by their partner to consent to a mortgagee's charge against the family home to secure the business debts of that partner, usually the man. This will occur during the currency of the relationship and may apply whether or not the home is vested in their joint names. Effectively, the House of Lords in *Barclays Bank v O'Brien* (above) recognised that where one partner (normally the wife) could show that she generally trusted and had confidence in her partner in financial matters a presumption of undue influence arises, placing a heavier burden on the mortgagee. If, in rare cases, the husband acts as the mortgagee's agent, then they will be unable to enforce the charge against the wife's equity. Otherwise, the ability to enforce would depend on whether or not the mortgagee was fixed with actual or constructive notice of the undue influence. The House of Lords made it clear that these principles would apply as much to cohabiting couples, whether heterosexual or homosexual. The case of *CIBC Mortgages plc v Pitt* [1994] 1 AC 200 where, unlike in *O'Brien*, the matrimonial home was in joint names and as far as the mortgagees were aware, the loan was purportedly for a joint holiday home, emphasised that in the *O'Brien* situation, where the home was in the man's sole name and the loan was for his business, the risk of undue influence was greater. In *Massey v Midland Bank plc* [1995] 1 All ER 929, CA it was confirmed that *O'Brien* applied to the cohabitation context, although the bank here were entitled to rely on the fact that they had required Ms Massey to seek independent advice. Furthermore, in *Barclays Bank plc v Boulter* [1999] 2 FLR 986, HL, it was confirmed (reversing the decision of the Court of Appeal) that it was for the wife to prove the bank had constructive notice of the undue influence, not for the mortgagee to disprove it, and that whether the land was registered or unregistered was irrelevant in cases of this nature. The question was whether the creditor had actual or constructive notice of the facts on which the equity to set aside the transaction was founded.

3.71 Thus, advisors need to be aware both of the potential conflict of interests between cohabitants and of their own professional position when advising in these situations and may find the decision in *Royal Bank of Scotland v Etridge (No. 2)* [1998] 2 FLR 843 in which helpful guidelines are set out as to the effect of legal advice in such cases particularly valuable.

GOOD PRACTICE CHECKLIST FOR ADVISORS OF COHABITANTS PURCHASING PROPERTY

• Take very full instructions as to the relationship, the contributions to the deposit, details as to whom any right to buy discount is attributable, anticipated contributions to the mortgage repayments, implications of any proposed improvements to the property.

• Ensure that a firm conclusion is reached in relation to the holding of the beneficial interests, whilst bearing in mind that certainty does not rule out flexibility. Include a declaration in the transfer or conveyance, making reference to a separate declaration of trust where a more complicated calculation of the beneficial interest is preferred. This may be particularly appropriate where one party is contributing mainly capital and the other intends to take prime responsibility for the mortgage repayments. Be aware that the communicated common intention of the purchasers at the time of purchase is critical, although deferred ascertainment of the beneficial interests is a permissible common intention.

- Consider the appropriateness of the life assurance arrangements in the light of anticipated contributions to the mortgage repayments and any dependency by one partner upon the other as well as the effect on other potential beneficiaries.

- Advise on the need to draw Wills, where appropriate, and the possibility of a cohabitation agreement.

4 Homelessness

3.72 The law governing the statutory duties owed to the homeless by local housing authorities is contained in Part VII Housing Act 1996 (HA 1996), which repealed Part III Housing Act 1985. It has implemented the major reforms foreshadowed in the Conservative government's Consultation Paper *Access to Local Authority and Housing Association Tenancies* (Department of the Environment, January 1994). Despite provoking widespread criticism, these were enacted, subject to fairly minor modifications, although following the recent Housing Green Paper ('Quality and Choice: A decent home for all' (DETR, 2000), this area of law is again under review. Indeed a new Homelessness Bill is currently before Parliament which, if enacted, will again increase the duties owed to the homeless. The main thrust of the 1996 reforms was to reduce the duties owed by local authorities to the homeless, principally by requiring them to provide accommodation only for a period of two years. The aim was thereby to remove the route into permanent accommodation through the homelessness legislation, and to introduce a housing register, governed by Part VI HA 1996, through which social housing is now allocated. It was argued that this would provide a more equitable system for all and would remove the perceived perverse incentive provided by the old legislation for people to make themselves homeless (para 2.8, *Access to Local Authority and Housing Association Tenancies*). If passed, however, the Homelessness Bill 2001 will abolish some of the harsher elements of the 1996 legislation including the minimum period for which an authority owes a duty to the homeless (see clause 6) and improve the security of tenure which the homeless must be offered in order to discharge the duty owed (clauses 7(1),(2) and (4)). It will also abolish the duty on housing authorities to maintain a housing register (clause 13) and instead provides authorities with new guidelines on how applications for housing should be treated and how housing can be allocated (clauses 14 and 15).

3.73 Regardless of the tenure of their previous accommodation, cohabitants may find themselves, either as a family unit or following breakdown of their relationship, without any accommodation at all. Part VII Housing Act currently gives local housing authorities duties to secure accommodation for a two-year period for certain categories of homeless people. As noted, this specified period will soon be abolished. In many instances cohabitants, particularly where they have children living with them, will fall within those categories and indeed one of the aims of the Homelessness Bill is to offer support to a wider range of homeless people including those who are not classified as having 'priority need' such as childless cohabitants who are not considered vulnerable (see clause 5). Homelessness arises in different ways, and how that situation arose may often determine whether or not a local authority has a duty to secure accommodation. Unfortunately, as will be seen, rooflessness of itself does not necessarily guarantee that a person is entitled to be found accommodation, even where there are dependent children. Homelessness has developed into a complex area of law and much of the case law under the old 1985 statutory scheme remains relevant now and will continue to do so following enactment of the current Homelessness Bill. Only an outline of the main provisions and cases relevant to the unmarried family is attempted here. Further details of provisions relevant to homelessness caused by domestic violence are given in Chapter 7.

(a) Procedure

3.74 The 1996 Act both increased the hurdles which must be overcome by a homeless applicant in order to show that they are owed a statutory duty under the Act; and at the same time reduced the nature of the duty owed to applicants successfully completing the course, to securing accommodation for a time-limited minimum period of two years. Whilst the latter minimum period is to be abolished, the extra hurdles will remain. Prior to the enactment of the 1996 reforms, great inroads had, however, already been made into the way in which the duty could be satisfactorily discharged under s 65 of the 1985 Act. In *R v Brent London Borough Council, ex p Awua* [1996] AC 55, the House of Lords held that, contrary to what had been previously understood and indicated in the Code of Guidance at that time, accommodation did not have to be 'settled' or permanent in order to discharge the duty to provide suitable accommodation, but merely must not leave an applicant threatened with homelessness in the sense that they were obliged to leave within 28 days. For the current Homelessness Bill to achieve its aim, this influential precedent also needs to be specifically addressed and this has been done in two ways. First, clause 7 specifically states that an offer of an assured shorthold tenancy from a private landlord (which offers very little security to a tenant) will not be sufficient to discharge the duty to a homeless person unless they specifically agree to accept the offer in the knowledge that they are under absolutely no obligation to do so. Second the clause imposes stronger duties on the Local Authority to only offer eligible homeless applicants accommodation which is suitable for them.

3.75 Under the 1996 Act, to be eligible to be housed for the minimum period of two years, the applicant must:

(i)   be eligible for assistance;

(ii)   be homeless or threatened with homelessness;

(iii)   have a priority need;

(iv)   not be intentionally homeless.

3.76 The Homelessness Bill does not seek to change these qualifying conditions. If a local authority has reason to believe an applicant is eligible for assistance, homeless and in priority need, it must provide temporary accommodation pending a final decision (s 188) whilst it completes its enquiries and decides whether all four conditions are met. Fortunately, the once widespread use of bed and breakfast accommodation as temporary accommodation has largely disappeared, other than as a very short-term measure, and has been replaced with private sector accommodation, often leased to the local authority.

3.77 Where cohabitants find themselves homeless or threatened with homelessness, they should be advised to apply to their local housing authority for accommodation pursuant to Part VII HA 1996. Where the authority has reason to believe that the applicant is homeless or threatened with homelessness, it has a duty to make enquiries (s 184(1)) and consider whether they are eligible for assistance and whether it owes a duty to secure them accommodation. If they also appear to be in priority need within the meaning of s 189 (see below), for example if they have dependent children who reside with them, the authority also has a duty to provide temporary accommodation pending completion of its enquiries (s 188). Thus, making an application can of itself provide a family with immediate help. There is no particular application form but most authorities normally require an applicant to attend their offices for an interview. However, their duties take immediate effect and cannot be avoided by closing the offices; and in the cities at least, they are expected to provide a twenty-four-hour service (*R v Camden London Borough, ex p Gillan* (1988) 21 HLR 114).

3.78 The Act sets out various steps to be followed by the local authority, and hurdles which the applicant must clear before proving entitlement to short-term accommodation. In addition the authority must also have regard to the Code of Guidance on HA 1996 Parts VI and VII issued by the Department for Transport, Local Government and the Regions (DLTR) and the National Assembly for Wales (s 182), which sets out matters to be taken into account. However, providing they have had regard to it, failure to comply with it will not of itself provide a basis for a valid challenge to an authority's decision (see *De Falco v Crawley Borough Council* [1980] 1 All ER 913).

3.79 The current edition of the Code of Guidance to Local Authorities on Allocation of Accommodation and Homelessness was published in April 1999 and was last updated on 4 December 2000 although it is still described as a Draft Code. It can be found on the Department for Transport, Local Government and the Regions' (DLTR) website at http://www.housing.dtlr.gov.uk/information/index03.htm#publications. It is a useful aid in negotiating cases with local authorities and has gone some way to soften the edges of the 1996 Act, which currently still very much embodies a Conservative government's housing policy.

3.80 Significantly, the 1996 Act introduced a right to request a review of any decision of the local authority under this Part of the Act (s 202) and, subject to having done this, a right of appeal on a point of law to the county court (s 204). This in effect means that the vast majority of decisions are no longer challengeable by way of judicial review, although the grounds for challenge and the remedies available to the court remain broadly the same. Here the court may quash, confirm or (unlike in judicial review) vary the decision (s 204(3)). Procedure on review is governed by s 203 and the Allocation of Housing and Homelessness (Review Procedures and Amendment) Regulations 1996 (SI 3122/96), and is considered in the Code of Guidance (see para. 19.6 – 19.21). An application for review must be made within twenty-one days of notification of the decision. Reviews are undertaken on the basis of written representations in most cases, although local authorities may hear oral representations if they wish (and must do so in some situations (see paras 19.14 – 19.15 Code of Guidance)) and should normally be carried out within fifty-six days. No public funding certificate is available for representation of applicants requesting review, other than, it seems, the limited and stringently means tested Legal Help advice and representation (check).

(b) Eligible for assistance

3.81 This is a controversial hurdle inserted by s 183 HA 1996 and those who are not eligible are defined in ss 185 and 186 Annex 7 of the Code of Guidance gives further details of those who are ineligible. Effectively, s 185(2) provides that persons from abroad subject to immigration control under the Immigration Act 1971 are ineligible and only British citizens, citizens of a European Economic Area country or Commonwealth citizens with the right of abode in the UK can effectively be eligible for assistance. A dependent partner or child who is an ineligible person from abroad will not be taken into account in determining whether their partner or parent is homeless or has priority need (s 185(4)). Section 186 goes on to indicate that an asylum-seeker (and any dependants) who are not ruled out by s 185, will still be ineligible for assistance if they have any accommodation in the UK, however temporary.

(c) Homeless or threatened with homelessness

3.82 This definition has been extended by s 175(1) HA 1996. Persons are regarded as 'homeless' if they have no accommodation in England and Wales or elsewhere which they, together with any person who normally resides with them as a member of their family or such other person for whom it is reasonable to reside with them, are entitled to occupy (s 175(1)).

3.83 The applicant's entitlement to occupy accommodation may take the following forms:

(i)   an entitlement to occupy by virtue of an interest in it or of an order of the court;
(ii)   an express or implied licence to occupy;

(iii) occupation as a residence by virtue of any enactment or rule of law giving him
the right to remain in occupation or restricting the right of another to recover
possession.

3.84 Section 177(2) provides that the accommodation must be such as is reasonable
for the applicant to occupy and in determining this the local authority may have
regard to the prevailing housing conditions in the local area. This is considered
further in relation to the test for intentional homelessness (see para 3.93).

3.85 Accommodation will not constitute 'available accommodation' if it is
available to the applicant only and not to other members of the family or other
persons normally and reasonably residing with him (s 176). In contrast to the 1996
edition of the Code, it now seems clear that both opposite and same-sex cohabitants
should come within the definition of a member of the other's family. The revised
2000 Code states, in now neutral terms, this:

> '. . . will clearly cover all persons who normally live as part of the applicant's household.
> As well as the applicant's partner, children (including foster children) and any other
> family members, this might also include a housekeeper, companion or a carer who lives
> with an elderly person or someone with a disability or illness'(see para. 11.3).

Thus this should be used by advisers should any reluctance be encountered from
housing authorities unconvinced that same-sex partners are to be regarded as family
members residing with an applicant.

3.86 Thus a cohabiting couple's needs as a unit should be taken into account in
determining whether accommodation is available for occupation. Similarly, where a
finding is made to secure accommodation for an applicant, the suitability of the
accommodation should be assessed according to their joint needs. Current policy
and practice as noted above is to place any tenancy granted in joint names. In
practice an authority could not prevent a cohabitant applicant who has a priority
need due to age or vulnerability (see below) from allowing his or her partner of the
same sex to live with them in permanent accommodation; but unless there is a joint
tenancy, the partner would have no right to succeed to the tenancy if it were secure,
nor if it were an assured tenancy granted by a housing association.

It has been held that occupation by way of licence of a battered wives refuge and a
night shelter, which could refuse admission if the shelter were full did not amount
to accommodation (see *R v Ealing London Borough Council, ex p Sidhu* (1982) 2
HLR 45 and *R v Waveney District Council, ex p Bowers* [1983] QB 238). These
examples predate the decision in *R v Brent London Borough Council, ex p Awua*
(above), in which Lord Hoffmann (at page 461) stated that the word 'accommodation' must mean a place which can fairly be described as such. A night shelter,
which is available only if there are bed-spaces and which excludes people during
the day, would seem to fail this test. The battered wives' refuge may not now be so
clear cut.

3.87 An applicant will also be homeless if unable to secure entry to the
accommodation or at risk from domestic violence from a person residing there
(s 175(2)(a)), as discussed in Chapter 7 below. A person is 'threatened with

homelessness' if they are liable to be made homeless within 28 days (s 175(4)), and, for the purpose of the subsequent duties imposed on the authority, there is no distinction made between these two categories of people.

(d) Priority need

3.88 Although not contained in the Homelessness Bill 2001, the DLTR are currently consulting on whether the homeless priority need categories should be reformed to include those fleeing harassment or domestic violence, those who have left local authority care, all 16 and 17 year olds, ex-prisoners and ex-service personnel (see http://www.housing.dtlr.gov.uk/information/index03.htm#initiatives) Any reform of these would not require primary legislation but would be effected by Order. For the time-being, however, a duty to re-house will be owed only to an applicant who is in priority need (s 189). Applicants in priority need are:

(i)   a pregnant woman or a person with whom a pregnant woman resides or might reasonably be expected to reside;

(ii)   a person with whom dependent children reside or might reasonably be expected to reside;

(iii) a person who is vulnerable as a result of old age, mental illness or handicap or physical disability or other special reason or with whom such a person resides or might reasonably be expected to reside;

(iv)   a person who is homeless or threatened with homelessness as a result of an emergency such as a fire or flood;

(v)   someone within a group of persons described as having priority need by the Secretary of State.

3.89 If homeless as a result of an emergency, cohabitants will automatically be considered to be in priority need although the nature of the emergency must be such as to cause physical damage. An illegal eviction is not an emergency (*R v Bristol City Council, ex p Bradic* (1995) 27 HLR 584, CA). A homeless cohabiting couple has nothing to lose from applying to the housing authority to see whether they can be classified in any of these categories. It has been held that it is not lawful for an authority to have a policy of excluding childless couples from falling within priority need (see *A-G (ex rel Tilley) v Wandsworth London Borough Council* [1981] 1 All ER 1162).

3.90 'Dependent children' normally means children under sixteen or still in full time education. The test is a question of fact: are there dependent children who reside or ought reasonably to reside with the applicant? An authority cannot, where the parents are separated, insist that the applicant produces a custody order before accepting that a priority need exists (see *R v Ealing London Borough Council, ex p Sidhu*, above). In *R v Lambeth London Borough Council, ex p Vagliviello* (1990) 22 HLR 392 the Court of Appeal confirmed that even a partial custody arrangement could indicate a priority need, as the test is one of whether children could reasonably be expected to reside with the applicant, not whether the applicant had sole custody. Since the advent of the Children Act 1989 (CA 1989) both these issues have increased significance. The 'no order presumption' in CA 1989 and its amendments to s 41 Matrimonial Causes Act 1973, which effectively removed the practice of automatically making orders relating to children on divorce, mean that cohabitants are less likely to have residence orders relating to children of previous relationships, yet such children may still give cohabitants a priority need for accommodation. In addition, s 11(4) CA 1989 specifically envisages that residence orders may be made in favour of two or more persons who do not live together and, thus, what would previously have been described as a 'partial custody' situation, has become more common, as discussed in Chapter 8. Indeed the Code of Guidance does now recognise this type of situation may give one or both parents a priority need and that each case must be carefully considered (para. 12.3).

3.91 The House of Lords decision in the joined cases of *R v Oldham Metropolitan Borough Council, ex p Garlick*; *R v Bexley London Borough Council, ex p Bentum*; *R v Tower Hamlets London Borough Council, ex p Begum* [1993] AC 509 decided, inter alia, that 'dependent children' were not normally capable of being 'applicants' and did not have a priority need in their own right through their vulnerability.

3.92 To show vulnerability, an applicant must be of retirement age, or vulnerable in some other way. This has been defined as being less able to both find and keep accommodation (see *R v Lambeth London Borough Council, ex p Carroll* (1987) 20 HLR 142, and *R v Kensington and Chelsea London Borough Council, ex p Kihara* (1996) 29 HLR 147). In *Carroll* the court indicated that an authority must reach its own decision on vulnerability and not merely rubber stamp a medical opinion unless that is decisive on the only relevant issues. Accordingly advisors should in appropriate cases advise the applicant to submit independent medical evidence to the local authority. Regard should also be had to the Code of Guidance (paras 12.1 – 12.23) which has been much expanded since 1996 and gives examples of the different categories of priority need and of vulnerability. The local authority must provide accommodation temporarily where there is a *prima facie* priority need, but thereafter they should make further enquiries to see if there is in fact such a need. Only if this is established will applicants proceed to the next hurdle.

(e) Intentional homelessness

3.93 It is this final hurdle which has spawned the most case law under the old law and undoubtedly causes hardship to people who fulfil the other criteria but are deemed to be the authors of their own misfortune. Where there is a finding of intentional homelessness, a local authority will not owe any duty to secure accommodation for the applicant, who may therefore literally be without a roof. The intentionality test has been made more stringent by the 1996 Act. A person is intentionally homeless if he or she does or fails to do anything which leads them to cease to occupy accommodation which is available and reasonable for them to occupy (s 191(1)). The definition of becoming intentionally 'threatened with homelessness' is subject to a similar test. An act or omission in good faith by a person unaware of a relevant fact such as security of tenure, the availability of assistance with rent or mortgage payments, or the validity of a notice to quit, is not to be treated as deliberate (s 191(2)). Section 191(3) is responsible for widening the ambit of intentional homelessness. It states:

> 'A person shall be treated as becoming homeless intentionally if—(a) he enters into an arrangement under which he is required to cease to occupy accommodation which it would have been reasonable for him to continue to occupy; and (b) the purpose of the arrangement is to enable him to become entitled to assistance under this Part; and there is no other good reason why he is homeless.'

Section 191(4) goes on to include as intentionally homeless persons who have received advice and assistance under s 197 as to where they can find suitable accommodation, but who have failed to secure this when they should reasonably have been expected to. These provisions aim to avoid collusion between friends, relatives, landlords and tenants with a view to obtaining accommodation, encouraging them instead to stay in 'unsettled' accommodation, for example with relatives, whilst they await accommodation through the housing register route. In addition, they can be seen to push people into making greater use of the private rented sector.

3.94 The issue of good faith (now in s 191(2)) arose in *R v Hammersmith and Fulham London Borough Council, ex p Lusi* (1991) 23 HLR 260, where a couple who gave up their London flat in order to pursue a business venture in Turkey which subsequently failed were found to be intentionally homeless upon their return. The Divisional Court found, however, that the local authority had misdirected itself in law by equating ignorance of relevant facts with bad faith and consequently quashed the decision, remitting it for further investigation of what was actually known or ought to have been known by the applicant. This approach was endorsed by the Court of Appeal In *R v Exeter City Council, ex p Tranckle* (1993) 26 HLR 244.

3.95 A person is not intentionally homeless if they give up accommodation which is not available for both the applicant and any person with whom they might reasonably be expected to reside (s 75). Thus, in *R v Peterborough City Council, ex p Carr* (1990) 22 HLR 206, QBD, a pregnant woman who left her accommodation with her sister due to her sister's refusal to allow her prospective child's father to live with her was not intentionally homeless. In *R v Westminster City Council, ex p Bishop* (1993) 25 HLR 459, the Court of Appeal found that accommodation was only available for the applicant's occupation if both the applicant and those members of her family who normally reside with her can reasonably be expected to occupy it. Thus, a finding of intentionality against an applicant who surrendered her tenancy on a problem estate where there was strong evidence of adverse effects from living there upon the applicant's daughter, was quashed.

3.96 Where one cohabitant has done an act, such as giving up a job, which has meant the loss of tied accommodation, then it may be possible for their spouse or cohabitant or another adult who usually and reasonably resides with them, to make the application under the Act in order to avoid a finding of intentionality (see *R v North Devon District Council, ex p Lewis* [1981] 1 WLR 328 and *R v Swansea City Council, ex p Thomas* (1983) 9 HLR 64). Each case will depend on its own facts, but to be successful the applicant must not have acquiesced in the act which led to the loss of accommodation. Thus, in *Lewis* above, although it was accepted that a cohabitant was entitled to make an application following her partner's quitting his job and losing accommodation, she was equally found to be intentionally homeless because she had acquiesced in his decision to leave. It would have been otherwise if she had done all in her power to prevent him from resigning.

3.97 Cases of mortgage and rent arrears may lead to intentionality findings, as do possession orders granted on the basis that the applicant has caused nuisance and annoyance to other occupiers. The Code of Guidance (see para. 13.7) suggests that a lenient view may be taken where arrears arise due to ignorance of the availability of welfare benefits. Where one party has spent the rent money on drink or caused nuisance and annoyance despite the attempts by the other to prevent it, the 'innocent' cohabitant or spouse can argue that they are not intentionally homeless, particularly if financially dependent on their partner, or for other reasons were not in a position to prevent the situation. It is submitted that this should be the case regardless of whether the parties are joint tenants or the tenancy is vested in the other's name. It has been held that mere knowledge of rent or mortgage arrears by a partner is not necessarily enough to constitute intentionality as they may not have learned of the situation until it was too late to forestall. However, where there is a joint tenancy, lack of knowledge may be difficult to uphold as both parties should be communicated with and served with proceedings. Many couples in severe financial straits may decide that what money is available should be spent on food rather than housing costs. They may be helped to some extent by the case of *R v Hillingdon London Borough Council, ex p Tinn* (1988) 20 HLR 305 where it was held that it could not be reasonable to occupy accommodation where to meet the mortgage repayments the family had to go without food and the other necessities of life. This approach was endorsed by the Court of Appeal in *R v Wandsworth London Borough Council, ex p Hawthorne* (1994) 27 HLR 59, where a mother was evicted for rent arrears which had accrued as a result of her electing to spend her benefit on food for the children rather than the rent after the imposition of a housing benefit ceiling. Indeed, the authority had considered the failure to pay rent a deliberate act without having applied itself to the question of what had caused the failure to pay rent as required by the Code of Guidance and consequently the intentionality finding was quashed.

3.98 Whether or not it is reasonable for an applicant to continue to occupy accommodation involves many questions, but an authority must take into account the housing conditions in its area in reaching a decision on reasonableness, and the worse these conditions are, the more an applicant is expected to put up with before quitting accommodation. In *R v Tower Hamlets London Borough Council, ex p Monaf* (1988) 20 HLR 529, it was held that the authority must perform a balancing exercise between the reasons for departure and housing conditions in that area. However, the authority must compare the applicant's actual housing conditions with those in the *authority's* area and not with the conditions of residents in the area or country where the applicant had left the accommodation (see *R v Newham London Borough Council, ex p Tower Hamlets London Borough Council* (1990) 22 HLR 298). Another important factor is that the authority can look beyond the immediate cause of homelessness to see if the real cause of the homelessness is intentional.

3.99 The House of Lords decision in *Awua* (above) removed the concept of 'settled accommodation' developed under the 1985 legislation and the fact that accommodation lost is not settled or permanent will not save an applicant from a finding of intentional homelessness unless the tenure was so precarious it rendered them liable to leave within twenty-eight days.

3.100 In *Din v Wandsworth London Borough Council* [1983] 1 AC 657, where a family ignored advice to remain in accommodation until the court order for possession expired, although it was accepted that by the time they applied to the authority they would in any event have been homeless unintentionally, the act of leaving available accommodation before being required to leave was sufficient to render them intentionally homeless in the view of the House of Lords. As none of the accommodation they had subsequently occupied had been settled, they were still intentionally homeless despite the fact that a considerable period of time had elapsed. A finding of intentional homelessness can only be redeemed after an applicant has lost subsequent settled accommodation *unintentionally*. In this regard *Awua* retained the concept of settled accommodation and it is now the position that, whereas leaving unsettled accommodation can warrant a finding of intentional homelessness, it seems an applicant cannot break the chain of causation and be considered as unintentionally homeless until they have gained settled accommodation and then lost it unintentionally. Thus cohabitants should not surrender accommodation which it is at that time reasonable for them to continue to occupy; clearly this has been very strictly interpreted by the courts and the 1996 Act provisions have made the test even more stringent.

3.101 However, the Code of Guidance does make it clear that authorities should not require mortgagors or tenants to fight possession actions where the mortgagee or landlord has a certain prospect of success (para 13.10). In *R v Newham London Borough, ex p Ugbo* (1993) 26 HLR 263, an assured shorthold tenant who ignored the council's advice to stay in the accommodation until after the possession order had been made, had a finding of intentionality made against her quashed by the Divisional Court, which found that the advice she had been given by the council was wrong. Given the increased use of assured shorthold tenancies to which tenants will rarely have any defence to possession proceedings, this is a significant development.

(f) Duties of local authorities; local connections; other routes to accommodation

3.102 Once an authority has made its decision it must notify the applicant, giving reasons if it finds no duty to secure accommodation or that there is a local connection elsewhere (s 184). If the authority finds there is no priority need, then advice and assistance, but nothing further, must be provided. One of the aims of the Homelessness Bill, however, is to extend the services provided to those who are homeless but not in priority need and thus in future accommodation may (although this is not, it seems a requirement) be provided (see clause 5). If there is priority need but the applicants are judged intentionally homeless, then accommodation must be provided for such period as will allow them to find other accommodation (typically twenty-eight days) and advice and assistance should also be provided. At this point, a family is often left unable to afford, or even find, private sector accommodation, yet nothing further has to be done by the local authority.

3.103 The harsh effects on a family of an intentionality finding, produced some imaginative attempts to secure housing under the 1985 Act by extending the principle established in *R v North Devon District Council, ex p Lewis* (above). The House of Lords decision in *R v Oldham Metropolitan Borough Council, ex p Garlick*; *R v Bexley London Borough Council, ex p Bentum, R v Tower Hamlets London Borough Council, ex p Begum* (above) was the result of three such attempts. They each sought to argue that a duty to house the families involved in each case arose where in the cases of both *Garlick* and *Bentum*; a dependent four year old child, and in *Begum*, a severely mentally handicapped adult daughter, neither of whom were 'tainted' with the intentionality of their parents (the original applicants), made fresh applications in their own names under the Act. However, the House of Lords rejected this argument upon the basis, *inter alia*, that a degree of understanding sufficient to appreciate the nature of the application was implicitly required by applicants under the Act, who needed to be able to decide whether or not to accept the accommodation offered. In the cases of the four-year-old dependent children, they were far too young to achieve this threshold and, in any event, had no priority need. Thus they could not be applicants under the Act. In the case of *Begum*, further evidence of her level of understanding would be required in order to determine whether she had the capacity to be an applicant.

3.104 In its deliberations, the court took the view that Parliament could not have intended intentionally homeless families to be housed 'through the back door'. It also took into account the fact that there were other statutory provisions which would assist in providing accommodation for children or a vulnerable person, namely s 20 CA 1989 and s 21 National Assistance Act 1948 respectively, although in both cases this would involve provision of accommodation by the state for the child or disabled person alone and not in the community with their families. Thus, intentionally homeless families may be faced with the invidious choice of accepting institutional care for their dependants or literally living with them on the streets.

3.105 Cohabitants with dependent children who find themselves in this situation, and who do not wish their children to be accommodated under s 20, may be able to obtain assistance by a request for assistance by Social Services under s 17 CA 1989. This places a duty on social services departments to safeguard and promote the welfare of children 'in need' within their area and to promote the upbringing of such children *by their families* where this is consistent with their welfare. This is to be done by providing a range of services including under s 17(6) 'assistance in kind or in exceptional circumstances cash' and thus may include accommodation. Services may be provided for the whole family under s 17(3) and may take the form of housing.

3.106 Providing a child can be shown to be 'in need', as defined by s 17(10), which involves showing that the child's health or development is likely to be significantly impaired or to fall below a reasonable standard without the provision of services, then the duty to provide assistance arises. It must be strongly arguable that any child who is literally roofless is 'in need' and that the assistance required to remedy this is accommodation. Unfortunately, social services departments no longer have their own housing stock. If they accept the need for assistance they may either provide cash for a deposit for private rented accommodation, although the section requires the circumstances to be 'exceptional' before such help can be forthcoming. Nonetheless, this may result in practice in the whole family being given emergency accommodation pending an assessment of the child's needs. However, in *R v Barnet LBC, ex parte Foran* (1999) 31 HLR 708, the Court of Appeal confirmed there was no absolute duty on Social Services to house homeless children together with their families. Furthermore, in *R ('G') v Barnet LBC* [2001] EWCA Civ 540, the Court of Appeal confirmed the duty in 517(1) CA 1989 LC promote the upbringing of children by their families, could be met by financing the family's return to their home country. Thus whilst there is power to accommodate, there is no duty to house a family, but only the children under s 20 CA 1989.

3.107 Prior to the Housing Act 1996, the House of Lords had been asked in *R v Northavon District Council, ex p Smith* (1994) 26 HLR 659 to consider whether the duty contained in s 27 CA 1989 requiring local housing authorities to co-operate with social services in carrying out functions under the 1989 Act, unless it is incompatible with their own duties and functions, extended to the provision of accommodation for a family previously found intentionally homeless, but whose children had subsequently been identified as 'in need'. They held that the housing authority were under no duty to provide permanent accommodation following the intentionality finding and that the applicants had no priority over others awaiting accommodation, either through the homelessness legislation or the waiting list route. All they therefore had to do was consider whether they could assist in preventing the children from suffering from lack of accommodation without prejudicing their other functions. If they could not, then it fell to social services to protect the children, either by financial assistance or by exercise of their other powers. The current Code of Guidance does emphasise the ability of Social Services to seek assistance from Housing Authorities (see para. 18.4) but often it may come down to an issue of resources.

3.108 Thus, following eviction from temporary accommodation, intentionally homeless families' best hope of assistance lies with social services, whose policies will vary from area to area and whose ability to assist them in finding and financing accommodation as a family is likely to be limited. Nonetheless, the duty in s 17(1) to promote the upbringing of children by their families is a powerful argument for advisors to use in favour of financial assistance, especially given the high cost of providing accommodation for children under s 20 CA 1989. Another possibility, where a family is on income support or income-based jobseeker's allowance, is for assistance to be provided in applying for a social fund budgeting loan for rent in advance (see Chapter 4).

3.109 If an applicant has succeeded in overcoming the hurdles contained in the homelessness legislation and described above, then the authority has a duty to secure suitable accommodation for a minimum period of two years (s 193). At the end of that period the authority may continue accommodation but are not obliged to do so providing the applicant is still in priority need, wants the accommodation to continue and there is no other suitable accommodation available (s 194).

3.110 In assessing suitability, which is now governed by s 200 HA 1996, the House of Lords has said this is primarily a matter of space and arrangement but that other matters, such as affordability of the rent, may be material. Under the 1985 legislation, the Court of Appeal has found that the physical structure of the building is not the only test and a vulnerability to violence in that location could be a factor (*R v Broxbourne Borough Council, ex p Willmoth* (1989) 22 HLR 118). In addition, personal factors of the applicant and those expected to reside with them are relevant (see *R v Brent London Borough Council, ex p Omar* (1991) 23 HLR 446). Accommodation at a rent which the applicant cannot afford from their own resources or with state assistance was not suitable (*R v Tower Hamlets London Borough Council, ex p Kaur* (1994) 26 HLR 597). It seems clear that assured shorthold private sector accommodation will be regarded as suitable, although it would still seem to be good law that the tenure or time element of suitability should reflect the circumstances of the case (*R v Wandsworth London Borough Council, ex p Wingrove* and *ex p Mansoor* [1997] QB 953, CA. As noted above, the Homelessness Bill if enacted will specifically prevent the offer of assured shorthold accommodation from discharging the duty to the homeless. In addition it intends to strengthen the homeless person's right to review the suitability of accommodation offered in discharge of the duty to secure accommodation (see clause 8).

3.111 If there is no local connection with the authority to whom they have applied, but there is with another authority, then s 198 provides that the applicant can be referred back to the authority with whom he or she has a local connection, providing the applicant does not run the risk of domestic violence in that area. Section 199 defines 'local connection' in terms of periods of residence (past or present), employment, family associations and special circumstances. Where an applicant does not have a local connection with any area but fulfils the other criteria, then the local authority to whom he or she has applied must secure suitable accommodation, although this may be done through another authority or housing body (see *R v Hillingdon London Borough Council, ex p Streeting* [1980] 3 All ER 413).

3.112 Homelessness on family breakdown due to domestic violence is a problem often affecting cohabitants with children, and is dealt with in Chapter 7.

Chapter 4

Tax, pensions and social security

4.01 It is in the areas of tax, pensions and social security that some of the greatest anomalies in the legal treatment of cohabitants become apparent. Despite statements of intent by politicians at various times to integrate the welfare benefit and tax systems, this has yet to be completely achieved. Nonetheless, some definite strides have been made in this direction by the Labour government during their first term and further changes have been announced. However, whilst the removal of some of the income tax advantages previously enjoyed by married couples has meant that the income tax position of heterosexual cohabitants is now virtually exactly the same as that of those who are married, this is not the case as regards their capital tax position. Similarly, whilst for means-tested or income-based welfare benefits there is no difference in the treatment of married and heterosexual cohabitants, this is not always the case in the context of contributory benefits in general and pensions in particular. Where parity has been achieved in the contributory benefit context, this has always been as a result of benefits previously extended to married claimants alone (such as an allowance for a dependant spouse) being removed, not by the inclusion of cohabitants in the definition of spouse. By way of contrast, same-sex couples are always treated as two separate individuals and thus they have an advantage over both married and heterosexual cohabiting couples in terms of their entitlement to income-based benefits. However, like heterosexual cohabitants they can gain no advantage from their partner's national insurance contributions in respect of pensions or other contributory benefits.

4.02 It is not proposed here to look at the substantive law in any great detail, but to outline the general principles, and points of particular relevance to cohabitants.

1 Income tax and tax credits

4.03 Both heterosexual and homosexual cohabitants are, and have always been, treated by the Inland Revenue as separate individuals for income tax purposes. The introduction of separate taxation for married couples in 1991 followed by the more recent abolition of the already devalued married couples allowance (other than for those over 65 and born before 6 April 1935) with effect from April 2000, means that there are now very few differences between the married and unmarried as far as income tax is concerned. Instead the focus has been switched to those with children and particularly to those working parents on low incomes. It should be noted that this transfer was not completely painless for those eligible for both entitlements. For during for the tax year 2000–2001, whilst the married couples' allowance and the additional personal allowance (which had been available to an unmarried parent) had been abolished (ss 31 and 33 Finance Act 1999), the new Children's Tax Credit was not yet available to families (s 20(2), (5) and Sch 3). However, Working Families Tax Credit and Disabled Persons Tax Credit were introduced at this point to replace certain welfare benefits (see Tax Credits Act 1999). It is perhaps also worthy of note that the introduction of tax credits available to married and unmarried couples with children does now mean that there is some integration of the tax affairs of cohabiting as well as married partners.

4.04 As of April 2001, where there are children of 16 or under there are two possible forms of tax credit available depending on your level of income and it is understood that these are to be merged into an Integrated Child Tax Credit in April 2003, although separate payment of the universal child benefit (discussed below) will remain. Currently, providing the highest earning parent is not a higher rate taxpayer and both parents are working, then either one of the parents is entitled to claim the Children Tax Credit (CTC) which can reduce the tax payable by up to £520 per year. In addition, providing one parent works a minimum of 16 hours per week, there is also available a means-tested Working Families Tax Credit (WFTC) which replaced the income-based benefit formerly known as "Family Credit" with effect from April 2000. This is aimed at low income working families. Like Children's Tax Credit, WFTC is operated by the Inland Revenue rather than the Department of Work and Pensions ((DWP) and formerly the DSS) and both are available to couples or single parents with children regardless of marital status.

4.05 Where cohabitants have no children, they will each receive a single person's personal allowance which they can set off only against their own income in each tax year. The single allowance for the tax year 2001/02 is £4,385. It should be borne in mind that everyone, regardless of age, is entitled to a personal allowance. Allowances are increased for those over 65; and children, however young, are entitled to a single person's allowance. However, since 1988, maintenance payments are no longer taxable in the hands of the recipient and thus do not constitute income for tax purposes (s 51A ICTA 1988). All payments must therefore be paid gross and there is no tax relief available in respect of maintenance payments to children including, now, of course, child support maintenance payable in accordance with the Child Support Act 1991 subject to the reforms to be implemented in April 2002 enacted in the Child Support and Pensions Act 2000 (see Chapter 9).

2 Children's Tax Credit

(a) Childrens Tax Credit

4.06 Cohabitants with one or more dependant children of 16 or under residing with them for all or part of the tax year can choose which of them claims CTC or may share it equally between them, providing neither of them is a higher rate taxpayer (see s 257AA and Sch 13B ICTA 1988). However, there is only one credit per family, regardless of how many children there are, or whether the children are children of the current or previous relationships, providing the latter are financially supported as part of that household. It is possible for a cohabitant to claim CTC for their own children (whether or not born inside marriage), an adopted child, a stepchild or "a child looked after at their own expense". This could include a partner's child by another relationship providing they bear at least half such expenses, although the parent partner would also of course be eligible to claim in their own right providing they were earning sufficient income. Generally, if only one partner is working, or only one of them earns sufficient to take full advantage of the tax credit, then that partner should claim it, to ensure full benefit is derived. Indeed both partners have to agree if the CTC is to be claimed by the lower earner. However, it is now possible for one partner to transfer any unused tax credit to the other after the end of the tax year. Where one partner is a higher rate taxpayer, earning more than £33,935, then the value of the tax credit is reduced at the rate of £1 for every £15 taxed at the higher rate. Where a partner earns in excess of £41,735 per year, then it is unlikely at current rates that any CTC will be payable, regardless of whether or not their partner is earning. Where there is a higher rate taxpayer, then they alone may claim the tax credit which cannot be shared with or transferred to the other partner. Any change of circumstances affecting the credit such as separation, loss of higher rate taxpayer status or the child no longer residing with cohabitants needs to be notified to the Revenue.

4.07 As previously observed, in principle, the partners in a couple can only make one claim between them as a claim can only be made by one partner in respect of each family. However, a new partner will only be able to claim a share of CTC if they are meeting at least half the total cost of maintaining the other partner's child by a previous relationship. Thus, if cohabitants each have qualifying children from former relationships and are each maintaining that child or children without their current partner's help, it seems that it may still be possible for them each to claim CTC. In addition, where a child from a previous relationship lives for part of the year with their other parent, then CTC may be divided between the parents as they agree or, in the absence of agreement, as decided by the independent General Commissioners for Income Tax. Their shared portion of the tax credit can then be shared again between current cohabiting or married partners. Thus it seems a tax credit could in theory be shared between three or even four adults who share the care of a child.

4.08 Another point to note is that, whilst the provisions are neutrally phrased in terms of "families" and "partners", the provisions only apply where "a husband and wife are living together or man and woman are living together as husband and wife" and thus same-sex cohabitants could, without question, each claim the allowance where there is more than one qualifying child being maintained wholly or partly by both partners.

4.09 Children over 16 and in full-time education do not entitle a parent to CTC. However, the child may be able to claim the means tested "Educational Maintenance Allowance" if they are living in a low-income family.

4.10 The Inland Revenue website at http://www.inlandrevenue.gov.uk is extremely helpful and contains information regarding eligibility for taxpayers and links to the relevant legislation. There is also a Children's Tax Credit Helpline on 0845 300 1036.

(b) Working Families Tax Credit

4.11 This tax credit has replaced the income-based benefit Family Credit with effect from April 2000. Where low income cohabitants who have a child under 16 or under 19 and in full-time education living with them, have combined savings of under £8,000 and one of them is working 16 hours per week or more they are entitled to claim Working Families Tax Credit. At 2001/02 rates, this entitles them to a basic credit of £59.00 per week where their income does not exceed £92.90 per week plus a further credit of £11.45 where one of them is working more than 30 hours per week. In addition they are entitled to a tax credit at the rate of £26.00 for each child under 16 and £26.75 for each child between 16 and 18. They will also be entitled to a child care tax credit of up to 70 per cent of the eligible child care costs (essentially for approved nurseries, after-school clubs and registered child minders) up to a maximum of £135 for one child and £200 for two or more children. Where income exceeds the £92.90 threshold, WFTC is reduced by 55 pence for each £1 above the threshold. There is an on-line calculator on the Inland Revenue website for those trying to assess entitlement in particular cases. Where a cohabiting couple are eligible, this will last for 26 weeks before they need to reapply. A same-sex couple who is responsible for a child normally living in their household must apply as single parents for WFTC. This has the advantage that savings and income of such a couple will not be aggregated in order to assess eligibility.

4.12 An important decision for cohabitants with regard to WFTC is which of them should make the claim as this may affect the method of payment. Unlike CTC, this tax credit cannot be shared between the couple. If the applicant is employed, his employer, as part of his pay packet, will pay him WFTC. If a partner who is not working makes the claim, it is paid directly to him. Whoever makes the claim, both partners will normally need to sign the claim form. Direct payments of WFTC will also be made to the self-employed.

4.13 Again the Inland Revenue website is helpful and there is a Tax Credits Helpline on 0845 6095000.

(c) Abolition of Mortgage Tax Relief

4.14 Cohabitants who purchased a property jointly before 1 August 1988 were, and still are, *each* entitled to mortgage interest relief on capital sums borrowed of up to £30,000 per person in relation to a property which was their only or principal residence, whereas married couples were limited to relief of a maximum of £30,000 per couple. Relief was then limited to a maximum of £30,000 *per property* but was abolished completely as of 6 April 2000 (s 38 Finance Act 1999).

3 Capital gains tax

4.15 The Taxation of Capital Gains Act 1992 (TCGA 1992) provides that capital gains tax is payable on all chargeable gains made in respect of chargeable assets, after deduction of all allowable losses and subject to an annual exemption of £7,500 for the tax year 2001/02. Cohabitants, unlike married couples, have always been entitled to an annual exemption each. However, with effect from 6 April 1990, married couples are similarly entitled to two exemptions and in addition, disposals between spouses are deemed to be neither at a loss or a gain. However, disposals between cohabitants do not attract any special treatment and are thus chargeable either as a gain or a loss as appropriate.

4.16 The main asset of most cohabitants is likely to be the home, although a sole or principal residence does not attract capital gains tax, and any profit made on a sale is not considered a gain (ss 222–224 TCGA 1992). A married couple can have only one sole or principal residence, whereas cohabitants may have one each. Accordingly, providing one property is vested in each of their names, and they can each satisfy the residence condition, it is possible to avoid paying capital gains tax on either property no matter when they are sold.

4 Inheritance tax

4.17 While no inheritance tax is payable on transfers between spouses, there is, again, no like treatment of cohabitants, who are treated as strangers. Inheritance tax is payable on "transfers of value", that is those which reduce the value of the transferor's estate, made either *inter vivos* or on death. However there is a threshold of £242,000 below which no tax is payable in respect of transfers made after 5 April 2001. Although this may seem a fairly large sum of money, there is, unlike capital gains tax, no exception in respect of the transferor's residence, and thus the value of the deceased's share of his or her property will be taken into account in calculating when the threshold is reached. Where jointly owned property is held as tenants in common in equity, the deceased's share forms part of the estate and tax will be payable in accordance with the terms of the Will.

4.18 Where there is an equitable joint tenancy, the deceased's share in the property will pass to the co-owner in accordance with the right of survivorship. However, although this share of the property will not form part of the estate, the surviving co-owner will be liable for any inheritance tax due in respect of the share.

4.19 After the first £242,000, tax is payable, currently at 40%, either by the estate or by the beneficiary. Thus where a cohabitant is the only beneficiary, his/her inheritance will be subject to tax where the total value exceeds this threshold. Where gifts are made before death, and providing the transferor lives for seven years after the making of the gift, then no inheritance tax is payable on such a gift and its value will not form part of the transferor's estate on death. Even if the transferor dies within the seven-year period, liability to tax will normally be reduced on a sliding scale, although if death occurs within three years of the gift, then tax is still payable at the full rate. If the donor survives three years but less than four, then 80% of the full rate of tax is payable; tax is payable at 60% of the full rate if the death occurs after four years but less than five; at 40% of the full rate after five years but less than six; and at 20% after six years but less than seven. In addition, there is an annual exemption of £3,000 which reduces liability on *inter vivos* gifts.

4.20 Cohabitants making Wills, perhaps even more than other clients, need to be advised of the inheritance tax implications of their proposed gifts, and to consider the advantages of making use of the annual exemption and of effecting life assurance for the benefit of their partner, as discussed in Chapter 1.

5 Council tax

4.21 Following unprecedented public dissatisfaction with the community charge, which had briefly replaced the domestic rating system, this form of local taxation was finally abolished and replaced with council tax by the Local Government Act 1992 (LGA 1992) as of April 1993.

4.22 Unlike the community charge, the council tax is a local tax levied on each "dwelling" (see s 3 LGA 1992) and is based on the assumption that the dwelling is occupied by two adults. It is payable by one or more of the residents (who must be over 18), where the dwelling is occupied as their sole or main residence. Where there is no such resident, council tax becomes payable by the non-resident owner. There is a hierarchy of residents, and the adult resident(s) liable for the tax will be the first to fall into the highest of the following categories (see s 6(1) LGA 1992:

- freeholder
- leaseholder
- statutory or secure tenant
- contractual licensee
- any other resident

4.23 Two or more residents falling into the same category (or owners in the absence of a resident) will normally be jointly and severally liable for the tax (s 6(2)). This will obviously affect cohabitants who are joint owners or joint tenants of a property. Furthermore, even where only one partner is ostensibly liable, s 9 provides that the partner of a liable person is (with the exception of a severely mentally impaired partner) also jointly and severally liable for the period of their residence if they are married or living with the liable person as their husband or wife. The consequence of this for opposite-sex cohabitants is that, on separation, it is vital for the cohabitant who leaves to inform the local authority that they are no longer resident in the property to avoid future liability. Same-sex cohabitants do not fall into this category and thus, unless there is joint liability upon the basis of equal residential status, they will not be deemed to be jointly and severally liable.

4.24 The amount of council tax payable depends on the valuation band into which the property has been placed and liability may be reduced if the dwelling is exempt, has less than two residents, is occupied by residents who are disregarded or are entitled to a status discount, or there is entitlement to council tax benefit (see ss 11 and 12 and Sch 1 LGA 1992 and SI 1992/552, SI 1992/2942, and SI 1993/149).

4.25 It should be noted that with regard to properties in multiple occupation, liability normally falls on the owner and not the individual residents. However, this entitles the owner landlord to include an element for council tax in the rent charged to tenants, which, although not reclaimable through council tax benefit, should form part of the rent eligible for housing benefit payments as discussed below.

4.26 It can therefore be seen that, whilst cohabitants are denied such tax benefits still given to married couples, joint liability where only one adult partner is ostensibly liable for council tax applies equally to both spouses and heterosexual cohabitants

6 Welfare benefits and pensions

4.27 The law is by no means even-handed in its treatment of heterosexual cohabitants in the area of welfare benefits and once again it is not possible here to do more than give a summary of the main points relevant to cohabitants. As has been noted in respect of imputed joint liability for council tax, there is a tendency to treat cohabitants in the same way as spouses where this is to the advantage of the state purse, but not when this would involve extra cost. As we have seen, the introduction of Working Families Tax Credit administered by the Inland Revenue heralds an attempt to integrate the tax and benefit systems and thus there is now no benefit available to working families as such. The Department of Social Security has been merged with parts of the Department of Education and Employment to become the new Department for Work and Pensions (DWP) and their website at http://www.dss.gov.uk provides claimants and advisers (there is a page dedicated to advisers) with guidance. There are various "New Deal" programmes which aim to get people back to work and provide them with advice and support, although unlike lone parents and the disabled, none of these is specifically directed at cohabitants. As in the taxation system, there is no recognition of cohabitants of the same sex, who are therefore always treated as separate individuals.

(a) Contributory benefits

4.28 Contributory benefits are those which are payable upon condition that sufficient National Insurance contributions have been made; they are not means-tested. In some circumstances, contributions by a person's spouse are taken into account in assessing entitlement to a contributory benefit, but this is never the case for cohabitants.

4.29 At the present time, a person entitled to a contributory benefit may in addition often need to claim either income related jobseeker's allowance (JSA) or income support (see para 4.40 ff) to supplement his or her income; these are non-contributory and means-tested benefit. It is most likely to be appropriate where the claimant has dependants for whom the contributory benefit does not provide or where the claimant is liable for mortgage repayments, which may be provided by income based JSA or income support. If accommodation is rented, then a claim for Housing Benefit (see para 4.65 ff) should be made to cover rent payments. Council Tax Benefit, as noted above, may also be applied for to cover Council Tax payments. Again, these are both non-contributory and means-tested, and are administered by the local authority rather than the DWP (formerly the DSS).

(i) Contribution-based jobseeker's allowance and other contributory benefits

4.30 It should be noted that unemployment benefit was replaced by the contribution-based jobseeker's allowance (JSA) with effect from 7 October 1996 and is governed by the Jobseekers' Act 1995. This benefit may be either contributory or non-contributory (income-based) and means that those people registered as unemployed will only have to claim JSA, removing the previous anomaly of having to make separate claims for both unemployment benefit and income support in many cases. Entitlement to contributory JSA depends upon the claimant's having paid sufficient class 1 National Insurance contributions, which are payable by those in employment only, and not by the self-employed. Other conditions of entitlement include being available for work, actively seeking employment and establishing that the unemployment is not voluntary. Once entitlement has been established, the claimant is paid contributory JSA for a period of up to six months at an age differentiated rate. The weekly rates for 2001/02 are £53.05 for those over 25, £42.00 for those between 18 and 24 and £31.95 for those under 18.

4.31 At the end of the six-month period, JSA becomes entirely means-tested. Furthermore, no adult dependant addition are payable as part of contributory JSA and thus where there are other dependants, or mortgage repayment costs, income-based JSA will be claimed in addition to contributory JSA providing the means test, which is the same as for income support, and other conditions can be satisfied. There has been a tightening of the availability for work and actively seeking employment tests and claimants must not be in remunerative work of more than sixteen hours per week, although their partner's work does not affect entitlement to contributory JSA. Claimants must be "capable of working", be under pensionable age and be in Great Britain. In addition, claimants are required to complete and sign a "Jobseeker's Agreement" as a condition of receiving benefit, in which they agree to identify, with the help of the Employment Service, the most appropriate steps back to work and allow their efforts to find work to be more closely monitored.

4.32 Other contributory benefits such as incapacity benefit (and formerly sickness and invalidity benefits which it replaced with effect from 13 April 1995), retirement pension, severe disablement allowance, and invalid care allowance similarly include no provision for dependants. Statutory sick pay is payable to employees by their employers for the first 28 weeks of sickness. It is paid at one standard rate and again, there are no additional payments for spouses or dependants of any kind. At the end of the 28 week period, incapacity benefit becomes payable for those who meet the contribution requirements and satisfy the "own occupation test" or the personal capability test" which assess continued capacity. Employers are also now responsible for statutory maternity pay, which again does not have any adult dependency additions. Those who are not eligible for this may qualify for maternity allowance, payable at a flat rate, without any adult dependant addition. There are also "Sure Start Maternity Payments" of £300 for those on low incomes. Again the DWP website is a useful resource to potential claimants and advisers alike.

(ii) Widows' benefits

4.33 Widows' benefits comprise a widows' payment on death of a lump sum of £1,000; widowed mothers' allowance where there are minor children; and widows' pension. There is also a non-contributory widows' pension. No payments of any of the benefits to which widows are entitled can be made to cohabitants on the death of his or her partner, no matter how long they lived together. However, it is important to note that if a widow receiving widows' benefit cohabits with a man, then her widows' benefits will be suspended. If cohabitation ceases, then the entitlement to widows' benefits revives. If the widow was cohabiting with another man at the time of her husband's death, then she is not entitled to the lump sum widows' payment. The definition of cohabitation or "living together as husband and wife" adopts the same criteria as for income-based jobseeker's allowance and income support (see para 4.47 below). It is for the "decision maker" (formerly the adjudication officer) to show that there is cohabitation.

(iii) pensions

4.34 Perhaps the biggest anomaly in the treatment of cohabitants and one about which people are least aware concerns pension payments made under the State Earning Related Pension Scheme (SERPS). Where a person qualifies, having made sufficient Class 1 National Insurance Contributions, the contributory pension payment is increased for a dependant spouse, but this does not extend to cohabitants, no matter how long the relationship may have lasted. This means that cohabitants are severely disadvantaged at this stage in the life-cycle and where each partner has not made their own pension arrangements, then the couple's only option is to apply for means-tested income support to top-up their other income (see below). In this context, of course, they are treated as a married couple and their income and capital will be aggregated in assessing eligibility. Even where a partner is contracted out of SERPS, cohabitants need to check the terms of their employer's or their own personal pension scheme to discover what the conditions of entitlement are for dependant cohabiting partners. Some schemes may improve upon the SERPS' position, others may require nomination of a joint beneficiary, many and probably most will, like SERPS, rule out payments in respect of a dependant cohabitant and thus a separate pension policy may need to be taken out by a dependant partner. This will almost certainly be the case where same-sex cohabitants are concerned. Since 6 April 2001, it has been possible to take out a stakeholder pension which most employers are required to set up where no occupational pension exists. Again, cohabitants need to check their entitlement under a stakeholder scheme. For a discussion of the difficulties specific to same-sex couples, see Rosenblatt, *'The Gay Pension'* [1999] *Fam Law* 784.

(b) Non-contributory benefits

(i) Child benefit

4.35 Child benefit is a universal benefit payable regardless of means in respect of all children under the age of 16 and those under the age of 19 undertaking non-advanced full-time education at a recognised establishment (ss 141 and 142 SSCB Act 1992. See also Child Benefit (General) Regulations 1976 as amended). The benefit is payable to the person who is responsible for the child and does not necessarily have to be a parent.

4.36 Responsibility comprises either having the child living with the claimant; or contributing to the expenses of the child at a rate no less than the weekly benefit payable (s 143(1) SSCB Act 1992). However, where one person contributes and another has the child living with him or her, the person with whom the child resides will be the person entitled to claim.

4.37 Cohabitants with children will normally be entitled to child benefit, for each child living with them. The Regulations provide that where parents are married, the wife is the person entitled to make the claim. Similarly, where the child lives with cohabitants who are both parents, it is the mother who must claim. However, where one cohabitant is a parent and the other is not, it is the parent who is entitled to claim. If neither partner is a parent, then it is for the couple to decide between themselves. From April 2001, £15.50 is payable weekly in respect of the eldest child, and £10.35 for other children. Where cohabitants each have children from previous relationships, it seems that there can be two eldest child payments.

4.38 The availability of an enhanced lone-parent rate of child benefit, totalling £17.55 in respect of the eldest child per week, is payable to a person who has sole responsibility for bringing up a child was controversially abolished for all new claims on 6 July 1998 but is still payable to those who were in receipt of the benefit on that date. Cohabitants, living together as husband and wife, were never eligible to claim this regardless of whether or not the claimant's partner was the child's other parent.

4.39 If a cohabitant was in receipt of lone parent benefit prior to beginning to cohabit, this will not now revive and only the standard rates of child benefit remain payable.

(ii) Income support and income-based JSA

4.40 Following the introduction of JSA in October 1996, this has become the principal benefit claimed by those who are not working. There are still two safety net means-tested benefits in respect of which both eligibility and entitlement are the same, save that those who are required to register for employment must now claim income-based JSA. This has led to income support being reserved for those not expected to be seeking work and the categories of people the state is prepared to sanction not to look for work have shrunk enormously. Principally, it is limited to those over 60, certain categories of sick and disabled people, who may claim it in addition to other benefits, those over 55 and unemployed, who have claimed income support for 15 years without being required to actively seek work, and lone parents claiming for a child under 16. All others must now claim income-based JSA. This particularly affects heterosexual couples, including cohabiting couples, as since 19 March 2001 often both, and always at least one of them, will be required to meet what are termed "labour marked conditions". This means they must attend a jobseeker interview and draw up a jobseeker's agreement, be available for work and meet the actively seeking employment conditions. As indicated above, claimants of JSA will be able to claim income-based JSA rather than income support whilst claiming contributory JSA in respect of their dependants and also for their mortgage interest repayments where appropriate, providing they satisfy the means test. Nonetheless, where one or both cohabitants qualify for contributory JSA, they will still be subject to separate eligibility rules if they need to additionally claim income-based JSA. The means test, payment of the benefit at a lower rate for those under 25 and other rules relating to eligibility for income-based JSA mirror those which apply to income support as described below, although the number of couples eligible for income support as opposed to income-based JSA has diminished, particularly in regard to couples. Both benefits can also be claimed as a supplement to a low income where less than sixteen hours per week are worked, or to contributory benefits where these alone amount to less than a claimant's entitlement to income-based JSA or income support.

4.41 For means-testing purposes in respect of both benefits, cohabitants who are living together as husband and wife are treated in exactly the same way as married couples The rationale for this is that to do otherwise would be to discriminate against married couples. On the other hand, married couples have a mutual and legally enforceable duty to maintain each other, whereas this is not the case as between cohabitants. For income-based JSA, couples are now divided into "joint claim couples" where both must fulfil labour market conditions as well as the means test, and "single claim couples" where only one member of the couple must meet the labour market conditions. A couple will only be classified as a "joint claim couple" where neither of them receives child benefit for a child or is caring for a child (s 1(4) JSA 1995; reg 3A(1) Jobseeker's Allowance Rgulations 1996) and thus will principally affect cohabiting couples who have no children living with them. Couples with children ("single claim couples") only need one partner to fulfil labour marked conditions. In both cases entitlement is to the same couples' allowance (£83.25 per week) although in the case of joint claim couples sanctions can be imposed in respect of either cohabitant's failure to meet conditions. In both single and joint claim cases benefit will only be paid to one member of the couple, but in joint claims, the couple must nominate who this is to be or a decision made by the Secretary of State in the absence of agreement. Thus whilst only one partner can be paid income-based JSA or income support on behalf of a couple, if one cohabitant fails to support the other from the benefit received, the partner has no legal redress.

4.42 Similarly, if one partner is employed, earning more than the JSA or income support that would be paid if the family had no income, but fails to support the partner, the unsupported partner may not claim JSA or income support. Co-operation is presupposed between the partners as it is between spouses, but cohabitants cannot bring pressure to bear by applying for a spousal maintenance order. In this situation, where the couple has been jointly assessed for JSA or income support, the aggrieved partner can either apply for the benefit to be paid directly to him or her instead of to the partner on the grounds of failure to maintain; or commence living in a separate household to gain individual entitlement to benefit. For those whose partners are in employment, the latter is the only option.

4.43 The so-called "cohabitation rule" was preserved in the Social Security Act 1986, which introduced the benefits of income support and family credit, although the word "cohabitation" was omitted from the statute, as it was thought to have pejorative overtones. Instead, references are made to unmarried couples living together in the same household as husband and wife and this is continued in current legislation (see s 137(1) SSBC Act 1992). The rule ensures that opposite-sex cohabitants are treated identically to married couples as far as means-tested benefits are concerned and their capital and income will be aggregated in order to assess entitlement to income-based JSA or income support. The capital limit is currently £8,000, although capital in excess of £3,000 is deemed to provide income of £1 for every £250 of capital over £3,000, which is taken into account in assessing income eligibility.

4.44 In general terms, income eligibility is assessed by deducting actual income from the total sum prescribed by the state as necessary to meet the needs of the particular family unit, and where there is a deficit the balance will be paid. Mortgage interest repayments will form part of a claimant's needs, but radical cuts in entitlement to benefit for the unemployed in respect of such payments have been introduced. There is a ceiling on mortgages in respect of which income support/JSA is payable of £100,000 for new claimants. However, as of 2 October 1995, existing borrowers who claim income-based JSA or income support for the first time get no help with their mortgage repayments whatsoever for the first eight weeks of their claim, and only one half of the interest element of the repayment for the next sixteen weeks. The position for borrowers who took out a mortgage after 2 October 1995 is even worse, as they are denied any benefit in respect of mortgage repayments for the first nine months of their claim.

4.45 The effect of this is that new borrowers are required to take out private insurance against unemployment at the time of taking out their mortgage. In any event, the mortgagee should be notified of the situation as even when the interest element becomes payable in full, it will not cover the whole mortgage repayment due in most cases and thus repossession could ensue unless an arrangement is made to defer the capital payments due with the mortgagee concerned. Similarly, where there is an endowment mortgage, payments of the insurance premium are not recoverable through income-based JSA or income support (see *R(SB) 46/83*) and both the mortgagee and insurer should be apprised of the situation.

4.46 Where an unmarried couple does not admit to living together as husband and wife, it is for the "decision maker", if the separate claims for income-based JSA or income support are to be rejected, to show that the couple cohabit in this sense and that the "cohabitation rule" should be applied. The factors to be taken into account have been developed through case law and DSS guidance pertaining to similar provisions in the legislation relating to supplementary benefit, the predecessor of income support and income-based JSA. The factors to be shown are as follows:

4.47 *The couple are members of the same household* The concept of sharing a roof but maintaining separate households is found in matrimonial law where separation is recognised for the purposes of the Matrimonial Causes Act 1973 if spouses live in separate households but not necessarily at different addresses (see for example *Mouncer v Mouncer* [1972] 1 WLR 321). For the purposes of social security law, there is no statutory definition of a household but there is much case law on the subject. If one member of the couple usually lives at another address, the cohabitation rule should not be applied. Liability for separate housing costs was held to be enough to show two separate households, regardless of living arrangements, in *R(SB) 13/82*. It is not possible for a person to be a member of more than one household at the same time, but the mere fact of marriage to another person does not prevent a person being a member of a household with a cohabitant as was indicated in *R(SB) 35/85*. The question of whether a person can be a member of one household for part of the week and a member of another for the remainder has not yet been decided.

4.48 The couple's reason for, and manner of, living together will be significant and the Decision Maker must not assume that people of different sexes living at the same address and in the same household are cohabiting as husband and wife.

4.49 In the cases of *Crake v Supplementary Benefits Commission, Butterworth v Supplementary Benefits Commission* [1982] 1 All ER 498, two cases which were reported at the same time, it was held that a person who moved in with a disabled friend to provide assistance and company did not become a member of the same household, living together as husband and wife. Neither was this the case where a woman and her children had moved in with a man for whom she acted as his housekeeper. However, in *R(SB) 30/83*, a couple were regarded as members of the same household notwithstanding that one of them lived away in order to attend a university course for thirty weeks of the year. It should be noted that the cases are not particularly consistent in applying this test

4.50 *The length and stability of the relationship* This is another critical factor and each case will turn on its own facts. If the relationship is brief or temporary, it should not fall within the category of living together as husband or wife. However, cohabitation of a few weeks is likely to be sufficient evidence of a couple's having formed a relevant relationship.

4.51 *Financial dependence* Where one partner is financially dependent on the other this is strong evidence of living together as husband and wife. Separate financial arrangements of themselves will not be conclusive as to the absence of cohabitation either, and evidence of how household expenses are shared will be taken into account.

4.52 *Sexual relationship* Although the Decision Maker is not permitted to ask direct questions about whether or not there is a sexual relationship, its assessment of the position will in practice be important in deciding whether two people are living together as husband and wife, as this is usually a normal facet of marriage. It will not, though, be conclusive, and evidence disproving such a relationship, such as separate sleeping arrangements, should be volunteered to the Decision Maker.

4.53 *Children* Where there are children of the relationship, or children of one of the parties who are cared for or have been maintained by the other, there is a strong presumption of living together as husband and wife.

4.54 *Public acknowledgment* Where two people held themselves out to be husband and wife, or where a woman has adopted a man's surname, this will be strong evidence that they are living as husband and wife. It is none the less also acknowledged that many couples who do not in any way pretend to be married, may be cohabiting.

4.55 If, having considered all the above factors, the Decision Maker decides a couple is living together as husband and wife, then only one couple's allowance for income-based JSA or income support can be made for the household, and any other benefit will be withdrawn. In the case of single claim couples, either of the partners may make the joint claim. As noted above, joint claim couples must both apply and nominate one of them to receive the couple's payment.

4.56 Where a couple wishes to dispute the decision, they may appeal within one month of the decision, and are entitled to reasons for the decision maker's decision. It is for the Decision Maker to prove that there is cohabitation. It is also possible to ask for the decision to be reviewed, and this will be particularly appropriate where the reasons for refusal show that an important fact has not been properly taken into account.

4.57 If partners separate, a new claim will have to be made. In practice, if they continue to live at the same address, it may be difficult to show that they are now living in separate households. In the case of married couples, the fact that a solicitor has been approached with a view to matrimonial proceedings will often back up the contention that a *de facto* separation has taken place. With cohabitants, this is, ironically, sometimes more difficult to prove, and separate arrangements for cooking, sleeping, shopping, washing and payment of bills may need to be shown to convince the Decision Maker of a change in the arrangements.

4.58 The "liable relative" procedure whereby the DWP (formerly the DSS) can seek a contribution to maintenance by issuing proceedings in the magistrates' court against a person liable to maintain a person or child dependent on income support, including an element for the carer of a child where there is no other liability to maintain (see *Barlow,* 1992, pages 89–90) are now contained in ss 106 and 107 Social Security Administration Act 1992. Whilst these provisions remain in force, given that courts no longer have the power to make maintenance orders for children in most cases (s 8(3) Child Support Act 1991), and it is not possible to claim a contribution in respect of a former cohabitant unless an order is being made in respect of a child, they have been largely rendered redundant, at least in so far as the position of former cohabitants is concerned. However, they can still be used in relation to families who fall outside the jurisdiction of the Child Support Agency and in respect of former spouses.

4.59 In addition to the "liable relative" procedure, it had always been the case that where there was a court maintenance order in favour of a claimant of a child whose carer is dependent upon income support or more recently income-based JSA, this sum would be deducted pound for pound from the IS or JSA entitlement of the person caring for the child. This is was also true where a child support maintenance assessment has been made, although the first £15 of child support or other child maintenance paid is now disregarded. Furthermore, a minimum amount of child support maintenance will be collected from a non-resident parent who is claiming income support or JSA and will be deducted automatically from their benefit, but is restricted to a maximum of £5.40 per week providing the non-resident parent does not themselves have care of a child, is over 18 and is not entitled to one of the benefits which would make them a "zero-rated" non-payer, exempt from child support payments. These include statutory sick pay, maternity pay, incapacity benefit, disability living allowance and Disabled Person's Tax Credit (see SSCB Act 1992, ss 151, 164, 30A, 129, and 71 respectively).

4.60 As the provisions of the Child Support Act 1991 are not restricted to children whose carers are in receipt of benefit, its structure and implications following its numerous past and proposed amendments will be discussed more fully in the general context of financial provision on relationship breakdown in Chapter 9 below. However, the Act has perhaps greater implications for separated parents where the carer and thus the child are dependent on income-based JSA or income support and these will be discussed here.

4.61 There is now at least a personal gain for the child or carer of £15 per week if child support becomes payable to a resident parent whilst on benefit and thus there is some incentive to co-operate with the Child Support Agency (CSA) alongside the increased disincentives not to. This maintenance disregard replaces the "back to work bonus" previously payable out of the maintenance paid during a claim if and when a claimant returned to work. By virtue of s 6(1) Child Support Act 1991 (CS Act 1991) the parent (or other person) with care of a child where the other parent or parents are non-resident (replacing the pejorative term "absent" with effect from April 2002) will be required by the CSA to authorise them to collect child support maintenance and to co-operate in assisting them to trace the non-resdent parent and to make an assessment unless this might reasonably cause harm or distress to the child or the resident parent. The implications of this for cohabitants may occur either on breakdown of the relationship or where one or both partners are non-resident parents in respect of children living with former partners. Even where there is a court order in existence, the CSA will require IS and income-based JSA claimants to co-operate in an assessment being made, and in virtually all cases this will result in a higher assessment of the maintenance, calculated in accordance with the rigid formula set out in the Act and Regulations and to be replaced with a simpler if not fairer assessment in April 2002 (see Chapter 9 below).

4.62 As discussed in Chapter 9, and of particular interest to cohabitants who are also absent parents, pre-April 1993 clean break settlements are taken into account in a broad-brush adjustment to the formula with effect from April 1995 and departure directions have been introduced by the 1995 Act enabling either parent to request for the consequences of a settlement to be taken into account. This is to be changed again with effect from April 2002 as discussed in Chapter 9 below. Currently, allowance for the housing costs of second families is now included in the calculation of exempt income, rather than just the protected income and further changes are forthcoming. However, at the present time, only costs in relation to a new partner and step-children (not, children of a cohabitant by a previous relationship) will be included in this category, although again this is to change.

4.63 Parents with care in receipt of income support or income-based JSA who fail to co-operate with the Agency, which includes not only failing to identify the absent parent but also failing to co-operate in assisting to trace them, may result in a "reduced benefit direction" in accordance with which forty per cent of the adult single person's income support allowance is deducted from their benefit for the first hundred and fifty-six weeks (reg 36 CS(MAP) Regulations 1992). This penalty has been made significantly harsher due to the belief that there is a high incidence of collusion between parents with care on benefit and absent parents. However, this can only be imposed after consideration has been given to the welfare of any child likely to be affected by the decision (s 2 CS Act 1991), although the welfare of the child is not the paramount consideration.

4.64 For a full assessment of the 1991 and 1995 Acts and the impact of the reforms contained in the Child Support and Pensions Act 2000 see Chapter 9

(iii) Housing benefit

4.65 This is another means tested benefit available to help pay rent. It is administered by the local authority, although the DWP will automatically notify the authority of a claimant's eligibility for housing benefit if they are in receipt of income support or jobseeker's allowance. Those on low incomes, or claiming WFTC or any benefit other than income support or JSA, must apply directly to the local authority for housing benefit (HB). Once again, couples living together as husband and wife are entitled to make only one claim in respect of their household, and their capital and income will be aggregated. Same-sex couples will be treated as separate individuals. For those who made their claims prior to 2 January 1996, the local authority must decide whether the rent or the size of the accommodation for your household is unreasonable. If neither is deemed unreasonable, then the HB should be paid in full. If either is deemed unreasonable, then they must consider whether the claimant is in a protected group, such as having care of a child or being over 60. If they are not in a protected group or they are but the local authority have deemed that there is suitable accommodation available and it is reasonable to expect them to move, then the rent will be restricted by them at their discretion. They may delay implementing the restriction and in assessing the amount of the restriction, must take relevant circumstances into account. Once applied, if the rent exceeds the determined reasonable rent, no benefit will be payable for the excess, regardless of the claimant's ability to pay from other sources.

4.66 From 2 January 1996, new claimants are subject to different rules but these are again based on the size in relation to the needs of the household and the level of the rent compared to other properties in the area. Essentially, a person is only able to claim housing benefit for the full rent "up to the average for similar properties in the area". This is known as the "local reference rent". Above average rents will only be reimbursed to the extent of 50% for those claiming HB continuously for the same property since 5 October 1997. Later claimants only get the lower of the claim-related rent (ie either what is paid or what is assessed is the appropriate rent for their needs and that property) and the local reference rent. However, the local authority has a discretion to pay more if it accepts there is "exceptional hardship". In addition, they have a separate discretion to increase benefit in "exceptional circumstances" where benefit has been reduced due to a non-dependant deduction or income above the applicable amount and this can be paid over and above the exceptional hardship payment. Those who take advantage of the New Deal programmes retain their previous higher entitlement to housing benefit for 52 weeks.

4.67 Eligibility is assessed in accordance with a specified calculation which takes account of prescribed personal allowances and premiums, earnings and maintenance disregards and contributions to housing costs assumed to be made by non-dependent members of the household. The capital cut-off limit is £16,000, although there is deemed income added to actual income in respect of capital in excess of £3,000 assessed at a rate of £1 per £250 excess.

4.68 Housing benefit is not payable in respect of mortgage repayments, although the interest element of such payments may be paid as part of a claim for income support or JSA. Recipients of Working Families Tax credit cannot claim any benefit to help with mortgage repayments.

(iv) Council tax benefit

4.69 Help with payment of council tax is by means of council tax benefit (CTB), which is itself administered by the local authority. It can be seen to resemble housing benefit in many ways and the income and capital limits and aggregation rules affecting cohabitants are the same, although there are some differences in the non-dependent deduction rules. There are two types of CTB. Main CTB may be applicable to cohabiting and separated couples. However, alternative maximum CTB comprises a second adult rebate, only applicable where there is a non-partner second adult living in the household who increases liability to the tax but makes no financial contribution to the household. Thus it could only be applicable to a former cohabitant.

4.70 Unlike its predecessor community charge benefit, main council tax benefit can result in a 100% reduction in a claimant's liability to the tax. The same rules apply to determine whether a couple lives together as husband and wife and only one partner can claim CTB in respect of the whole bill

4.71 The second adult rebate operates to reduce the claimant's liability by between seven and a half per cent and 25% after any status reduction, depending on the second adult's income. The claimant's capital is ignored for these purposes unless they are also eligible for main CTB. Where there is dual eligibility for main CTB and the second adult rebate, the higher of the two benefits is payable

(v) The social fund

4.72 By virtue of s 32 Social Security Act 1986 (now s 167 SSCB Act 1992), the social fund replaced the previous grant based system of single payments and urgent needs payments. It introduced a much narrower grant system for specific circumstances, and, more controversially, crisis and budgeting loans which are repayable. However, there have been some recent changes to the operation of the fund. For the purpose of determining eligibility, married and cohabiting couples are once again treated alike

4.73 The fund is divided into two distinct parts. The first consists of non-discretionary payments in relation to maternity, funeral and cold weather expenses. For the purpose of what is now known as the "Sure Start Maternity Payment", currently limited to £300, the claimant or their partner must be in receipt of income-based JSA, income support Working Families Tax Credit or Disabled Persons Tax Credit. The claim must be made within three months of the birth (and extends to still births) and any capital over £500 will be deducted from the payment. Those with capital over £700 will be ineligible.

4.74 Funeral expense payments and cold weather payments are subject to a similar capital deduction rule. Cold weather payments are available only to households claiming income-based JSA or income support for at least one day during the cold weather period and who are in receipt of pensioner or disability premium or have a child under five; whereas funeral expense payments are payable to those in receipt of any of the means-tested welfare benefits referred to above who take responsibility for a funeral. A Funeral Payment no longer has an absolute ceiling but is intended to cover the cost of "a simple, respectful, low-cost funeral".

4.75 All other payments from the social fund are discretionary. In general terms, community care grants are payable to those coming out of institutional care, or where a payment will prevent institutional care being necessary. These are not repayable.

4.76 Budgeting loans are available only to those who have been in receipt of income-based JSA or income support for at least 26 weeks, to meet intermittent and specified categories of expenses, including furniture and household equipment, clothing, rent in advance and removal expenses to secure accommodation, improvement, maintenance and security of the home. There are strict criteria, and any loan is repayable, although interest free. Crisis loans are available to all those who do not have sufficient savings to meet expenses incurred as a result of an emergency and have no other means of meeting the expense. Such a loan will not be made unless the claimant is able to repay it. Where a loan is made, it can be recovered both from the person to whom it was made, and from a person for whose benefit it was made. This may be of particular relevance to cohabitants.

4.77 The DWP web-site at http://www.dss.gov.uk is again a useful resource for claimants and advisers alike, although in challenging any decisions made in respect of welfare benefits or WFTC, the Child Poverty Action Group's *Welfare Benefits Handbook 2001/2002* is invaluable.

Chapter 5

Inheritance and succession

5.01 The desirability of unmarried couples making Wills and taking out life assurance has been discussed in Chapter 1. Cohabitants, whether of the same or opposite sexes, are vulnerable on the death of their partners if no provision has been made by Will to cover such an eventuality. Where a cohabitant dies intestate, the distribution of the estate is governed by s 46 Administration of Estates Act 1925 (AEA 1925). Any children of the deceased, including those of the relationship, will inherit from the estate under these provisions unless there is a surviving spouse and the value of the estate is less than £125,000, in which case the whole estate passes to the spouse. This remains the position, despite the Law Commission's recommendation contained in *Distribution on Intestacy* (Law Com No 187 (1989)) that the whole of the estate should automatically pass to the surviving spouse on intestacy. Such a reform would obviously have adversely affected the succession rights of children, but was rejected and not included in the Law Reform (Succession) Act 1995. The Act did, however, introduce a new statutory rule that a surviving spouse must have survived the deceased for at least twenty-eight days to inherit where the death occurs after 1 January 1996. Although the Family Law Reform Acts 1969 and 1987 have effectively given children of unmarried parents the same succession rights as those of married parents, the deceased's partner will never be a beneficiary on intestacy under s 46 and may not take out letters of administration in respect of the estate.

5.02 The surviving cohabitant may, however, have a claim under the Inheritance (Provision for Family and Dependants) Act 1975 (I(PFD)A 1975) for financial provision to be made out of the deceased's estate and their position has recently been enhanced by amendments to the Act following the Law Reform (Succession) Act 1995 as discussed below. However, even where a Will has been made, benefiting a cohabitant and any children of the relationship, should the deceased also leave behind a spouse, or former spouse who was being maintained by the deceased, or any children by other relationships, they may all, by virtue of the same statute, have a claim against the deceased's estate. This could of course substantially reduce the provision the deceased believed would be available for his or her partner and their children. If the deceased had had the necessary means, life assurance could have ensured provision was made for all those to whom the deceased owed financial responsibility. Unfortunately, such foresight is rare. The first part of this chapter will therefore deal with the claims that can be made under I(PFD)A 1975, either by or against a deceased cohabitant's partner.

5.03 The cause of death may have a bearing on the financial provision available to those left behind. Where it can be shown that death resulted from the fault of a third party, then the partner may well, and any children of the relationship certainly will, have a claim for compensation against the third party under the Fatal Accidents Act 1976 (FAA 1976) as amended. As will be seen, this is true for heterosexual cohabitants only, and a minimum period of cohabitation of two years is required by the statute as a prerequisite for a claim. The second part of this chapter will therefore consider the law relating to FAA claims, as it affects cohabitants, and here it should be noted that the Law Commission has recently recommended that its provisions should be extended to other dependants including same-sex partners (*Claims for Wrongful Death,* 1999 Law Com. No.263). Similarly, the Criminal Injuries Compensation Authority has revised its scheme as of April 2001 and now entitles same-sex cohabitants of two years' standing to claim following a partner's fatal injury as discussed below.

1 Inheritance Act claims

5.04 Following recommendations made by the Law Commission in *Distribution on Intestacy,* (Law Com No. 187, Part III), cohabitants have finally been included by the 1995 amendments as a separate category of applicant entitled to apply for provisions under the 1975 Act. However, it should be borne in mind that the inheritance situation will always be more complex where the deceased partner has left a surviving spouse or children from outside the cohabitation relationship. In broad terms, the I(PFD)A 1975 enables claims to be made by specified categories of person against a deceased's estate, where either the deceased's Will or the law on intestacy does not make satisfactory provision for them. The rules as to what sort of provision should be made vary according to the category of person. It should be remembered that on intestacy, although cohabitants never inherit from their partners (s 46 AEA 1925) and may therefore need to make a claim under the 1975 Act, any children of that relationship will usually inherit on a parent's intestacy regardless of the fact that their parents never married.

5.05 Where there is no surviving spouse, the deceased's estate will be divided equally between his or her children, regardless of whether those children were born inside or outside marriage. Thus account will be taken of all the deceased's children. If there is a surviving spouse, (and significantly this definition includes a spouse in the process of divorcing until the time a decree absolute is pronounced), then the first £125,000 will go to the spouse, who will also have a life interest in one half of the remainder of the estate (s 46(1) AEA 1925). The other half of the residuary estate is held upon the statutory trusts for the deceased's children in equal shares, and on the death of the spouse the children become entitled to the spouse's half share also. These rules apply regardless of the ages of the children. Only where the deceased's estate passes *bona vacantia* to the Crown because there are no beneficiaries at all on the deceased's intestacy, may a surviving cohabitant, at the discretion of the Crown (see Chapter 1), receive provision out of the deceased's estate without having to apply under the 1975 Act.

5.06 Should the deceased's children have been omitted from their parent's will as beneficiaries, if they are to receive provision out of the estate, they also must make a claim under the Act; in this situation whether or not they are minors is significant, as will be discussed below.

(a) Claims by cohabitants

(i) Eligible applicants

5.07 Providing a cohabitant can show he or she is an eligible applicant under the Act, the claim will proceed to be considered on the merits. Until the 1995 amendments, cohabitants did not constitute a separate category of eligible applicant under the 1975 Act. However, in line with the Law Commission's recommendations, cohabitants who have lived with the deceased as his or her spouse in the same household for at least two years immediately prior to their death may now apply to the court for reasonable provision to be made out of their estate for their maintenance (see ss 1(1)(ba) and 1A). The biggest change to the law is that cohabitants who meet the two-year cohabitation requirement will no longer have to show dependency upon the deceased in order to obtain provision. The wording of the added subsection follows that included in the amendments to the Fatal Accident Act 1976 and is part of a trend where a period of cohabitation is stipulated by statute as a qualification for rights resulting from a cohabitation relationship. However, proof of cohabitation throughout the two-year period is required and this itself could in some cases create difficulties. An added s 3(2A) gives some indication of the factors that will influence the court in determining the amount of reasonable provision for a cohabitant's maintenance. It states:

> "Without prejudice to the generality of paragraph (g) of subsection (1) above, where an application is made under s 2 of this Act by virtue of s 1(1)(ba) of this Act, the court shall, in addition to the matters specifically mentioned in paragraphs (a) to (f) of that subsection, have regard to—(a) the age of the applicant and the length of the period during which the applicant lived as husband and wife of the deceased and in the same household as the deceased; (b) the contribution made by the applicant to the welfare of the family of the deceased, including any contribution made by looking after the home or caring for the family."

5.08 This extension of the categories of eligible applicants was recognition of the growing numbers of couples who cohabit as man and wife, although there has not to date been a great deal of case law testing the impact of these reforms. Given the decision in *Fitzpatrick v Sterling Housing Association Ltd* [1997] 4 All ER 705 (see Chapter 3) which interpreted the phrase "living as husband or wife" as being exclusively heterosexual, it seems unlikely that this provision will be interpreted by the courts so as to include same-sex cohabitants (see eg Roberts, *Fitzpatrick v Sterling – a case with wider implications?* [2000] Fam Law 417). However, in the case of *Re Watson (Deceased)* [1999] 1 FLR 878, the Chancery Division did have to consider what could amount to "living as husband and wife" in the heterosexual context. Here a couple who had in their youth been romantically involved and sexually intimate had never married or cohabited at that time preferring instead to care for their respective elderly parents. Some 20 years later, the applicant (the woman), moved into the deceased's home as a companion and also kept house for him. Her own home remained unoccupied and she paid half the household bills arising out of the shared occupation of the deceased's home until he died some 10 years later. As he had no surviving relatives and had made no Will, on his death, his estate passed *bona vacantia* to the Crown. Subsequently the applicant applied under the 1975 Act claiming she had lived with the deceased as his wife and was entitled to provision. Perhaps surprisingly, Neuberger J allowed her claim, stressing that in order to judge whether a couple were living as husband and wife, the court should ask whether they would be considered so to be in the opinion of a reasonable person with normal perceptions. He stressed that consideration of that question should not ignore the multifarious nature of marital relationships, but listed the cooking, cleaning and washing tasks performed by the applicant alongside the mutuality of life shared by the couple despite the lack of both shared bedroom and sexual relationship, which he found would not be unusual for a married couple in their mid to late 50s. Thus here, the lack of any sexual relationship during cohabitation was not fatal to the claim and companionship plus performance of wife-like housekeeping tasks coinciding with the patriarchal expectations of the marital relationship were sufficient, at least for a couple in this age group. On the facts, the applicant could not easily claim to have been financially dependant on the deceased under s 1(1)(e) (discussed below) and thus her only possibility of a claim was as a cohabitant.

5.09 If a cohabitant's claim is successful, the provision available is still limited to "maintenance" and is therefore less generous than the provision that can be made in favour of a spouse where no such limitation applies. Nonetheless, where there has been a long term cohabitation relationship with children of the deceased forming part of the family unit, the courts now have scope to give substantial weight to these factors, which mirror those to be taken into account in respect of applications by spouses and former spouses (see s 3(2)). These must still be considered in the light of the other factors set out in s 3 (discussed below), such as the size of the estate, the financial needs and resources of the applicant and any other applicant or beneficiary under the estate.

5.10 Prior to the 1995 amendments, the only avenue open to a cohabitant to make a claim under the 1975 Act was to show that they fell within the category specified by s 1(1)(e) and required an element of dependency by the survivor on the deceased. This therefore remains the only possibility for both the surviving gay cohabitant and the heterosexual cohabitant who cannot meet the two-year cohabitation qualification stipulated by the amendment. Subsection 1(1)(e) of the 1975 Act provides that an application for provision may be made by any person ". . . who immediately before the death of the deceased was being maintained either wholly or partly by the deceased".

5.11 Thus, cohabitants can make a claim under this subsection only if they can show that they were financially dependent upon the deceased, and such dependence must have existed immediately before the death. It was considered by Megarry V-C in *Re Beaumont, Martin v Midland Bank Trust Co Ltd* [1980] 1 All ER 266 (at page

272b) that a temporary interruption of maintenance just before death would not necessarily defeat the claim, as what the court had to decide was whether there was in existence a settled arrangement between the deceased and the claimant at the time of death. This reasoning was considered fully and followed in *Kourkgy v Lusher* (1981) 4 FLR 65. A man who had left his cohabitant returned to live with his wife just nine days before he died. This alone was not fatal to the cohabitant's claim. However, as there was evidence which revealed that the deceased had slowly been divesting himself of responsibility towards the applicant over a much longer period, this defeated her claim to maintenance out of the estate. It is not at all clear that this applicant would have faired any better under the amended statute. For this requires a cohabitant to have lived with the deceased "for the whole of the period of two years ending **immediately** before the date when the deceased died". The Act provides further definition of the necessary degree of maintenance. Section 1(3) goes on to state:

> "For the purposes of subsection (1)(e) above, a person shall be treated as being maintained by the deceased, either wholly or partly, as the case may be, if the deceased other than for full valuable consideration, was making a substantial contribution in money or money's worth towards the reasonable needs of that person."

5.12 Although it might seem that the Act creates two categories of claimant – those who were actually being wholly or partially maintained by the deceased, and those who could be construed as so being by virtue of the test in the later subsection – this was held in *Re Beaumont* (above) not to be the correct approach. In that case, the deceased was a woman with whom the applicant had lived for some twenty-six years. She died leaving him nothing in her Will. She had owned the bungalow in which they lived, paid all the outgoings and performed the domestic chores. He owned a car in which he used to drive the deceased around; paid for his accommodation; contributed to the shopping bill and did gardening and repair jobs around the home. Megarry V-C held that s 1(3) qualified s 1(1)(e), and was not an alternative. Accordingly, the applicant's claim failed as the maintenance of the claimant by the deceased was a substantial contribution to his needs for full valuable consideration.

5.13 Again, in the leading case of *Jelley v Iliffe* [1981] Fam 128, the Court of Appeal held that rent-free accommodation provided for the applicant by the deceased was capable of being a substantial contribution to his needs. Whether or not this was for full valuable consideration depended on whether the applicant's contribution to household expenses equalled or outweighed the value of the deceased's contribution by virtue of the accommodation. Thus where cohabitants make equal contributions, or indeed where the surviving partner was maintaining the deceased, no claim is available under this subsection. A degree of financial dependency must be established.

5.14 In *Bishop v Plumley* [1991] 1 All ER 236, the Court of Appeal held that in order to decide whether the deceased had been making a substantial contribution, the matter had to be looked at in the round, and a common sense approach applied, avoiding fine balancing computations involving the value of normal exchanges of support in the domestic sense. Interestingly, Butler-Sloss LJ commented that it could not have been Parliament's intention to place an applicant who was less devoted and contributed less to the deceased partner's needs in a more advantageous position than a more caring applicant. Thus, although the wording of the Act appears to be capable of leading to an anomalous position, in this case, the applicant was allowed to proceed and have her application considered on the merits. She was herself in poor health and 64 years of age, and had lived in a property owned by the deceased with whom she had lived for ten years, performing the domestic chores and caring for him during years of bad health.

5.15 As noted above, the wording of the added subsection almost certainly post-*Fitzpatrick* excludes homosexual cohabitants. However, providing they can show the necessary degree of dependency immediately before death, they would seem to fall within the category of eligible applicants specified in s 1(1)(e). Similarly, the new amendments do not exclude use of this subsection by cohabitants who fail to meet the two-year cohabitation requirement, providing dependency can be established. Given that the duration of the cohabitation relationship is a factor which the court must specifically weigh in relation to applications made under s 1(1)(ba), the court may be reluctant to make orders where the period of cohabitation is less than two years. A claim under this head may however assist a dependant and very recently deserted cohabitant or a former cohabitant who was being voluntarily financially supported post-separation by their former partner. Much may depend on how many competing claims there are in respect of the estate and it is worthy of note that neither the Law Commission nor Parliament appear to have had any deliberate intention to restrict applications by cohabitants who are dependent yet do not meet the two-year requirement.

(ii) Criteria relevant to the claim

5.16 The next hurdle an applicant must overcome is to show that the distribution of the deceased's estate, either in accordance with any Will or pursuant to the law on intestacy, "is not such as to make reasonable financial provision for the applicant" (s 2(1)). In the case of a cohabitant this has to be considered in the light of s 1(2)(b) which defines reasonable financial provision as "such financial provision as it would be reasonable in the circumstances of the case for the applicant to receive for his maintenance". This is deliberately less generous than the test applicable to spouses, where provision is not limited to that needed for maintenance (see below). In addition, it will not be sufficient for a cohabitant to show that he or she needs maintenance, but also that it was objectively unreasonable in the circumstances of the case for the deceased to have failed to make provision. Thus in *Re Coventry, Coventry v Coventry* [1980] Ch 461, the Court of Appeal held that an adult son who was undoubtedly in need of maintenance and whose father died intestate, resulting in a fairly small estate devolving to his wife, received an award of only £2,000. It was stressed that each case will depend on its own facts, but it is not for the court to decide how the deceased's assets should have been fairly divided, but rather whether it is unreasonable that the estate does not provide reasonable maintenance for the applicant.

5.17 Section 3(2) sets out the principal factors to be taken into account by the court deciding whether the estate has provided "reasonable financial provision". These can be summarised as follows:

- the financial resources and needs the applicant, any other applicant and any beneficiary of the deceased's estate have or are likely to have in the foreseeable future;
- any obligation and responsibilities the deceased had towards any applicant or beneficiary of the estate;
- the size and nature of the net estate;
- any physical or mental disability of any applicant or beneficiary of the estate; and
- any other matter including the conduct of the applicant or any other person, which in the circumstances of the case the court may consider relevant.

5.18 These factors echo those to be taken into account by a court when making an order for financial relief on divorce as set out in s 25(2) Matrimonial Causes Act 1973. However, whereas the provision relating to conduct has been amended in the matrimonial situation to limit its scope to conduct which it would be inequitable to disregard, the 1975 Act has not. "Relevant conduct" had been narrowly interpreted by the courts and it is submitted that this interpretation of relevant conduct may well be imputed into the workings of the 1975 Act in the future. Generally, it can be seen that the relative needs and resources of all the potential beneficiaries have to be weighed against each other and the existence of life assurance benefiting one or more of them will be of great relevance. In addition the size of the net estate will be critical to the approach and outcome of any claim.

5.19 As discussed above (para 5.07), the 1995 amendments have inserted further factors to be weighed into the equation when the court considers applications by cohabitants under s 1(1)(ba) with regard to the duration of the cohabitation and the contribution made to the welfare of the family of the deceased, which are similar to those applying to applications made by spouses or former spouses. Where an application is being made under s 1(1)(e), s 3(4) provides that the court also has to take into consideration "the extent to which and the basis upon which the deceased assumed responsibility for the maintenance of the applicant and . . . the length of time for which the deceased discharged that responsibility." In *Jelley v Iliffe* (above), it was held that the provision of rent free accommodation over a period of time did reveal an assumption of responsibility.

5.20 The relevant date for assessing the factors is the date of the hearing not the date of death. The right to bring a claim under the Act is a personal one and it cannot therefore be continued by the applicant's personal representatives should the applicant die before the court has determined the application.

(b) Claims by children

5.21 Children of the deceased are eligible as of right to bring an action against the deceased's estate, claiming that the reasonable financial provision has not been made for them out of the deceased's estate (s 1(1)(c)). The relevant criteria for assessing whether or not reasonable financial provision has been made are as set out above, but with some important distinctions. In particular, s 3(4) does not apply to children and thus no assumption of responsibility needs to be shown. Provision is however again limited to maintenance and, of course, minor children (as opposed to adult children) are likely to be treated far more generously as there is no duty to maintain an adult child. In most of the cases where adult children have succeeded, they have shown a moral obligation on the part of the deceased to provide for them (see eg *Re Pearce* [1993] 2 FCR 179 and *Re Goodchild, Pearce v Davis Pearce* [1996] 1 WLR 694), although this is not necessarily a pre-requisite (see *Re Hancock (Deceased) Goodchild v Goodchild* [1993] 1 FLR 500). Indeed, in *Espinosa v Bourke* [1999] 1 FLR 747 CA, the court effectively overrode the clear wishes of the deceased to leave his estate to his student grandson on the basis that he had helped his daughter more than enough during his lifetime. He had been financially assisting his adult daughter who had previously helped care for him but later abandoned him. He had also promised his late wife that he would leave a portfolio of shares to the daughter. At the time of her father's death, she was in difficult financial circumstances, whereas the grandson (her own son) had lesser needs and the court found an obligation towards the daughter existed.

5.22 It should also be noted that whilst s 1(1)(d) includes as a separate category of applicants, step-children treated by a step-parent as a child of the family, children who are not the natural children of a cohabitation relationship but have been regarded by their parent's cohabitant as "children of the family" have no claim under the Act against their parent's cohabitant's estate, other than as a person who was wholly or partly maintained by the deceased for two years immediately prior to the death under s1(1)(e).

(c) Orders available to the court

5.23 The court, by virtue of s 5, has power to make interim orders in favour of an applicant who is "in immediate need of financial assistance". This is likely to take the form of periodical payments, but a lump sum may be made if the circumstances merit it.

5.24 The final orders available to the court, which are set out in s 2, once again resemble those which can be made on divorce and are:

- periodical payments;
- lump sum;
- transfer of property;
- settlement of property; and

- acquisition of property not comprised in the estate out of property which is so comprised for transfer or settlement to or settlement on the applicant.

5.25 Notwithstanding that an order in favour of a cohabitant can extend to reasonable provision for his or her maintenance only, this can still take the form of any of the orders listed above. Unlike the provisions on divorce contained in the Matrimonial Causes Act 1973, the court can actually order that specific property be acquired for the benefit of a claimant. For example, a smaller home may be ordered to be purchased rather than transferring the existing home to the applicant.

5.26 In addition, under s 9, the court has a discretion to order that the deceased's severable share of a beneficial joint tenancy be treated as part of the net estate, but the court must rule on this when it is deciding the preliminary issue of whether or not reasonable financial provision had been made and not when it is making the final orders. Further this can be done only where the application is brought within the initial six-month time limit for bringing an action as discussed below. The effect of this rule is that where the deceased was a co-owner of a property his share in which would normally pass to the other co-owner by virtue of the rule of survivorship, the court can rule that the deceased's share of the property should, for the purposes of the Act, be deemed to form part of his net estate. Severance of a joint tenancy will be ordered only where it is "just in all the circumstances of the case" and only in so far as is necessary. Thus, if some but not all of the value of that share is needed, the balance will still pass to the co-owner by right of survivorship.

Legal Aid and Inheritance Act claims

5.27 Following the coming into force in April 2000 of the Access to Justice Act 1999, the Legal Services Commission (LSC) has replaced the Legal Aid Board. In addition, the Funding Code Criteria, Procedure and Guidance now contain information relevant to clients seeking public funding for Inheritance Act claims, which may take the form of Legal Help, General Family Help or Legal Representation. The Funding Code and relevant forms are available on the Legal Services Commission website at http://www.legalservices.gov.uk www.legalservices.gov.uk and paras 80 – 85 of the Guidance deal specifically with the eligibility criteria in Inheritance Act cases. A useful article on the impact of the legal aid reforms in the family context is Burrows, *Legal Aid and the Family Lawyer* [2000] Fam Law 834.

5.28 Of particular concern is the impact of the statutory charge which has always applied to such claims. Where a successful claimant is publicly funded, the legal aid statutory charge will apply to any moneys or property exceeding £2,500 in value recovered or preserved as a result of work carried out under the public funding certificate (reg 44(1)(d) and (2)(b) Community Legal Service (Financial) Regulations 2000 SI 2000/516). Usually, but not necessarily, an order for costs will be made against the estate where a claimant is successful. However, this will affect the size of the estate available to be distributed and thus may be taken into account in evaluating the appropriate sum to be awarded. Any costs not recovered by a publicly funded claimant from the estate but incurred under the certificate will have to be paid to the LSC by the claimant; again this will affect the amount ultimately in the hands of the claimant. Where property which the court has ordered is to be used as a home for the claimant or their dependants is transferred, the LSC may, if satisfied that the property will provide adequate security for the sum which is the subject of the charge, agree to defer the enforcement (reg. 52). Application for the charge to be deferred must be made on Form CLSADMIN1. The Commission will take a legal charge over the property, and simple interest will accrue to the initial sum charged at a rate of eight per cent per annum from the date of registration of the charge. In addition if a sum is recovered by a publicly funded claimant under the 1975 Act which the court orders is to be used to purchase a home for the claimant or their dependants, the Commission may again, on the same conditions, agree to postpone enforcement by taking a legal charge over the property purchased. Where the Commission does agree to postponement and the claimant subsequently wishes to move to a new home, reg 52(2) gives the LSC discretion to accept a substitute charge on the new property.

5.29 The form of the court order is critical to the Commission's agreement to deferment of the statutory charge, and practitioners must ensure that it clearly states that the property transferred or to be purchased is to be used as a home by the publicly funded party or his/her dependant(s). A suggested form of words for inclusion in an order to comply with the requirements of the regulations is:

> "...and it is certified that for the purpose of Regulation 52 of the Community Legal Service (Financial) Regulations 2000 the lump sum of £ has been ordered to be paid to enable the [dependant] to purchase a home for himself/herself or his/her dependants/that the property at has been preserved/recovered for the [dependant] for the use as a home for himself/herself or his/her dependants".

5.30 The Commission will require the assisted person to agree in writing to the conditions of deferment of enforcement. No interest will actually have to be paid until the legal charge in favour of the Commission is redeemed, although the Commission will of course accept any repayment which the assisted person wishes to make and will deduct this from the total sum repayable. Statements of interest accrued are issued each year by the Commission.

(d) Defending a claim

5.31 Defending a claim will arise only where the deceased's Will benefits his or her cohabitant and/or children of their relationship but fails to provide reasonable financial provision for other eligible applicants – principally a spouse, a former spouse who has not remarried, other children of the deceased and any other adult dependants falling within s 1(1)(e), discussed above.

5.32 The terms of the Act are to the effect that a spouse (who remains such until the day any decree absolute of divorce is pronounced) is able to receive more generous provision than any other type of applicant. The test is whether reasonable provision, and not reasonable provision *for his or her maintenance*, has been made by the estate. However, all the circumstances of the case, including, it seems, the existence of any divorce proceedings, will be taken into account, as well as the general factors set out above and contained in s 3. A spouse is likely to receive provision similar to that which he or she would have received on divorce and this may, following the House of Lords decision in *White v White* [2000] 2 FLR 981, become more generous where assets exceed needs. (For a discussion of the effect of this landmark decision on Inheritance Act claims see the two-part article by Ross, 'The Implications of *White v White* for Inheritance Act Claims' [2001] *Fam Law* 547 – 550 and 619 – 623). Any other person who is supporting the spouse will of course be relevant, as will any provision which has been made by way of life assurance, and the size of the estate.

5.33 A former spouse is in a much weaker position, as the question of financial provision between the spouses will have been decided by the court (see *Barrass v Harding and Newman* [2001] 1 FLR 138 for a recent application of the principles). Indeed many orders made on divorce specifically preclude an application under the 1975 Act.

5.34 Any children of the deceased may likewise make a claim against the estate.

5.35 Where a cohabitant beneficiary is faced with a claim, it is clearly preferable to reach agreement by negotiation. Although this is not an area where legal aid litigants are required to attempt mediation, litigation is costly and will quickly deplete the estate available for distribution. Although costs will normally be awarded to the successful party against the loser(s), where a claimant is publicly funded, any order for costs is likely to be unenforceable in any event.

(e) Procedure

5.36 An important requirement in relation to inheritance claims is that they comply with a strict time limit. Section 4 stipulates that applications must be made within six months of the date on which representation (a grant of probate or letters of administration as appropriate) with respect to the estate of the deceased was taken out, unless the court grants permission for a late application. Good reason will be needed for a late application, and an application for leave must set out the grounds for the request.

5.37 Following the Civil Procedure Reforms, these applications are governed by Civil Procedure Rules Practice Direction (CPR PD) 8B and claimants must use the Part 8 procedure. Thus the claimant must file the Part 8 claim form together with a statement/affidavit in support and any written evidence on which he or she intends to rely including an official copy of the grant of representation and of every testamentary document admitted to proof. The proceedings will be treated as being allocated to the Multi-track and the defendant must acknowledge service within 14 days of being served. However, a hearing date for directions is usually (in practice) sought (CPR PD 8A para 4.1) at the time the claim form is issued, but in any event the court will give directions after the defendant has filed the Acknowledgement of Service or after the time for filing it has expired (CPR-PD-8, para 4.2).

2 Fatal accident claims

5.38 Following amendments introduced by the Administration of Justice Act 1982, a cohabitant who can show dependence on the deceased may well be able to bring a claim under the Fatal Accidents Act 1976 (FAA 1976) against a third party who was responsible, due to a wrongful act, for the death of the partner. The act needs to be such as would have entitled the deceased to bring an action and recovered damages if death had not ensued. Thus where a cohabitant dies due to a road accident or an accident at work caused by another party's negligence, a claim will lie. A child of the deceased who was dependent on him or her at the date of the death also has a right of action under the Act. The Law Commission has recently reviewed the operation of the 1976 Act and has made recommendations for amendment (see *Claims for Wrongful Death,* 1999, Law Com No 263).

5.39 A quite separate action brought by the personal representatives of the deceased in his or her name under the Law Reform (Miscellaneous Provisions) Act 1934 for compensation for loss incurred up to the date of death, may also benefit a cohabitant and any children who are beneficiaries under the deceased's Will. However, any damages payable are assessed quite independently of any claim under the 1976 Act, and will not be taken into account in assessing quantum in a successful Fatal Accidents Act claim.

5.40 Section 1(3) of the FAA 1976, as amended, provides that an application may be made by any person who:

(i)   was living with the deceased in the same household immediately before the date of death; and

(ii)   had been living with the deceased in that household for at least two years before that date; and

(iii) was living during the whole of that period as the husband or wife of the deceased.

5.41 This definition of cohabitants was the first in English law to impose a two-year qualification period as a means of identifying "stable relationships" and is one which, following *Fitzpatrick v Sterling Housing Association Ltd* (above), is limited to heterosexual cohabitants at least until the Law Commission's proposals for reform are implemented. As we have seen, the same qualification period is now required to make a claim under s 1(1)(ba) I(PFD)A 1975 but is not necessary in relation to succession of assured or Rent Act protected tenancies or with regard to the new domestic violence legislation (see Part IV FLA 1996).

5.42 Section 3(4) of the Act goes on to provide that the fact that such an applicant has no enforceable right to financial support by the deceased as a result of their living together must be a consideration. Thus in determining the appropriate multiplier to be applied in assessing damages, the fact that either party could have determined the relationship at will, without any right to maintenance ensuing, will be taken into account and is likely to reduce awards made to cohabitants as opposed to spouses. It is thought that the greater the degree of stability of the relationship shown, the greater the award. Any cohabitation agreement could be of great significance in such a situation. Apart from this additional consideration, damages will be assessed in accordance with the normal principles of tort.

5.43 Cohabitants are not at present entitled to statutory bereavement damages (currently £7,500) for deaths occurring after 1 April 1991, which are automatically awarded to a spouse where liability is proved under the 1976 Act. However, interestingly, the Law Commission recommended that bereavement damages should not only be increased to £10,000 but that they should also be available to long-term partners, both same and opposite sex regardless of whether or not they were in any way dependant on the deceased (Law Com 263 para 6.11 – 6.31). Under this proposal, a surviving cohabitant (whether same or opposite sex) will have the right to apply for statutory bereavement damages subject to a maximum of £30,000 being available to be shared among all eligible applicants. Where there is dependency, an action for further damages will also be available (see below), but where there is no whole or partial dependency by the survivor on the deceased cohabitant, then a free-standing claim for bereavement damages alone will be able to be made. This would be a considerable improvement in the law from the point of view of cohabitants and shows that the Law Commission at least is prepared to recommend changes in the law to better reflect the plurality of modern-day family structures.

5.44 Some moves to improve the position of surviving cohabitants have also been made by the courts. Even before the 1982 amendments to the Act, the courts, in *K v JMP Co Ltd* [1976] QB 85, had sought to assist a cohabitant who was the mother of the three children of the relationship and where the couple and their children had lived together as a family unit before the death of the children's father. Only the children could at that time bring a claim. However, in assessing the multiplicand, the Court of Appeal deducted a sum in respect of the deceased's expenses, but decided not to deduct a sum in respect of the applicant's expenses previously paid by the deceased, resulting in a larger sum to be paid to each of the children. Although the award went to the children, it was recognised that the children could not without their mother do certain things, such as visiting their relatives in Ireland, and provision was made for her expenses in this regard. The court was clearly keen that she should have this assistance.

5.45 This decision is not entirely redundant. There will be cases where a cohabitant has the responsibility of bringing up the child of the deceased, but cannot make a claim under the Act because they had not lived together for two years. In such a situation, it might be felt appropriate to increase provision for the children in accordance with the reasoning in *K v JMP Co Ltd* (above).

5.46 Other than in respect of statutory bereavement damages, not presently available to cohabitants, dependency is also a prerequisite of a successful claim under the Act for all categories of applicant. Any dependant child of the deceased will also have a claim under the FAA 1976, but any child who cannot prove dependency will not be eligible. The Law Commission proposals aim to extend the classes of applicants to a wider range of dependants including same-sex cohabitants and children of the deceased's cohabitant. However, having considered the possible ways of achieving this, they have recommended that rather than add specific groups, a general dependants' clause should be added to the current categories. The wording suggested echoes the I(PFD)A 1975 and will add to the list of claimants:

> "any person not falling within any of paragraphs (a) to (g) above who was being wholly or partly maintained by the deceased immediately before the death or who would, but for the death, have been so maintained at a time beginning after the death" (clause 1(2) draft Bill).

5.47 Similarly, the suggested definition in the draft Bill of "being wholly or partially" maintained borrows from the Inheritance Act 1975 in that it will be fulfilled if the other person, "otherwise than for full valuable consideration, was making a substantial contribution in money or money's worth towards his reasonable needs". This would be likely to encounter similar difficulties regarding tests of whole or partial dependency as was recognised by the Law Commission, who felt that the decisions of *Jelley v Iliffe* (above) and *Bishop v Plumley* (above) reflected the way in which they wished the Bill to be interpreted (see Law Com No 263 paras 3.31-3.46).

5.48 At the present time however, cohabitants of the same sex are specifically excluded by the prerequisite in the FAA 1976 that the claimant and the deceased were "living together as husband and wife". As was seen in Chapter 3, this has been held to exclude couples of the same sex in the context of succeeding to a tenancy (see *Fitzpatrick v Sterling Housing Association* (above) and *Harrogate Borough Council v Simpson* (above)) and the Act does not currently provide for any residual category of dependant similar to that found in s 1(1)(e) I(PFD)A 1975. Thus, notwithstanding dependency, only a heterosexual cohabitant who fulfils all the conditions can make a claim under the 1976 Act as things stand.

Procedure and Legal Aid

5.49 Fatal Accident Act claims are currently governed by CPR PD 16 which sets out what a claimant must include in the particulars of claim. Where a claimant is publicly funded, the statutory charge will apply to any damages recovered and, in contrast to Inheritance Act claims, the first £2,500 is not exempt.

3 Criminal Injuries Compensation Scheme

5.50 This is another area where strides have been made for cohabitants and perhaps foreshadows the direction the law will take in other areas in the future. Cohabitants used to be specifically excluded from recovering compensation where a partner dies as a result of a violent crime but now certain cohabitants are eligible to apply. The scheme itself has been the subject of controversy and review culminating in the Criminal Injuries Compensation Act 1995, which introduced a new tariff measure of compensation for injuries with effect from 1 April 1996. The rules of the scheme itself, application forms and a guide to the scheme are available from the Criminal Injuries Compensation Authority (CICA) at Tay House, 300 Bath Street, Glasgow G2 4GR (Tel: 0141-331-2287, Fax 0141-331-5579), and can be found on their website at http://www.cica.gov.uk. CICA have finally dealt with all cases under the pre-1996 scheme and have revised the scheme with effect from April 2001.

5.51 The 1995 Act extended the scheme in the case of fatal injuries to (heterosexual) cohabitants who had lived with the deceased in the same household for two years immediately prior to the date of death (para 38). Since April 2001, this has been further extended to include same-sex partners. The new definition of qualifying claimants who are surviving cohabiting partners is now as follows:

> "38(a) the partner of the deceased, being only, for these purposes:
> (i) a person who was living together with the deceased as husband and wife or as a same sex partner in the same household immediately before the date of death and who, unless formally married to him, had been so living throughout the two years before that date."

5.52 A child of the deceased, including a child of the family or a dependant child, is also a qualifying claimant. All claims must be made within two years of the incident in respect of which the claim is made, although this limit may be waived if there is good reason for the delay and it is in the interests of justice to do so. The compensation payable will normally be in the form of a lump sum assessed on the tariff scale plus, where the claimant was dependent upon the deceased, and providing the deceased's only normal income was not from social security benefits, a further payment based on a loss of earnings calculation will also be made. Where there is only one qualifying claimant a level 13 tariff sum of £11,000 is payable. Where there is more than one, each claimant is awarded a level 10 sum of £5,500 (para. 39).

5.53 Reasonable funeral expenses are also payable and, in assessing these, account should be taken of the religious and cultural background of the victim and his family (para 37 and para. 21 Guidance).

5.54 The scheme only requires an application to be completed on the appropriate form and sent to the CICA for consideration. There will not normally be a hearing and the assessment of the compensation will be determined by the Authority and notified through the post to the applicant. However, it should be noted that there may be delays in processing compensation claims. The scheme is discussed further in the context of domestic violence (see Chapter 7 below).

Chapter 6

Cohabitants and matrimonial proceedings

1 Introduction

6.01 Many cohabiting couples, particularly in the early stages of their relationship, have at least one partner who, although separated, remains married to another party or, although divorced, has on-going matrimonial proceedings relating to unresolved issues concerning the children or financial matters. Given that it is now clear that the divorce reforms contained in Part II Family Law Act 1996 (FLA 1996) will not be implemented, the Matrimonial Causes Act 1973 (MCA 1973) will continue to govern divorce proceedings for the time being. However, whilst the piloting of the Act showed that there were many difficulties with divorce under the 1996 Act, one of its legacies is a far stronger mediation culture and the possibility of a mediated solution is one which practitioners are now more likely to suggest. Indeed in the legal aid context, the possibility of mediation often has to be explored before public funding can be made available for family law litigation (see Funding Code Procedures C27–28). With effect from 1 May 2001 the LSC has introduced a new 'willingness test' allowing a recognised mediator to first make enquiries of the other party to see if they are willing to attend a mediation assessment meeting (before offering an appointment to the applicant for a public funding certificate). If not, the mediator can confirm that the case is unsuitable for mediation allowing the applicant to make an application straight away for a certificate. If the opponent is willing to attend mediation then no application can be made until after a meeting has taken place and the mediator has assessed whether or not the case is suitable for ongoing mediation. Thus a cohabitant who is still in the throes of divorce from a previous partner may be encouraged to take part in mediation with their former partner.

6.02 On the other hand, what was the Ancillary Relief Pilot Scheme has now been implemented nationally with effect from 5 June 2000 and affects the procedure governing financial provision on divorce. Cohabitants going through a divorce from a former partner need also to be aware of the sweeping change that has come about in the approach to financial provision on divorce following the landmark House of Lords decision of *White v White* [2000] 2 FLR 981, which, at least in cases where there has been a fairly long marriage and where assets exceed the needs of the parties, has introduced the need to examine proposed divorce settlements against asset division based on 'a yardstick of equality'. This affects cohabitants to the extent that what is paid or received as financial provision from a previous relationship may limit or extend the financial resources available in the new cohabiting relationship.

2 Cohabitants and the divorce

6.03 There is not now to be any immediate switch to a purely no-fault system of divorce and thus cohabitants involved in divorce proceedings will most commonly use or be responding to the quicker but fault-based grounds of adultery (s 1(2)(a) MCA 1973) or behaviour (s 1(2)(b) MCA 1973). The alternative is to wait until the parties have been separated for two years when divorce will be granted on the basis of two years' separation providing the respondent consents to the divorce (s 1(2)(d) MCA 1973) or five years' separation where the respondent's consent is not required (s 1(2)(e) MCA 1973). Divorce following desertion of a period of two years is of course still available to the party deserted (s 1(2)(c) MCA 1973), but is in practice little used.

6.04 Under the current law, cohabitation with another party can be cited as evidence of adultery based on inclination and opportunity sufficient to prove irretrievable breakdown of marriage under s 1(2)(a) MCA 1973. Traditionally, the cohabitant would be named and joined as co-respondent to the proceedings. Court rules now permit divorce proceedings to be brought on this ground without the need to name a co-respondent or serve them with the proceedings (see rule 2.7(1) Family Proceedings Rules 1991). However, they may still be named and joined as a party at the election of the petitioner. Thus, a married cohabitant who is to be the respondent in the divorce proceedings may wish to negotiate to agree to admit the adultery upon the basis that the petitioner will not name the co-respondent in the petition. It should be noted that, where the cohabitant is named as a co-respondent in divorce proceedings, this renders the cohabitant and their partner's spouse 'associated' for the purposes of the domestic violence legislation under s 62(3)(g) FLA 1996. In this situation alone, a cohabitant could if necessary apply for a non-molestation order against the spouse or vice versa.

3 Cohabitants and children

(a) Residence and contact

6.05 The existence of a cohabitant is obviously of significance in relation to disputes relating to children of one of the parties from a previous marriage, both in terms of the child support assessment and other possible claims for financial provision by the children discussed in Chapter 9. It is also of significance in terms of the residence and contact arrangements for those children, which need to be agreed or decided by the court following divorce. Such disputes will be resolved as between both married and unmarried parents in accordance with the principles laid down in the Children Act 1989 (see Chapter 8), the most notable of these being that the welfare of the child is paramount (s 1(1) CA 1989).

6.06 How does this translate into the effect a cohabitation relationship can have on the decisions made by the courts in relation to children of a previous relationship?

6.07 The extent to which cohabitation is relevant depends on the nature of the orders sought. Cohabitation may be taking place at the time of the divorce proceedings or one or both parents may begin a cohabitation relationship some time after the arrangements for children have been agreed. This often leads to renewed hostility between the parties, making any agreed arrangements difficult to achieve or maintain and necessitating court orders or variation of existing orders to determine residence and contact (s 8 CA 1989).

6.08 Broadly, and particularly where the cohabiting parent is seeking a residence order, the court will be most concerned to examine the suitability of the cohabitant as a parent (see for example *S v S* [1986] 1 FLR 492) as well as the stability of the cohabitation relationship (see *Stephenson v Stephenson* [1985] FLR 1140). Usually, where a welfare report is ordered (now carried out by a child and family reporter under the auspices of the Child and Family Court Support Advisory and Support Service (CAFCASS) as discussed in Chapter 8 below), it will include an assessment of these matters for the court, and a cohabitant who did not want to hinder their partner's case would normally need to co-operate with this process.

6.09 Where there are contact and residence disputes and one parent is involved in a gay cohabitation relationship, this is, of course, a factor to be examined in the light of the likely effect this will have on the child's welfare. Certainly as far as lesbian mothers are concerned, the courts have in recent years accepted that it may still be in a child's best interests to live with their mother in her new circumstances despite the social difficulties the child may encounter in addressing other people's perceptions of that relationship. In *B v B* [1991] 1 FLR 402, research findings indicating that children brought up in such relationships are unlikely to be adversely affected and that there was no evidence of stigmatisation of such children by their peers were taken into account by the High Court before awarding an exemplary mother who understood the needs of her children custody. In *C v C* [1991] 1 FLR 223, the Court of Appeal, held that the mother's lesbian relationship was an important factor to be put into the equation when determining what was in the best interests of the child, but did not of itself constitute a bar to her caring for her child. More recently in *G v F (contact and shared residence: applications for leave)* [1998] 2 FLR 799, a case where shared residence of a child was sought following the breakdown of a same-sex relationship, Bracewell J., was clear that in her view there was no room for discrimination on the basis of sexual orientation in such a case. She stated:

> 'It would be entirely wrong. . .and unsustainable to seek in any way to reflect against the applicant by reason of the nature of her relationship with the respondent'(at p. 805).

However, it is perhaps significant here that this was not a case where the child's father was a party objecting to residence or contact. To date there have not been any cases of a homosexual father applying for custody or residence of children.

6.10 With regard to orders for contact, there is a presumption that it is better for the child to know both parents (see *Re H (Minors) (Access)* [1992] 1 FLR 148 and *Re W (A Minor) (Contact)* [1994] 2 FLR 441) and thus, generally, the existence of a cohabitation relationship by the partner seeking contact should not of itself prevent contact taking place, even where the court has concerns about the suitability of contact between the child and contact parent's cohabitant. Conditions can be attached to any s 8 order (see s 11(7) CA 1989) and some form of contact should nearly always be possible. This point has been underlined in the Court of Appeal decision of *Re O (a minor) (contact: imposition of conditions)* [1995] 2 FLR 124.

6.11 The impact of the Human Rights Act 1998 (HRA 1998) may be felt quite keenly in this area, particularly as regards same-sex cohabitants. Article 8 of the European Convention on Human Rights protects the right to private and family life and any thoughts that a same-sex parent's contact with their own child could be automatically outlawed on the basis of their sexual orientation was held to constitute a breach of Article 8 in the case of *Salgueiro da Silva Mouta v Portugal* (1998) Application No 33290/96.

(b) Change of surname

6.12 Where a child comes to live with one parent and their cohabitant, they will not be a child of that family as there is no marriage between the adults. It has already been noted that such a child does not have any direct claim against the estate of their parent's cohabitant, although if dependency can be proved they may fall within the residual category of applicants under s 1(1)(e) I(PFD)A 1975. However, a child in that situation may want to change their surname to that of the cohabitant. Although any person with unfettered parental responsibility might have been thought to be able to independently change a child's name, as discussed in Chapter 2, case law has now made it clear that consent or a s 13 or specific issue order needs to be obtained (see *Dawson v Wearmouth* [1999] 1 FLR 1167). Even where only one parent has parental responsibility, whilst *Re PC (Change of Surname)* [1997] 2 FLR 730 suggested they may act independently to change a child's name, with the other parent needing a prohibited steps or specific issue order, dicta in the House of Lords in *Dawson v Wearmouth* and the Court of Appeal in *Re W, Re A, Re B* [2001] Fam 1 have indicated that consent of the other parent or leave of the court is required before a surname can be changed, although given the wording of s 2 CA 1989, the authority for this is unclear as is the penalty for failing to obtain consent. Where a residence order is in force, either the written consent of every person with parental responsibility is required or leave of the court must always be obtained (s 13(1) CA 1989). Where the children's names are to be changed by deed poll, the Practice Direction of December 1994 (see [1995] Fam Law 209) still governs the procedure and essentially requires written consent of all persons with parental responsibility to be produced, or the matter will be referred back to the court or the Master of the Rolls in cases of doubt as appropriate. If the change is objected to and there is no residence order in force, a specific issue order should be sought (s 8 CA 1989) and the criteria for making the decision relate to the child's welfare *(Re F (child:*

surname) [1994] 1 FLR 110, CA). Where a residence order is in force an application under s 13 CA 1989 must be made. In such a case, as the child's welfare was paramount, the s 1(3) checklist was a useful *aide-memoire* whereas it applies directly in s 8 applications.

6.13 In *Re B (minors) (Change of Surname)* [1996] 1 FLR 791 the Court of Appeal was refused an application on behalf of children to change their surname to that of their stepfather, despite there being little contact with the natural father, and the teenage children's clear wishes to adopt their stepfather's surname which they had already done informally. However, in *Re S (change of surname)* [1999] 1 FLR 672, it was made clear the views of a *Gillick* competent child should be given the most careful consideration where a change of surname application was concerned. Again in *Re C (minor) (change of surname)* [1994] 1 FCR 110, the Court of Appeal accepted that to change a name which had been in informal use for a long period of time may well not be in a child's best interests. *Dawson v Wearmouth* (above) and subsequent cases have affirmed that the courts do regard change of surname by children to be an extremely important issue which will not be done lightly, and the courts lean towards retaining the status quo, even in the face of strong feelings by older children themselves, making it now extremely difficult to change a child's surname.

(c) Child support and maintenance

6.14 As discussed in Chapter 9, a cohabitant is not expected to maintain the children of his/her partner's former relationship and thus, on relationship breakdown, no maintenance will be payable in respect of these quasi-step-children, either as child support or as maintenance ordered by the court, even though their parent's partner has maintained them throughout the relationship.

6.15 At the present time, the effect of a new cohabitation relationship upon child support calculation, depends upon whether the non-resident parent is dependent upon their partner or vice versa and whether there are any children of that new relationship. The juxtaposition of the first and second families within the child support assessment has been the subject of much controversy which has led to the numerous changes to the original child support formula, culminating first in the Child Support Act 1995 and now in the reforms contained in the Child Support, Pensions and Social Security Act 2000, which come into force for new cases in April 2002 as discussed below (see Chapter 9). At the moment, and in general terms, where the non-resident parent is supporting a new partner, the calculation of exempt income makes no allowance for an adult dependant or, indeed, for children who are not the natural or adopted children of the non-resident parent and living with them, although the housing costs calculation for the protected income levels does take this into account. This will change following implementation of the 2000 Act reforms. In addition, the changes introduced in April 1995 currently ensure that no one pays more than 30% of net income and that housing cost calculations do not assume that an adult dependant can meet their share of the costs.

6.16 Conversely, a new partner's income is not taken into account directly for the purposes of calculating the net income, although where there are children of the new cohabitation relationship, any income of their partner will act to reduce the absent parent's exempt income and thus increase the sum to be paid. The changes to regulations introduced with effect from April 1995 acted to remove any presumed contribution to housing costs by a non-resident parent's partner. However, the Child Support Act 1995 provides such a contribution as a departure ground which entitles a parent with care to apply for a sum greater than that produced by the formula (see Chapter 9 below). Finally, it is worthy of note that account can now be taken of clean break settlements ordered before 5 April 1993 in one of two ways and these reforms may affect cohabiting couples either as absent parents or parents with care. Whereas these were originally not taken into account at all, public pressure has resulted in this being made a departure ground and in the earlier introduction of a broad brush allowance which has been retained as follows.

6.17 Firstly, it is necessary to establish the value of the deemed capital transfer. An allowance of £20 in exempt income is then added for every £5,000 attributable to the absent parent's share of the transfer up to a ceiling of £25,000.

6.18 It seems property or capital transfers will remain a ground for 'variation' (which will replace departure directions) under the 2000 Act reforms, although generally the grounds will be narrower than currently exist. How cohabitants will be affected by the new scheme will depend on their individual circumstances, but crucially only the non-resident parent's income will be taken into account under the new formula, regardless of how much the other parent or partner is earning and there will be a flat rate contribution which does take into account all the children that a non-resident parent is maintaining. On the downside, actual housing costs will not be taken into account. Clearly some will gain and some will lose, but at least, as will be seen in Chapter 9, all will benefit from knowing where they stand.

4 Cohabitation and financial provision on divorce

6.19 The existence of a new cohabitation relationship by one or both parties to financial provision proceedings is, of course, a significant factor when the court is deciding financial provision on divorce. Of itself, cohabitation is not conduct which it would be inequitable to disregard (s 25(2)(g) MCA 1973) when deciding ancillary relief applications. Unlike remarriage, cohabitation does not have any direct effect on the court's jurisdiction to make any of the orders for periodical maintenance and poses the question as to the weight to be given to this factor when deciding lump sum and property adjustment orders, particularly given that there is no legal obligation on cohabitants to maintain each other either during or after the relationship. The court is under a duty to have regard to all the circumstances of the case (s 25(1) MCA 1973), and cohabitation is undoubtedly one important circumstance to be weighed in the equation.

6.20 Where a formerly dependant spouse is now cohabiting with another partner, that partner's resources are not directly relevant and whatever his or her current circumstances, due regard must be had, *inter alia*, to the age of the parties, the duration of the marriage and the contribution made to the welfare of the first family by the spouse when making financial provision and property adjustment orders (s 25(2)). The court has a duty to consider whether a 'clean break' can be achieved (s 25A(1)) and, where there is cohabitation on the part of a formerly dependant spouse, it is much more likely that a clean break will be ordered, although much may depend on the length of the marriage as well as the stability of the new relationship.

6.21 Nonetheless, the existence of a cohabitation relationship will have an indirect effect upon the financial provision to be ordered, in so far as a new partner's resources or need for support will always have an impact upon the financial position of the former spouse involved in matrimonial proceedings. For example, where one party to proceedings is being provided with accommodation by their new partner, this may mean that the court is more likely to transfer property to the other spouse who has care of the children of the family, given that the children's welfare is the court's first consideration (s 25(1) MCA 1973). Conversely, in *Suter v Suter and Jones* [1987] Fam 111, a cohabitant living with a woman and three children from her previous marriage was expected to make a contribution to the family's housing costs and thus periodical payments payable to her by her former husband were reduced on appeal. Even unenforceable moral obligations to maintain a new cohabitant and their children may amount to a relevant circumstance and act to reduce the resources the court considers available to maintain a former spouse as in *Roberts v Roberts* [1970] P 1, although generally the needs of the former spouse and any children of the first family will not be subjugated to those of the second.

6.22 In *A v A (financial provision: variation)* [1995] 2 FCR 353 at page 359, Thorpe J summarised the principles to be applied when dealing with ancillary relief applications where there is a new cohabitation relationship:

> 'First, cohabitation is not to be equated with marriage. In performing its functions under the Matrimonial Causes Act 1973 (as amended) the fact of cohabitation is not to be given any decisive weight.
> Second, cohabitation is, however, a relevant factor in that it bears upon the financial circumstances, particularly upon the assessment of the wife's financial needs.
> But it seems to me above all that the court should strive to discern the realities in determining what weight to give to the factor of cohabitation, particularly since the subjective presentation of the parties often seeks to disguise or distort the realities.'

Thus, there are no hard and fast rules as to the extent to which the existence of a cohabitant will affect proceedings. In this case, the former wife's periodical payments were reduced in proportion to the contribution to the living costs her cohabitant was making or was able to make in the view of the court. Clearly, no order should be made which can only be met by a former spouse from the resources of his or her cohabitant and the court should be satisfied that any order made can be met out of the party's own resources (see *B v B (periodical payments) (transitional provisions)* [1995] 1 FLR 459).

6.23 Cohabitation is of great importance where a divorce settlement provides for payment of maintenance (or indeed other provision such as occupation of the family home) 'until remarriage or cohabitation with another person' for a specified period of time. Here what exactly amounts to cohabitation is critical and the courts have looked to the reality of the situation. In *K v K (Enforcement)*[2000] 1 FLR 383, such a maintenance clause had been agreed. The wife had formed a relationship with an American and they became engaged. The new partner had his own accommodation but spent several nights a week with the wife helping to run her Bed and Breakfast business. Evidence of this was provided by the husband's enquiry agent and formed the basis of his refusal to continue to pay maintenance to the wife. The court found that the reality was that the wife and her fiancé had been cohabiting and whilst the husband was ordered to pay the arrears, maintenance should cease. The court went on to enumerate a list of factors based on s 137(1) Social Security Contributions and Benefits Act 1992 and other authorities which were of assistance in determining whether there was cohabitation. These were:

- *Living together in the same household* Where, as was found here, the separate accommodation was aimed at retaining the maintenance payments, this did not mean they always had to live under the same roof, although this was the normal meaning;
- *A sharing of daily life* Here the couple shared both professional and personal tasks that amounted to this;
- *Stability and a degree of permanence* A passing relationship such as a holiday romance is not sufficient;
- *Shared Finance* Here the couple pooled their resources to some extent;
- *Children* Here the fiancé had formed a close relationship with the wife's son as a 'second father';
- *Intention and motivation* The deliberate avoidance of losing the maintenance by finding her fiancé separate accommodation and attempting to get the best of both worlds showed the wife's true intentions; and
- *The opinion of the reasonable person with normal perceptions* To the outside world the couple appeared committed to each other.

6.24 Thus cohabitation remains a matter of fact and may mean different things in different contexts. This case contrasts, for example, with that of *Re Watson (Deceased)* [1999] 1 FLR 878 discussed in Chapter 5. However, in the post-divorce maintenance context the courts seem keen to show they are alert to avoidance tactics and cohabitants should beware of litigating on the basis of sham arrangements.

6.25 In terms of procedure, there are now new rules governing ancillary relief cases introduced by the Family Proceedings (Amendment No. 2) Rules 1999 (SI 1999/3491) which amend the FPR 1991. As was the case with the Woolf Reforms, which introduced the 1998 Civil Procedure Rules, the aim is to reduce delay, facilitate settlements and limit costs. The parties are under a duty to fulfil the court's expectations which include parties making offers and proposals, and giving these proper consideration. The court is also now more interventionist in its approach with the aim of encouraging co-operation and mediation where appropriate and speeding matters along by identifying the issues early on, regulating the extent of disclosure and expert evidence and fixing timetables as well as giving directions. Under the old rules, a cohabitant could not it seems, be ordered to file an affidavit of means prior to the hearing (*Wynne v Wynne and Jeffers* [1980] 3 All ER 659) and there is still no specific provision for cohabitants to co-operate with the court in their partner's divorce proceedings in this way.

6.26 Problems may arise where a partner has (or claims to have) no knowledge of their new partner's financial position in their Form E, although that party can be ordered to file an affidavit in respect of what they do know about their partner's means and such a stance may not be advisable in the new ancillary proceedings atmosphere which emphasises co-operation. A cohabitant, whether or not a co-respondent, cannot be joined as a party for the purpose of ancillary relief application, but may have intervened and become a party. However, discovery against them will only be ordered if it is relevant to the issue being tried (*S v X (intervenors)* [1991] FCR 39). Nevertheless, the Family Proceedings Rules 1991 as amended (FPR 1991) empower the district judge hearing an ancillary relief application to order the attendance of any person for examination or cross-examination and to order the discovery and production of any document or require further affidavits (rule 2.62(4)).

6.27 In addition, *Frary v Frary* [1994] 1 FCR 595 gives guidance as to the way in which the court can compel a cohabitant to produce evidence of their means in respect of an application for financial provision where their partner indicates they have no knowledge of their means. Providing the cohabitant is to be called as a witness, rule 2.62(7) FPR 1991 (SI 1991/1247) permits the court to order any person to produce at an 'inspection appointment' any document necessary for the disposing fairly of the application for ancillary relief or the saving of costs. The leading case of *Livesey* (formerly *Jenkins*) *v Jenkins* [1985] AC 424 has clearly stated that disclosure in ancillary relief cases must be full and frank to enable the court to properly exercise its discretion under s 25 MCA 1973 and the new rules clearly now embody this approach.

6.28 The piecemeal approach of the courts to cohabitation in this context stems from the confused recognition of cohabitation relationships generally. Given there is no duty to maintain, the court is forced to look at the reality of the situation and make judgments about the stability of the relationship and sometimes even to the veracity of the information placed before the court. The notion of an earned contribution from the assets of the former marriage also adds to the scope for different approaches to their relevance and post-*White* there is seemingly an even bigger difference in approach between 'big money' and other cases where assets do not exceed needs and a needs-based approach will remain. Nonetheless, there is an increased willingness to look at the financial position of cohabitants in divorce proceedings.

Part II

Relationship breakdown

It is on relationship breakdown that legal advice is most often sought by cohabitants. As has been noted in Chapters 1 to 6, the legal position of cohabitants on breakdown of the relationship depends to a large degree on any legally binding arrangements that have been made between them. At the present time there is no "divorce law equivalent" for those who have not made pre-emptive arrangements by entering into full or partial cohabitation agreements as discussed in Chapter 1 or who cannot otherwise reach agreement on breakdown. Whilst the need for change in the law in this field has been recognised by both the Law Society and the Solicitors' Family Law Association who have put forward comprehensive proposals for reform affecting both same and opposite-sex cohabitants (see Law Society, 1999 and SFLA, 2000), the Law Commission's long-awaited recommendations on the property rights of cohabitants are not due to be published before Spring 2002 at the earliest. Whilst in London, same- and opposite-sex cohabitants can register their partnerships (see the Mayor of London's website at http://www.london.gov.uk/mayor/partnerships/), this is little more than symbolic, proving the commitment involved in the relationship. Registration has no legal effect other than perhaps being useful evidence that one cohabitant is dependant on the other or that each cohabitant classifies themselves as a member of the other's family for the purposes of applications under the Inheritance Act 1975 (see Chapter 5) or tenancy succession under the Rent Act 1977 (see Chapter 3). Furthermore, as noted in Chapter 1, the Relationship (Civil Registration) 10 Minute Rule Bill currently before Parliament is not expected to become law. However, if it did, it would treat same and opposite-sex cohabitants who registered their relationships as if they were married, whilst also permitting them to make and register their own agreements.

Under current law the fall-back position for cohabitants is the general law applicable to the area or areas of dispute. As a rule, the more comprehensive the arrangements which have been made between cohabitants, the less scope there should be for lengthy and bitter litigation. However, most cohabitants fail to make any arrangements at all. Faced with this situation, as in divorce, the aim should be for the parties to reach agreement without having to resort to the courts, particularly in relation to the arrangements for any children. The new legal aid scheme also means that the viability of mediation must be explored by former cohabitants before public funding is made available to litigate disputes relating to children and the rented family home , although not property disputes brought under s 14 Trusts of Land and Appointment of Trustees Act 1996.

Legal advice on the appropriateness of tentative agreements reached between the parties is often sought. This can place the advisor in the position of having to indicate that the agreement is not in the client's best interests. Whilst there is a duty to explain why this view has been formed, it is also important for practitioners to explain that, despite this, bitter litigation rarely allows amicable relations between the parties in the long term. Nonetheless instructions must be followed, subject to the requirements of the Legal Services Commission (and the codes of conduct of the Law Society, the SFLA or the Family Bar Association where appropriate). Yet no client should be allowed to agree to an arrangement which would severely prejudice his or her long-term future unless all the other options have been explained, explored and rejected. Solicitors are often criticised for tending to exacerbate the tension between parting couples. The possibility of counselling, conciliation or mediation for cohabitants on relationship breakdown may be overlooked. The availability of such services will depend on the area in which the couple live, but, particularly in relation to disputes about children, this is an avenue of help of which the client should at least be aware.

The Lord Chancellor's Department's Marriage and Relationship Support Programme, provides funding to organisations under s 22 Family Law Act 1996 who will promote the programme's of "positively promoting the provision of high quality, cost effective services in the vital area of marriage and relationship support to ensure that as many couples as possible can benefit". This programme in its latest form at last recognises that all relationships, not just marriages, are deserving of such support (notwithstanding the wording of s 22 FLA 1996), and clearly intends to provide services to non-marital families including all opposite-sex cohabitants. Indeed, it does not appear either to exclude services to same-sex cohabitants, and particularly where the interests of children would be served by such support, same-sex couples should be able to take advantage of the services available. Five million pounds will be allocated to organisations around Britain able to provide such services in 2002–2003. This should make mediation and other support services for cohabitants and parents more readily available in the longer term and this climate change encouraging support and mediation in all family law work is probably one of the less expected yet sustainable legacies of the ill-fated Family Law Act 1996.

A list of agencies who may be able to assist is set out in Appendix III and it should be noted that LCD-funded new-style "Family Advice and Information Networks", enabling couples to access a range of services including mediation and advice for separating couples, are being piloted in England. Amicable settlement is not, however, always possible. The prime example is a case of domestic violence. Here the only remedy available may be prompt court action. This area of law underwent radical reform following the Law Commission's recommendations (*Report on Domestic Violence and Occupation of the Family Home*, Law Com No 207, 1992) and the dramatic last minute withdrawal of the Family Homes and Domestic Violence Bill 1995, culminating in its inclusion in revised form as Part IV Family

Law Act 1996. This is addressed next, in Part II of this book. Disputes about the children will be considered in the following chapter, and the law relating to child support, financial provision for children, and housing and property rights between cohabitants, which have all undergone significant changes since the last edition of this book, will be considered in later chapters.

Another radical overhaul affecting practitioners acting for cohabitants undergoing relationship breakdown is that of the new legal aid regime. Whilst the new rules and regulations are noted where appropriate in each of the following chapters, the overall impact of the new scheme in the context of relationship breakdown is now summarised.

New-Style Legal Aid

Following the implementation of the Access to Justice Act 1999, on 1 April 2000, pursuant to s 1 of that Act, the Legal Services Commission (LSC) was created with the Legal Aid Board transferring all responsibility for the provision of public funding of legal services (what was known as legal aid) to it. Section 4(2) of the Act describes in very general terms the levels of service which may now be funded by the LSC. The definitions of each level of service are to be found in the funding code criteria at Section 2.1.

The fundamental difference with the new system of funding is that under the Access to Justice Act 1999 there is no entitlement to public funding.

With the introduction of the General Civil Contract (Solicitors) – a contract between the LSC and solicitors (or other suppliers of service) – it is only firms who hold a franchise in a relevant category of legal work who will be able to undertake work in that area if such work is to be funded by the LSC.

The levels of service are as follows:

(1) *Legal help* – essentially "advice and assistance" work (formerly the green form/Claim 10 scheme).

(2) *Help at court* – authorises help and advocacy for a client in relation to a particular hearing without formally acting as legal representative in the proceedings.

(3) *Approved family help* – authorising help in relation to a family dispute including assistance in resolving that dispute through negotiation or otherwise. It includes the services covered by legal help as well as the issuing of proceedings and representation in proceedings necessary to obtain disclosure of information from another party or to obtain a consent order following settlement of part or all of the dispute and related conveyancing work. This is a wholly new level of service and an application to the LSC for a certificate is required before help can be provided. There is no provision for emergency applications for approved family help which is sub-divided into Help with Mediation (limited to advice in support of family mediation, help in drawing up any agreement reached in mediation and, where appropriate, help in confirming such an agreement in a court order and related conveyancing work, charged at the old ABWOR rates and the only level of service where the statutory charge does not apply) and General Family Help (which can best be described as an old style limited legal aid certificate eg in cases under the revised ancillary relief procedure general family help will be appropriate for all work required up to and including at the Financial Dispute Resolution Appointment but not including the final hearing).

(4) *Legal representation* – the most similar to the old style full legal aid certificate and sub-divided into investigative help (effectively legal representation limited to investigation of the strength of a proposed claim and which level of service is not available in family proceedings) and *Full Representation* – a grant of legal representation including emergency representation and full representation.

(5) *Family mediation* – available only to approved mediators and authorises mediation of a family dispute including assessing whether mediation is suitable to the dispute and the parties and all the circumstances.

Many familiar elements of civil legal aid and advice and assistance remain (albeit in a modified form) including rules on financial eligibility, the statutory charge and limited protection against an opponent's costs. There are some fundamental differences however and some of the more significant are as follows:

(1) A solicitor carrying out work under the legal help/help at court scheme pursuant to a contract with the LSC is from May 2001 able to carry out £500 (excluding VAT) worth of work before approaching the LSC for an extension to the financial limit.

(2) As an extension of Section 29 of the Family Law Act 1996 the funding code procedures C27 to C29 as recently amended require a recognised mediator to determine whether or not the case is suitable for mediation and whether the opponent is willing to attend for mediation before an application can be made for general family help or for legal representation in the following family proceedings:

(a)   Matrimonial Causes Act 1973 (other than s 37 of that Act);
(b)   The Domestic Proceedings and Magistrates' Courts Act 1978;
(c)   Parts I to III Children Act 1989 (including Sch I to that Act).

(3) Article 3(1) of the Community Legal Services (Funding) Order 2000 confirms that, as from 1 April 2001, a civil certificate cannot be granted unless the solicitor is authorised to provide such work as would be carried under the certificate by a contract with the LSC.

(4) Solicitors who have a franchise in the area of family law work under contract with the LSC therefore to undertake such work are able to exercise devolved powers to grant a certificate of emergency representation eg in the case of an urgent injunction required under Part IV Family Law Act 1996. The LSC will return, by fax or post, emergency applications to solicitors where, in the view of the LSC, devolved powers should have been exercised to grant the certificate by the solicitor.

(5) The government has now proposed increasing the £2,500 exemption from the statutory charge to £3,000, such change scheduled to be effective as from 3 December 2001. Regulation 52 of the Community Legal Service (Financial) Regulations 2000, SI 2000/516 confirms that interest is charged from the date of registration of the statutory charge at 8% on the lesser of either the value of the charge or the value of the property at the time of recovery. The Lord Chancellor's Department however has proposed changing the rate of interest from 8% (which level has prevailed since 1994) to 1% above the Bank of England base rate. Interest will continue to be calculated on a simple basis and the rate of interest will only change if there has been a variation of 1% or more (in the Bank of England base rate) in the last 12 months before the date of application of the charge. This proposed change is likely to be effective from December 2001.

For further information in relation to the levels of service funded by the LSC and for full details of the Funding Code and the General Civil Contract, readers should consult the three volumes of the Legal Services Commission's manual and the chapter on public funding in Butterworths looseleaf *Family Law Service* which is updated quarterly and which covers the current and proposed eligibility criteria for all levels of funding and the rates of remuneration for all work undertaken under the Scheme.

Chapter 7

Domestic violence and the family home

7.01 The home is at times violent for some families, married or unmarried. Indeed, domestic violence cases comprise 25% of all assaults, making it the single largest category of violent crime (see Mirless-Black, 1999). Although less publicised and researched, violence can also be found in relationships between couples of the same sex. Even after couples separate, violence may still occur. Depending on the effects of an assault, criminal and/or civil remedies may be available to a cohabitant victim, although the traditionally half-hearted police response to "domestic" crime is well documented. Unmarried victims have been shown in practice to experience a more positive police response to domestic violence than married victims, as the public policy factor of recognising the unity of those bound in marriage does not apply (see J. Pahl, *Police Response to Battered Women* [1982] Journal of Social Welfare Law 337). Nevertheless, other factors, which have traditionally been cited by the police as justification for declining to bring charges against violent spouses, have undoubtedly also deterred the bringing of charges against violent cohabitants. Examples are an alleged propensity for victims to change their minds about pressing charges, and reluctance to testify against their partners, although these have never been insuperable hurdles in the cases of cohabitants who have always been compellable witnesses.

7.02 In recent years, many initiatives have been taken in different parts of the country to highlight domestic violence as a crime to be taken seriously by the police and public alike. Changes to policing practice in relation to domestic violence incidents such as those recommended in Home Office Circular 60/1990 have resulted in a less negative view of police protection available where there is violence in the home, although a Home Office Research Study (Grace, 1995) found that a third of police officers were unaware of the Circular, despite it having been sent to all Police Authorities. More recently, the Home Office has given the issue of domestic violence a much higher profile and has a webpage dedicated to this issue (see http://www.homeoffice.gov.uk/domestic_violence/). As part of their new approach, it has commissioned research with a view to finding better solutions. In 2000, in the light of research findings, it issued updated guidance (see *A Choice By Right* Home Office, 2000 and *Multi-Agency Guidance for Addressing Domestic Violence,* Home Office, 2000) and a new Circular (Home Office Circular 19/2000). This shows a clear intention to strengthen police involvement in domestic violence and suggests that there should be an arrest in all cases of domestic violence unless there are exceptional circumstances.

7.03 These initiatives are to be welcomed, and it is clear that the recommendations aim to lower the threshold at which police intervention in domestic disputes occurs, and to enhance support for victims. Public awareness of the problem has also been raised by media initiatives over the years, one of the first being launched during 1994, the International Year of the Family. More recently, in response to the 1997 European Parliament resolution on the need to establish a European Union wide campaign for zero tolerance of violence against women, the European Commission conducted a European campaign to raise awareness on violence against women in 1999/2000, which was fully supported by the Home Office. Publicity leaflets aimed at victims produced by the Home Office for free distribution at courts and other public places, now provide easier access to contact points for victims (see for example, *Domestic Violence: Break the Chain*, Home Office, 2000). However, research also shows that, despite such initiatives, the police response to domestic violence still varies tremendously from area to area and that the recommendations in the 1990 Home Office Circular have not always been followed (see Grace 1995).

7.04 However, whilst there is no room for complacency, the police should now in most areas have policies in place which give much more positive help to victims of domestic violence, including at the very least a willingness to arrest where this is appropriate as well as support for victims. There should either be a specialist domestic violence unit, which has a significant numbers of women police officers, or specially trained officers who have an understanding of the often difficult choices facing victims of domestic violence. Indeed, the enactment of new powers under the Protection from Harassment Act 1997 – aimed at protecting victims of stalkers, but of wider application – has also served to promote readier police intervention in domestic violence cases more generally. Unfortunately, there was, for a long time, no new investment in the provision of refuges for victims of violence, although lottery funding has more recently been made available to assist for better provision in some areas. The lack of a safe address unknown to the abuser will make many victims reluctant to use the criminal remedies available or even avail themselves of civil remedies for fear of reprisals. Although victims of domestic violence are compellable witnesses in criminal proceedings, generally speaking, and despite new Home Office guidance directed at zero tolerance of domestic violence by the Police, it has not been the policy of the Crown Prosecution Service to use these powers, which would otherwise act as a big disincentive to report such incidents.

7.05 Thus, whilst the number of arrests has increased, the number of convictions has remained fairly constant (National Inter-Agency Working Party, 1992). The Home Office has suggested that it might be appropriate to prosecute even where the victim does not want to give evidence and that the CPS should consider such a policy (Home Office, 2000a). In all cases where a victim withdraws, the CPS has been instructed to investigate to ensure such withdrawal is genuine (Home Office, 2000a). Part of the impetus for the Home Office review of domestic violence has been the implementation of the Human rights Act 1998 (HRA 1998). It is clear that the state has a duty to protect its citizens from torture or inhuman or degrading treatment (Article 3 ECHR) and this includes prevention rather than cure (see *A v United Kingdom (human rights: punishment of child)* [1998] 2 FLR 959. It is interesting and important to note in this context that other initiatives in the homelessness field are also aimed at protecting both adults and children from violence and that in both England and Wales, victims of domestic violence are to become a priority need category under the Homelessness Bill 2001. Furthermore, both the DLTR and the National Assembly for Wales have endorsed new Draft Codes of Guidance on Homelessness (available on their respective websites) which are aimed at fostering good practice by local authorities who should readily provide housing in safe areas to victims of family violence.

7.06 Unfortunately, Part IV Family Law Act 1996 (FLA 1996), whilst providing an improved range of civil remedies, has not included the recommendation made by the Law Commission that the police, where they have been involved in an incident, be able to take out civil injunctions to protect a victim of domestic violence on their behalf where this is the victim's wish (see *Domestic Violence and Occupation of the Family Home*, 1992, Law Com No. 207, para 5.20). This would have had the effect of removing the blame for injunctions being obtained against an abuser away from the victim and on to a third party, the police, arguably reducing the likelihood of the abuser seeking revenge against the victim. Thus, even under the 1996 scheme of legislation, a victim still has to choose whether to agree to testify in a police prosecution in the event of the abuser pleading not guilty, or personally to seek protection in the form of civil remedies. As will be discussed below, this is now a choice that is available to cohabitants of the same sex as well as heterosexual cohabitants.

1 Criminal proceedings

(a) Prosecution

7.07 Although not always appropriate, there may be circumstances in which both victim and perpetrator may benefit from the knowledge that domestic violence is increasingly viewed by the police as a serious criminal offence warranting prosecution.

7.08 The proceedings which may be brought, whether victim and aggressor are of the same or the opposite sex, are identical, but how effective they are usually depends on the police response, and the seriousness of the assault. The most serious incidents of domestic violence involve charges of murder or manslaughter. The Offences Against the Person Act 1861 enables prosecution for assaults occasioning actual bodily harm (at least bruising usually—s 47); grievous bodily harm (very serious harm—s 18); or wounding (some puncturing of the skin—s 20). In *R v Ireland v Burstow* [1998] AC 147, the House of Lords accepted that harassing conduct could amount to "assault" and that "bodily harm" was not restricted to physical harm but could include psychological injuries. Section 30 Criminal Justice Act 1988 also provides a statutory offence of common assault for which the police themselves will now often prosecute, rather than, as was their previous policy, suggesting that the victim take out a magistrates' court summons for common assault. Although the latter is still an option, it is rarely appropriate as legal aid is not available, leaving the victim to bring his or her own case.

7.09 The recent change in police policy towards domestic disputes has meant an increase in the number of prosecutions brought in domestic disputes to the point that some victims then find that they cannot withdraw the charges should they wish to effect a reconciliation. Yet there are many reasons why a cohabitant may not want his or her partner prosecuted, as where the victim is financially dependent upon their assailant, particularly if there are children. Pressure is often brought to bear on victims in these situations to withdraw the charge, although the victim, having made a statement and been summoned to give evidence, can be jailed for contempt, however frightened about his or her personal safety, if he or she does not attend court.

7.10 One advantage of calling the police and allowing the perpetrator to be charged is that it will almost certainly result in the court's imposing a bail condition that the defendant must not contact the victim pending trial. This is often an effective way of keeping the violent partner at bay, allowing time to dwell on the seriousness of the situation. On the other hand, prosecution can result in a guilty plea and the matter being dealt with by the magistrates' court on the day after the incident, with nothing more than a fine being imposed, particularly if it is a first offence. This may leave the perpetrator at large, angry and vengeful, placing the partner in a vulnerable position and in need of the additional protection of the civil law. Another difficulty with bail conditions is that a victim may not be made aware that bail conditions have been changed or even that the case has been dealt with. Given that the victim is not a party to the criminal proceedings but merely a witness, victims are often not informed of developments. It also seems that in some cases the existence of bail conditions may be used to justify the refusal of legal aid for civil injunctions (see Crisell, "Injunctions v Bail Conditions" [1995] Fam Law 85) upon the basis that this would involve the unnecessary duplication of proceedings which have the same effect at the expense of public funds. Yet the protection offered by bail conditions is only ever temporary, and is protection which is likely to be withdrawn by the court without even hearing from the victim or giving him or her notice of this. Thus, this line of argument should be fiercely resisted. However, when applying for a certificate for emergency representation (or considering the use of devolved powers to grant such a certificate) a solicitor must enquire whether the police have been informed about the assault and, if so, whether any action will be, or has been, taken. If the police have charged and placed the perpetrator on police bail, depending on the terms of such bail, emergency representation may be refused. If the police have not been informed then the victim may be asked to contact the police first, and only if the police decline to act, will a certificate be granted.

7.11 One other important development in this field is the Protection from Harassment Act 1997, which was aimed at stalkers but applies more widely and creates a summary arrestable offence of harassment. This is defined in s 1 in relation to its effect upon the victim and measured against the objective standard (see s 7(2)) of whether "a reasonable person would have realised that this behaviour would cause the alleged victim to fear the use of violence or to be harassed, alarmed or distressed".

7.12 Section 1 states:

"(1) A person must not pursue a course of conduct—

(a) which amounts to harassment of another, and
(b) which he knows or ought to know amounts to harassment of the other.

(2) For the purposes of this section, the person whose course of conduct is in question ought to know that it amounts to harassment of another if a reasonable person in possession of the same information would think the course of conduct amounted to harassment of the other."

7.13 Thus it is no defence to claim that the defendant was unaware of the harassing nature of their conduct if they ought to have known. It is a defence to show, *inter alia*, that the conduct was reasonable in all the circumstances or necessary for the detection or prevention of a crime (s 1(3)).

7.14 However, to be guilty of an offence under s 2, such conduct must have occurred on at least two occasions (s 7(3)). In *Lau v DPP* [2000] 1 FLR 799, the issue arose whether there had to be a nexus between the two incidents to amount to a "course of conduct" under the Act and the court found that there did. Thus the fewer the occasions and the wider they are spread, the less likely it will be that a finding of harassment can be reasonably made. In this case, only two separate incidents four months apart were proven by the prosecution, with three intervening matters (which would have assisted the claim to a course of conduct) not found to be proved to the court's satisfaction. Again, as illustrated in the more recent case of *R v Hills* [2001] 1 FLR 580, this requirement of a course of conduct also arises in connection with the more serious offence under s 4 (discussed below). Here a conviction for two assaults some six months apart by a cohabitant on his partner of 18 months standing was quashed as, on the evidence the necessary cogent link between the two assaults had not been made out and there was therefore no course of conduct. These two cases vividly illustrate some of the pitfalls and difficulties in using the 1997 Act in domestic violence cases, where the criminal standard of proof applies and evidence will often be no more than the word of one party against the other.

7.15 Once s 1 is made out, then an injunction restraining the conduct can be issued. Section 3 provides that an actual or apprehended breach of s 1 may be the subject of a claim in civil proceedings by the victim and damages may be awarded for among other things "anxiety caused by the harassment". Section 4 of the Act also creates the indictable offence of putting people in fear of violence, which is committed where such a course of conduct has occurred on at least two occasions (note *R v Hills* (above)) and where he or she knows or objectively ought to know the behaviour will put the victim in fear of violence. It carries a maximum penalty of five years' imprisonment and/or a Level 5 fine. This is of potential importance to cohabitants who wish criminal prosecution to be pursued and is again subject to defences of being pursued for the prevention or detection of crime or where it was reasonable for the protection of the offender or another or their property. However, both offences have been criticised for not clearly defining the behaviour sought to be criminalised. It was feared that the lack of a clear statutory definition of the behaviour being targeted may result in courts and juries being unwilling to convict, and this seems to have been born out.

7.16 Any decision made by a victim of domestic violence in relation to pressing charges must be an individual one, but where possible it should be one made in the fullest possible knowledge of the benefits and disadvantages at that time and in the future. It is to be hoped that the new Home Office guidance promoting a zero tolerance arrest policy in such cases, is applied with consideration of the victims genuine wishes, although the removal of the decision to prosecute from the victim is one which in many cases is likely to be welcomed.

(b) Compensation for criminal injury

7.17 A criminal court, on conviction, has power to make a compensation order pursuant to s 35 Powers of Criminal Courts Act 1973 in a domestic violence case where the victim has been injured. However, the defendant's means are taken into account and where the assailant is on a low income an order is unlikely to prove very satisfactory from the victim's point of view. Such orders are usually payable by instalments and their effectiveness is subject to the defendant's regularity of payment.

(c) The Criminal Injuries Compensation Authority

7.18 One advantage of using the criminal law against a violent partner is the possibility of obtaining compensation for injuries under the Criminal Injuries Compensation Scheme. The Criminal Injuries Compensation Act 1995 implemented the scheme on a statutory footing. It also finally succeeded in introducing a tariff basis for assessment of compensation for injuries which applies to all applications received after 1 April 1996, regardless of when the injuries occurred, with the rules of the scheme and the tariffs having been reviewed as regards applications made after 1 April 2001. Thus, the scheme is no longer based on the common law rules for assessment of damages in personal injury cases. As noted in Chapter 5, it is now administered by the Criminal Injuries Compensation Authority (CICA), which replaced the old Board. Claims are assessed by claims officers, reviewed by adjudicators and appeals go to the Criminal Injuries Appeals Panel. The working of the scheme is kept under review by the Secretary of State. From an advisor's point of view, the most important point to note is that applications must be made as soon as possible and in any event within two years of the injury, unless the limit is waived because it is in the interests of justice to do so. The time limit under the pre-1996 scheme had always been three years, in line with that for a civil claim for personal injuries. Compensation is awarded on a tariff basis with twenty-five levels of compensation having currently been specified. A table of the tariff of injuries is appended to the details of the scheme and can be viewed on the CICA website at http://www.cica.gov.uk.

7.19 The scheme does allow a claim for compensation where the victim and the person responsible for the injuries were, at the time of the injuries, living in the same household as members of the same family providing the injury was not sustained prior to 1 October 1979. This definition includes a man and woman who are living together as husband and wife, but not, it seems, same-sex couples who would not in this context (and in contrast to fatal injury cases under the scheme) be regarded as family members, even if they are living in the same household (see para 17 of the scheme).

7.20 However, for the victim to qualify for compensation, the assailant must have been prosecuted, unless the Authority considers there are good reasons why this has not happened. In addition, where the incident involves violence between adults in the family, they must have ceased living together before the application was made and seem unlikely to resume cohabitation again. Where a child is the victim of abuse, the award of compensation must not be against the minor's interests.

7.21 Where a criminal compensation order or a civil award of damages has been made, then any compensation awarded under the scheme will be reduced by the sum received from that other source. If such sums are awarded after compensation has been paid under the scheme, they must be paid over to the Authority.

7.22 Applications for compensation must be made within two years of the incident that gave rise to the injuries, and compensation is awarded on the basis of the tariff injuries table. The only special damages payable relate to loss of earnings and certain restricted out of pocket expenses.

7.23 Claims are limited now to those meriting a minimum award of £1,000. Thus, if a victim has suffered minor bruising and no loss of earnings, he or she may not receive any compensation, as their entitlement is to less than the minimum, after the deduction of any social security payments paid as a direct result of the injuries. The tariff injuries table now gives a guide to the injury threshold at which compensation begins to become payable.

7.24 Advisors should be aware of the existence of the scheme, despite the minimum level rule and will find the CICA website of assistance with any potential claim. Legal costs are not recoverable and where advice is given under the Legal Help scheme, the statutory charge applies and costs are deductible from compensation obtained. Application forms are obtainable from CICA, Tay House, 300 Bath Street, Glasgow G2 4GR, (Tel: 0141-331-2287, Fax 0141-331-5579), and can be found on their website at http://www.cica.gov.uk together with a guide to the new scheme.

7.25 Criminal prosecution may serve only to exacerbate a victim's vulnerability when the partner is once again outside the confines of the criminal justice system, and compensation under the CICA scheme will not of itself remove the threat of violence. Thus additional remedies may be required. Even where the victim wishes the criminal law to be used, civil proceedings may also be appropriate. The housing situation may also need urgent consideration by the victim's legal advisor. The numerous inconsistencies between the various civil remedies available to victims of domestic violence have been heavily criticised over a number of years. Many of the difficulties with the old legislation from the point of view of cohabitants were outlined in the first edition of this book (see Barlow, 1992, pages 114–124). In its report *Domestic Violence and Occupation of the Family Home*, (Law Com No 207, 1992) the Law Commission described the existing remedies as "complex, confusing and lack[ing] integration" (para 1.2). The report's recommendations have largely been included in Part IV FLA 1996, subject to a greater distinction being drawn in relation to new-style occupation orders between married and cohabiting couples as will be discussed below. Whilst the new legislation has removed many of the sources of complaint with respect to the old law, and has undoubtedly extended the classes of victims who can avail themselves of its protection, it has unfortunately failed to fully integrate the role of the police, either in assisting the victim in applying for civil remedies as noted above, or in facilitating consistent enforcement of such remedies through the power of arrest. Nonetheless, as shall be seen, progress has been made, although perhaps not as much as had been hoped the reforms would achieve.

2 Civil remedies

7.26 Part IV FLA 1996 (with the exception of s 60) came into force in October 1997 ahead of the earlier Parts of the Act. It provides for the first time a uniform code of domestic violence remedies available, in the main, in all courts with jurisdiction in family proceedings. The introduction of this legislation was not without drama. The Conservative government's small majority enabled eight back-bench Conservative MPs (prompted by the *Daily Mail*, see eg 23 October 1995) to exert enough pressure to get the Family Homes and Domestic Violence Bill (FHDVB 1995) withdrawn due to their concerns that privileges relating to the family home and previously reserved to married couples were being extended to unmarried cohabitants. Although some concessions were made to this point of view in the revised legislation reintroduced in Part IV FLA 1996, it remained relatively faithful to the intentions of the Law Commission. The new law was arguably a great step forward in terms of its approach, which is much more victim and child centred than its predecessors, concentrating on the harm being suffered within the household, and removing to some degree the discrimination against cohabitants, and most notably against gay cohabitants, in this area of law. It repealed and replaced the whole of the Domestic Violence and Matrimonial Proceedings Act 1976 (DVA 1976), together with the relevant parts of the Domestic Proceedings and Magistrates Courts Act 1978 (DPMCA 1978) (ie ss 16–18, s 28(2) and para 53 to Sch 2). In addition, the whole of the Matrimonial Homes Act 1983 (MHA 1983) was repealed, although much of this was re-enacted in amended form in the new Act. The 1996 Act also aimed to plug a serious gap in the previous law by providing a procedure for the transfer of tenancies between cohabitants (other than gay cohabitants) who do not have children of the relationship, but in contrast to the withdrawn 1995 Bill, it failed to extend s 17 of the Married Women's Property Act 1882 (MWPA 1882) beyond formerly engaged couples to cohabitants, which is to be regretted.

(a) The new law – Part IV Family Law Act 1996

7.27 Part IV of the Act introduced two types of order:

(i)   non-molestation orders (s 42) and
(ii) occupation orders (ss 33–4).

7.28 Non-molestation orders are available to specified classes of applicant called "associated" persons, defined in s 62(3), and ranging far beyond spouses and cohabitants who had exclusive access to the statutory remedy under the old law. The occupation order remedy is in a sense more complex than the old-style ouster and exclusion orders it replaced. Different types of occupation orders are available depending, firstly, on whether or not the applicant is an "entitled" applicant, entitled in their own right to occupy the family home, in which case a s 33 occupation order can be sought by any "associated" person; and, secondly, ss 35 and 36 occupation orders where the respondent but not the applicant is entitled to occupy the family home, in which case the remedy is limited to former spouses, heterosexual cohabitants and former cohabitants who are "non-entitled" applicants. There are also two residual categories of occupation order where neither party is entitled to occupy under ss 37 and 38. These are available to former spouses and cohabitants/former cohabitants respectively as discussed below. As will be explained, different criteria must be applied by the court to different categories of applicant when determining their applications.

7.29 Although provisionally both non-molestation and occupation orders are available in all courts, s 59 denies magistrates' courts jurisdiction to hear cases involving determination of a dispute as to beneficial interests or occupation rights in respect of a property. Where there is no dispute, or where it is not necessary to determine the dispute, the magistrates' court does have jurisdiction. This means that, in contrast to their position under the old law, cohabitants are able to apply to the magistrates' court for domestic violence remedies. It is also open to the Lord Chancellor to specify proceedings under the Act which may only be commenced in a specified level of court (s 57) as is the case with Children Act proceedings.

(i) Non-molestation orders

7.30 The aim of such an order remains to restrain a party from molesting the applicant or any relevant child. In line with the Law Commission's recommendations, the term "non-molestation order" was retained in the 1996 Act and is designed to convey that violence *per se* is not a pre-requisite for obtaining an order. There is no definition of "molestation" contained in the Act; a deliberate omission designed to ensure that the current level of protection is not reduced. Thus, authorities such as *Vaughan v Vaughan* [1973] 1 WLR 1159, where "pestering", by a man who called upon his estranged wife morning and evening, at home and at work, making a thorough nuisance of himself, and *Spencer v Camacho* (1983) 4 FLR 662, where, following a series of other incidents a man rifling through his partner's handbag, were both held to amount to molestation, remain good law.

7.31 In essence, where any conduct harassing the victim, violent or non-violent, which warrants intervention by the court could and can still be the subject of an injunction, and both physical and mental harassment fall within the scope of the 1996 Act as they did under the 1976 legislation. However, in *Johnson v Walton* [1990] 1 FLR 350, the court took the view under the 1976 Act that in addition to the actual harassment not amounting to violence, there must also be an intent to cause distress or alarm for it to amount to molestation. In most cases, such an intention will be apparent, yet is questionable as to whether the difference in approach between actual violence and harassment should be sustained. If, where there has been actual violence, the harm caused rather than the actual intention is the test, as decided in *Wooton v Wooton* [1984] FLR 871, where violence during epileptic seizures amounted to molestation, why should a similar harm-based approach not be taken to other forms of harassment? It is also hoped that non-molestation orders will be thought appropriate even where the parties intend to continue to live together, in contrast to the approach taken in *F v F (protection from violence: continuing cohabitation)* [1989] 2 FLR 451, where a non-molestation order was refused on these grounds. There is nothing in the wording of the 1996 Act to indicate that such restriction was intended, although this was equally true of the old law. Such restrictive interpretation appears unnecessary, as there may be situations where parties genuinely feel that a non-molestation order may be an effective means of saving a relationship from further violence and they should be given the opportunity to test this with the protection of an order.

7.32 Section 42(6) also makes it clear that molestation of both a general or specific nature may be prohibited by an order, and advisors in drafting orders should consider both specifying particular types as behaviour from which protection is required whilst at the same time also prohibiting molestation of a more general nature, to maximise the victim's protection.

I CRITERIA

7.33 In terms of the criteria for granting a non-molestation order, the Commission's recommendation that a broad statutory criteria as opposed to an attempt at exhaustive definition has been adopted. Consequently, s 42(5) provides that, in deciding whether to exercise its powers under this section and, if so, in what manner, the court shall have regard to all the circumstances including "the need to secure the health, safety and well-being" of the applicant and any relevant child. The term "well-being", it is hoped, is sufficiently wide to ensure that courts do not feel restricted to making orders only in cases where violence or threat of violence can be proven. What has become clear following the high-profile case of *C v C (non-molestation order: jurisdiction)* [1998] 1 FLR 554 is that the motive for the conduct allegedly amounting to molestation may be relevant to whether or not the court is prepared to grant a non-molestation order. In this case the husband's application for a non-molestation order preventing his estranged wife from making revelations about her husband to the press was refused on the basis that her intention was not to harass him but rather to give a public airing to her side of the story. Thus in contrast to the approach of the Protection from Harassment Act 1997 which considers the effect of the conduct upon the victim, here the respondent's actions had to amount to more than an intrusion of the applicant's privacy in order to constitute molestation, which it was said must be "some quite deliberate conduct which is aimed at a high degree of harassment of the other party" (per Sir Stephen Brown at pp 556H–557A).

7.34 The term "relevant" child is defined in s 62(2) and extends beyond children residing with the applicant who were protected by the 1976 Act. It includes any child who lives or might reasonably be expected to live with either party to the proceedings, any child in respect of whom an order under the Adoption Act 1976 or the Children Act 1989 is in question in the proceedings and any other child whose interests the court considers relevant. This is wide and might encompass a situation where, for example, a child came to stay with an applicant on contact visits, or was cared for during the day by an applicant, although did not reside with them.

II WHO MAY APPLY?

7.35 *Own motion powers* A non-molestation order (in contrast to an occupation order) may be granted by a court in any family proceedings to which the respondent is a party without an application having been made for one. Where the court considers that an order should be made for the benefit of any other party to the proceedings or any relevant child, it can of its own motion make a non-molestation order (see s 42(2)(b)). This, of course, follows the approach found in the Children Act 1989 with respect to the making of s 8 orders and the definition of family proceedings in ss 63(1) and (2) FLA 1996 follows that in ss 8(3) and (4) of the 1989 Act. Family proceedings include actions involving:

- The inherent jurisdiction of the High Court;
- Parts II and IV Family Law Act 1996;
- Matrimonial Causes Act 1973;
- Adoption Act 1976;
- Domestic Proceedings and Magistrates Court Act 1978;
- Part III Matrimonial and Family Proceedings Act 1984;
- Parts I, II and IV Children Act 1989; and
- Section 30 Human Fertilisation and Embryology Act 1990.

It should be noted that a non-molestation order made in other family proceedings will cease to have effect should these proceedings be withdrawn or dismissed (s 42(8)).

7.36 *Eligible applicants* Freestanding applications under Part IV FLA 1996 may, of course, also be made by eligible applicants. The range of potential applicants under the 1996 Act is far wider than spouses and cohabitants living as husband and wife encompassed within the 1976 Act and this is perhaps the most radical of the Act's reforms. However, as discussed below, it has not included all the categories of applicant recommended by the Law Commission, and has followed the recommendations of the Home Affairs Select Committee made in March 1993 in this regard (see [1993] Fam Law 307 for summary). The Act does, however, remedy some of the more glaring defects of the old legislation.

7.37 Those entitled to apply for non-molestation orders must be "associated" with the respondent. "Associated" persons are defined by s 62(3) to include:

- spouses and former spouses;
- heterosexual cohabitants (s 62(1)(a) defines "cohabitants" as a man and a woman living as husband and wife, thus excluding gay cohabitants) and former cohabitants;
- those living or having lived in the same household otherwise than merely by reason of one of them being the other's employee, tenant, lodger or boarder. This could include gay cohabitants;
- those falling within a defined group of close relatives, in respect of whom cohabitants are equated with spouses for the purpose of ascertaining the relationship (see s 63(1));
- those who have at any time agreed to marry each other;
- parents with a child of the relationship or a child in respect of whom they both have or have had parental responsibility;
- those who are both parties to the same family proceedings other than proceedings brought under Part IV FLA 1996.

7.38 Furthermore in *G v F (non-molestation order: jurisdiction)* [2000] 2 FCR 638, Wall J. held that where it was not entirely clear whether or not the parties were associated, s 62(3) should not be interpreted so as to exclude borderline cases but should be given purposive construction to offer as much protection as possible to domestic violence victims. Here a couple who, for social security purposes, had represented that they had not been cohabiting but had spent several nights a week together were found by Justices at first instance not to be associated, leaving the woman without a remedy under the Act. On appeal, the Family Division found that the evidence when viewed as a whole was sufficient to support the proposition that the parties were cohabitants within the meaning of the Act as three of the "signposts" set out in *Crake v Supplementary Benefits Commission* [1982] 1 All ER 498 were present – ie sexual relationship, living in the same household and a joint bank account.

7.39 Whilst the statutory definition includes a far wider range of applicant than under the previous law, one important and arguably very vulnerable group have been denied protection. The Law Commission recommended (see para 3.24 Law Com No 207, 1992) that persons in a romantic relationship such as boyfriend/girlfriend, who have had a sexual relationship (whether or not involving sexual intercourse), should have a remedy against molestation. However, as they do not now fall within the definition of "associated" persons, they cannot avail themselves of the protection of the Act unless they happen to fall into one of the categories of associated persons specified in s 62(3). This leaves those who have had a relationship but have not had a child together, not cohabited, not lived in the same household nor made an agreement to marry relying on the often inadequate remedies offered by the law of tort (see para 7.115 below) or the criminal law. This would have been the position of the applicant in *G v F* (above) had they not have been found to have been cohabiting on appeal. Thus, it is to be regretted that although they are a group whom it was acknowledged by the Law Commission may well be subject to behaviour by their partner or former partner which amounts to molestation, and have as great if not greater need for protection, they are still without a remedy under the 1996 Act.

7.40 From the perspective of cohabitants, there have however been significant strides made. Firstly, although the Law Commission did not include same-sex couples within the definition of "cohabitants" and, indeed, specifically excluded them (s 62(1)(a)), they do fall within the more general category of those who have lived together in the same household other than on a commercial basis. The Law Commission foresaw that the test for determining whether people are "living together in the same household" would be that developed in the matrimonial law context to establish the degree of community of life between them (see for example *Fuller v Fuller* [1973] 2 All ER 650 and *Mouncer v Mouncer* [1972] 1 WLR 321). Although there may be difficulties in interpretation of the definition of the same household with regard to persons who have not had a sexual relationship, such as friends who are also flat-sharers, it is submitted that in the case of gay cohabitants they should be able to show that they are or have been living in the same household. Thus, although all the authorities relate to married or heterosexual cohabiting couples, the existence of an intimate relationship together with shared meals and domestic arrangements should bring them within the definition. Indeed, the Law Commission report specifically refers to homosexual couples as falling within this "family relationship" in the broader sense in its report (para 3.19).

7.41 The extension of the categories of eligible applicants has overcome several difficulties for which the old law was heavily criticised. Thus the inclusion of both former cohabitants and former spouses obviates some of the more glaring inadequacies of the previous legislative scheme. In addition, the fact that the "same household" category includes those who *have lived* in the same household and does not require people to remain living in the same household in order to take advantage of the law avoids the need for strained interpretation by the courts to reach a just decision, as was arguably the case in *Adeoso v Adeoso* [1980] 1 WLR 1535, CA.

7.42 It is worthy of note that whereas s 44 stipulates the means by which an agreement to marry must be proven (it must be evidenced in writing unless it can satisfy the court that there has been the gift of an engagement ring or an engagement ceremony witnessed by at least one person), there is no statutory guidance on acceptable evidence of cohabitation. There is clearly no minimum period of cohabitation or, indeed, of living in the same household required before an applicant within these categories of associated person may apply. However, should an applicant be unable to show that they are a person associated with the respondent on the grounds of cohabitation, advisors should always clarify whether they may fall within one of the other categories of associated person set out above. Where parties are associated, it seems that they apply for a non-molestation order even though the harassment is not prompted by their family relationship. Thus in *Chechi v Bashir* [1999] 2 FLR 489 in the case of two brothers, who were therefore associated, the court had jurisdiction to grant a non-molestation order even though their dispute concerned business matters, although in fact the order was refused.

7.43 Another significant change introduced by the 1996 Act is that children under 16 may apply for a non-molestation or occupation order but only with leave of the court. This may be granted where the court is satisfied that the child has sufficient understanding to make the proposed order (s 43). Given that non-molestation orders may be made against close relatives, whether or not living in the same household, it is logical that children with sufficient understanding should have the same *locus standi* here as they have in respect of applications under the Children Act 1989. Applications by children for leave have to be made to the High Court pursuant to s 43 FLA 1996.

7.44 One lacuna, which may affect cohabitants, is the inability of a person to apply for a non-molestation order against their partner's former partner/spouse. The formation of new relationships often sparks vengeful acts amounting to violence or harassment against the new partner as well as the former spouse or cohabitant. Given that they are not associated unless both are parties to the same family proceedings, such molestation would have to be addressed either through the law of tort or the criminal or civil remedies available under the Protection from Harassment Act 1997.

(ii) Occupation orders

7.45 Part IV of the 1996 Act replaced both ouster orders under the DVA 1976 and the Matrimonial Homes Act 1983 and exclusion orders under the DPMCA 1978 with a new form of order known as occupation orders. These may be either declaratory or regulatory and are detailed in ss 33–41 FLA 1996. Whilst the changes brought in by Part IV were widely welcomed, many feel that in practice not as much has been achieved as had been hoped (see eg Humphries, "Occupation Orders Revisited" [2001] *Family Law* 542). As will be seen, the most significant distinction under the provision is between "entitled" and "non-entitled" applicants. Both can obtain occupation orders, although the ability to seek them, as well as the scope of the order is more restricted in the case of non-entitled applicants. Although the 1996 remedies put heterosexual cohabitants on a more equal footing with spouses in most respects, there is a marked distinction between the criteria to be applied in the case of non-entitled applicants and the lack of commitment of marriage must always be a relevant factor (s 41). It should be noted that occupation orders are only available to same-sex cohabitants who can show that they are "entitled" applicants.

I SECTION 33 OCCUPATION ORDERS AND ENTITLED APPLICANTS

7.46 To be able to apply for a s 33 occupation order, an applicant must be able to show two things: firstly, that they have an entitlement to occupy the accommodation and, secondly, that the accommodation either was or was intended to be their home jointly with a person with whom they are associated. Section 33(1) defines entitlement to occupy, either through having a legal or beneficial estate or interest, or by virtue of contractual or statutory rights including "matrimonial homes rights" defined by s 30 and not extending to cohabitants. Therefore, both heterosexual and gay cohabitants who are sole or joint owners, or tenants (whether contractual or statutory) in the rented sector may apply for an order against their partner or former partner regardless of their partner's legal status in relation to occupation of the home. This is because an order can be sought against any person with whom the applicant is associated within the meaning of s 62(3) and, as discussed above, gay couples will fall within the "same household" category of association.

II NATURE OF THE S 33 OCCUPATION ORDER

7.47 Section 33(3) sets out the nature of s 33 occupation orders, which can do any of the following:

(a) enforce the applicant's entitlement to remain in occupation as against the respondent;

(b) require the respondent to permit the applicant to enter and remain in the dwelling-house or part of it;

(c) regulate the occupation of the dwelling house by either or both parties;

(d) where the respondent has entitlement to occupy the home other than by virtue of matrimonial home rights, prohibit, suspend or restrict the exercise by him/her of his/her rights to occupy the dwelling-house;

(e) where the respondent has matrimonial home rights in respect of the dwelling house, restrict or terminate those rights;

(f) require the respondent to leave the dwelling-house or part of it; and

(g) exclude the respondent from a defined area in which the dwelling-house is included.

7.48 The court therefore has great flexibility in terms of the type of declaratory and regulatory orders that can be made and extends to all entitled applicants remedies that were previously only all available to spouses under the MHA 1983. It must be seen as a great improvement that the nature of the order that can be made is no longer purely dependent upon whether or not the parties are married to each other or upon the court to which the applicant happens to have applied. It should be noted, as discussed below, that additional provisions in respect of matters such as maintenance of the property, taking care of furniture and payment of rent, mortgage or other outgoings can be included in a s 33 occupation order (see s 40 and para 7.81 ff below), although this is one area where the effectiveness of the 1996 legislation has proved not to be as effective as had been hoped.

III CRITERIA FOR MAKING A S 33 OCCUPATION ORDER

7.49 A major distinction between occupation orders and ouster injunctions under the DVA 1976 was thought to be that a violent situation was not a necessary pre-requisite to the making of an order, and that orders could be made more readily.

In *Wiseman v Simpson* [1988] 1 FLR 490, the Court of Appeal had emphasised the "draconian nature" of ouster orders under the old law, restricting them in effect to extreme situations. Ironically, the 1996 Act has now been interpreted in a similar vein. In *Chalmers v John* [1999] 1 FLR 392, Thorpe LJ, indicated that in his view there had been little or no change:

> "The gravity of an order requiring a respondent to vacate a family home, an order overriding proprietary rights, was recognised in cases under the Domestic Violence and Matrimonial Proceedings Act 1976 and a string of authorities in this court emphasise the Draconian nature of such an order, and that it should be restricted to exceptional cases. I do not myself think that the wider statutory provisions contained in the Family Law Act 1996 obliterate that authority. The order remains Draconian ... It remains an order that overrides proprietary rights and it seems to me that it is an order that is only justified in exceptional circumstances."(at p 397 E–F)

7.50 Sections 33(6) sets out the matters to which the court must have regard in considering whether to make an occupation order but these are subject to a "balance of harm" test introduced in s 33(7). The court is directed to have regard to all the circumstances including:

(a)   the respective housing needs and housing resources of the parties and relevant child;

(b)   the respective financial resources of the parties;

(c)   the likely effect of any order, or of any decision by the court not to exercise its powers to make an order on the health, safety or well-being of the parties and of any relevant child, and;

(d)   the conduct of the parties in relation to each other and otherwise.

7.51 However, the application of these standard criteria is subject to s 33(7), which states that if it appears to the court that the applicant or any relevant child is likely to suffer significant harm if an order is not made, then the court *shall* make the order unless:

(a)   the respondent or any relevant child is likely to suffer significant harm if the order is made; and

(b)   the harm likely to be suffered by the respondent or child in that event is as great or greater than the harm likely to be suffered by the applicant or child if the order is not made.

7.52 This is known as "the balance of harm test" and it creates a presumption in favour of an order where a child or the applicant is likely to suffer significant harm without one. This can only be avoided where it can be shown that *as great or greater* harm is likely to be suffered by the respondent or child if an order is not made. The interaction of these two subsections was considered by Thorpe LJ in *Chalmers v John* (above), who indicated that they implied a two-tier approach. Firstly a court must decide whether the applicant or a relevant child is likely to suffer significant harm attributable to the conduct of the respondent if an order is not made. If it concludes in the negative, then the making of an order is discretionary in accordance with the criteria in s 33(6). If on the other hand, it considers that significant harm is likely, only then must it make an order unless balancing likely harm to the respondent against the likely harm to the applicant under s 33(7), the likely harm to the respondent is as great or greater, in which case it reverts to being a matter of discretion for the court.

7.53 The term "significant harm" is borrowed from the CA 1989 and it was confirmed in *Chalmers v John* (at p 398) that its meaning in s 33(7), coincided with that in s 31 CA 1989 and considered by Booth J in *Humberside County Council v B* [1993] 1 FLR 257, namely harm that was "considerable, noteworthy or important". "Harm" is defined in s 63(1) FLA 1996 as meaning ill-treatment or impairment of health and, in the case of a child, development. What is significant may be judged in the context of its effect on the victim and is clearly not confined to physical health. It must, however, be attributable to the respondent's conduct but does not have to be intentional conduct (*G v G (occupation order: conduct)* [2000] 2 FLR 36). However, once an applicant has reached this threshold of significant harm, then the occupation order must be made unless the respondent or relevant child would suffer equal or worse significant harm if the order were to be made. As was noted in the second edition of this book, "Depending on where the threshold is placed, this is potentially a welcome shift towards a harm centred approach to the application of this remedy" (pp 126-127).

7.54 In *B v B (occupation order)* [1999] 1 FLR 715, heard after *Chalmers v John*, Butler-Sloss LJ indicated that men or women who treat their partners with domestic violence causing injury or driving them from the family home will generally be made subject to an occupation order (at p 724F-H). This case also illustrates how the balance of harm test should work in practice. Here, the parties were married and joint tenants of their council home in which they lived with the husband's six-year-old son by a previous relationship and their own baby daughter. The wife was driven to leave the home with the daughter by the husband's violence and moved to bed and breakfast accommodation, where she would have to stay until an offer of alternative accommodation was made by the council in several months time. The husband and son remained in the home, located near the son's school. He had been advised by the council that should an occupation order be made against him, he would be considered intentionally homeless and would face either a move away from the area to only temporary accommodation, forcing the son to change schools. His only other option was the placement of his son in local authority accommodation. The Court of Appeal, overturning the occupation order made against the husband at first instance, held that whilst the trial judge had been entitled to find that the wife and baby were likely to suffer significant harm attributable to the husband's conduct if an order was not made, he had not taken sufficient account of the son's interests and thus had not correctly applied the balance of harm test:

". . .whilst in no sense underestimating the difficulties and frustrations of living with and caring for a toddler in bed and breakfast accommodation, the essential security for a child of [the baby's] age is being with her mother. Furthermore. . .[the wife's] residence in bed and breakfast accommodation is likely to be temporary. For [the son] the position is much more complex. His security depends not just on being in the care of his father, but on his other day-to-day support systems, of which his home and his school are plainly the most important." (at pp 723-4 per Butler-Sloss LJ).

7.55 Nonetheless, *Chalmers v John* has seemingly placed the harm threshold back exactly where it was under the old law, limiting both the granting of occupation orders and the application of the presumption in favour of an order in s 33(7) to "extreme" cases, at least. The shift in this direction can be seen to have been prompted at least in part by the facts in *Chalmers v John*. The parties were cohabitants of some 25 years standing whose relationship was described as "tempestuous". They had two children, one of 25 and the other only seven. Despite several incidents of violence over the years in connection with which both parties had suffered minor injuries, there had been police involvement and the respondent had been prosecuted unsuccessfully, Thorpe LJ took the view that this was "in the range of domestic violence a slight case" (at p 396H). It was not one where the applicant and the younger child (who had by then left the family home and moved to temporary accommodation much further from the child's school) were likely to suffer significant harm if the order was not made. Thus the court, applying the standard criteria, declined to make an occupation order in the applicant's favour, not even one regulating occupation of the home as between the parties. The fact that other matters of dispute between the parties were to be heard by the court within two months was also an influential factor, with Thorpe LJ commenting, "As a matter of generality, it seems to me that a court should be cautious to make a definitive order at an interlocutory stage with a final hearing only six or seven weeks distant" (at pp 396–397).

7.56 The reluctance to make occupation orders other than in extreme cases, where there has been physical violence, was again endorsed by Thorpe LJ in the more recent case of *G v G (occupation order: conduct)* [2000] 2 FLR 36, where he made clear that an occupation order could only be warranted where something over and above the normal tensions surrounding the process of relationship breakdown exist. Here he reiterated (at p 41):

> "...this was not a case in which the wife had suffered any violence at the hands of the husband. It has been said time and time again that orders of exclusion are Draconian and only to be made in exceptional cases."

7.57 At least in this case, the imposition of conditions of occupation under s 33(3)(c) by the trial judge was endorsed. Again in *Re Y (children) (occupation order)* [2000] 2 FCR 470, Sedley LJ indicated that occupation orders should be seen as "a last resort in an intolerable situation" (at p 480). Overall, short of further legislation or a change of direction by the House of Lords in future cases, it seems that little has changed in terms of the availability of occupation orders in the domestic violence context, although advisors should seriously consider whether an applicant's situation can be improved by imposing conditions on each parties' continued occupation of the home.

7.58 Another possible exception may arise where, although there is not violence as between family members, the granting of an occupation order would serve another meritorious purpose, such as promoting the interests of a child. Thus in *S v F (occupation order)* [2000] 1 FLR 255, a case where no violence was alleged between the parties, an occupation order was granted to a father enabling him to continue to occupy the London family home with his son who wished to remain in London to complete his education and therefore did not wish to move away from London with his mother and siblings. Outside the domestic violence context at least then, occupation orders may have provided more scope for regulation of the family home than permitted by the predecessors.

7.59 The standard criteria in s 33(6)(a)–(d) are common to all occupation orders. They are those which, broadly speaking, the courts had been taking into account in making ouster orders under the DVA 1976 since *Richards v Richards* [1984] AC 174 required courts to apply the criteria set out in s 1(3) MHA 1983 to such applications, and which were extended to applications by cohabitants in *Lee v Lee* [1984] FLR 243. The housing needs and resources of the parties and any affected child are obviously critical, and financial needs and resources affect the ability to secure accommodation elsewhere. The current homelessness legislation now found in Part VII Housing Act 1996, which reduces the duties of local housing authorities to providing only temporary accommodation for a maximum period of two years to those with priority need, has increased the attractiveness of staying in the family home, and no longer does a party with priority need have automatic access to alternative permanent accommodation, although the Homelessness Bill 2001 seeks to reverse this as noted in Chapter 3. In terms of how the court will exercise its discretion in non-mandatory (ie s 33(6) not s 33(7)) cases, it is probably still the case that the court is more likely to grant an occupation order excluding the respondent if the applicant can show that the respondent can easily find other accommodation with a member of his or her family, or has the means to rent other accommodation (see *Baggott v Baggott* [1986] 1 FLR 377).

7.60 The 1996 Act criteria can be seen to focus more clearly on the effect of the harm likely to be suffered, and this was certainly the Law Commission's intention. It was not, though, their intention that the conduct of the parties, a relevant factor under s 1(3) MHA 1983, should also be included, precisely because it wanted the harm suffered to be the guiding principle. However, it was added in the passage of the Bill through Parliament and has obviously opened the door for the minutiae of a relationship to be included in affidavits and debated in court. Generally speaking, the courts have tried to minimise the amount of public "mud-slinging" undertaken to that which is necessary. However, the drafting of the statute seems to encourage evidence of both good and bad conduct and, given the potentially long term effects of this order and consequent repercussions for an excluded party, the courts may have difficulty in limiting what is put before them, as was seen in both *Chalmers v John* and *G v G*. Nonetheless, the relevance of conduct should not distract the courts from dealing quickly and appropriately with such cases.

IV DURATION OF S 33 ORDERS

7.61 Occupation orders under this section may be made for a specified period, or until a specified event or further order (s 33(10)). Thus, in contrast to ss 35, 36, 37 and 38, where an occupation order is limited to a maximum period of six months in the first instance, and also to the *Practice Direction* [1978] 1 WLR 1123 under the old law limiting the making of ouster orders to a period of three months in the first instance, no statutory time limit has been imposed where an applicant is entitled.

V NON-ENTITLED APPLICANTS AND S 36 OCCUPATION ORDERS

7.62 The House of Lords finally decided in *Davis v Johnson* [1979] AC 264 that cohabitants who had no estate or interest in the family home were able to obtain ouster orders against their partner under the DVA 1976. However, their legal position as against third parties remained precarious, and difficulties arose as a result of the court's inability under this statute to make orders, for example with respect to payment of outgoings in respect of the property or removal of furniture. Part IV FLA 1996, whilst falling short of automatically conferring matrimonial homes rights upon all cohabitants, considerably enhances the position of what it terms "non-entitled" cohabitants, former cohabitants and former spouses in this regard. Indeed, given that a violent situation is not a pre-requisite for the making of an occupation order, it may be a useful tool for a deserted non-entitled former cohabitant who quickly needs to assert their status in relation to a third party such as a mortgagee or landlord. There seems to be no reason why orders cannot be made to safeguard the position of an applicant in this way pending final resolution of matters between the parties, and the decision in *S v F* (above) shows that occupation orders may be made to regulate occupation of the family home outside the domestic violence context. However, despite the Law Commission's recognition of the unsatisfactory nature of the previous law as concerned heterosexual cohabitants, former cohabitants and former spouses (see para 4.15), it has been prepared to leave same-sex cohabitants, who have no estate or interest in the family home vested in their partner (arguably a very vulnerable group), without a remedy.

VI WHO MAY APPLY FOR A S 36 ORDER?

7.63 Applications are limited to non-entitled cohabitants and former cohabitants (defined heterosexually in s 62(1)(a)) and do *not* extend to any other category of "associated" persons. Non-entitled former spouses may apply for a s 35 occupation order, which is subject to criteria similar to that applicable to s 33 orders including the balance of harm test where a s 35(5) occupation order is to be made (s 35(8)).

7.64 Where one cohabitant or former cohabitant has a legal or statutory right of occupation as defined by s 36(1)(a) FLA 1996 in respect of the family home and is thus entitled to occupy it, but their partner/former partner has no such right, then, provided they live or lived together as husband and wife or intended to do so, in that dwelling-house, the partner without a right of occupation may apply for a s 36 occupation order as against their partner or former partner. There is no qualifying period of cohabitation required for applicants to be able to avail themselves of this remedy, but proof of cohabitation may become an issue as was the case in *G v F* (above), although here the court indicated eligibility for domestic violence remedies should be construed inclusively rather than restrictively.

7.65 Where a person claims to have an equitable interest in the home or the proceeds of sale thereof, but has no legal estate, they may be treated as having no right to occupy for the purpose of applying under s 36, without prejudice to the right of any such person to apply under s 33 if such a right to occupy does exist.

VII NATURE OF A S 36 OCCUPATION ORDER

7.66 By ss 36(3) and (4), depending on whether or not the applicant is in occupation, every s 36 occupation order must contain a provision either giving the applicant the right not to be evicted or excluded from the dwelling-house or part of it by the respondent and prohibiting the respondent from evicting or excluding the applicant during the period of the order, or giving the applicant the right to enter into and occupy the dwelling-house for the period specified in the order and requiring the respondent to permit the exercise of that right. Thus, for the period of the order, the occupant is given personal rights of occupation equivalent to the matrimonial homes rights set out in s 30(2) as against the respondent. In addition, a s 36 occupation order may by virtue of s 36(5) contain any of the provisions in s 33(3)(c), (d), (f) and (g) ("restriction or exclusion provisions") as listed at para 7.47, regulating the occupation by one or both parties, restricting or suspending the exercise of the respondent's right to occupy, requiring the respondent to leave all or part of the dwelling-house and/or excluding the respondent from a defined area.

7.67 In deciding whether or not to include a restriction or exclusion provision, s 36(7) directs the court to have regard to matters specified in s 36(6)(a)–(d), which are the standard criteria also found in s 33(6), These are, namely, the housing needs and resources of the parties or any relevant child, the financial needs and resources of the parties, the likely effect of any order or decision not to make an order on the health, safety or well-being of the parties and any relevant child and the conduct of the parties in relation to each other. In addition, it must have regard to the question posed in the balance of harm test as contained in s 33(7) (para 7.51 above). However, in contrast to the position of entitled applicants and non-entitled former spouses it does *not* require the court to impose such a provision where it appears that an applicant or relevant child is likely to suffer significant harm if it is not included. This remains a matter for the court's discretion and is an example of how revisions made in Part IV FLA 1996 sharpened the distinctions between the remedies available to cohabitants as opposed to spouses following the withdrawal of the FHDVB 1995.

7.68 A major change to the position of a successful applicant for a s 36 occupation order as opposed to the position of a non-entitled cohabitant who obtained an ouster injunction under the 1976 Act, is contained in s 36(13) of the 1996 Act. This, for the first time, actually extends to cohabitants, former cohabitants and former spouses, in whose favour a s 36 occupation order has been made, some of the effects of matrimonial homes rights protection as set out in s 30(3)–(6). This only lasts for the period of the occupation order, a maximum of six months in the first instance, extendible only once for a further maximum six-month period. The rights in this context are personal and do not operate as a charge on the respondent's estate in the same way as matrimonial homes rights do pursuant to s 31 and thus cannot be registered as a Class F land charge or a notice under the Land Registration Act 1925, although, of course, the applicant will be in actual occupation.

7.69 The effect of s 36(13) is perhaps most striking in relation to the applicant whose partner or former partner is a tenant as it elevates for some purposes the occupant's status to that of occupation by a spouse. This, together with s 40 (see below), enables the occupant to make rent and mortgage payments or other outgoings without fear of them being refused on the grounds of their lack of legal status. It particularly avoids the problem of statutory tenants under the Rent Act 1977 and the Rent (Agriculture) Act 1976, meets the principal home test for HA 1985 and Part I, HA 1988 (discussed further in Chapter 10) as well as dealing with the position where occupation is under a trust. In all these cases, the non-entitled applicant's occupation under a s 36 order will be treated as if it were occupation by the entitled respondent. Thus, whereas a non-spouse in whose favour an ouster injunction had been made under the DVA 1976, and who occupied accommodation in which they had no estate or interest, was completely vulnerable to a possession action by a third party such as a landlord for non-payment of rent, this is no longer the case for cohabitants, former cohabitants and former spouses. Section 36(13) now gives them the right contained in s 30(3) to make payments for rent or other outgoings in respect of the accommodation to third parties, regardless of whether any order to make such payments has been made pursuant to s 40 (see below).

7.70 Thus, whilst falling short of simply giving non-entitled cohabitants s 30 matrimonial homes rights for all purposes, and despite, as developed below, having made concessions to drawing sharper distinctions between the married and unmarried applicant, Part IV FLA 1996 has resolved many of the difficulties of non-entitled heterosexual cohabitants.

VIII CRITERIA FOR MAKING S 36 OCCUPATION ORDERS

7.71 In addition to the common criteria set out in s 33(6)(a)–(d) and repeated in s 36(6)(a)–(d), other factors must also be taken into account under s 36 and thus the applicant arguably has a more difficult task than under s 33. Thus, the standard criteria of all the circumstances, including the housing needs and resources of the parties or any relevant child, the financial needs and resources of the parties, the likely effect of any order or decision not to make an order on the health, safety or well-being of the parties and any relevant child and the conduct of the parties in relation to each other apply and, as discussed above, the ability of the respondent to find alternative accommodation will be a very important factor. However, when considering a s 36 application, the court must, in the case of cohabitants and former cohabitants, also have regard to further matters specified in s 36(6)(e)–(i):

(e)   the nature of their relationship;
(f)   the length of time during which they have lived together as husband and wife;
(g)   whether there are or have been children of both parties or in respect of whom both have or had parental responsibility;
(h)   the length of time that has elapsed since the parties ceased to live together;
(i)   the existence of any pending proceedings between the parties:

(i)   for orders for financial relief against parents under para 1(2)(d) or (e) to Sch 1 CA 1989; and

(ii)   relating to the legal or beneficial ownership of the dwelling house.

7.72 It is probably likely that the closer the relationship approximates to a marriage with children, the more likely it is that an application will be successful, although the degree of harm likely to be suffered by the applicant and any relevant child, which may not be a child of the relationship, must also be a powerful factor.

7.73 Furthermore, s 41 goes on to require the court to have regard to the fact that they have not given each other the commitment involved in marriage, when required to consider the nature of the parties' relationship. This is again the product of the political compromise struck to salvage the main body of the Law Commission's proposals following the withdrawal of the FHDVB 1995.

7.74 As noted above, restriction or exclusion provisions may be imposed under s 36(5), although the balance of harm test question need only be had regard to and there is no direction to impose them where otherwise significant harm is likely to be suffered by the applicant or relevant child.

IX DURATION OF S 36 ORDERS

7.75 Unlike s 33 occupation orders, which may be made for an indefinite period, those made under s 36 are limited to a period of six months in the first instance, with one single possible extension for further maximum period not exceeding six months (s 36(10)). The position also contrasts with orders made in favour of former spouses under s 35, which, although limited to six months in the first instance, may be extended on one or more occasion for further maximum periods of six months at a time (s 35(10)). This is the position in which the 1995 Bill intended to place cohabitants, but the disparity is another example of how the 1996 Act was revised to privilege protection to those who have chosen to marry.

X OCCUPATION ORDERS WHERE NEITHER COHABITANT IS ENTITLED TO OCCUPY – S 38 – ELIGIBLE APPLICANTS

7.76 Section 38 occupation orders are appropriate where neither cohabitant is entitled to occupy the family home by virtue of any beneficial estate or interest or contractual or statutory rights. It will therefore only apply to a small category of people, such as squatters and bare licensees, who, providing they were spouses or cohabitants, were in fact protected under the DVA 1976. Section 37 now applies to spouses or former spouses where neither is entitled to occupy the home and marriage can again be seen to be privileged. For here only the standard criteria in s 33(6) and the balance of harm test presumption (s 33(7)) applies. In addition, the occupation order, although initially for six months, may be extended on one or more occasion for further maximum periods of six months at a time. Under s 38, applications can be made by cohabitants and former cohabitants providing they live or lived together in the accommodation.

XI NATURE OF S 38 OCCUPATION ORDERS

7.77 It was obviously not appropriate to extend the declaratory provisions neither of s 30(3)-(6) to this category of applicant (nor indeed to s 37 applicants) and thus no declaration of occupation rights will be made as part of the order. However, the court can make the regulatory orders contained in s 33(3)(b)(c)(f) and (g) requiring the respondent to permit the applicant to enter and remain, regulating the occupation by one or both parties, requiring the respondent to leave all or part of the dwelling-house and/or excluding the respondent from a defined area.

XII CRITERIA FOR MAKING A S 38 OCCUPATION ORDER

7.78 Sections 38(4) and (5) apply the standard criteria to the making of an occupation order as applied to both entitled and to non-entitled cohabitants under s 33(6)(a)–(d) and s 36(6)(a)–(d) (housing and financial resources, likely effect of the order and the conduct of the parties), as discussed above. Interestingly, the additional criteria applied to cohabitants in s 36(e)–(i) (nature of the parties' relationship, whether there are children, length of time since cohabitation ceased and existence of pending proceedings under Sch 1 CA 1989) are not to be applied by the court in deciding whether to make a s 38 order, where the respondent has no property rights in the family home. However, once again, although the balance of harm test criteria must be taken into account, there is no requirement to make an order, even though the court concludes that significant harm is likely to be suffered by the applicant or relevant child. The matter rests, as in s 36 applications in the court's discretion.

XIII DURATION OF S 38 ORDERS

7.79 Section 38(6) provides for the same duration as under s 36, namely a maximum of six months in the first instance which can be extended for one further maximum period of six months.

XIV INTERRELATIONSHIP OF DIFFERENT TYPES OF OCCUPATION ORDER

7.80 It should be noted that ss 36 and 38 do not prevent cohabitant applicants from claiming an interest in property in subsequent proceedings for example under s 14 TLATA 1996 or Sch 7 FLA 1996 (s 39(4)). Furthermore, if an application is made for an occupation order under one section, but the court considers it has no power to make it under that section but does have power to make an order under one of the other sections, then it can do so (s 39(3)). Thus, in an appropriate case a s 36-occupation order can be made when a s 33-occupation order has been applied for.

XV ADDITIONAL PROVISIONS—S 40

7.81 In order to meet some of the criticisms of the former law, particularly as it applied to cohabitants, the court may now make additional provision to regulate certain matters between the parties relevant to the occupation of the accommodation after the making of an occupation order. These provisions only apply for the duration of the order. However, in terms of their practical effectiveness, lacunae have been exposed by case law as discussed below.

7.82 On making an occupation order under ss 33, 35 or 36 (but not ss 37 and 38) or, it should be noted, at any time thereafter, the court may:

(a)   impose on either party obligations as to repair and maintenance of the dwelling-house or the discharge of relevant rent or mortgage payments or other outgoings;

(b)   order a party occupying the dwelling-house or part of it (regardless of whether or not they are entitled to occupy the accommodation in their own right) to make periodical payments in respect of the accommodation to the other party, who, but for the order would themselves be legally entitled to occupy the accommodation;

(c)   grant either party possession or use of furniture or other contents of the dwelling house;

(d)   order either party to take reasonable care of any furniture or other contents of the dwelling-house; and

(e)   order either party to take reasonable steps to keep the dwelling house, furniture or other contents secure.

7.83 In deciding how the court should exercise its powers under this section, s 40(2) provides that the court should have regard to all the circumstances of the case including:

(a)   the financial needs and financial resources of the parties; and

(b)   the financial obligations which they have or are likely to have in the foreseeable future, including financial obligations to each other and any relevant child.

7.84 Advisors must therefore carefully think through exactly what their client will need to do to effectively occupy the accommodation or to be compensated for their loss of it. Enquiries must be made of clients to ascertain details of rent and mortgage payments and other outgoings. A priority must be to ensure that these payments continue to be paid either by the occupant or by the excluded partner. Where the property is rented, attention should be turned to whether housing benefit needs to be transferred or applied for. In all cases, information as to the parties' respective means and financial commitments will need to be available in a way that was not at all relevant under the DVA 1976. Close attention should be paid to the question of maintenance and repair needs in the case of an owner occupied property, as well as ensuring that one or both parties will meet the necessary ground rent and service charge payments where appropriate.

7.85 Thus, whilst consideration of these matters should not prevent or delay the relief required in emergency cases, occupation orders are, at least in principle, qualitatively different from ouster orders under the 1976 Act for cohabitants, although in practice enforcement of s 40 orders is not possible as revealed by *Nwgobe v Nwgobe* [2000] 2 FLR 744. In this case the applicant was granted an occupation order and the respondent was consequently ordered to pay the rent, rent arrears, council tax and water rates on the former matrimonial home, which he subsequently failed to pay. The applicant therefore applied for him to be committed to prison for contempt of court. However, the Court of Appeal found that the respondent could not be committed to prison as payments under s 40 FLA 1996 did not fall within any of the exceptions to the Debtors Act 1869, which abolished imprisonment for unpaid debt. Furthermore, it did not accept that committal could be made as if it were a breach of the occupation order itself, as this would have meant an implied repeal of s 5 Debtors Act 1869. Neither could it be enforced under the Attachment of Earnings Act 1971, as it was not listed in Sch 1 to that Act. To add insult to injury, the applicant could not even enforce the order through conventional means as the payments were due to a third party rather than the applicant herself. Whereas in the case of spouses, making a periodical maintenance order could circumvent this situation, this is of no use in the cohabitation context. Clearly, a fatal flaw in the court's powers has been exposed which, as the Court of Appeal noted, requires legislative intervention. As things currently stand, whilst the court can undoubtedly make orders ancillary to an occupation order under s 40, this may be of little use to a cohabitant where their former partner fails to comply.

7.86 In terms of what orders the court can make, it is clear that it can make an order for periodical payments of what may be termed an "occupation rent" to the excluded party, regardless of whether or not the occupant is entitled in their own right to occupy the property. This extends a provision previously only available against a non-entitled spouse under the MHA 1983 to all occupying pursuant to a s 33, s 35 or s 36-occupation order. How this is to be calculated, is a matter that has not yet been authoritatively decided by the courts in relation to equitable accounting following separation, where both parties have a beneficial interest in an owner occupied property (see discussion in Chapter 11). In the context of an occupation order, however, cases where such periodical payments should be ordered may prove to be the exception rather than the rule, given that beneficial entitlement will normally be ascertained later in separate proceedings if necessary and an equitable accounting exercise performed. However, orders for an occupation rent are not restricted to the dispossessed owner-occupier and may be appropriate where the family home is rented. The Law Commission report offers no guidance on this issue and expresses surprise that respondents to the working paper did not make separate comment on this proposal (see Law Com No. 207, para 4.39).

7.87 Where an occupant is dependant on housing benefit, although payment of the rent could be claimed following an occupation order, no extra payment of any type of benefit would be available for payment to the respondent. The excluded party could in these circumstances be relieved of the rent payments and it is submitted no further order for payment of an occupation rent would be appropriate. Given the payments must be periodical, it does not seem to be possible for the court to order a lump sum equivalent to a deposit on rented accommodation to be paid to the respondent where the parties' means permitted and such a payment appears appropriate. It should be noted here that, as discussed in Chapter 10 below, separating cohabitants may now apply for transfer of tenancy orders pursuant to s 53 and Sch 7 FLA 1996, where the family home was rented. In this context, compensation may be awarded to the cohabitant whose interest is transferred, and would be in the form of a lump sum.

7.88 Although occupation orders can be seen to be qualitatively different from ouster orders under the DVA 1976 and grant a much more secure occupational status for potentially longer periods of time to cohabitants and former cohabitants, they are still in essence a temporary remedy. It is therefore imperative that where an occupation order is made, that thought is given to what form the final resolution of the position between the parties is to take if there is no reconciliation. It is probable that even under s 33, where an indefinite period is a possibility, the courts will in most situations make occupation orders for a specified period of time. Although in some cases extension of orders may be obtained, this is not to be relied upon, particularly under s 36, where two six-month periods is the absolute maximum. Thus, whilst not suggesting that unnecessary pressure be put upon the occupant, it is vital that advisors ensure that a s 33 or s 36 occupant is aware of the final remedies available and that the appropriate applications are made in good time for a transfer of tenancy order or an order under s 14 TLATA 1996.

(iii) Urgent applications—ex parte non-molestation and occupation orders

7.89 Under the 1976 Act, the use of *ex parte* orders in the absence of statutory guidance had been restricted by case law to emergency situations where the interests of justice or the protection of the applicant or a child clearly demanded the court's immediate intervention (see *Ansah v Ansah* [1977] Fam 138, CA). This approach was made arguably more stringent by a Practice Note (see [1978] 2 All ER 919) which stated that such orders should not be made unless there was "real immediate danger of serious injury or irreparable damage" and whilst courts could in some situations be persuaded to grant *ex parte* non-molestation orders, the Court of Appeal in *G v G (ouster: Ex p application)* [1990] 1 FLR 395 indicated that this should be the exception rather than the rule and that in any event orders should only be made *ex parte* to retain the *status quo*.

7.90 Section 45 FLA 1996 now states that both non-molestation and occupation orders may be made *ex parte* when the court considers it is "just and convenient to do so". To determine appropriate cases for exercising this power, the court shall have regard to all the circumstances including:

(a) any risk of significant harm to the applicant or a relevant child if the order is not made immediately (s 45(2)(a));
(b) whether it is likely the applicant will be deterred or prevented from pursuing the application if an order is not made immediately (s 45(2)(b)); and
(c) whether there is reason to believe that the respondent is deliberately evading service and that the applicant or a relevant child will be seriously prejudiced by the delay involved in effecting service of the proceedings in the magistrates' court or effecting substituted service in any other court (s 45(2)(c)).

7.91 Where *ex parte* orders are made, s 45(3) provides that the respondent must be given an opportunity to make representations relating to the order as soon as just and convenient at a hearing on notice.

7.92 Whilst the statutory guidance is arguably less stringent than under the previous law, the powers under the 1996 Act must now be construed in the context of the need of the court as a public authority to comply with the provisions of the Human Rights Act 1998. It is certainly arguable that the making of an *ex parte* occupation order was a breach of the respondent's right under Article 6 of the European Convention to the right to a fair and public hearing. But it could argued that the limited duration of the ex parte order (usually seven days until the return date) and the need to offer the alleged victim and any children safety and freedom from the risk of real or alleged violence would outweigh possibly any short-term inconvenience to the respondent. Further, it is usual when making ex parte occupation orders for the court to also include a provision that the respondent may apply to have the order set aside on 48 hours' notice.

7.93 The Law Commission decided against recommending that different criteria be applied to *ex parte* applications for non-molestation orders as distinct from occupation orders (see paras 5.5–5.9) on the grounds that these remedies are usually sought together. Instead, they have considered that there are particular situations where the making of an *ex parte* order may be particularly meritorious and these have been drawn to the court's attention in s 45(2). "Significant harm" in s 45(2)(a), and also adopted in the balance of harm test, is a term borrowed from the Children Act 1989. "Harm" is defined in s 63(1) as follows:

(a)   in relation to a person who has reached the age of eighteen years, means ill-treatment or the impairment of health; and
(b)   in relation to a child, means ill-treatment or impairment of health or development.

7.94 In both cases "health" includes physical or mental health. In relation to a child, the same subsection provides that "ill-treatment" includes sexual abuse and forms of ill-treatment which are not physical and "development" means physical, intellectual, emotional, social or behavioural development. What will amount to "significant" harm is not specified in relation to an adult. However, where a child's health or development is involved, s 63(2) indicates that the question of whether the harm suffered is significant should be determined by comparison with the health and development reasonably expected of a similar child. These definitions follow those found in s 31(9) and (10) CA 1989. Section 45(2)(b) covers the situation where an applicant is so terrified of the respondent that they will not proceed with the application unless they have the court's protection first. However, that is not to say that the court cannot be persuaded of other appropriate situations for the making of an order *ex parte*. Whenever an *ex parte* order is applied for, it will be important to be able to explain to the court why it is inappropriate or impossible for the application to be made on notice. It may also be possible to apply for abridgement of notice in appropriate cases. It should also be noted that the presumption in favour of a power of arrest (s 47(2)) does not apply to orders made *ex parte* (see s 47(3)), as will be discussed more fully below.

(iv) Powers of arrest and other methods of enforcement of non-molestation and occupation orders

7.95 This is another area where the 1996 Act has, in theory at least, improved upon the position under the old law. Whereas previously, a power of arrest could only be attached where the respondent had caused actual bodily harm and was likely to do so again (s 2(1) DVA 1976), s 47(2) FLA 1996 provides that on making a non-molestation or occupation order, the court *shall* attach a power of arrest "where it appears ... that the respondent has used or threatened violence against the applicant or a relevant child" *unless* the court is satisfied in all the circumstances that they will be adequately protected without such a power of arrest. Thus, the burden of proof has been reversed. Only where adequate protection without a power of arrest can be shown will the court not impose one, meaning that in most cases, a power of arrest will be attached to one or more provisions of the order. This makes a compromise through undertakings doubly attractive from a respondent's point of view, and is a good reason for a vulnerable victim not to be persuaded to agree to an undertaking where an order will be granted. For a power of arrest is by far the quickest and most effective method of enforcement of a non-molestation injunction, enabling a police officer to arrest the respondent without a warrant where there is reasonable cause to suspect that the terms of the order to which the power of arrest has been attached, have been breached (s 47(6)). Interestingly, this change to the law was recommended by the Law Commission after responses to its Working Paper (*Domestic Violence and Occupation of the Family Home*, (1989) Working Paper No. 113) revealed a weight of opinion favouring such an option (see para 5.12-5.13, Law Com No. 207, 1992). Advisors should note that a *President's Direction (Family Law Act 1996: attendance of arresting officer)* [2000] 1 FLR 270 was issued with the consent of the Lord Chancellor on 9 December 1999, and governs court procedures in the case of arrests made for breach of non-molestation orders under s 47(7).

7.96 However, this almost mandatory direction to attach a power of arrest to orders has raised problems in practice. Firstly, there is anecdotal evidence that the courts are showing a reluctance to attach powers of arrest (see Humphries, 2001, (above)). In *Re B–J (a child) (non-molestation order: Power of Arrest)* [2000] 2 FLR 443 it was made clear by the Court of Appeal (overruling *M v W (non-molestation order: duration)* [2000] 1 FLR 107) that the duration of a non-molestation order should be decided before and in isolation from consideration of whether a power of arrest should be attached. The need to attach the latter should not reduce the length of the former. Indeed it was perfectly possible to attach a power of arrest of shorter duration than that of the non-molestation (or occupation order) itself, notwithstanding the lack of express words in the statute. However, in the unusual cases of *Chechi v Bashir* (above) involving a business dispute between two brothers, where it was felt that a non-molestation order was justified and the conditions for making a power of arrest applied, the court took the view that the existence of power of arrest would undoubtedly be abused by the victim. Thus, as happend here, it may be appropriate for the court to accept undertakings to which no power of arrest could be attached.

7.97 Another difficulty with the provisions relating to powers of arrest came to light in the case of *Re H (a minor) (respondent under 18: power of arrest)* [2001] 1 FLR 641. Here it was argued that the court could not attach a power of arrest where the respondent was a minor. The Court of Appeal dismissed this, confirming that the wording of s 47(2) was clear and provided no exceptions to the mandatory duty where there would have been no adequate protection for the applicant and child without the power of arrest. However, the court drew attention to the fact that they had no powers to deal with contemnors under 18 and this required the urgent attention of policy makers.

7.98 This presumption in favour of a power of arrest does not apply to orders made *ex parte*. In this situation the court has a discretion to attach a power of arrest where the respondent has used or threatened violence to the applicant or relevant child *and* there is a risk of significant harm to either of them if the power of arrest is not attached immediately (s 18(3)). This is again a significant improvement on the old law, where there was great reluctance to use a power of arrest in relation to *ex parte* orders (see *Ansah v Ansah* (above)).

7.99 Where no power of arrest has been attached to the order or to that part of it which has been breached, a warrant of arrest supported by evidence on oath may now be applied for at the court which made the relevant order. Thus, Part IV of the 1996 Act has extended the enforcement powers of the High Court and county court in this regard although a warrant will only be issued if the court has reasonable grounds for believing the respondent has failed to comply with the order (s 47(9)). One potentially serious difficulty is, however, that the new warrant procedure only applies where the court has not attached a power of arrest to the order or that part of the order which has been allegedly breached. This assumes that the power of arrest will always provide a victim with an effective remedy who consequently will not need to avail themselves of the warrant procedure. However, there is only a *power* and not a *duty* to arrest for breach at the discretion of the police officer. This leaves a victim who has had a power of arrest attached to the order unable to use the warrant procedure where the police have declined to make an arrest, leaving committal proceedings as the only remedy. Ironically, in these circumstances, a victim with an order without a power of arrest is in a better position than a victim with a power of arrest, exercise of which has been declined by the police. All three courts also now have power to remand the respondent in custody or on bail where a respondent arrested on a warrant cannot be dealt with immediately (see s 47(10)-(12) and Sch 2). New powers to remand for medical reports or a report under s 35 Mental Health Act 1983 were also included in Part IV FLA 1996 (s 48) and magistrates' courts were granted extended powers of committal and suspended committal orders (s 50). The need to comply precisely with procedural requirements when applying for committal combined with the court's heightened awareness of its duty to protect the contemnor's European Convention rights was underlined by the case of *Couzens v Couzens* [2001] 2 FLR 701, when the courts' failure to serve the suspended committal order in accordance with Form N79 prevented the court from activating the term of imprisonment following a further breach. Another development in this area occurred in *Harris v Harris* [2001] 2 FLR 955, where the court agreed to exercise its common law power to suspend the remainder of a nine month sentence, after an appeal against sentence and two attempts to purge the contempt had failed.

7.100 No maximum time limits for the duration of non-molestation orders, s 33 occupation orders or, indeed, for powers of arrest have been included in the 1996 Act. Thus, in principle non-molestation orders and powers of arrest may exceed what had become the normal three-month period following the *Practice Note* [1981] 1 WLR 27 under the old law.

(v) Undertakings

7.101 Undertakings were a common method of compromise between parties under the 1976 Act, providing protection equivalent to a non-molestation order, whilst avoiding the need for an applicant to prove their case and permitting a respondent to "save face" with no finding of molestation having been made by the court. The use of undertakings in this way has been criticised for being used to put pressure on a victim who then loses the opportunity of the best form of protection; a power of arrest.

7.102 Amendments made to the FHDVB 1995 during its passage through the House of Lords added provisions relating to undertakings and these have been preserved in the 1996 Act. Section 46 permits undertakings to be accepted by the court in any case where the court has power to make a non-molestation or occupation order. Section 46(2) makes it clear that, as was the position under the old law (*Carpenter v Carpenter* [1988] 1 FLR 121), no power of arrest may be attached to an undertaking, although it is enforceable in the same way as an order by means of committal proceedings (see s 46(4)). Whether the warrant procedure under s 47(8) extends to undertakings is still a moot point and has not been tested in the courts. Section 46(2) makes it clear that the court must not accept an undertaking where a power of arrest would otherwise be attached, although this was the solution adopted in the case of *Chechi v Bashir* (above) and considered appropriate by the court of appeal on its unusual facts.

7.103 This prohibition on the acceptance of undertakings places the court in a difficult position where parties are keen to resolve the matter by means of undertakings. For, in order to judge whether a power of arrest would be attached, the court has to form a view on whether or not the respondent has used or threatened violence (s 47(2)). In principle, if on reading the affidavit evidence or statements, the court forms a *prima facie* view that a power of arrest would be attached, the court must proceed to hear the case and decide this issue, regardless of the wishes of the parties. Whilst fully accepting that undertakings could be used to pressurise a victim, it is questionable whether a forced hearing of the evidence can be justified on public policy grounds, and it seems courts are still inclined in practice to accept undertakings. It is to be regretted that Parliament has not taken the opportunity to change the law to enable powers of arrest to be attached to undertakings. Where parties are keen to compromise, a consent order incorporating a power of arrest could avoid a protracted hearing, but does not of course shield the respondent from a finding that there has been violence or threat of violence.

7.104 The 1996 Act has therefore given the court a more pro-active role and in appropriate cases it should refuse to accept undertakings until after evidence has been heard and where appropriate make an order with a power of arrest attached in accordance with the direction in s 47(2), other than in the most unusual circumstances. As discussed above, powers of arrest should be attached to orders much more frequently than under the old law, but this does not always coincide with current practice (see Humphries, 2001). Conversely, undertakings should have become a much less commonly used means of compromise, although proved useful on the unusual facts in *Chechi v Bashir*. Whether or not applying for a warrant can enforce breach of an undertaking under s 47(8) is still unclear and will turn on statutory interpretation of the interrelationship between s 46(4) and s 47(1) and (8). In the author's view, it is arguable that the warrant procedure described above may be used in case of breach of an undertaking. Section 46(4) provides that an undertaking accepted on an application for a non-molestation or occupation order is "enforceable as if it were an order of the court". Section 47(8) provides the remedy of a warrant procedure for breach where the court has made a "relevant order" (defined in s 47(1) as an occupation or non-molestation order) but not attached a power of arrest.

7.105 Given that the warrant procedure is a method of enforcement, and undertakings, whilst specifically prevented from having powers of arrest attached, are otherwise enforceable as orders of the court, only a very literal interpretation of what is meant by "relevant order" in s 47 should prevent undertakings being enforced by the warrant procedure. If this does prove to be the interpretation decided upon by the courts, then undertakings will only be enforceable by means of committal proceedings with the attendant difficulties experienced under the old legislation.

(vi) Procedure

7.106 Both non-molestation and occupation orders may be made by all three courts with the proviso in the case of the magistrates' courts that they cannot hear applications for occupation orders where there is a dispute about either party's legal entitlement to occupy the family home (s 59(1)). In addition, the magistrates' court may decline jurisdiction if it considers the case can be more conveniently dealt with by another court (s 59(2)). In s 57, power has also been reserved to the Lord Chancellor to specify the level or class of court in which certain proceedings must be commenced or to which they must or can be transferred. Thus, a regime similar to that applying to the Children Act now applies.

7.107 Part IV applications are restricted to courts with family jurisdiction and geographical limits for commencement will not apply as is the case with both divorce and Children Act proceedings, although where there are other related family proceedings pending, applications should be made to the same court.

7.108 There is a comprehensive joint application form (Form FL401) modelled on the style of the current Children Act forms, for both non-molestation and all types of occupation order. This should be accompanied by a sworn statement and filed at court and served upon the respondent personally not less than two clear days before the hearing, although abridgement of this period can be ordered by the court before service. It requires details of the parties, the type of relationship, any relevant children, other family proceedings, whether an *ex parte* application is to be made and the reasons for this, the family home, any mortgage and the types of orders applied for. The same form should also be used for applicants under 16 years of age, although this will be treated as an application for leave to the High Court in the first instance and if leave is granted may, if appropriate be transferred to the county court. There is to be a separate and simpler form where variation, extension or discharge of an order is sought.

7.109 Where an occupation order is made on an application under s 33 or s 36, any mortgagee or landlord must be served with a copy of the order by first class post. Any orders made must be served personally on the respondent.

7.110 District judges may hear applications under Part IV, which will be heard in chambers. Bail applications on behalf of a person arrested pursuant to an attached power of arrest may be made orally or in writing, with the details to be included in a written application set out in the rules.

7.111 It should be noted that s 60 FLA 1996 is novel in that it indicates that rules of court may provide for a representative to apply for an occupation or non-molestation order on behalf of the victim. This has, however, still not been brought into force.

7.112 Emergency representation will usually be appropriate where protection is sought under these provisions and may if necessary be granted by solicitors' firms either using devolved powers or by the LSC via fax application or over the telephone. Guidance from the LSC provides that letters should be written trying to prevent the behaviour complained of before injunction proceedings are issued and a certificate of public funding granted save where protection is required as a matter of urgency. In this situation it should also be considered whether an approach should be made to the police . This will often not be appropriate and may just serve to exacerbate the situation and leave the applicant without protection. Delay in bringing proceedings could prejudice the outcome of an application and this should be borne in mind by advisors.

(b) Injunctions ancillary to the Children Act 1989

7.113 Given the extended categories of "associated" persons, the broad definition of "relevant child" and the ability of the court to make non-molestation orders of its own motion in family proceedings, Part IV FLA 1996 has largely removed the need for cohabitants or former cohabitants to seek protection from molestation or attempt to exclude another party ancillary to the CA 1989. It is to be remembered, however, that the county court and High Court can grant non-molestation injunctions ancillary to a s 8 order to protect the child and residential parent pursuant to ss 38 and 39 County Courts Act 1984 and s 37 Supreme Court Act 1981, although no power of arrest can be attached.

7.114 It should also be noted that s 52 and Sch 6 FLA 1996 amend the CA 1989, inserting new ss 38A and 44A, which enable a court making an interim care order or an emergency protection order to exclude a suspected abuser (rather than the child) from the home, leaving the allegedly abused child living in their home surroundings. In addition the court may attach a power of arrest to such an exclusion order.

(c) Injunctions in tort actions

7.115 Although, for the majority of cohabitants, it is no longer necessary to contemplate these remedies, they remain of some assistance to same-sex couples, where only the abuser has a legal right to occupy the family home. Although non-molestation orders are available to all cohabitants, as noted above, only s 33 occupation orders where the applicant is entitled are available to same-sex cohabitants. Thus, where violence occurs in a gay relationship and is perpetrated by the partner, who is also the sole legal occupier, there is no remedy through which to preserve occupation of the home under the 1996 Act, or exclude them from an area around the home. This has left this category of victims in the same position as former heterosexual cohabitants prior to the 1996 legislation. Ironically, the Act has therefore left a most vulnerable group without any from of direct protection.

7.116 The only possible remedies available for this group of cohabitants and, indeed, for those who have had a relationship where there has not been cohabitation, an agreement to marry, or a relevant child, are those offered by the law of tort. In recent years this has developed remedies for harassment and to which has now been added the statutory tort of harassment under s 3 Protection from Harassment Act 1997. A victim of violence may apply for an injunction ancillary to an action for damages in tort for assault, battery, trespass or nuisance whereby the court can restrain the other party from behaviour which amounts to assault, battery, trespass or nuisance.

7.117 Developments in the case law in this field had enabled an action to be taken in nuisance for behaviour amounting to harassment which usefully extended the applicability of this remedy beyond obvious cases of physical violence and trespass. It was found that verbal harassment not strictly amounting to a threat was actionable if it could be shown to cause the victim to suffer mental or physical illness and despite the victim having no proprietary interest in the property at which the offending persistent telephone calls were being made (see *Khorasandjian v Bush* [1993] 3 All ER 669, CA and *Burnett v George* [1992] 1 FLR 525, CA). However, in *Hunter v Canary Wharf Ltd, Hunter v London Docklands Development Corpn* [1997] 2 All ER 426, the House of Lords overruled *Khorasandjian v Bush* in so far as it held that a mere licensee could sue in private nuisance. Despite Lord Cooke delivering a dissenting judgment on the point, saying that for him occupation of the property as a home was an acceptable criterion for entitlement to sue in private nuisance and one which was consistent with international standards, it seems that the usefulness of this remedy in the family context has been greatly reduced for those unable to use the domestic violence legislation, leaving the Protection from Harassment Act 1997 as the best avenue to explore, despite the attendant difficulties of having to prove a "course of conduct" as discussed above.

7.118 The improved remedies available under Part IV FLA 1996 have proved, as we have seen, to contain unexpected gaps but they have made a significant difference to the protection available. However, although s 42 FLA 1996 non-molestation orders are a useful way to protect "associated persons", which include gay and heterosexual cohabitants and former cohabitants, as a power of arrest can be attached, they cannot be used to protect a former non-entitled gay cohabitant by restraining their former partner from coming within an area of their new address, as no occupation order is available and the property is not in any event the former family home.

7.119 Another consideration is the possibility of civil proceedings under the Protection from Harassment Act 1997. Section 3 provides that an actual or apprehended breach of s 1 harassment may be the subject of a claim in civil proceedings by the victim, and damages may be awarded for among other things "anxiety caused by the harassment". This has effectively created a new statutory tort of harassment breach of which, in contrast to s 42 FLA 1996, provides a civil remedy regardless of whether or not the individuals concerned are "associated", and makes a claim for damages available. The county court and High Court when hearing a civil action also has power to grant injunctions to restrain the harassment. This civil remedy is a welcome addition to the limited remedies available for harassment under the law of nuisance following developments in the case law in *Khorasandjian v Bush; Hunter v Canary Wharf Ltd; Hunter v London Docklands Development Corpn* and *Burris v Azadani* [1996] 1 FLR 266, CA. Breach of the civil injunction requires an application for a warrant before an arrest can be made and thus for cohabitants and former cohabitants able to seek a s 42 FLA 1996 non-molestation injunction with power or arrest attached, it is an inferior remedy where a non-molestation injunction can effectively target the behaviour complained of.

7.120 To bring an action under the general law of torts, it must be shown that a tortious act has been committed, and the extension of the tort of nuisance to include harassment or molestation now permits actions to redress such behaviour in addition to the use of the torts of assault, battery and trespass where appropriate.

7.121 The procedure for applying for protection in this way involves an application on Claim Form N1 including details of the claim/matter complained of and a statement of truth out of the appropriate High Court or county court for the district where the claimant or defendant resides. An injunction can be applied for without a claim for damages or other relief by virtue of s 38 County Court Act 1984. Such free standing injunction applications are governed by the Civil Procedure Rules 1998. The Civil Claim Form N1 is supported by an N16A injunction application in the county court or an application notice Form N244 in the High Court. An injunction may be granted if the other party behaves in an unconscionable manner or threatens to do so, or if an order is necessary to protect a person from the invasion of a legal or equitable right.

7.122 Applications may be made without notice on affidavit, and, unlike hearing under Part IV FLA 1996 or the CA 1989, the matter will be heard in open court, not in chambers. Two days' notice is otherwise required for an injunction application. It is not clear whether an exclusion order can be made other than where there is an action for trespass, and no power of arrest can be attached to these injunctions. Breach of an injunction will again be punishable as contempt and in such a situation, committal proceedings can be issued and pursued and a warrant of arrest can be granted also in respect of a breach.

3 Emergency accommodation

7.123 Often the most urgent need of a victim of domestic violence is a safe place to live, either permanently or temporarily, until court orders affording some protection against violence can be obtained. Many victims are reluctant to go and stay with relatives or friends, as these are likely to be the violent partner's first port of call on discovering that they have fled the home. There is now a fairly wide network of women's refuges offering temporary accommodation and the local Women's Aid will provide details of possible refuges. However, such accommodation, whilst safe, often leaves a great deal to be desired and can only ever be temporary. National Lottery money to expand the network of refuges in accordance with recommendations made by the Home Affairs Select Committee was awarded in October 1995 has improved the situation in some areas. However, the ability of victims of domestic violence to obtain permanent rehousing under the homelessness legislation was removed with the implementation of Part VII Housing Act 1996. As discussed in detail in Chapter 3, this repealed the law contained in Part III HA 1985 and now only requires local housing authorities to provide the statutory homeless with temporary accommodation for a minimum of two years (s 193(3) HA 1996). These reforms are set to be reversed, however, if the Homelessness Bill 2001 is enacted in its current form (see clause 6).

7.124 The hurdles which the homeless have to overcome to be a beneficiary of the currently reduced duty under the HA 1996 have been increased. Applicants must show that they are eligible for assistance and not excluded by being an asylum seeker or a person from abroad subject to immigration control (see ss 183(2), 185 and 186). They must now also have not failed to take reasonable steps to secure that accommodation is available (s 197(3)). This is in addition to having to show they are homeless or threatened with homelessness (s 175), unintentionally homeless (see s 191) and in priority need (s 189). A local authority must make enquiries under s 184 to see whether a duty is owed to secure accommodation. Where there is an apparent priority need, there is a duty to provide accommodation pending their enquiries (s 188). A victim of domestic violence in need of urgent accommodation, regardless of whether or not they are the tenant or owner of accommodation, may still be homeless within the meaning of the Act.

7.125 Section 177(1) specifically indicates that a person is homeless if they have accommodation which it is not reasonable for them to occupy because it is "probable" that this will lead to domestic violence against them or a person who might reasonably be expected to reside with them. Clause 10 of the Homelessness Bill 2001 will amend s 177(1) to include violence other than domestic violence, widening its scope and extending it to encompass violence between same-sex cohabitants, as they will be "associated" as required by the Bill's definition of other violence in this context. In determining whether it would be reasonable for the person to continue to occupy accommodation regard may be had to the general circumstances prevailing in relation to housing in the area (s 177(2)). In addition s 175(2) treats a person as homeless if they have accommodation but cannot secure entry to it, although this provision under the 1985 legislation offered in practice nothing more than short term temporary accommodation as authorities required a person to use their legal remedies to re-enter or be found intentionally homeless.

7.126 Domestic violence is defined in s 171(1) as violence or threats of violence likely to be carried out made by a person with whom the applicant is "associated" which is given the same meaning as in Part IV FLA 1996. Thus, a person who would succeed in getting a non-molestation order due to harassment not amounting to violence or threats of violence would not be assisted by this provision, which effectively requires the applicant's physical safety to be in jeopardy, although the violence need not have occurred within the home. As with re-entry, local authorities have in the past expected victims of domestic violence to use their legal remedies and apply for non-molestation and occupation orders, saying that failure to do so will result in a finding of intentional homelessness. Whilst there may be situations where an authority may reasonably require an applicant to use their domestic violence remedies (as in *R v Eastleigh Borough Council, ex p Evans* (1984) 17 HLR 515), a policy that all such applicants must be challengeable. The current DLTR Code of Guidance acknowledges that injunctions will not necessarily deter people and applicants should not be found intentionally homeless if they have not pursued domestic violence remedies on account of "a well-grounded fear of reprisal". In such cases applicants should not be pressured into taking out such orders and should not necessarily be asked to return to their home, having obtained such orders (para 13.7(iii)). Unfortunately, although authorities must have regard to the Code of Guidance, it does not have the force of law. However, advisors should attempt to resist such pressure upon their clients, and particularly where injunctions have been breached in the past or where the violence is so serious that a further attack should not be risked or where, perhaps, it can be shown that an injunction with a power of arrest attached will be no deterrent. Nonetheless, providing priority need can be established, emergency accommodation should be available pursuant to s 188 where there has been or is likely to be actual or threatened violence.

7.127 Victims of domestic violence are arguably always in priority need in their own right on account of being vulnerable within the meaning of s 189(1)(c) as a result of a "special reason"and changes following implementation of the Homelessness Bill 2001 will give priority need to victims of domestic violence as set out in the Draft Homelessness (Priority Need for Accommodation) (England) Order 2001. The meaning of vulnerability in this sense under the current law was broadened when considered in *R v Kensington and Chelsea London Borough Council, ex p Kihara* (1996) 29 HLR 147, and victims of violence are referred to specifically in the Code of Guidance as an example of vulnerability of this nature (see para 12.22). However, an applicant can also establish priority need under s 189 if they are pregnant; have dependent children residing with them or who might reasonably reside with them; or are vulnerable as a result of old age, mental illness or handicap or physical disability or other special reason, or if such a person might reasonably reside with the applicant. The current Draft Code of Guidance (December 2000) (available on the DLTR website) is issued by the Secretary of State pursuant to s 182 for the assistance of local authorities. In terms of showing that a separated applicant has dependent children it is reasonably expected should reside with him or her, the code acknowledges that a court order may post-Children Act 1989 often not exist and should not be required as a general rule (para 12.3). This was confirmed by the Divisional Court in the case of *R v Ealing London Borough Council, ex p Sidhu* (1982) 2 HLR 45, which also indicated that accommodation available at a women's refuge to the applicant did not prevent her being homeless.

7.128 The hurdle, of showing that the applicant is not intentionally homeless (s 191), is the most litigated and is the factor which will determine whether the applicant will be secured accommodation. Readers are referred back to the discussion in Chapter 3. The current provision under s 191(4) whereby a finding of intentionality will be made if advice and assistance is given but fails to secure suitable accommodation where it was reasonably expected they would do so is potentially very serious and could leave vulnerable victims of domestic violence literally on the streets with nowhere to go unless they are carefully advised that positive action on their part is required in seeking out accommodation.

7.129 Aside from this, the critical factors in the domestic violence context are, firstly, whether to avoid a finding of intentionality applicants will be pressured to use their domestic violence remedies where they have no right of occupation in the short term, and where they in fact wish to live somewhere other than the former family home, in which they will often feel that they remain vulnerable to their former partner; and, secondly, whether given the ability of cohabitants and former cohabitants now to apply for transfer of tenancy orders on relationship breakdown under Sch 7 FLA 1996 in addition to using Sch 1 CA 1989 where there are children and s 14 TLATA 1996 in the owner occupation context (see Chapters 10 and 11), they will be expected to pursue such final remedies even where the prospects of success are poor.

7.130 Given that the homelessness legislation no longer provides a direct route into permanent accommodation (although this is set to be reversed post-Homelessness Bill 2001), it may be that applicants will be keener to pursue a remedy in relation to the former family home in any event. However, there must be a risk of victims of domestic violence being forced to litigate against their will. In some situations, refusal of legal aid to pursue an application with little prospects of success, may assist in achieving the client's desired outcome.

7.131 It is likely that the degree of violence will have a great bearing on the authority's approach to a victim who has interest in former accommodation. Even where the hurdles set out above are successfully overcome, the applicant may be referred to another authority with which he or she has a local connection pursuant to s 198. Advisors should be aware that where the applicant, or a person reasonably expected to reside with the applicant, runs the risk of domestic violence in that other district, no referral should be made—s 198(2)(c). This will be strengthened by the Homelessness Bill 2001 (see clause 10(2)).

7.132 Applicants must be advised in writing of the local authority's decision and the reasons for the decision where a duty to secure accommodation is denied pursuant to s 184(3) of the Act. The letter must also inform the applicant of their right to request a review under s 202 within twenty-one days of notification of the decision. This right to review is a pre-requisite to the right of appeal to the county court under s 204 on a point of law. Thus, whereas before, all challenges to homelessness decisions were made by way of judicial review, in most cases use is now made of the county court, which is to be welcomed. On appeal the court can confirm, quash or, significantly, vary the decision of the local authority giving the county court slightly wider powers than those available to the High Court on judicial review. It is still the decision letter which will form the basis for the appeal, subject to the review procedure having been unsuccessfully pursued. As under the previous law, advisors should ensure that they request copies of the information on the local authority's file to which the applicant or advisor is entitled and from which the strength of the review or legal challenge.

7.133 Another option where a violent partner and the victim are joint tenants of public sector rented accommodation is for the victim to give notice to quit the accommodation, as notice by one joint tenant is valid to terminate the tenancy, even though the other joint tenant does not know and would not wish the tenancy to be terminated; this was established by the House of Lords in *Hammersmith and Fulham London Borough Council v Monk* [1992] 1 AC 478. Normally this action may render the notice giver intentionally homeless but it is a device used where the local authority agrees to it in consideration of their providing alternative accommodation in their area. This device, which is likely to be available only to local authority, or possibly housing association tenants will be discussed further in Chapter 10, where permanent housing solutions for cohabitants will be considered.

However, it should be noted here that this approach of collusion between a social landlord and domestic violence victim is not always straightforward although its efficacy has now been further endorsed by the House of Lords in *Harrow London Borough Council v Johnstone* [1997] 1 FLR 887. New grounds for possession are now available in the independent housing sector, inserted by s 145 HA 1996 in relation to secure tenancies and s 149 HA 1996 in relation to assured tenancies where the landlord is a registered social landlord or housing trust can be used. This enables the landlord to gain possession where one partner has left the accommodation because of violence or threats of violence made by the other towards them or towards a member of their family living with them. Thus, the landlord can recover the accommodation from the violent partner.

7.134 Anti-social behaviour injunctions can be used by Local Authorities to assist former cohabitants in council accommodation (s 152(3) HA 1996. However, the case of *Manchester City Council v Worthington* [2000] 1 411 makes it again clear that there are Human Rights Act pitfalls with committal proceedings. In this case, which involved serious violence and frequent breaches of the order, the rapidity and cursory nature of the committal hearing led to the respondent's appeal being allowed and a re-hearing ordered.

CHECKLIST IN DOMESTIC VIOLENCE SITUATIONS

I Non-molestation orders

7.135

- Check nature of cohabitation relationship and ensure parties are "associated" and whether there are any relevant children in need of protection.
- Consider in the light of this whether the court will be required to attach a power of arrest (s 47(1)).
- Consider whether the application should be made *ex parte*, whether there is a risk of significant harm attributable to the respondent's conduct, whether the applicant will be deterred otherwise and whether service is being evaded. Are the more stringent grounds met for imposing a power of arrest *ex parte* (s 47(3))?
- Has the Applicant notified the police? Is or will any action be taken by the police? Is the Respondent subject to bail conditions?
- Seek emergency legal aid where appropriate.
- Grant a certificate of emergency representation or make fax application to the LSC.

II Occupation orders

7.136

- Take full instructions on the nature of the relationship, the difficulties that have arisen, whether there is a risk of significant harm if no order is made and the possibility of alternative accommodation available to both parties.

- Consider whether an occupation order is appropriate to regulate right of occupation of the family home, and/or to permit entry for the applicant and/or restrict occupation/access by the respondent of the home and surrounding area.
- Establish that the property concerned is the family home, identify its tenure and further establish the respective rights of occupation of the parties in respect of it.
- If the applicant is "entitled", application for a s 33 occupation order will be appropriate, regardless of whether the cohabitants are of the same sex or heterosexual. Take instructions on the standard criteria set out in s 33(6) (housing and financial needs and resources, effect of an order or no order on health, safety and well-being of parties and children, and the conduct of the parties) and apply the balance of harm test in s 33(7).
- If the applicant is heterosexual, not entitled to occupy the home in his/her own right but the respondent is so entitled, apply for a s 36 occupation order and take full instructions on the standard and additional criteria set out in s 36(6) concerning the nature of the relationship, duration of cohabitation, presence of children, length of time since cohabitation ceased and existence of any pending proceedings between the parties. Have regard to the balance of harm question (s 36(7)). Consider also the impact of s 41 that the commitment of marriage has not been given.
- Where neither party is entitled, apply s 38 (heterosexuals only).
- Take instructions on appropriate ancillary orders to be applied for under s 40.
- Consider public funding position.
- If time-limited order granted, diary for need to make renewal application.
- Consider and advise on possibilities for final resolution of matter, and consider issuing appropriate proceedings and applying for order restraining service of notice to quit by excluded joint periodic tenant as soon as possible.
- Notify mortgagee or landlord of outcome of application or intended further application where appropriate.

III. Other remedies

7.137
- Where the 1996 Act does not provide a remedy, consider the possibility of injunctions in tort and any criminal or civil remedy under the Protection from Harassment Act 1997.

Chapter 8

The status of children on relationship breakdown: resolving disputes under the Children Act 1989

8.01 When a relationship breaks down, any children of the relationship all too frequently become a focus for the dispute between their parents. Both parties often seek legal advice as regards their respective positions in relation to the children. The introduction of the CA 1989 radically altered the approach of the law to such disputes in both the married and the unmarried contexts. Indeed, an important achievement has been to establish a common statutory code available to the courts to resolve issues relating to children on relationship breakdown, regardless of the marital status of the parents.

8.02 Much has happened in terms of the support available to parents in dispute, including cohabiting parents, since the last edition of this book. At that time, the fear was expressed that the implementation of the divorce reforms contained in Part II Family Law Act 1996 (FLA 1996) and the likely increased demand on mediation and support services by divorcing couples would make such services virtually inaccessible by cohabitants.

8.03 In fact, developments since the final announcement that the divorce reforms are not now to be implemented, are favourable to cohabitants going through relationship breakdown. For it seems that there are to be more relationship support and mediation services in general, and the pure marriage focus contained in the FLA 1996 has been lost. Indeed it is fair to say that despite the demise of the pro-mediation Family Law Act, the fact that it was extensively piloted and much has been learned by the legal profession during this process, has led to a sea-change in the approach to family disputes, particularly those concerning children.

8.04 Mediation is now being promoted both by the courts and the Community Legal Service (part of the Legal Services Commission) as well as the Law Society and the Solicitors' Family Law Association (SFLA) in their codes of conduct. Furthermore, the Lord Chancellor's Department has just announced its programme for Marriage and Relationship Support, which is no longer restricted to married couples. This again indicates that the marriage-centric view of family disputes is waning. The National Family and Parenting Institute launched in 1999 has now set up a telephone help-line for parents called "Parentline" and another help-line "Parentline Plus" aims to support the well-being of disadvantaged families, whether married or not. It runs parenting classes and its website on http://www.nfpi.org offers help and support to parents and information and training for professionals working with parents and children. Thus it appears that it is now much better recognised that unmarried cohabiting parents have similar needs and concerns to married parents, with the welfare of the children in either style of family being uppermost for all involved.

8.05 Thus, whether or not a client is publicly funded, advisors of unmarried parents in dispute about their children's future arrangements on relationship breakdown should, in the first place (except where there are concerns about violence within the relationship), suggest a mediation appointment to see whether differences can be resolved by reaching an out of court agreement. Where appropriate, this can be translated into a consent order in court proceedings. Many family courts now have conciliation or mediation schemes which include disputes between unmarried parents, and there are many more out of court schemes. Public funding by way of a Certificate of General Family Help or legal representation will often be contingent upon the possibility of mediation having been explored, (Funding Code Procedures C27-29) although other forms of funding will be available for mediation in such cases. These include (for the mediator) Family Mediation and (for the client's solicitor) legal help or in some cases Help with Mediation (if a client is participating in family mediation or has successfully reached agreement or settlement as a result of such mediation) and is in need of legal assistance (to perhaps draft minutes of agreement for approval by the court). However, the mere fact that a mediation session takes place will not in itself justify the provision of this level of funding. The appropriateness of mediation will have to be considered, as well as the willingness of the parties to participate, but the possibility of resolving a dispute concerning children by this means should always be examined at the outset before harmful litigation is launched. Family Mediation is now widely available and both National Family Mediation and the Family Mediators Association as well as the UK College of Family Mediators should be able to advise on the availability of mediators in local areas (see Appendix III for details). In addition, the SFLA and the Law Society can advise of where to find lawyer mediators, who will obviously not be able to act as both mediator and legal representative to either party (see Appendix III). They also run training courses for lawyers wishing to become mediators. The Community Legal Service Directory lists mediators who undertake publicly funded mediation.

8.06 Note also that the Children Act Advisory Committee 's (CAAC's) Handbook of Best Practice in Children Act cases is still available and the SFLA and Law Society publish codes for their family specialist members on good practice in children cases. The Lord Chancellor's Department has also produced a Guide to Family Mediation for those who may require or be required to use mediation services, entitled 'Sorting things out together – How family mediation can help you'. This is available on-line on the LCD web-site at www.lcd.gov.uk.

8.07 When relationships break down, the key issues to be decided in connection with the children are those of residence and contact, which are, of course, the concepts adopted by s 8 CA 1989 Act to replace the old notions of custody and access. Section 8 also provides for prohibited steps orders and specific issue orders to be made where the context requires in such disputes. However, one additional issue that can arise only in the unmarried context under the 1989 Act is that of parental responsibility.

8.08 Whereas all married parents are automatically endowed with parental responsibility in respect of their children, currently only mothers, not fathers, have this status automatically conferred on the birth of a child where the parents are unmarried (see Chapter 2). Thus, unless a s 4 parental responsibility order or agreement has been made before the parents' relationship breaks down, fathers may at this juncture seek to acquire parental responsibility and this will be considered below.

8.09 First, however, the general principles of the Act which to a large extent govern the way in which disputes between parents relating to their children are decided, will be considered.

1 General principles—s 1 CA 1989

8.10 Part I of the Act is an attempt to translate into practice the underlying philosophy of the CA 1989 as expressed by the Law Commission in their Report *Review of Child Law: Guardianship and Custody* (1988, Law Com No. 172); and it is in s 1 that the main guiding principles for determining disputes are to be found. There has been considerable clarification by case law on how those principles, which differ from those established under the old law, are to be applied in practice by the courts. Where the CA 1989 has in effect encapsulated previously established principles, then pre-Children Act case law (discussed in some detail in the first edition of this book) may still be of relevance (see Barlow, *Living Together: A Guide to the Law,* 1992, pages 136–139).

8.11 Prior to the implementation of the Human Rights Act 1998 (HRA 1998), there was some concern as to whether the welfare principle conflicted with the right to private and family life in Article 8 of the European Convention on Human Rights. Whilst the rights of children are protected by the Convention, so are the rights of the adults in the family and these require careful balancing where there is a dispute between family members. Was legislation, which clearly prioritised the rights of children, therefore incompatible with the Convention? In *Scott v United Kingdom* [2000] 1 FLR 958, the European court of Human Rights concluded that it was not. Here the making of a freeing order and the dismissal of a progressing mother's application for increased contact with her child was not a breach of Article 8 on the basis that Article 8 was not an absolute right and is qualified by Article 8(2) which permits interference on certain grounds. Article 8 states:

'1. Everyone has the right to respect for his private and family life, his home and his correspondence'.
2 There shall be no interference by a public authority with the exercise of this right except such as is in accordance with the law and is necessary in a democratic society in the interests of national security, public safety or the economic well-being of the country, for

the prevention of disorder or crime, for the protection of health or morals, or for the protection of the rights and freedoms of others.'

8.12 Thus the balancing of the rights of family members fell within the state's margin of appreciation and here the welfare principle could be justified "for the protection of the rights and freedoms of others". Therefore, whilst in principle each family members' rights start with equal protection, this has to be measured in each case against the justifications for interference with those rights, including the need to protect the rights of others.

8.13 In addition to the welfare principle, the 1989 Act introduced a welfare checklist (s 1(3)), a statutory principle of no delay (s 1(2)) and, perhaps most radical of all, a presumption that the courts would make no order unless it could be shown that the order would bring some positive advantage to the child (s 1(5)). These will each be considered in turn as they provide the background against which all disputes relating to children on parental relationship breakdown are decided.

2 Parental responsibility on relationship breakdown

8.14 Parental responsibility is defined in s 2 as "all the rights, duties, powers, responsibilities and authority which by law a parent of a child has in relation to a child and his or her property". It is given automatically on the birth of a child, jointly to both parents where they are married to each other, but only to the mother where they are unmarried. Although the government have committed themselves to legislate to give all parents, who jointly register the birth, joint parental responsibility whether or not they are married, as part of the Adoption and Children Bill 2001 (see Chapter 2), this will not be retrospective.

8.15 Thus, unless a s 4 parental responsibility order or agreement (see Chapter 2) has been made earlier, fathers may seek to acquire parental responsibility after the parents' relationship has broken down, in addition to resolving the obvious issues of residence and contact. Where an unmarried father obtains a "residence order" whereby the child lives with him following breakdown of the relationship, the court must make a s 4 order giving him parental responsibility (s 12(1)), and this cannot be brought to an end whilst the residence order remains in force (s 12(4)).

8.16 Perhaps surprisingly, despite the s 1(5) no order presumption, the courts have for the most part been ready and willing to grant parental responsibility orders wherever the father is seeking contact. One reason for this approach can be found by comparing the position of married parents with unmarried parents. Following breakdown of the relationship, where both parents have "parental responsibility" arising out of marriage, they retain it, even though a residence order is made in favour of one parent alone.

8.17 In the case of married parents, parental responsibility cannot be withdrawn from either parent, although the making of residence, contact, specific issue or prohibited steps orders can restrict it. In the case of unmarried parents, this is also true of the mother. Thus even where an unmarried father becomes the sole resident parent and a s 4 order is accordingly also made, the mother will retain parental responsibility, which cannot, by virtue of s 2(9), be surrendered or transferred. However, as the unmarried father can acquire parental responsibility only by virtue of s 4, his parental responsibility can, subject to s 12(4), be terminated in accordance with s 4(3), upon the application of himself or of any other person who has parental responsibility for the child or, with leave of the court, on the application of the child. It should also be stressed that s 2(8) states that the fact that a person has parental responsibility for a child shall not entitle them to act in any way which would be incompatible with any order made under the Act. Thus, although a non-resident parent may retain parental responsibility and thus may approach the child's school, or consent to medical treatment, it does not entitle him or her to take the child to live with him or her where there is a residence order in favour of the child's other parent.

(a) Summary of options for unmarried parents

8.18 The options with regard to parental responsibility on relationship breakdown, although almost always linked to issues of residence and contact, are as follows.

(i) Where a father does not have parental responsibility on relationship breakdown

8.19 *The parties can make their own arrangements for residence and contact, without seeking a formal court order or making a parental responsibility agreement* This leaves an unmarried father in a vulnerable position, as only the mother has parental responsibility and he has no legally recognised status *vis-à-vis* his child. This could present difficulties with third parties even if there are no problems with the child's mother. From the father's point of view, this is the least favourable option, and one, it is suggested, which is inappropriate where the parents have cohabited and undertaken joint parenting for any length of time. It does, however, leave the mother in a position of theoretical complete control unless and until such time as the father makes applications for parental responsibility or residence or contact.

8.20 *The parties can enter into a parental responsibility agreement and make their own arrangements for residence and contact, without seeking to formalise these in a court order* If the arrangements break down, s 8 orders will have to be sought at that stage. Alternatively, a consent order could be sought, but the court could refuse to make it on the basis of the s 1(5) no order presumption if arrangements have been made and are working well, as discussed above. In *Re X (minors) (parental responsibility agreement)* [2000] 1 FLR 517, the Court of Appeal confirmed that the parents' ability to enter into a Parental Responsibility Agreement was an important part of their right to respect for private and family life under Article 8 of the European Convention on Human Rights. Thus even where the child was in care and the local authority objected to the father having parental responsibility for the child, the mother could not be prevented from entering into the agreement under s 4 CA 1989, and, in contrast to a Parental Responsibility Order, the welfare principle is not applicable in the case of a Parental Responsibility Agreement.

8.21 *The parties can agree neither arrangements nor the issue of parental responsibility and thus the only option is for the father to apply for s 8 orders and, if he wishes, a parental responsibility order* The court could make a parental responsibility order in any event and must do so if a residence order is made in favour of the father (s 12(1)). This cannot be brought to an end whilst the residence order is in force (s 12(4)). Where a father applies for contact and parental responsibility, the recent trend in the courts, as indicated below, is that the father should almost always be granted the status of parental responsibility despite objections by the mother, although in *Re H (parental responsibility)* [1998] 1 FLR 855, the Court of Appeal stated that this does not amount to a presumption in favour of granting parental responsibility. There is also some evidence from research that the dropping of applications for parental responsibility orders are being used as a bargaining tool in negotiations relating to contact (see Butler *et al*, *The Children Act 1989 and the Unmarried Father* (1993) 5 JCL 157 and [1993] Fam Law 90). An alternative is for a mother to cross-apply for a residence order, even though there is no dispute about residence as opposed to contact, to ensure that s 2(8) will prevent any inconsistent use of the father's parental responsibility. However, the no order presumption will have to be overcome by showing that this would provide the child with a positive benefit. Whether the resident parent's peace of mind would supply this is questionable, although if the child itself were expressing a desire to have its permanent home settled by the court, this would presumably be sufficient.

(ii) Where a father has previously acquired parental responsibility

8.22 *Both parents retain parental responsibility and no further orders are made, with all arrangements for residence and contact being made between the parents by agreement* This places the parents in the same position as most married parents, and may become more common where an agreement has been reached following successful mediation. A consent order could be sought to formalise the agreed arrangements, but the court could refuse to make it on the basis of the s 1(5) no order presumption if arrangements have been made and are working well, as discussed above. A deed of separation could be used to formally record the arrangements. Alternatively, should arrangements break down, appropriate s 8 orders can be sought at this later time.

8.23 *Both parents retain parental responsibility but subject to orders for contact and/or residence* Where there is a dispute as to the arrangements for the children at the time of the relationship breakdown, this is the most likely scenario. In the normal course of events, even though an unmarried father's parental responsibility is capable of being terminated by the court (s 4(3)), it is highly unusual for this to happen. The no order presumption (s 1(5)) predicates against it and it would have to be shown that such a step was required in the interests of the child. In *Re P* *(terminating parental responsibility)* [1995] 1 FLR 1048, FD, it was stated that there was a presumption that parental responsibility would continue. It should be noted that if contact only, rather than the place of a child's residence, is in issue, the court may feel it inappropriate to make a residence order in view of s 1(5). If the resident parent or a child feels insecure, given the other parent's parental responsibility, it could be argued that a residence order would be in the child's interests, given the resultant restrictions of s 2(8) on the exercise of parental responsibility.

8.24 *Mother retains parental responsibility but father's parental responsibility is terminated by order of the court* This is unlikely to happen unless the father has shown complete disregard to the child's welfare. In *Re P (terminating parental responsibility)* (above), where the father, unbeknown to the mother, had seriously injured the child, it was confirmed that the welfare principle (s 1(1)) applied to an application to terminate parental responsibility and that the same tests of attachment and commitment between father and child as applied on an application for parental responsibility were to be used to assess an application to terminate it. It was useful to consider whether the court would have granted parental responsibility, if the father did not already have it.

(b) The case law

8.25 How live an issue the factor of acquiring parental responsibility has become, can be judged from the burgeoning case law, some of which relates to the disadvantaged position of unmarried fathers without parental responsibility whose children are placed in the care of the local authority or are being considered for adoption. Although the European Court of Human Rights has confirmed that it is not a breach of Article 8 nor is it unjustifiably discriminatory under Article 8 of the European Convention not to grant parental responsibility to all fathers (see most recently *B v United Kingdom* [2000] 1 FLR 1), the government is committed to reform, and legislation will, it seems be introduced to give parental responsibility to fathers who jointly register their child's birth with the mother. However, this is not to be retrospective and even after the implementation of the proposed legislation, there will also be fathers who do not jointly register the birth and thus do not automatically acquire it in this way. Thus the ability to enter into a parental responsibility agreement and to apply for a parental responsibility order will remain important.

8.26 Recently, the Court of Appeal has made clear that is considers parental responsibility to be a status which does not interfere with the day-to-day care of a child and is, accordingly, a status which should normally be granted to a father who has shown commitment and attachment to his child. Where there has been cohabitation by a child's parents, this will normally be straightforward, as in the absence of matters which would prejudice the child's welfare, a father will usually have done enough. In *Re S (a minor) (parental responsibility)* [1995] 3 FCR 225, CA, Ward LJ said that the essence of granting a parental responsibility order was the grant of status. He indicated that is was wrong to concentrate on an applicant's rights and powers and said it was the status given to a father by fatherhood that should be concentrated upon. This is perhaps to underestimate the empowering effect of parental responsibility in practical terms, although this can be restricted by other orders of the court (see s 2(8)). Nonetheless, this approach is a departure from the pre-CA 1989 law and aims to reduce the isolation of non-resident parents from their children. What then is the test for making a parental responsibility order?

8.27 In *Re H (minors) (illegitimate children: father: parental rights)(No 2)* [1991] 1 FLR 214, it was held, pre-CA 1989, that a father whose children were in care and about to be placed for adoption should be granted an old-style parental rights order, providing the court was satisfied as to the degree of commitment which the father had shown towards the children, the degree of attachment between father and children and the reasons for the father applying for the order.

8.28 This has become the accepted test approved by the Court of Appeal many times since the coming into force of the CA 1989 in the context of parental responsibility orders (see eg *Re G (a minor) (parental responsibility order)* [1994] 1 FLR 504, CA). In *Re C and V (minors) (parental responsibility and contact)* [1998] 1 FLR 392, a father of a child with special medical needs, which only the mother had been trained to meet, was refused contact but granted the status of parental responsibility to reflect his commitment.

8.29 Further guidance was given in *Re P (a minor) (parental responsibility order)* [1994] 1 FLR 578, where it was held that the fact that parents cannot co-operate is not a reason for refusing a parental responsibility order, for the effect of s 2(8) is to prevent a person with an order interfering with the day-to-day management of a child's life where the child lives elsewhere. Thus a mother's objection is not a reason to refuse an order, although in light of s 2(8) it would be a reason for seeking s 8 orders to carefully regulate other matters. Furthermore, although financial commitment to the child may be a factor, and in *Re S (a minor) (Parental Responsibility)* [1995] 2 FLR 648, Butler-Sloss LJ stated that a father showing real commitment ought to cement it by sharing the burdens as well as the pleasure of looking after a child, in *Re H (a minor) (parental responsibility order: maintenance)* [1996] 1 FLR 867, the Court of Appeal made it clear that the court should not refuse to make a parental responsibility order as a means of coercing a father to pay maintenance. The thrust of these cases is that nearly all unmarried fathers will obtain parental responsibility if they want it, and this gives credence to the argument that all parents should get parental responsibility for their children regardless of their marital status.

8.30 Nonetheless, more recently the Court of Appeal has confirmed that there is no presumption in favour of a father being granted parental responsibility (*Re H (parental responsibility)* [1998] 1 FLR 855). Clearly the welfare principle applies to any application for a parental responsibility order, and will be refused where a father's misconduct shows a lack of commitment to the child. In *Re H (parental responsibility)* [1998] 1 FLR 855, the Court of Appeal refused to grant an order to a father who had deliberately harmed his son and in *Re P (Parental Responsibility:*

Change of Name) [1997] 2 FLR 722, a father who had been imprisoned on numerous occasions as a result of his criminal activities had thereby demonstrated a lack of commitment to his child. The motive for applying for parental responsibility may also be relevant. In *Re P (Parental Responsibility)* [1998] 2 FLR 96, it was indicated that an order should be refused where the father's reasons for applying were demonstrably wrong and improper and where s 8 orders were not likely to prove an effective barrier. Here a father who planned to use parental responsibility to interfere with and possibly undermine the mother's care of the child was refused an order. Such motives and ineffectual nature of s 8 orders will not, however, always be easy to prove.

8.31 A parental responsibility order can be an important means of an unmarried father obtaining *locus standi* in other proceedings. In *Re H (a minor) (parental responsibility)* [1993] 1 FLR 484 a court granted an order to a father whose child had moved to Scotland and whose stepfather now intended to adopt, in order to protect his position in these proceedings.

8.32 In *Re E (a minor) (parental responsibility blood test)* [1995] 1 FLR 392 where a father, whom the mother feared might remove the child from the jurisdiction, had enjoyed frequent contact but was refused staying contact, the Court of Appeal stated that the approach to any application for a parental responsibility order by a father who had shown the degree of attachment and commitment to a child as this father was that *prima facie* an order would be for the welfare of the child. There would have to be cogent evidence that the child's welfare would be adversely affected for the order to be refused. In *Re T (parental responsibility: contact)* [1993] 2 FLR 450, CA, it was held that where there had been intense hostility by the father towards the mother, showing her hatred and serious violence and showing no regard for the child's welfare (going so far as to fail to return the young child after contact for nine days), the court was right to refuse, *inter alia*, a parental responsibility order.

(c) Other issues

8.33 It seems important that, on relationship breakdown, fathers are made aware of the potential significance of not acquiring parental responsibility. For example, they will not be automatically entitled to notice of certain types of proceedings, such as adoption proceedings, discharge of care order proceedings or unless they have lived with the child for a period of at least three years, s 8 proceedings. This in itself may in some cases raise human rights issues under Articles 8 and 14 of the European Convention, were a child to be adopted rather than placed with a potentially committed father, as almost happened in *Re O (a minor) (custody: adoption)* [1992] 1 FLR 77. In other circumstances, their status as a parent of the child may require that they be given notice. This is the case with emergency protection orders (s 44(1)), care orders (s 31), child assessment orders (s 43(1)) and applications for appointment of a child's guardian (s 5(1)). From a mother's point of view, a parental responsibility order made on breakdown may give rise to feelings of insecurity, although her position is no less secure than that of any married mother, *vis-à-vis* her children on divorce. In practice, a father who is likely to abuse the arrangements agreed or decided upon by the court is likely to do so regardless of whether or not parental responsibility is granted. Abuse, which blatantly disregards the welfare of the child, may well be sufficient to found an application to terminate parental responsibility, as discussed above.

8.34 The issue of disputed parentage may arise in relation to both parental responsibility and contact applications as well as in the context of child support. The Child Support and Pensions Act 2000 has now brought about major reform to this area with a view to making it compliant with the European Convention on Human rights. It has introduced, with effect from April 2001, a new integrated mechanism for obtaining a declaration of parentage in all contexts and has replaced the two procedures formerly available under the Child Support Act 1991 (CSA 1991) and the (FLA 1986) (see amended s 27 CSA 1991 and new s 55A FLA 1986). Anyone with sufficient interest may now bring an application for a declaration of parentage and thus the prohibition on declarations of illegitimacy (s 58(5)(b) FLA 1986) is abolished. Where a child is concerned the court has power to refuse to hear the application if it considers this is not in the child's best interests and no subsequent application can then be made without leave (ss 55A(5) and (6) FLA 1986). In addition, s 23 FLA 1986 was finally brought into force alongside these reforms and now permits other bodily samples to be taken to resolve parentage disputes including DNA testing. Crucially, it has also amended s 21 (3) Family Law Reform Act 1969, enabling the court to consent to a test where it believes it to be in the child's best interests, where the resident parent refuses to do so. Previously, blood tests could not be ordered to determine parentage other than when needed to decide an ancillary issue such as contact and could not be ordered in respect of a child where the person having care and control did not consent (see *Re E (parental responsibility: blood tests)* [1995] 1 FLR 392, CA). In *Re R (blood test: constraint)* [1998] 1 FLR 745, it was suggested that s 21(3) Family Law Reform Act 1969 could be circumvented by a court ordering the child to be handed over to the Official Solicitor who could then consent to blood tests. Hale J also suggested that the inherent jurisdiction could be used to give effect to and order for tests where the parent refused to consent. However, in *Re O and J (a child) (paternity: blood tests)* [2000] 1 FLR 418 this approach was rejected and Wall J considered that there was no power to compel a parent to comply with an order for blood tests. This has ultimately led to reform reversing the position in the 2000 Act, enabling the court to consent where it feels it appropriate for the child.

8.35 Thus, it is no longer necessary for the court to draw inferences from either party's refusal to consent. The welfare test has always applied to such applications (see *O v L (Blood Tests)* [1995] 2 FLR 930, CA) and it has been said that every child has the right to know the truth about their parentage (see *Re H a minor (blood tests: Parental Rights)* [1997] Fam Law 89, CA). However, the recent case of *Re T (Paternity: Ordering Blood Tests)* [2001] *Fam Law* 738 (discussed below) has now considered the position post-2000 Act reforms and in the context of the competing human rights under Article 8 of the Convention of the child, the social and the natural parents. In *Re O and J (above)* Wall J stated that the law in England and

Wales on this issue failed to comply with Article 8 of the European Convention on Human Rights. Arguably, a child's right to family life is predicated upon them knowing who exactly that family comprises. Similarly, the law infringed Article 7 of the United Nations Convention on the Rights of the Child which indicates that children should as far as possible have the right to know their parents. For a discussion and call for reform on these issues see Sharp, "Paternity Testing – Time to Update the Law", [2000] Fam Law 560. It is perhaps unsurprising therefore that DNA tests were ordered in *Re T* (above) and confirmed that the approach in *Re H* (above) was still good law. Here the mother and husband were unable to have children and the mother had had relationships with four men with a view to becoming pregnant and a child was born in 1994. The applicant publicly proclaimed that he was the father but an order for tests was refused in 1995. Following the introduction of the HRA 1998, he applied again and here the court granted the application, ordering DNA tests on the basis that they were in the child's best interests. Here, where the child had the right to respect for his private and family life in the sense of knowing his true identity, it conflicted with a competing right to respect for a private and family life within the stability of his mother's social family unit. Nonetheless where as here the disputed parentage was in the public domain and there was a risk of the child learning of it, certainty of parentage was in the child's best interests even when balanced against the rights of the mother and husband, whose relationship was thought stable enough to withstand the testing. It was also stated that the child's interests in knowing his identity carried the most weight and any interference with the mother and husband's rights under Article 8 was proportionate to the legitimate aim of providing the child with the knowledge of his true roots.

3 The welfare of the child post-CA 1989

(a) The welfare principle

8.36 Section 1(1) CA 1989 states that the child's welfare shall be the court's "paramount consideration" when determining any question regarding the upbringing of the child or the administration of a child's property. "Upbringing", however, it should be noted, is defined as including the care of the child, but not its maintenance (s 105(1)).

8.37 There is nothing radical about this principle, which has proved to be a restatement of the well-established welfare principle previously contained in s 1 Guardianship of Minors Act 1971 (GMA 1971), despite the slightly different wording. Various issues relating to the working of the principle have now been clarified in case law. Perhaps of greatest significance is the finding that it is not in breach of the right to family life protected by Article 8 of the European convention on Human Rights as considered in *Scott v United Kingdom* (discussed above). For elaboration of the potential difficulties surrounding potential incompatibility see Vine "Is the paramountcy principle compatible with Article 8?" [2000] *Family Law* 826.

8.38 Importantly, the welfare of the child is *not* the court's paramount consideration, although it is important, on an application under s 10(9) for leave to apply for a residence order, as otherwise some of the matters in that subsection would be otiose (see *Re A and W (minors) (residence order leave to apply)* [1992] 2 FLR 154 and *Re C (residence: child's application for leave)* [1995] 1 FLR 927, CA). By analogy, this must also be the case in relation to all applications for leave to apply for contact or any of the other s 8 orders.

8.39 However, in *Oxfordshire County Council v M* [1994] 1 FLR 175, the Court of Appeal held that under the 1989 Act and in wardship where the child's interests are paramount, legal professional privilege attaching to medical reports has to yield to that overriding principle. As a matter of practice, any leave granted for medical reports to be obtained is usually upon condition that the report is disclosed to all parties, forcing practitioners to make a tactical decision as to its likely impact on their client's case. Clients need to be carefully advised as to the advantages and disadvantages of obtaining this kind of evidence.

8.40 Issues have arisen in the public law arena as to how to resolve situations where the welfare of one child conflicts with that of another, an issue that could equally arise in the private law sphere. In *Birmingham City Council v H (No 3)* [1994] 1 FLR 224, where both mother and baby were children, the House of Lords established the principle that it was the best interests of the child who was the subject of the application which should prevail. However, in *Re F (a minor) (contact: child in care)* [1994] 2 FCR 1354, where a child in care sought contact with siblings not in care and who were opposed to contact, the Court of Appeal held that in respect of an application under s 34 (for contact between the child in care and another person), the child in care's welfare was paramount, although a contact order could not in practice bind the siblings. Yet, on a s 8 application by the child in care for contact with siblings, it was the siblings' welfare which was paramount. In *Re T and E (proceedings: conflicting interests)* [1995] 1 FLR 581, it was agreed that where applications involved different welfare tests, and in this instance the Adoption Act 1976 which makes the child's welfare the first consideration applied in respect of one child and the CA 1989 in respect of the other, then the welfare of the child subject to the 1989 Act prevailed due to the paramountcy principle. In *Re S a minor (Contact: Application by Sibling)* [1998] 2 FLR 897, where an application for contact was brought by an adopted child for contact with her birth sister who had also been adopted, it was made clear that it is the welfare of the child who is the subject of the application, here the birth sister and not the applicant, which will be paramount. Where all other things were equal however, and a conflict of welfare demands arises, the test is to provide the situation of least detriment to all the children.

8.41 Finally, in *Gibson v Austin* [1993] 1 FCR 638, argument to the effect that s 1(1) CA 1989 had overruled the *ratio* in *Richards v Richards* [1984] AC 174 making the child's welfare paramount in applications for ouster orders under the DVMPA 1976, rather than just one of a number of factors, was firmly rejected by the Court of Appeal. As noted in the last chapter, the draconian nature of the new remedy of occupation orders has similarly once again been emphasised post-1996 in *Chalmers v John* [1999] 1 FLR 392.

(b) The welfare checklist

8.42 Section 1(3) states:

> "In the circumstances mentioned in subsection (4), a court shall have regard in particular to—
> (a) the ascertainable wishes and feelings of the child concerned (considered in the light of his age and understanding);
> (b) his physical, emotional and educational needs;
> (c) the likely effect on him of any change in his circumstances;
> (d) his age, sex, background and any characteristics of his that the court considers relevant;
> (e) any harm which he has suffered or is at risk of suffering;
> (f) how capable each of his parents, and any other person in relation to whom the court considers the question to be relevant, is of meeting his needs; and
> (g) the range of powers available to the court under this Act in the proceedings in question."

8.43 This welfare checklist broke new ground by introducing, in statutory form, a set of priorities which the court must have particular regard to; but this is confined by s 1(4) to two specific situations. It applies firstly where the court is deciding whether to make, vary or discharge a s 8 order and this is opposed by any party to the proceedings. Thus, if the parties are agreed and the application is unopposed, the court does not have to apply the checklist, and, subject to the welfare principle and the no order presumption contained in s 1(5) (discussed below), the court cannot reject agreements made between parties on the basis of the checklist considerations alone. The wishes and feelings of a child, not a party to the proceedings would not, for example, therefore normally be an issue in a consent application. Nonetheless, although the court does not have to have regard to it in other situations, given it is for the most part a restatement of matters which courts have traditionally considered in the context of the welfare principle, matters contained in the checklist may well be taken into account when applying s 1(1). Indeed, it has been described by the Court of Appeal as "a useful *aide memoire*" (see *Re B (minors) (change of surname)* [1996] 1 FLR 791). The other context in which the checklist is mandatorily applied is where the court is considering whether to make a care or supervision order under Part IV of the Act. Here, agreement cannot oust the court's power to intervene and apply the checklist. Yet, care and supervision orders can be made only on application to the court by a local authority or other authorised person such as the NSPCC. Section 37 enables the court to order an investigation of the child's circumstances by the local authority where it feels it may be appropriate for a care or supervision order to be made, but the court has lost its power to make a care or supervision order of its own motion in family proceedings where it is troubled by the unsatisfactory nature of the arrangements proposed by the parents. Although an application can be made for a care or supervision order, either as an end in itself or in other family proceedings (s 31), the court's loss of power to intervene in this way is a sign of the shift made in the 1989 Act towards leaving responsibility for children much more with their parents and free from state interference.

8.44 From the point of view of cohabitants on relationship breakdown, the checklist is likely to be of most significance on s 8 applications where the parties cannot agree arrangements for the children following breakdown. It aimed to give a consistency of approach to the court's consideration of all the matters relevant to such applications, but the weight given to these individual factors is still a matter for the discretion of the individual court. It should be noted at this stage that where disputes concerning children do culminate in litigation, the court welfare officers (CWO's) reporters used to prepare reports in private proceedings and guardians *ad litem* appointed to represent the child's interests in public law proceedings have been renamed as "children and family reporters" and "children's guardian" respectively. With effect from April 2001 they are now all governed by a new agency, the Children and Family Court Advisory and Support Service (CAFCASS), introduced by the Criminal Justice and Court Services Act 2000.

8.45 A body of case law has grown up around the matters specified in the checklist and now provides useful indicators of how courts are likely to view the issues raised.

(i) Ascertainable wishes and feelings

8.46 Although this heads the list that is not to say that any greater weight is to be given to these than to any of the other checklist considerations (*Re W (a minor) (medical treatment: court's jurisdiction)* [1993] 1 FLR 1, CA). It is, however, the matter which best illustrates a departure from the approach under the old law towards a more child-centred approach. The fact that the wishes must be ascertainable and must be considered in the light of the child's age and understanding, indicate that the maturity of the child is critical to the weight which will be given by the court to these factors. In *Re P (a minor) (education)* [1992] 1 FLR 316, the Court of Appeal held that it was the court's duty to take the wishes and views of older children into account, especially if they were sensible, mature and intelligent. Nonetheless, the wishes of younger children may be ascertainable through indirect means, such as observation by a children and family reporter of behaviour with the adults involved. The maturity of the child must also be assessed in the context of the issue which was to be decided. Thus in *Re E (a minor)* [1993] 1 FLR 386, a 15-year-old Jehovah's witness who wished to refuse a blood transfusion in the knowledge that he might die, was nonetheless adjudged by the court to not be able to fully appreciate the implications of his decision, despite being found to be mature enough to make decisions about his own welfare generally. This underlines the fact that although the wishes and feelings must be had regard to where the child is sufficiently mature, that is not to say that they are paramount where these conflict with their own welfare. In *Re P (wardship: care and control)* [1992] 2 FCR 681, Butler-Sloss LJ made the principle clear:

> "[I]n all family cases it is the duty of the court to listen to the children, ascertain their wishes and feelings and then make decisions about their future, having regard to but not constricted by those wishes."

8.47 Some illustrations in context are useful. In *Re F (minors) (denial of contact)* [1993] 2 FLR 677, the Court of Appeal found that great weight was correctly given to the views of brothers aged 12 and 9 who did not want to have contact with their transsexual father. In cases where leave is sought to remove a child permanently from the jurisdiction, the wishes and feelings have often been critical. In *M v M (minors) (jurisdiction)* [1993] Fam Law 396, the Court of Appeal found that a trial judge who granted leave to a mother to take two articulate children to Israel against their wishes was wrong and had failed to sufficiently consider the wishes and feelings of the children and the views of the welfare officer. Again, in *M v A (wardship: removal from jurisdiction)* [1993] 2 FLR 715, a mother, with whom the children had their principal home, (although their care was shared with their father), was refused leave to take two boys aged 12 and 9 permanently to Canada in view of their wish to remain in England with their father despite finding that they loved both homes.

8.48 A change of approach has been taken by the Court of Appeal in relation to the weight to be given to children's views on a change of surname. In *Re F (child surname)*, CA, it was confirmed that this was an important issue not to be taken lightly and to be decided in accordance with the child's welfare; and in *Re B (minors) (change of surname)* [1996] 1 FLR 791, it was held that although the wishes and feelings of adolescent children usually prevail in issues of residence or contact, this did not extend to a formal change of surname from that of their father to stepfather. It should be noted that this application was treated as an application under s 13 CA 1989 given the existence of an old-style custody order and not as a s 8 application for a specific issue order. The court was not therefore specifically directed to the checklist, although the court described it as a useful *aide memoire*.

8.49 How the court ascertains children's views may vary, although the usual course would be through a children and family reporter's report. Whether it is appropriate for the judge to see the child personally in private remains a matter of discretion for individual judges, although increasingly the view is being taken that the child should be heard from directly, given their right to a fair hearing reinforced by the HRA 1998 (Article 6). It is anticipated that there will be an increase of cases in which children are themselves represented in order to avoid potential breach of Article 6 of the European Convention on Human Rights which a court, as a public body, has a duty to prevent under the 1998 Act. If leave is granted, then children of sufficient understanding may become parties to proceedings (s 10(8)), and in private law proceedings, it is for the court to decide whether they must be represented through a next friend (see rule 9.2A FPR 1991) or whether, in the case of older children, they may instruct a solicitor directly. In *Re CT (a minor) (wardship: representation)* [1993] 2 FLR 278, a 14-year-old girl, whose solicitor was satisfied she had sufficient understanding to give instructions in relation to her application for a residence order in favour of her aunt and grandmother, should not have been warded and the court had no power to impose a Guardian ad Litem (GAL) on her. The principles set out in *Re S (a minor) (independent representation)* [1993] 2 FLR 437 at page 448 in relation to whether a child could proceed without a GAL were held in *Re C (residence: child's application for leave)* [1996] 1 FCR 461 to be equally applicable to applications for leave to seek a s 8 order. A useful article on how professionals may judge the capacity of children to participate in family proceedings is Sawyer, "The competence of children to participate in family proceedings" [1995] CFLQ 7(4) 180. As noted, however, the implementation of the HRA 1998 and the applicability to children of Article 6 guaranteeing access to a court and to a fair hearing is predicted to increase the number of cases in which children are separately represented.

(ii) The child's physical, emotional and educational needs, the ability to meet them, the risk of harm and the effect of change

8.50 Many of the checklist factors are matters which in the context of the arrangements on relationship breakdown, overlap and may be more or less influential depending on the nature of the order sought. Advisors need to assess their client's proposals for a child in this overall context. They need then to compare them with the proposals of any other party to the proceedings in order to present their client's proposals as the arrangements most likely to promote the child's welfare.

8.51 In terms of a child's physical needs, unless a child has particular medical or special needs (in which case the availability of appropriate facilities to meet these within reach of each parent's proposed home will be a very significant factor), the major issue is likely to be the accommodation which a resident parent can offer. That is not to say that the parent who can offer the most materially is at an advantage, as often the court is in a position to equalise the effects of such imbalance through maintenance and transfer of property orders or settlements under Sch 1 CA 1989 (see Chapters 9 to 11). However, a parent with unsatisfactory or undetermined accommodation is at a disadvantage as compared with one whose arrangements are clear and satisfactory. Stability in terms of the home will always be an important factor and the arrangements proposed for the child's education, particularly if these involve a move to a new school will be examined. The effect of any change in the child's circumstances is another factor to which the court is directed to have particular regard (s 1(3)(c)) and thus any change that is proposed by a parent needs to be as positive as possible for the child. However, the quality of day-to-day care available probably carries most weight, which is a matter which links in with the question of how capable each of the parents is in meeting the child's needs (s 1(3)(f)). Continuity of care has always been considered an important factor and there is a tendency for courts to want to retain the *status quo* if possible. Thus, all other things being equal, the parent who has the children immediately after relationship breakdown places themselves in a position of advantage, particularly if a long time elapses before the matter is heard (see eg *Re A (a minor) (custody)* [1991] 2 FLR 394). Courts are also extremely reluctant to split up brothers and sisters (see eg *Re P (custody of children) (split custody order)* [1991] 1 FLR 337).

8.52 In terms of the child's emotional needs, the closeness of the relationship that each parent has with the child and the ties between a child and his or her brothers and sisters will be powerful factors. The ability of the resident parent to meet the child's needs, including the need to have contact with the other parent, can be critical to the decision as to which parent should be the resident parent (see *Re A (a minor) (custody)* [1991] 2 FLR 394 per Butler-Sloss LJ at page 400). More recently, in *Re D (minors) (family appeals)* [1995] 1 FCR 301, the Court of Appeal refused to interfere in the decision of the lower court to place young children with a working father as it was not plainly wrong, given, it seems, the mother's underestimation of the importance of a father to the children, whereas the father had a proper recognition of the importance of a mother. Generally speaking, there is a rebuttable presumption of fact that a very young child would be better off with the mother, as this was what the natural position would be (*Re W (a minor) (residence order)* [1992] 2 FLR 332, CA).

8.53 Where one parent is working and the other not, this can prove to be an advantage to the parent able to offer full-time care. However, if for example, the children are used to going to a nursery or childminder and are happy there, a change from this routine to remaining at home with one parent may not be viewed so positively.

8.54 Finally, the important factor of whether a child has suffered or is at risk of suffering harm (s 1(3)(e)) has been deliberately widely drawn to ensure that it is capable of encompassing both physical and emotional "harm". This must be judged in the context of the individual child and the history of the family. There has been something of a change in the approach of the courts as to harm to a child that is indirect, at least in contact applications. Where there has been domestic violence directed by one parent at the other parent (usually the mother) but not the child, the child's right to know both parents overrode in most cases, in the court's view, any negative impact the mother's fear would have on the child. However, recently the Court of Appeal has indicated that family courts need to have a heightened awareness of the existence of and consequences to children of exposure to domestic violence between their parents and experts' reports on the issue will be critical (see *L, V, M, H (contact: domestic violence)* [2001] FAM 260). In the case of residence being sought by a parent now in a gay relationship, this is a factor to be taken into account (see *C v C (a minor) (custody: appeal)* [1991] 1 FLR 223). It is likely to be argued that a child's exposure to such a situation would put them at risk of suffering "harm". However, as was successfully done in *B v B (minors) (custody, care and control)* [1991] 1 FLR 402, advisors should consider calling expert evidence to persuade the court that there is no such risk of harm in the sense of an increased risk of homosexuality or damage resulting from teasing by other children in relation to their atypical home circumstances.

8.55 Whether a matter is likely to cause harm is not always obvious. In *Re W (Residence Order)* [1999] 1 FLR 869, the trial judge had taken the view that the mother and her new partner's lack of inhibitions towards nudity in front of the children would be harmful to them. However, the Court of Appeal held that there was no clear evidence that this behaviour would be harmful and thus should not have been taken into account.

(iii) Age, sex, background and other relevant characteristics

8.56 As has been discussed, a young child may well be better off with their mother, whereas an older child may be quite capable of making a mature decision about whom they wish to live with. The sex of a child, particularly during the difficult years of puberty, may mean that a child should be placed with the parent of his or her own sex.

8.57 A child's background and other relevant characteristics obviously encompass religious upbringing and cultural differences between parents which may be lost once the family splits up. The range of orders available to the court should enable exposure to valuable features of a child's life to be preserved on relationship breakdown. A specific issue order can determine the child's religious education following breakdown and conditions on residence and/or contact orders could ensure contact with parents of different religions during important religious festivals or cultural events. Similarly, particular interests, which have always been undertaken with the non-resident parent, can be preserved by attaching conditions to contact orders, if this is necessary to ensure any such activities continue.

(iv) Range of powers available to the court

8.58 This factor draws attention to the fact that the court may make various orders under the CA 1989 in "family proceedings" of its own motion, regardless of whether there is an application for such an order before the court. Thus, it may make a s 8 order in any "family proceedings" (see s 8(3)) in which a question arises with respect to the welfare of the child if it considers it right to do so (s 10(1)(b)). Furthermore, the court has various options if it is concerned about the arrangements and making no order at all (s 1(5)) does not resolve the situation.

8.59 Section 7 does give the court power, of its own motion, when considering any question with respect to a child under the Act, to seek welfare reports from a children and family reporter or a local authority on specified matters relating to the welfare of the child. It has been underlined that the ordering of a report where the court has taken into account the relevant factors such as delay, is a matter for the court's discretion. It is highly unlikely to be "plainly wrong" and reversed on appeal (*Re W (welfare reports)* [1995] 2 FLR 142). Thus, if a court was dissatisfied about the agreed arrangements in respect of which s 8 orders were being sought by the child's parents, the court has power to order a report with a view, if appropriate, to the local authority's then applying for a care or supervision order. Alternatively, as will be discussed below, the court can in exceptional circumstances make a "family assistance order" pursuant to s 16 of the Act, requiring a children and family reporter or local authority officer to advise, assist or befriend any person named in the order providing the adult parties agree. Finally, as mentioned above, where they feel a care or supervision order may be appropriate, the court can order a s 37 investigation by the local authority.

(c) The principle of no delay

8.60 Section 1(2) requires the court to have regard to the general principle that delay in determining a question relating to the upbringing of a child is likely to prejudice the welfare of the child. This was an attempt to give statutory force to an already established principle that delay in children's cases is a bad thing. Section 11 goes on to direct that in s 8 proceedings a timetable must be drawn up by the court to determine the matter without delay and to give directions to ensure adherence to the timetable as far as possible and there is a similar provision in respect of care and supervision proceedings in s 32. The practical procedures are now contained in r. 4.15 FPR 1991 (High Court and county court) and rule 15 FPCR 1991 in respect of Family Proceedings Courts. Courts have taken a fairly robust attitude to these duties and the *Practice Directions (children cases time estimates)* [1994] 1 WLR 16 and *(family proceedings: case management)* [1995] 1 WLR 332 and Best Practice Guidance (Handbook of Best Practice in Children Act cases) June 1997 reinforce this. After some doubt, it has been established that these also apply to the Family Proceedings Court and the same practice should be adopted here (see *Re S and P (discharge of care order)* [1995] 2 FLR 782). Generally, inaccurate time estimates were found to be causing inordinate delay in urgent cases and all legal advisors must consider the time needed for documents, opening and closing speeches and judgment.

8.61 Delay is, however, still very much a problem that caused much concern to the CAAC (now the Children Act Committee of the Family Law Advisory Board), which has observed an increase in waiting time since the coming into force of the Act. This has become even more pertinent since the implementation of the HRA 1998, given that Article 6 of the Convention requires matters to be heard within a reasonable time frame. In the CAAC's Annual Report 1994/5, Dame Margaret Booth's study on delay in public law cases commented that many of its findings would be equally applicable to private law cases. A summary of the interim report can be found at [1995] Fam Law 511. Firmer judicial control of the proceedings with closer liaison between court staff and others involved has been recommended with unnecessary requests for welfare reports and other experts' reports finding criticism. Inconsistency of approach between courts in the transfer of proceedings from the family proceedings court to the county court, was often the cause of many months' delay, with the late joinder of parties to an action also occasioning delay. Inexperienced legal advisors was one other matter identified as a problem, as was lack of adequate resources. Some of these issues have been addressed as a consequence of the wider civil procedure reforms and are likely to be kept under review given the Human Rights Act concerns.

8.62 However, although courts are becoming increasingly reluctant to allow departure from the prescribed timetable on the one hand, where there is good reason for delay which might actually promote the child's welfare, practitioners should not be deterred from applying for further time. Two decisions illustrate this. In *C v Solihull Metropolitan Borough Council* [1993] 1 FLR 290, it was stated that, whilst delay is normally inimical, a planned purposeful delay may well be beneficial to the welfare of the child. In *Re B (a minor) (contact: interim order)* [1994] 2 FLR 269, the Court of Appeal held that delay occasioned purposively by the CWO supervising trial basis contact does not offend the no delay principle and should have been allowed by justices. Further problems may arise where a children and family reporter who has made a report is unable to attend the date fixed for hearing. The court must then decide whether attendance is necessary and whether the harmful effects of delay outweigh the benefit to be gained from the attendance of the welfare officer. In *Re CB (Access: attendance of court welfare officer)* [1995] 1 FLR 622 and *Re C (Section 8 Order: court welfare officer)* [1995] 1 FLR 617, the Court of Appeal found that although it is desirable that a CWO should be present if either party so wishes, a court was nonetheless entitled to hear a case in their absence upon the basis of the no delay principle, but should not depart from the recommendation of the CWO without having heard their oral evidence. In all cases, the court will have to balance whether the child's interests are best served by proceeding on the basis of incomplete evidence or by yet further delay. The same principle must still apply to children and family reporters given that they now perform the same role as Court Welfare Officers in private law proceedings.

(d) The no order presumption

8.63 Section 1(5) broke with tradition by limiting the court's power to make orders in respect of children to situations where making the order is better for the child than making no order at all. Thus, the traditionally interventionist role of the court has been checked by this provision. The change is most starkly noticed in the divorce context, where current practice as governed by the amended s 41 MCA 1973 is to leave both parents with unfettered parental responsibility where agreement has been reached about the residence and contact arrangements. By analogy where unmarried parents both have parental responsibility, the court's approach is likely to be the same, meaning that it will only be when arrangements cannot be agreed that one or both parents will need to seek a court order. However, as discussed below, it is now quite clearly established that this presumption will not routinely prevent a court from making a parental responsibility order where a father has shown appropriate commitment, nor be used to refuse a contact order (see *Re R (a minor)* [1993] 2 FLR 762).

8.64 One practical problem, which the no order presumption embodies, is that of the agreement of arrangements for a child which all parties wish to have formalised by way of consent order. In the divorce context, it is the practice of many courts to take the view that the no order presumption prevents the making of these "insurance" orders. Yet objections to a consent order which all parties truly wish to have made should be able to be overcome by showing that the imposition of an order risks prejudicing the working of the arrangements themselves. Further weight must be given to the benefits of a consent order settling the arrangements between unmarried parents where there is no parental responsibility agreement or order. As where the father has no parental responsibility or contact order, they effectively have no legal right to see their child, and conversely, the child has no legal tie with that parent. Furthermore, a father who does not have parental responsibility and intends to care for the child or even enjoy substantial contact following relationship breakdown will have no proof that, for example, he is entitled to make decisions about medical treatment on behalf of the child or meet the child from school even if the child's mother has verbally delegated parental responsibility for these purposes. Accordingly, there are very good practical reasons for an order to be made. In *B v B (a minor) (residence order)* [1992] 2 FLR 327, the Court of Appeal recognised this in the context of a grandparent carer without parental responsibility, who was encountering difficulties in making arrangements for the child with the Education Authority. Although in the absence of an issue upon which the court's intervention was necessary, the court would usually decline to make the order even though the order was sought by consent, where the child's carer did not have parental responsibility, a residence order would be better for the child than making no order at all.

8.65 Thus, whilst in general, a positive benefit to the child must be shown in order to rebut the no order presumption, this may in practice be easier in the unmarried as opposed to the married context. It should perhaps also be said that the practical application of s 1(5) in relation to consent orders may vary from court to court. Interestingly, research shows that the no order presumption may be deterring applications (see Bailey-Harris *et al*, 1999) and certainly the Lord Chancellor's Department's statistics show that the number of applications to the court for residence orders has fallen as compared with the number of pre-Children Act custody applications (*Judicial Statistics*, LCD, 2000).

4 Section 8 orders

8.66 Section 8 CA 1989 sets out the orders that can be made with respect to children in family proceedings and these are known as s 8 orders. It introduced residence and contact orders, which have replaced orders for custody and access both under s 9 GMA 1971 and in matrimonial proceedings. In addition, s 8 provides for prohibited steps and specific issue orders, which may be used to control where appropriate and necessary, the steps which can and cannot be taken by a parent in relation to a child following breakdown of the parents' relationship.

8.67 On breakdown of an unmarried relationship where there are children, in order to clarify any arrangements and ensure they are as far as possible acknowledged in law and enforceable, it may still be necessary for the parents to seek s 8 orders, although those seeking public funding may be required to resolve issues through mediation in the first instance. This section defines the orders that can be made with respect to children in "family proceedings", which, by virtue of subs 3, means wardship proceedings and proceedings under Parts I, II and IV of the 1989 Act; the Matrimonial Causes Act 1973; the Adoption Act 1976; the Domestic Proceedings and Magistrates' Court Act 1978; Part III of the Matrimonial and Family Proceedings Act 1984 and proceedings under s 30 Human Fertilisation and Embryology Act 1990 (HFEA 1990). Following the coming into force of Part IV of the Family Law Act 1996 (FLA 1996), this replaces the references to the DVA 1976 and the MHA 1983 (Sch 8, para 60 FLA 1996).

8.68 In applications under Pt IV FLA 1996 where there are children of the relationship, in addition to granting injunctions and declaring rights of occupation, the court can of its own motion make orders under s 8 if a question arises with respect to the welfare of a child and the court considers the order should be made, even if there has been no application (s 10(1)(b)).

8.69 Section 8 orders are defined as follows by s 8(1):

> "*a contact order*' means an order requiring the person with whom a child lives, or is to live, to allow the child to visit or stay with the person named in the order, or for that person and the child otherwise to have contact with each other;
> '*a prohibited steps order*' means an order that no step which could be taken by a parent in meeting his parental responsibility for a child, and which is of a kind specified in the order, shall be taken by any person without the consent of the court;
> '*a residence order*' means an order settling the arrangements to be made as to the person with whom a child is to live; and
> '*a specific issue order*' means an order giving directions for the purpose of determining a specific question which has arisen, or which may arise, in connection with any aspect of parental responsibility for a child."

(a) Applicants

8.70 Applications for s 8 orders are not restricted to parents. In addition to any parent or guardian of the child, any person granted a residence order with respect to the child may apply as of right for any s 8 order (s 10(4). A further group may apply as of right just for residence and contact orders (s 10(5)) as follows:

> "Any party to a marriage in respect of which the child is a child of the family;
> Any person with whom the child has lived for three out of the past five years, providing that period of time has not ended more than three months prior to making the application; and
> Any person who has the consent of each of the persons who does have a residence order or has parental responsibility where there is no residence order, or, where the child is in care, the consent of the relevant local authority."

8.71 Any person not included in these categories, including the child him/herself, providing the court considers he or she has sufficient understanding, may also apply with the court's leave (s 10(8)). In line with the *Gillick* principle (see *Gillick v West Norfolk and Wisbech Area Health Authority* [1986] 1 FLR 224) the older a child, the more significant their wish to take proceedings becomes. However, in *Re S (a minor) (independent representation)* [1993] 2 FLR 437, the Master of the Rolls made it clear that age is not the only indicator of understanding. He observed:

> "Children have different levels of understanding at the same age. And understanding is not absolute. It has to be assessed relative to the issues in the case." (At page 444H)

8.72 How courts and solicitors should judge a child's understanding is a difficult issue (see *Re CT) (a minor) (wardship: representation)* (above)), and one already raised in the context of a child's wishes and feelings (see para 8.49). Rule 9.2A FPR 1991 governs the procedural position of children making applications for leave in their own right or through a solicitor and is not without difficulties (see Burrows, "A Child's Understanding", [1994] Fam Law 579 for a discussion of the problems).

8.73 One issue that has recently been clarified is that the paramountcy principle in s 1(1) CA 1989 does not apply to applications for leave, and thus considerations other than the child's welfare may hold sway in granting or refusing applications for leave (see *Re H (residence order: child's application for leave)* [2000] 1 FLR 780). On such applications the court will, in addition to deciding whether the child is mature enough to bring the application, also consider whether the matter is sufficiently serious to justify a court hearing and/or whether it ought rather to be resolved by the family themselves. In *Re SC (a minor) (leave to seek section 8 orders)* [1994] 1 FLR 96, a 14-year-old wanted to go abroad on holiday with her friend's family and also wanted to go and live with them. The issue of the holiday was not considered sufficiently serious to warrant court intervention and her wish to move in with another family was felt to be something which the family ought to resolve rather than the court. The court must also judge the likely success of the application for leave, and the fact that the proposed application is not hopeless is a factor in favour of granting leave. However, if the issues the child's application raises are already being raised by one of the adult parties, then even post-Human Rights Act, it seems this is likely to be a reason to refuse the application (see *Re H (residence order: child's application for leave)* [2000] 1 FLR 780).

8.74 Whilst the child's welfare is not paramount in such applications, leave was refused where it was thought not to be in the child's interest to hear the evidence of his bitter and hostile parents (*Re C (residence: child's application for leave)* [1996] 1 FCR 461. The implications of the HRA 1998 on the need for children to have a voice in court proceedings about their future have yet to be fully tested. However, there have been indications that Article 6 of the Convention is likely to lead to an increase in the number of cases where children are separately represented and this may in turn give rise to greater number of leave applications being granted to children to bring s 8 applications in their own right. This was acknowledged by the Court of Appeal in *Re A (a child) (contact: separate representation)* (2001) *Times*, 28 February where it was said that children who needed someone to orchestrate the investigation of the case on their behalf may need party status and legal representation. However, the CAFCASS Practice Note also makes clear that in most private law cases the child's interests will be best served by a welfare report under s 7 CA 1989 undertaken by a children and family reporter. In cases where there is a significant foreign element, or where the child has been refused leave to instruct a solicitor direct under FPR 9.2A but continues to wish to do so, it might be appropriate to grant party status to a child (see CAFCASS Practice Note, 1 April 2001, *Officers of CAFCASS Legal Services and Special Casework: Appointment in Family Proceedings* available on their website at www.cafcass.gov.uk). Those representing children are also referred to the SFLA's *Guide to Good Practice for Solicitors Acting For Children*.

8.75 Section 8 orders can be sought or made by the court of its own motion in any family proceedings (s 10(1)), as defined above, or where there are no family proceedings, on the application of any person who is entitled to apply for a s 8 order or who has been granted leave to do so (s 10(2)). These provisions are subject to s 9, which prevents a court making a s 8 order, other than a residence order, with respect to a child who is in the care of a local authority; prevents a local authority from applying for a residence or contact order; and prevents such an order being made in favour of an authority. Normally, a person seeking to remove a child from care would apply to discharge the care order pursuant to s 39. However, an unmarried father without parental responsibility is not eligible to make such an application. Thus his only course would be to apply for a s 8 residence order, for, once a residence order is made in relation to a child who is in care, this automatically discharges the care order (s 91(1)).

(b) Residence orders

8.76 Residence orders are used to settle where and with whom a child should live, usually, but not exclusively, on the breakdown of a child's parents' relationship. As has been seen above, although in the context of the unmarried family it is likely to be the child's parents who will be the parties to the proceedings and who will be seeking the order, applications for s 8 orders are open to a wide range of people. Where parents agree the arrangements, the court does not have to, but may have regard to the checklist set out in s 1(3). However, where the court feels there is cause for concern, welfare reports or a s 37 investigation can be ordered, or a family assistance order made under s 16. This power should not be exercised unless the court is satisfied that the circumstances are exceptional. The effect of such an order is discussed below (see para 8.140).

8.77 Although residence orders must be judged in accordance with the welfare principle, the checklist and the no order presumption, other relevant circumstances including financial considerations may be looked at. In *Re R (Residence: Financial Considerations)* [1995] 2 FLR 612, the Court of Appeal held that a judge who ordered that a 3-year-old child should live with her father during the week and her mother most weekends was entitled to look at the case realistically in the round and anticipate the likely effect of the mother giving up work and drawing state benefits. As noted above, where all other things are equal, a parent's attitude to contact with the other parent may be influential in deciding who should become the primary carer, given the importance of maintaining contact with both parents (see *Re d (minors) (appeal)* (above)).

(i) Residence orders, parental responsibility and s 1(5)

8.78 As indicated in the section on parental responsibility above, the approach of the courts and indeed the parents themselves may vary according to whether the father has already acquired parental responsibility. That is not to say that in s 8 applications the presence or absence of parental responsibility is more influential than the nature of a child's relationship with their father or his actual commitment to the child, but rather that the options available to the court in terms of the orders they may make may be viewed differently. The 1989 Act leaves parental responsibility with both married parents after the making of a residence order. Where an unmarried father becomes the resident parent on breakdown, s 12(1) directs that the court shall also make a s 4 order giving him parental responsibility. As the court cannot take away a mother's parental responsibility, both parents will in this situation have parental responsibility for the child subject to the s 8 orders. Where a s 4 order or agreement has been made granting the father parental responsibility, it is open to the mother (or, with leave, the child) to apply to discharge the s 4 order on breakdown. However, as discussed above the presumption is that it will be retained (see *Re P (terminating parental responsibility)* (above)). Any person who is not a parent but in whose favour a residence order is made, is automatically given parental responsibility while the residence order remains in force by virtue of s 12(2). However, their parental responsibility is limited to the extent that they are specifically denied power to consent or refuse to consent to adoption, and cannot appoint a guardian for the child (s 12(3)).

(ii) Shared residence orders—s 11(4) CA 1989

8.79 Another break with the principles established under previous case law is the acknowledgement in s 11(4) that a court may under s 8 make a residence order in favour of two or more persons who do not live together.

8.80 This, on the face of it, represented in the married context a reversal of the old authorities such as *Riley v Riley* [1986] 2 FLR 429 where the Court of Appeal refused to approve a joint custody, care and control arrangement which had been in existence for some five years without any apparent adverse effect on the child. Shortly before the coming into force of the CA 1989, the Court of Appeal in *J v J (Minor) (Joint Care and Control)* [1991] 2 FLR 385 took a different approach, endorsing an arrangement for joint custody, care and control stating that although in the majority of cases such an order would mean a child would not know where their home was, in this case the child was left in no doubt where she was going to be. However, such orders were stated to be "wholly exceptional". It had not in any event been possible to make joint orders in respect of unmarried parents, but s 11(4) has changed this. Furthermore, it provides that where more than one person is granted a residence order, the order may specify, although this is not a requirement, the periods in which the child is to live in the households concerned. Thus, an order may now be made granting one parent residence during term time and the other residence for the duration of the school holidays, or that the child spends Monday to Thursday with one parent and Friday to Sunday with the other.

8.81 This obviously opened up the possibility of the courts making shared residence orders wherever one parent was having a substantial amount of staying contact. However, the courts, perhaps predictably, were slow to move away from the idea that it is best for a child to know that they have one settled residence. Shared residence orders in the main, remain very much the exception rather than the rule, although recently there has been a new approach to this issue. In *Re H (a minor) (shared residence)* [1994] 1 FLR 717 an application for an order where there had been *de facto* shared residence in the past was refused, with Cazalet J stating at page 726:

> "[S]uch an order should not be made in the normal conventional circumstances of parents who have separated. It may be that there will be cases where a shared residence order can be made which will assist because it will reduce the differences between the parties. But, almost invariably circumstances require that a child should make his settled home with one parent rather than the other."

8.82 In *A v A (minors) (shared residence order)* [1994] 1 FLR 669, the Court of Appeal confirmed that *Riley v Riley* (above) was no longer good law, although the *Riley* view that for a child to have competing homes would cause confusion and stress, would hold good in many situations. It went on to set out general principles to be applied when considering the issue of shared residence:

(i)   the case must have some unusual feature which justifies a shared order;
(ii)   the shared residence order must offer some benefit to the child before the unusual circumstances can justify an order;
(iii)   the court must be guided by the welfare principle (s 1(1)) and the welfare checklist (s 1(3));
(iv)   the decision is at the discretion of the judge on the individual facts of the case;
(v)   a shared order is unlikely where concrete issues are still arising between the parties;
(vi)   a general "exceptional circumstances" condition was not to be imported into the s 11(4) test.

8.83 These principles are not without difficulty (for a discussion of this see Helen Conway, "Shared Residence Orders" [1996] Fam Law 435) and in practice, the cases most likely to be successful appear to be those where a shared residence arrangement is already working. However, in the recent case of *D v D (shared residence order)* [2001] 1 FLR 495, the Court of Appeal confirmed a shared residence order where the arrangements had broken down. They also indicated that contrary to earlier case law, it is not necessary to show that exceptional circumstances exist before a shared residence order may be granted, neither is it probably necessary to show a positive benefit to the child. However, the order must be in the interests of the child in accordance with s 1 CA 1989. They went on to say that while guidance from the Court of Appeal should be valuable to courts of first instance, they were still free to make the right decision in the interests of the children on the individual facts of each case. Here the children, over a number of years, had divided their time between their parents' homes, despite a high level of animosity between the parents. When the arrangements broke down the father applied for a shared residence order which was granted notwithstanding the hostility between the parties and with a view to attempt to lessen the animosity and help them co-operate better over the arrangements. Thus this appears to have taken the concept of shared residence orders back to what the Law Commission had originally intended.

8.84 Where both parents have parental responsibility, there is arguably no need for a shared residence order. In *A v A* (above), however, it should be noted that the court imposed a shared residence order where the children were effectively sharing their time between the two homes despite the mother's opposition, no other areas of dispute between the parties, and despite the no order presumption. Interestingly, although the parents were married and thus both had parental responsibility, the court took the view that there was a positive benefit to the children in having a court order reflecting the well-established arrangements, which allowed the father to play an important role in their lives. This may serve as persuasive authority in cases where a consent order is sought, and is an approach that was followed more recently in *D v D*.

8.85 Another possible use of shared residence orders is to enable parental responsibility to be given to a cohabitant who is not the natural parent of the child, but who has treated the child as a child of the family and wishes to continue to play a role on breakdown. In *Re H (shared residence: parental responsibility)* [1996] 3 FCR 321, the Court of Appeal stated that where there were circumstances which justified a shared residence order under s 11(4), then the fact that this would also confer parental responsibility on the 'step'-father was an additional ground for making the order. However, in *Re WB (minors) (residence orders)* [1995] 2 FLR 1023, Thorpe J held that a shared residence order would only be appropriate if the shared regime was most likely to promote the interests of the child. It was not appropriate where the sole purpose was to vest full parental responsibility in the stepfather, when in reality the child lived with the mother and had contact with the father. Yet in *Re AB (adoption: joint residence)* [1996] 1 FLR 27, FD the court held it was appropriate, having made an adoption order in favour of the foster father, to grant a joint residence order in favour of cohabitants of twenty years who had jointly fostered a child for five years and wanted to adopt, but were prevented from jointly doing so by s 14(1) Adoption Act 1976. Where a same-sex couple have children born into the relationship as a result of AID or other fertility treatment, on breakdown of that relationship residence and contact orders may be sought more frequently in order to create a legal relationship between the child and the non-resident partner. In this situation only a shared residence order can give the "social parent", as opposed to the birth parent, parental responsibility even where the parties agree that this is what they wish to achieve. Indeed, even in the case of a transsexual father, the denial of the right to apply for a parental responsibility order or make an agreement did not constitute a breach of Article 8 of the European convention on Human Rights (see *X, Y, and Z v United Kingdom* [1997] 2 FLR 892). However, in *G v F (contact and shared residence)* [1998] 2 FLR 799 the practical parenting problems which arose on the breakdown of a same-sex relationship were dealt with sympathetically by the court which granted leave to apply for a shared residence order to the "social" parent.

8.86 The effect of a shared residence order is that each parent will have or will acquire parental responsibility but cannot exercise it in a way that is incompatible with any conditions of that order or indeed any other orders made under the 1989 Act (s 2(8)). It should also be noted that a shared residence order specifically gives the right to remove the child from local authority accommodation under s 20 of the 1989 Act. Overall, unlike in the USA, the courts have not to date embraced the potential of shared residence orders as fully as perhaps they might have and are not prepared to make them wherever there is a substantial contact situation. Although they were officially seen as a means of "remov[ing] any impression that one parent is good and responsible while the other is not" (*The Children Act 1989 Guidance and Regulations* (HMSO, 1991) *vol. 1: Court Orders*, para 2.28), the courts continue to prefer as the normal expectation that one parent will become the child's primary carer and certainly do not feel that substantial staying contact will warrant a shared residence order in most cases. However, there does seem to be a greater acceptance of the potential of shared residence orders, and it may be that the decision in *D v D* (above) will be a turning point which will mean more parents who have been sharing in the upbringing of their children since separation will continue to share residence sanctioned by a court even when difficulties arise.

(iii) Interim and ex parte residence orders

8.87 Following *Re B (a minor) (residence order: ex p)* [1992] 2 FLR 1, where the Court of Appeal confirmed that despite clear guidance in the Family Proceedings Rules 1991, interim residence orders could in exceptional circumstances be made *ex parte*, r 4.4(4) and r 4.21(7) FPR 1991 and the equivalent provisions in the FPCR 1991, were amended to enable all s 8 orders to be made *ex parte*. In *Re G (ex p interim residence order)* [1993] 1 FLR 910, it was confirmed that an *ex parte* order would rarely be appropriate but might be appropriate in a "snatch" situation or its equivalent. Thus, the door is open in serious situations for such orders to be made, but the normal route to any form of residence order is an application on notice. This is underlined by the requirements of Article 6 of the European Convention on Human Rights, which guarantees a fair and public hearing and implies that there should be "equality of arms" as between the parties. This must make orders made by courts in *ex parte* hearings potentially subject to challenge.

(iv) Effects of a residence order

8.88 Should a child's parents resume cohabitation for a period exceeding six months, then any residence order that has been made will lapse. When a residence order is in force, no person may cause the child to become known by a different surname, or remove the child from the UK, without either the written consent of every person who has parental responsibility for the child, or leave of the court (s 13(1)). However, a resident parent may now take the child out of the UK for a period of up to one month (s 13(2)) without consent or leave; and the court may grant leave for other proposed visits out of the UK, either generally or for specified periods or places, when making the residence order (s 13(3)). Thus s 13 in fact imposed on unmarried parents restrictions in these two respects which were not previously automatically imposed with orders for custody or access. Opposition to holidays abroad by one parent (usually the non-resident parent) normally arises where it is feared that the children will not be returned to the jurisdiction.

8.89 However, in *Re S (leave to remove from jurisdiction: securing return from holiday)* [2001] 2 FLR 498 it was made clear that to prevent such a trip a parent must satisfy the court that there was a real risk of the children not being returned, which the father had not done in this case. Nevertheless, the court took the view that there was a need to safeguard the children's interests and their human rights by ensuring they would be returned from their proposed holiday to visit relatives in India, a country which is not a party to the abduction Conventions. The children were therefore made wards of court and the mother was required to provide the father with copies of the return airline tickets and only apply for tourist visas which she must not seek to extend, nor must she apply for Indian passports for the children. The orders were then served on the Indian High Commission and the Foreign and Commonwealth Office.

8.90 Although the requirements of s 13 now apply to children of unmarried, as well as married, parents, the anomalous need for leave to be sought to take the child to Scotland or other parts of the UK, not a part of the jurisdiction of England and Wales—a restriction that many parents did not realise in any event—has at least been removed. Holidays abroad for a period of up to one month where the child is to travel with the resident parent are now possible, but it seems that school holidays abroad require the consent of every person who has parental responsibility. Advisors might give thought to whether a blanket consent for such trips should be sought at the time a residence order is being made.

8.91 Separate issues arise where, following separation, the resident parent wishes to take the child permanently out of the jurisdiction which is not permitted without leave of the court where a residence order has been made. This has prompted much case law, of late. In many cases where arrangements for children between cohabitants have been made amicably, only the mother will have parental responsibility or possibly both parents will have unfettered parental responsibility. It now seems that despite this and notwithstanding the wording of s 2(7) CA 1989, agreement of the other parent or leave of the court may well be needed in both these situations. This has fuelled a view that a "duty" to consult the other parent has arisen in some (not yet closed) categories of cases, such as change of surname, change of school, circumcision, sterilisation and, arguably, permanent removal of a child from the jurisdiction (see Maidment, *Parental Responsibility: Is There a Duty to Consult?* [2001] *Family Law* 518).

8.92 It has always been the case in the married context that agreement or leave was necessary, but now in the unmarried context and particularly post-Human Rights Act, the courts must be seen to be balancing and protecting the right to family life of all family members. In *Re A (permission to remove child from jurisdiction: human rights)* [2000] 2 FLR 225, a mother who wished to take up a new life in New York, where she believed she would be able to better pursue her musical career, was granted leave to take her 10-month-old child with her. The Court of Appeal confirmed the order despite the father's opposition and claim that it would breach Article 8 rights of both himself and his daughter in that they would effectively be denied contact with each other. It made clear that the Convention rights of the father and child had to be balanced against the mother's conflicting Article 8 right to private life and that the careful and conscientious balancing of these rights by the judge at first instance could not be challenged on Convention grounds in the Court of Appeal as this had been carried out in a way that was "beyond attack". The mother's wish to move away was reasonable. She did however give undertakings to litigate any issue relating to contact in the English courts, return the child to England at least twice a year and allow additional contact if she were in England in addition to facilitating e-mail and postal contact.

8.93 In another Court of Appeal decision, *Re C (leave to remove from jurisdiction)* [2000] 2 FLR 457, a mother was refused leave to remove her 6-year-old from the jurisdiction to go and live in Singapore, the home of her new husband, who wished to practise medicine there. The trial judge had found that the presumption of the mother's reasonable plans to go abroad were outweighed by the fact that a permanent move would severely limit the child's contact with her father, despite the effect this would have on the new family who would be separated. The Court of Appeal (with Thorpe LJ dissenting) felt it was not entitled to interfere with the decision of the judge who had heard all the evidence at first hand and had properly applied the law. The dissenting opinion of Thorpe LJ took the view that the risk of emotional harm to the child consequent upon the break up of her new family unit had not been given proper weight.

8.94 It seems clear, however, that this was not a decision which changed the way in which such cases are judged but emphasises the broad discretion allowed to judges at first instance and the inability of the Court of Appeal to interfere on the merits of a case even if it would have reached a different conclusion. It only has power to intervene where there has been a misapplication of the law (see *G v G (minors) (custody appeal)* [1985] FLR 763). However in *Payne v Payne* [2001] 1 FLR 1052, there was some distancing by the Court of Appeal of any endorsement of a presumption in favour of the resident parent's plans. In *Re H (application to remove from jurisdiction)* [1998] 1 FLR 848, a consistency of approach to such cases had been called for and it had been stated that where the resident parent's plans were reasonable then the court will not ordinarily interfere unless there was some compelling reason in the child's best interests to the contrary. In *Payne,* the Court of Appeal, however, made it clear that there was no presumption in favour of the resident parent created by s 13(1)(b) CA 1989. Yet the reasonable proposals of the parent with a residence order wishing to live abroad carry great weight. Such proposals must be carefully scrutinised and it must be clear that the motivation to relocate is genuine and not one intended primarily to terminate the child's contact with the other parent. Furthermore the effect upon the new family and the child is also very important as is the effect of the denial of contact and the opportunity to continue contact notwithstanding the move may be critical. The court also stated that the HRA 1998 does not require a new approach to relocation cases and the approach applied since *Poel v Poel* [1970] 1 WLR 1469 and reaffirmed in all the cases discussed above remains valid. It should also be noted that relocation by a parent within the UK may also be subject to challenge in exceptional cases (see *Re H (Residence Order: Relocation) The Times*, August 29, discussed at para 8.117).

8.95 Another aspect of these applications is the operation of the no order presumption. In *Re X and Y (leave to remove from jurisdiction: no order principle)* [2001] 2 FLR 118, heard just before *Payne,* this issue was considered in a case concerning cohabitants, where the mother wished to return to live near her family abroad. Here leave was granted and it was made clear that the court has to apply the welfare principle alongside the no order presumption having regard to the s 1(3) checklist. Thus the applicant parent must show a positive case that it is in the child's interests to relocate and there can be no presumption in favour of the resident parent. Nonetheless, it seems clear that outcomes are bound to vary, despite the attempt to provide a consistency of approach.

8.96 Section 14(1) provides a sanction where a residence order is in force and any person, including a person in whose favour there is also a residence order, breaches the terms of the order. Providing the person has been served with a copy of the residence order, then the offended resident parent may enforce the residence order as if it were an order requiring the other person to produce the child to them under s 63(3) Magistrates' Courts Act 1980. This enables justices to impose a fine of £50 per day up to a maximum of £1,000 whilst the breach continues, or a sum not exceeding £5,000, or to sentence the person to imprisonment of a maximum of two months or until the breach is remedied. This is the only remedy available where the residence order was made in the magistrates' courts, but where the order was made in the county court or High Court, it can be enforced in the usual way for contempt of court.

(c) Contact orders

8.97 Contact orders are the successors to access orders, but are more wide-ranging as they specifically contemplate contact other than visits. Contact can include letters and telephone calls, as well as visits and stays with the other parent and has been used with considerable flexibility. Although contact orders will not be made automatically on relationship breakdown where both parents have parental responsibility, the Court of Appeal has made it clear that this does not entitle a parent to take a child away from their settled home or to refuse to return a child after a contact visit (see *Re B (minors) (residence order)* [1992] 3 All ER 867; *Re H (a minor) (interim custody)* [1991] 2 FLR 411). In practice, therefore, a non-resident parent with parental responsibility should be advised that the courts are likely to view such abuse of parental responsibility as tantamount to "snatching", whatever their technical position in law.

8.98 Whilst the child is with the contact parent, if the parent does not also have parental responsibility, the parent may nevertheless do what is reasonable to promote or safeguard the welfare of the child (s 3(5)); a contact parent with parental responsibility may do anything that a parent may do provided it is not inconsistent with any residence or other order under the Act (s 2(8)).

(i) The right of the child

8.99 The received wisdom of the old law that contact is the right of the child (a right which is underlined in the United Nations Convention on the Rights of the Child), rather than the right of the parent has unquestionably survived the transition. This has been made clear in a number of cases (see eg *Re R (A Minor) (Contact)* [1993] 2 FLR 762). In *Re D (a minor) (contact: mother's hostility)* [1993] 2 FLR 1, Balcombe LJ stated at page 3:

> "One starts with the premise that it is the child's right to know both its parents but there may be cases . . . where there are cogent reasons why the child should be denied that opportunity."

8.100 However, recently, as noted above, whilst there has not been a reversal of this position, there is an increased willingness by the court to take the effect of contact on the resident parent into account particularly where there has been domestic violence (see *L, V, M, H (contact: domestic violence)* [2001] FAM 260, discussed further below). Whereas previously mothers who objected to contact were automatically seen as the villains and were castigated as "implacably hostile", the courts are now encouraged to consider the validity of such hostility and perhaps require a positive change in the violent partner's behaviour prior to granting contact. As noted above, applications for contact orders are increasingly being sought in conjunction with parental responsibility orders in the unmarried context, and the authorities now make it clear that the latter will nearly always be granted. Whether or not contact is in the child's interests has to be judged in accordance with the welfare principle, and checklist where the application is opposed.

(ii) Implacable hostility to contact

8.101 Much case law has developed with regard to how the courts should deal with contact applications where the resident parent is hostile to contact. Some of the principles that have been established by Children Act case law seem themselves in recent post-Human Rights Act Court of Appeal decisions to be subject to revision and refinement and the seminal case in the contact context is that of *Re L (Contact: Domestic Violence); Re V (contact: domestic violence); Re M (contact: domestic violence); Re H (contact: domestic violence)* [2001] FAM 260 in which the Court of

Appeal signalled the need to discourage the use of presumptions in Children Act cases and revisited the approach to contact where the mother had been the victim of the father's violence. Fear of violence is often the reason a mother is "implacably hostile" to contact and, as shall be seen, any presumptions in favour of contact are not now seen as appropriate at least in this context. The Lord Chancellor's Family Law Advisory Board have also consulted on the issue of contact and domestic violence and have also signalled the need for a change of approach (see *Report to the Lord Chancellor on the Question of Parental in cases where there is Domestic* Violence, April 2000, the Stationery Office, following the *Consultation Paper on Contact between Children and Violent Parents*, 1999, The Stationery Office), which the Court of Appeal has now endorsed, as noted below.

8.102 Generally speaking, some difference can be seen in how the right of a child to know and see their father has been interpreted, depending on whether or not their father was married to their mother. In *Re SM (a minor) (natural father: access)* [1991] 2 FLR 333, an unmarried father who had had regular contact with his child for nearly two years, but whom the child did not know was her father, was denied an access order because the mother wished her to continue to grow up regarding her stepfather as her father and the court agreed that continued contact would destabilise the new family unit and not be in the best interests of the child. This has subsequently been described as "on its facts, a high watermark case" (see *Re H (contact: principles)* [1994] 2 FLR 969, CA) but must now surely be revisited given the need for a child to know their family as a pre-requisite to their right to family life guaranteed under Article 8 European Convention on Human Rights.

8.103 In *Re D (a minor) (contact: mother's hostility)* [1993] 2 FLR 1, a mother's implacable hostility to a father to whom she had not been married was sufficient to displace what was then safely described as the normal presumption of contact after the child had reacted badly to attempts to re-introduce contact. However, against this trend, in *Re P (a minor) (contact)* [1994] 2 FLR 374, the Family Division did not reverse the justices' decision to grant an unmarried father contact despite expert evidence that this would adversely affect the mother's mental health. In fact, following *Re L (contact: domestic violence); Re V (contact: domestic violence); Re M (contact: domestic violence); Re H (contact: domestic violence)* (above) the Court of Appeal has now laid great store by the need to pay heed to expert evidence on the effect of contact with a violent parent on the resident parent victim and arguably such a principle may extend beyond cases involving violence where the deterioration of the resident parent's health and well-being will impact negatively upon the child.

8.104 This decision involved four appeals heard together in each of which the father had been violent to the child's mother and had been refused contact with their child at first instance. It is essential reading for any advisor acting in such a case. The Court of Appeal, in refusing the appeals in all four cases, had the benefit of both the Family Law Advisory Board's Report (summarised at [2000] *Fam Law* 388) and of the expert report prepared by two consultant psychiatrists (detailed at [2000] *Fam Law* 615). It held that there was no presumption against contact where domestic violence was alleged or proved, but violence was one highly material factor which the court must consider in the balancing exercise required by the application of the welfare principle and the welfare checklist in s 1(1) and (3) CA 1989. It went on to say that in appropriate circumstances, it could offset the "assumption" in favour of contact with the non-resident parent. Thus there is some evidence of downgrading of the child's right to contact from a presumption to a lesser assumption. Furthermore, it made clear that family judges and magistrates needed to have a heightened awareness of the effect of children being exposed to domestic violence of one parent against the other and allegations ought to be investigated and findings of fact made before the contact application is heard. Where interim contact is sought, the court should give particular consideration to the likely risk of harm if contact is granted or refused, and take steps to ensure the risk of harm is minimised and the safety of the child and the residential parent secured before, during and after contact. On hearing a contact application where there are such allegations, the court should consider the conduct of the parties towards each other and the child; the effect of contact on the child and the residential parent, and the motivation of the parent seeking contact.

8.105 Outside the violence context, there is still an assumption if not a presumption in favour of contact, which does not sit easily alongside the no order presumption in s 1(5) CA 1989. In *Re H (a minor) (contact; principles)* [1993] Fam Law 673, the Court of Appeal found no reason not to order contact where a child had not seen her natural father (her mother's ex-husband) for three years and regarded her mother's cohabitant as her father. It stated here and again in *Re H (a minor) (contact: principles)* (above) that the question in deciding whether to refuse a contact order was whether there were cogent reasons for denying the contact.

8.106 Another important issue is how the no order presumption in s 1(5) affects the willingness of the courts to make a contact order where the resident parent is implacably hostile to contact. In *Re H (a minor) (parental responsibility)* [1993] 1 FLR 484, CA, it was stated that it was not necessary to show positive benefit for the child before making a contact order, although in this case the stepfather's threat to leave the mother should a contact order be made, in fact forced the court (which did grant the father parental responsibility) not to make the contact order it would otherwise have made. In *Re W (a minor) (contact)* [1994] 2 FLR 441, the Court of Appeal made it clear that the mother had no right to deny the child contact with her father (and mother's ex-husband) and it was an abdication of responsibility for the court to make no order simply on the basis that the mother would not obey it. Although the child was three and a half, had not seen her father since she was three months old and regarded her stepfather as her real father, supervised contact was ordered. Yet in *Re J (a minor) (contact)* [1994] 1 FLR 729, CA, whilst stating that courts should be reluctant to allow implacable hostility to deter them from making contact orders, the court indicated there would be times when courts had to inflict injustice upon the non-resident parent and made no order. In this case the parents had been married but a court welfare officer's report indicated that a contact order would place great stress on the child.

8.107 In *Re O (contact: imposition of conditions)* [1995] 2 FLR 124 the Court of Appeal went as far as saying it was almost always in the interests of the child to have contact with the non-resident parent and for a while mothers hostile to contact (for whatever reasons) were viewed with increasing impatience by the court. In *F v F (contact committal)* [1998] 2 FLR 237 the court indicated (at page 240), when making a suspended committal order, that there was "a clear obligation upon the mother to assist the children to come to terms with having contact with their father". There followed withdrawal from this hard-line position in cases prepared to follow the approach in *Re D (contact: reasons for refusal)* [1997 2 FLR 48 where an appeal by a father against a refusal of direct contact was confirmed on the basis that he posed an indirect risk to the child through harm to the mother.

8.108 In *Re P (minors) (contact: discretion)* [1998] 2 FLR 696, and in *Re K (contact mother's anxiety)* [1999] 2 FLR 703 well founded fears by mothers were recognised as valid reasons for refusing contact, and even irrational fear which genuinely affected the mother may prove sufficient. Following the recent drawing back from an absolutist approach in favour of contact and culminating in *Re L (contact: domestic violence); Re V (contact: domestic violence); Re M (contact: domestic violence); Re H (contact: domestic violence)* (above), it seems that so-called implacable hostility to contact now needs further investigation, particularly in the context of domestic violence between the parents and this will impact on the readiness of the court to grant interim contact in such cases (see now *Re M (interim contact: domestic violence)* [2000] 2 FLR 377).

8.109 Overall, implacable hostility places advisors of both parties in difficult positions. However, the courts' old certainty that contact is always in a child's best interests has gone. Obviously, the father's behaviour to the child and the mother are likely to be critical. The marital status of the parents should not affect the court's decision, but in practice, as has been seen married fathers have in the past fared better, as illustrated above. An interesting article sets out the history of implacable hostility cases and considers the new approach of the courts in Kaganas and Day Sclater, "Contact and Domestic Violence – The Winds of Change?" [2000] Fam Law 630.

(iii) Enforcement of contact orders

8.110 In terms of the powers available to the courts to punish non-compliance with contact orders, the CAAC confirmed in its 1994/5 report that it is of the view that the powers available to the courts were sufficient. They also made it clear that penal enforcement of such orders was not seen as the best way forward in these difficult cases and was unlikely to be in the interests of the child (see page 36). Nonetheless, an example where committal to prison for contempt successfully induced a change of mind in an implacably hostile mother can be found in *Z v Z (refusal of contact: committal)*, a county court decision, noted at [1996] Fam Law 255. Whilst it is to be hoped after the recent reconsideration of contact and domestic violence cases that such a scenario will not be revisited, in *A v N (committal: refusal of contact)* [1997] 1 FLR 533 the Court of Appeal held that in such committal proceedings the child's welfare was "material" rather than paramount and dismissed the mother's appeal against her committal to prison for breach of an order for supervised contact with a violent father. These issues were considered recently by the European Court of Human Rights in *Hokkanen v Finland* [1996] 1 FLR 289 and *Glaser v United Kingdom* [2000] 3 FCR 193. In *Hokkanen* it was held that Finland was in breach of its obligations under Article 8 of the Convention because it had failed to provide a means by which a father could enforce his right to contact. However, in *Glaser,* the court accepted that if the only means of enforcement were imprisonment of the residential parent or changing residence, this might provide justification for failing to enforce the right of contact. In *Re M (contact order: committal)* [1999] 1 FLR 810, it has been suggested that treatment, such as family therapy or even changing residence, rather than imprisonment may be appropriate and should be explored, and this was underlined by Thorpe LJ in the leading case of *Re L (a child) (Contact: domestic violence)* (above).

8.111 The threat of an order for costs should not be used to pressurise a mother into agreeing to contact (see *Re R (a minor) (contact: consent order)* [1995] 1 FLR 123), as the 1989 Act had laid down relevant criteria relating to the child's welfare and any short cut which would prejudice that enquiry should be avoided.

(iv) Interim contact orders

8.112 The court has power to make interim orders for contact pursuant to s 11(3) CA 1989. Guidance was been given in *Re D (contact: interim orders)* [1995] 1 FLR 495, which confirms that caution should prevail where there are unresolved issues. This has been reaffirmed by the need to be wary of granting interim contact in domestic violence cases and the need to ensure protection for mother and child as noted in *Re M (interim contact: domestic violence)* [2000] 2 FLR 377 and *Re L (contact: domestic violence); Re V (contact: domestic violence); Re M (contact: domestic violence); Re H (contact: domestic violence)* discussed above. Where the principle of contact has been accepted, then interim contact is likely to be appropriate. Where the principle of contact is not agreed, then the welfare test must be applied and any interim order should not prejudge the issue and would normally be used as part of the adjudication process, unless the court already had sufficient information to conclude that interim contact was in the child's interests. Normally, this would only arise after hearing oral evidence and having received a children and family reporter's report.

(v) Dismissing applications for contact

8.113 Even when courts feel that contact is not appropriate, it has been made clear that applications to dismiss contact (s 91(4)) should only be made where there are truly exceptional circumstances (see *Re M (Contact)* [1995] 1 FLR 1029), although this must now be reconsidered in the light of the "assumption" rather than any presumption in favour of contact set out in *Re L (contact: domestic violence)* discussed above. Certainly, there is now more focus on how the father (typically) can change his behaviour if he is to gain contact, rather than any automatic assumption that he should be awarded contact where his conduct is found to have been harmful to the other parent and child. An order refusing contact was made in *Re T (parental responsibility: contact)* [1993] 2 FLR 450, CA, where a father had, amongst other things, failed to return the child for nine days after contact, and *Re P (terminating parental responsibility)* [1995] 1 FLR 1048, where the father, unbeknown to the mother, had caused non-accidental injury to the child. In *K v M (paternity: contact)* [1996] 1 FLR 312, FD, the court made an order under s 91(4) restricting further applications for contact without leave in respect of a man who thought he might be the father of a child born to a married woman with whom he had had an affair. The court here also confirmed that blood tests were not necessary to decide the issue of contact and concluded that it was not in the child's interests to disturb the settled relationship of the child with the mother and her husband. Yet now the need to know who the child's family are, in order to protect the Article 8 right to family life, may lead to a change of approach in such cases.

8.114 A child's opposition to contact may lead to an application being dismissed or no order made. In *Re C (contact: no order for contact)* [2000] Fam Law 699, it was accepted that a child was terrified of his father and this justified an order prohibiting even indirect contact. Where a child is mature enough to make her own decisions, it has been accepted that there is little the law can do to force compliance with court orders defining contact very specifically and thus a "no order" may be appropriate (see eg *M v M (defined contact application)* [1998] 2 FLR 244).

8.115 When deciding such cases, the court must make it clear whether it is dismissing the application or making no order (*D v D (Application for Contact)* [1994] 1 FCR 694).

(vi) Other issues

8.116 Contact orders will not of course be made in relation to parents with the benefit of a joint residence order. As with residence orders, contact orders cease to have effect if the child's parents live together for a period of more than six months. Clients should be advised that if a reconciliation takes place, the whole procedure for residence and contact orders will have to be gone through again should the reconciliation last for more than six months but prove not to be permanent.

(d) Conditions on residence and contact orders

8.117 Section 11(7) permits the court to both give directions on how a residence or contact order is to be carried into effect and also to impose conditions which must be complied with by specified persons (s 11(7)(b)). This needs also to be considered in the light of s 10(5) which provides that specific issue and prohibited steps orders should not be made with a view to achieving a result which could be achieved by making a residence or contact order. Case law has developed which has shed some light on the sort of conditions that can legitimately be imposed and the inter-relationship of the four different s 8 orders. In an exceptional case where the welfare of the child demanded such an approach, a condition could be attached to a residence order to prevent the resident parent's relocation to another part of the UK with the child. This was due to no leave being required to relocate under s 13 CSA 1989 (see *Re H (Residence order: Relocation)* (2001) *The Times* August 29). There is no power to impose conditions which effectively order parents to have contact with each other (*Croydon London Borough Council v A* [1992] 2 FLR 341), and any conditions must not be inconsistent with a residence order *(Birmingham City Council v H* [1993] 1 FCR 247). Thus a condition may be imposed that contact take place at a Child Contact Centre where other venues are not available or appropriate.

8.118 A condition may also specify indirect contact, rather than direct contact and providing there are not cogent reasons for denying contact, there is an assumption (but not a presumption) that there should be contact, albeit indirect, although there may now be greater emphasis on showing a positive benefit to the child before indirect contact will be granted following the decision in *Re L (contact: domestic violence)* (above) and in contrast to earlier decisions such as *Re H (minors: access)* [1992] 1 FLR 148). In *Re P (Contact: Indirect Contact)* [1999] 2 FLR 893, it was stated that it would be most unusual for a court to decide that even indirect contact would be inappropriate. An illustration of what indirect contact can mean is found in *Re M (A Minor) (Contact: Conditions)* [1994] 1 FLR 272, FD, where the court considered it appropriate to grant an unmarried father serving a prison sentence contact by post with his two and a half year old child, despite the child not really knowing his father, the father's violence towards the mother and his imprisonment for robbery, burglary and theft. With regard to the imposition of conditions, Wall J felt that whilst there was possibly jurisdiction to order the mother to implement contact by reading the letters to a child who could not read provided the mother agreed, an order compelling the mother to read the contents of any letter could not stand and had to be subject to a right of censorship. The view was taken that the court could not by virtue of s 11(7) order the mother to write progress reports, as this would effectively order contact between the parents. It was felt that indirect contact should be carefully drawn to define the number of letters and phone calls.

8.119 In *Re O (contact: imposition of conditions)* [1995] 2 FLR 124, however, the Court of Appeal examined the ambit of s 11(7). At first instance the judge made an order for indirect contact requiring the mother to send photographs of the child every three months, copies of all nursery reports, information about serious illness and to accept delivery of cards and presents for the child through the post, to read and show the child any communication and give him any presents. The mother appealed upon the basis that the court did not have jurisdiction to make such an order, relying on the dicta in *Re M (a minor) (contact: conditions)* (above). However, her appeal failed and the court took the opportunity to set out the principles involved:

- as contact was usually in the child's interests, indirect contact should be ordered where direct contact was not appropriate, so that the child could grow up knowing the absent parent. The court did have powers to enforce contact;

- s 11(7) gives the court a wide discretion which is not subject to limitation and it did not accept propositions based upon *Re M (a minor) (contact: conditions)* (above) that the court could not impose positive obligations such as reading letters to the child or providing transport or travel costs for direct contact. It was reasonable to require the mother to read the letters and this should not be subject to any right of censorship;
- the court should not automatically define the indirect contact by prescribing a number of letters to be sent; and
- the court has ample power to compel one parent to send photographs, school and medical reports in order to promote meaningful contact between father and child and in a proper case could compel the mother to write reports.

8.120 This approach is less pragmatic than that in *Re M (a minor) (contact: conditions)* (above). However, its message is clearly aimed at encouraging responsible behaviour between parents, however deeply entrenched their hostility to contact, but must now be tempered by the decision in *Re L (Contact: Domestic Violence)* (above), given that indirect contact is often a feature of cases brought against a domestic violence background. Practically speaking, it also remains the case that penal enforcement of breach of contact orders is not encouraged.

8.121 Other limitations on the use of s 11(7) are as follows. There is no power to impose conditions on persons other than those specified in s 11(7)(b). Thus, a local authority cannot be required to supervise contact by such a direction (*Leeds City Council v C* [1993] 1 FLR 269) and there is no power under this provision to override the adults' proprietary rights in the family home (see *Pearson v Franklin* [1994] 1 FLR 246 and *Re D (minors) (residence: conditions)* [1996] 2 FLR 281). A condition specifying the address the resident parent must reside at was not appropriate in *Re E (residence: imposition of conditions)* [1997] 2 FLR 638, CA. Finally, s 11(7) does not entitle these powers to be used so as to interfere with the exercise of other statutory or common law powers by the local authority or police, for example (see *D v D (jurisdiction: injunctions)* [1993] 2 FLR 802, CA) or in the place of other orders such as a non-molestation order (see *D v N (contact order: conditions)* [1997] 2 FLR 797.

8.122 The court may define contact in the order, and thought should be given to whether definition which could be in the child's best interests, is desired by either parent, although the general principle that no order should be made unless it is better for the child than making no order at all will apply (s 1(5)), and may prove an obstacle. Other types of conditions can be attached to a contact order and the relationship between conditional residence and contact orders and prohibitive steps and specific issue orders is discussed below.

(e) Prohibited steps orders, specific issue orders and wardship

8.123 The two remaining s 8 orders, prohibited steps orders (s 50) and specific issue orders (s 10), are defined as follows:

"'*a prohibited steps order*' means an order that no step which could be taken by a parent in meeting his parental responsibility for a child, and which is of a kind specified in the order, shall be taken by any person without the consent of the court;

'*a specific issue order*' means an order giving directions for the purpose of determining a specific question which has arisen, or which may arise, in connection with any aspect of parental responsibility for a child."

8.124 One of the aims in introducing these new orders was, according to the Law Commission, to incorporate into the statutory code the most valuable features of the wardship jurisdiction (see Law Com No. 172, 4.20). The definitions of the two orders allow the court to give negative and positive directions to any person in relation to the exercise of aspects of parental responsibility. Thus it can prohibit a person without parental responsibility from doing any act which could be done by a person with parental responsibility. For example, an unmarried father without parental responsibility could, it seems, be prevented from contacting the child's school even though, strictly, this is an act that only a parent with parental responsibility should do. Wardship, however, has not been abolished and remains available for use by individuals, in contrast to local authorities whose use of the inherent jurisdiction has been severely curtailed.

8.125 In wardship, parental responsibility is vested in the court, so that no important step can be taken in relation to the child without leave of the court. Although there is no general embargo as in wardship, by using these two orders the court can define matters upon which it wishes to be consulted before action is taken. This can be achieved by imposing a prohibited steps order and/or giving directions on any matter in dispute by means of a specific issue order.

8.126 Although neither of these orders should be imposed with a view to achieving a result which could be obtained by making a residence or contact order (s 9(5)(a)), they may be made where no residence or contact order is being sought. Thus, a prohibited steps order could be made preventing the child being taken out of the jurisdiction by a non-parent where there is no residence order; and a specific issue order could be made in relation to the appropriate schooling or religious education for a child where there is no agreement between the parents. These orders can also be made supplemental to residence and contact orders and can be applied for not only by parents but by any other person eligible to apply for a s 8 order pursuant to s 10(2), although they may need leave of the court to make the application.

8.127 The relationship between these two s 8 orders and conditional residence and contact orders is still being clarified. Section 11(7) enables the court to impose conditions when making a s 8 order on, *inter alia*, any parent or person with parental responsibility, and to "make such incidental, supplemental or consequential provision as the court thinks fit". It is difficult to think of a wider discretion for attaching conditions, and where a residence and/or contact order is being made, almost any result desired by the making of a prohibited steps or specific issue order, could probably also be achieved by attaching conditions to the residence or contact order and thus separate orders need not be made – in line with s 9(5). These orders are therefore most likely to be sought other than in the context of relationship breakdown, or possibly where disputes arise some time after breakdown, when the issues of contact and residence have already been resolved. Case law has now shed some light on both the ambit of the orders and when it is inappropriate to make them.

8.128 In *Nottinghamshire County Council v P* [1994] FAM 18, the Court of Appeal confirmed that an application for a prohibited steps order by a local authority that a father should vacate the household and have no contact save under local authority supervision could not be made as it contravened s 9(5) and was in fact seeking disguised residence and no contact orders. In *Re H (prohibited steps order)* [1995] 1 FLR 638, the local authority sought to prevent the mother's cohabitant, who was not a party to the proceedings but whom they now suspected of abusing children living with the mother, from having contact with them. The Court of Appeal held that a prohibited steps order against the mother, preventing her allowing the cohabitant contact, amounted to a "no contact" order and offended s 9(5). However, it took the view that a prohibited steps order could have been made against the cohabitant even though he was not a party to the proceedings, provided he was given liberty to apply (s 11(7)(d)). Thus, although a "no contact" order could not be properly made against him, as it could only be directed at the person with whom the children lived, a prohibited steps order could be directed and enforced against him. A "no contact" order against the mother, on the other hand, could only be enforced against the mother and did not protect the children when they were not under her control.

8.129 A prohibited steps order cannot be used to prevent contact between parents, as it does not relate to parental responsibility (*Croydon London Borough Council v A* [1992] 2 FLR 341). Similarly, it cannot be used to restrain one parent from assaulting another (*M v M (residence order: ancillary jurisdiction)* [1994] Fam Law 440), or to oust one parent from the family home (*Pearson v Franklin* (above)).

8.130 In *Re B (minors) (residence orders)* [1992] 3 All ER 867, it was held that a specific issue order requiring the return of a child after a "snatch" was inappropriate in view of s 9(5) as the same result could be achieved by a residence order with appropriate directions and conditions attached pursuant to s 11(7). In *Re HG (specific issue) (sterilisation)* [1993] 1 FLR 587, it was confirmed that provided there was a question to be answered, there did not have to be a dispute between the parties before a specific issue order could be made. Another situation in which a specific issue order was deemed appropriate involved an application by a solicitor defending the father in criminal proceedings who wished to interview the children about incidents they had witnessed. However, in *Re J (specific issue order: leave to apply)* [1995] 1 FLR 669, Wall J dismissed an application for leave to make an application for a specific issue order deeming J to be a child in need pursuant to s 17 CA 1989 on the grounds both that this was a matter delegated to the discretion of the local authority and that it was not an issue relating to parental responsibility.

8.131 It was confirmed in *Dawson v Wearmouty* [1999] 1 FLR 1167 (above), that where there was no residence order (in which case s 13 applies), a specific issue order was the correct procedure for an application to change a child's surname, and would have to be used if the child themselves wanted to made such an application, subject to leave being granted. In *Re C (a child) (HIV test)* [2001] Fam 48, the Court of Appeal endorsed a specific issue order requiring a baby to undergo an HIV test against her parents' wishes.

8.132 The court can again make these orders of its own volition in any "family proceedings" (s 10(1)). However, the Act specifically prevents their being used in any way that is denied to the High Court by s 100(2) in the exercise of its inherent jurisdiction. Section 100(2) essentially prohibits the court using the wardship jurisdiction for the purpose of placing a child in the care or under the supervision of a local authority, or in relation to a child already in care. Neither can it be used to confer on a local authority power to determine any question relating to parental responsibility for a child. Thus specific issue and prohibited steps orders cannot be used to circumvent the deliberate restriction of a local authority's powers in this regard. It should also be noted that no local authority may seek to invoke the wardship jurisdiction without leave of the court (s 100(3)), ensuring that authorities are largely confined to the powers specified in Parts III and IV of the Act relating to care proceedings and emergency protection of children – matters outside the scope of this book.

8.133 Where a child is not in care, however, wardship remains an option both for parents and non-parents in relation to specific matters concerning the child's upbringing. The prohibitive cost does not make this an easy option, but one advantage where a non-parent is seeking the assistance of the court is that no application for leave will be required in order to ward the child. As regards matters between parents themselves, s 8 orders may be applied for without leave, and in most cases, there need be no thought of wardship proceedings. It should be noted, however, that even though there is no restriction on wardship proceedings being issued by private individuals, and that this offers a uniquely speedy form of protection which may be of particular importance in child abduction situations, wardship proceedings should not be allowed to continue where the statutory framework provided by the CA 1989 is just as effective. In *Re CT (a minor) (wardship: representation)* (above), where Thorpe J took the view that the services of the Official Solicitor were needed in a case where an adopted child wished to apply to live permanently with her aunt, and directed that wardship proceedings should be issued, the Court of Appeal did not agree that wardship was the right jurisdiction. Waite LJ stated (see [1993] 4 All ER 518 at page 524) that although the court undoubtedly had discretion to allow wardship to go forward in suitable cases, they had a duty in loyalty to the 1989 Act scheme only to do so in appropriate situations. Examples given were, where issues cannot be resolved under Part II CA 1989 in a way that secures the best interests of the child; or where the minor's person is in a state of jeopardy and can only be safeguarded through wardship; where wardship can protect the child more efficiently from external influences, such as intrusive publicity or where the sanctions provided by wardship are a more efficient deterrent than ordinary contempt of court.

8.134 In practice, therefore, it seems that the wardship has probably greatest value when dealing with child abduction, although other situations where the court's overall control could have advantages include the management of a child's property in the event of their parents' death. A useful discussion of the use of wardship and the court's wider inherent jurisdiction can be found in White *et al*, *The Children Act in Practice*, 2nd edition, 1995, Butterworths, pages 267–283.

(f) Duration of s 8 orders

8.135 As noted above, interim s 8 orders may be made as the Act states that where the court has power to make such an order it may do so regardless of the fact that it is not in a position finally to dispose of the proceedings (s 11(3)). Thus an order can be made until the date of the next hearing or a specified event (see also s 11(7)(c)). Judicial guidance has been given on the making of interim residence orders, which are no different in their effect from that of final orders. Courts should be mindful on making them of the no delay principle and not make them longer than necessary (see *Re O (minors) (leave to seek residence order)* [1994] 1 FLR 172 and *Re Y (a minor) (interim residence order)* [1994] Fam Law 127). The appropriateness of interim contact orders has been discussed above.

8.136 It has also been seen that contact and residence orders cease upon the child's parents resuming cohabitation for a period of six months. Section 9(6) provides that no court shall make any s 8 order which will continue to be effective after the child is 16 unless it is satisfied that the circumstances are exceptional. Thus normally residence and contact orders will be expressed to continue until the child attains the age of 16. After this, the *Gillick* principle, that young people of this age are well able to make up their own minds on these issues, comes into play under the Act. Section 9(7) goes on to say that no s 8 order, other than one varying or discharging an existing order shall be made in relation to a child who is already 16 unless the court is satisfied that the circumstances are exceptional. It is thought that exceptional circumstances would certainly include a child who is mentally handicapped, for example. Similarly, where unorthodox medical treatment with potentially serious repercussions is being considered for or by a 17-year-old, it may still be appropriate to make a specific issue order.

8.137 Where a s 8 order does continue in respect of a child beyond the age of 16, it shall then cease on the child's reaching the age of 18 (s 91(11)). If a care order is made in respect of a child, this automatically discharges any s 8 orders relating to the child (s 91(2)).

(g) Directions and conditions

8.138 In proceedings where the question of making a s 8 order arises, the court must draw up a timetable with a view to determining the question, and give appropriate directions to ensure adherence to that timetable (s 11(1)). Rules of court specify appropriate periods for particular steps. The court may give directions of its own motion or on written (or oral if urgent) request subject to certain procedural requirements (FPR 1991, r4.14(2), (3) and (4); FPC (CA 1989) r1991, r14(2)(5) and (6). A written request for directions is made on Form C2. As to the directions which may be given (eg as to timetable for the proceedings submission of evidence or transfer of proceedings to another court) practitioners must have regard to FPR 1991, r4.14(2); FPC (CA 1989) r1991, r14(2). As to timing of proceedings, practitioners must have regard to FPR 1991, r4.15; FPC (CA 1989) r1991, r15. As to attendance at the directions hearing, practitioners must refer to FPR 1991, r4.16; FPC (CA 1989) r1991, r16. As noted above, the court is given very wide discretion, when making s 8 orders to impose conditions on any parent or person with parental responsibility or with whom the child lives (see s 11(7)). The wide ambit of this provision has been confirmed by the courts in *Re B (a minor) (residence order)* [1992] Fam 162, CA and *Re O (Contact) (Imposition of Conditions)* (above). However, some restrictions on the use of conditions have been noted in the context of the discussion about contact and residence orders above (see 8.117ff).

5 Appointment of guardians, parental responsibility and residence orders

8.139 The interrelation of parental responsibility and residence orders has already been canvassed both in this chapter (see paras 8.78ff) and in Chapter 2. It should be noted that, once a residence order has been made, where the non-resident parent retains parental responsibility, this does not postpone the effectiveness of the appointment by the resident parent of a testamentary guardian in the event of death (s 5(7)). However, the guardian would have parental responsibility jointly with the surviving non-resident parent. Any appointment of a testamentary guardian by a parent where the surviving parent has parental responsibility and no residence order has been made, or where a residence order has been made in favour of the deceased parent and the surviving parent jointly, will not take effect until after the death of the surviving parent.

6 Family assistance orders

8.140 The Act introduced a new family assistance order, which can be distinguished from supervision orders previously available to the court on making orders for custody, and from supervision orders under the 1989 Act discussed below. As will be seen, supervision orders can now be made only upon the application of the local authority and not of the court's own motion. Section 16 gives the court power in any family proceedings, where the court has power to make a s 8 order and regardless of whether or not it does make such an order, to make a family assistance order requiring a probation officer or local authority officer to advise, assist and (where appropriate) befriend any person named in the order. Such orders can be made only where the court is satisfied that the circumstances are exceptional and where every party named in the order, other than the child, consents.

8.141 Such orders may require a person named in the order to keep the officer informed of the address of any person named in the order and to allow them to visit.

An order will last for a maximum of six months. It enables the officer to refer to the court the question of a variation or discharge of a subsisting s 8 order.

8.142 It is perhaps surprising that the consent of older children is not required before such an order is made, particularly as the main distinction between this order and a supervision order is the voluntary nature of the new order. However, advisors should be aware that clients do not have to consent to these orders, although it may be that the consequence of refusing to consent will be for welfare reports to be ordered if this has not already been done and the appropriate local authority applying for a supervision or care order pursuant to s 31, following a direction from the court to investigate the child's circumstances pursuant to its power under s 27.

8.143 In practice, family assistance orders have been little used. They cannot be misused, so as to provide an indirect way of providing someone to accompany a child to visit his father in prison (*S v P (contact application: family assistance order)* [1997] 2 FCR 185, but one was appropriate to assist a child and her grandparents, with whom it was decided the child should reside, to establish a new life together (*Re U (application to free for adoption)* [1993] 2 FLR 992. They can also be a good means of involving the local authority in the supervision of contact (see *Leeds City Council v C* [1993] 1 FLR 269). One important difficulty with the order, however, came to light in *Re C (a minor) (family assistance order)* [1996] 1 FLR 424, FD. Here the court was in effect unable to compel a local authority to comply with a family assistance order where they claimed they had inadequate resources so to do.

7 Welfare reports

8.144 As has been seen above, s 7 gives the court power of its own motion, and at its absolute discretion (see *Re W (welfare reports: appeals)* [1995] 2 FLR 142, CA) when considering any question with respect to a child under the Act, to seek welfare reports from a children and family reporter or a local authority on specified matters relating to the welfare of the child. In *Re K (contact: psychiatric report)* [1996] 1 FCR 474, CA, it was held that the court had no power to order a local authority to instruct a child psychiatrist to provide a report under s 7(1)(b)(ii) and parties should either have been invited jointly to instruct such an expert or RSC Order 40 had to be invoked.

8.145 The provision of welfare reports has caused greatest concern in the context of the inherent delay and inadequate resources, as discussed above. On referral the courts are asked to specify the areas of concern to be reported on and the reasons for requiring a report. The probation service brought in *National Standards for Probation Service Family Court Welfare Work* as of January 1995, which, *inter alia*, stated that ten weeks from receipt of the papers was the prescribed target for a s 7 report. It is to be hoped that CAFCASS will improve upon this.

8.146 Care and supervision orders can now be made only on application to the court by a local authority or other authorised person such as the NSPCC (s 31); and such an order can no longer be imposed by the court of its own motion. The only course open to the court is a family assistance order, which is dependent upon the consent of the relevant parties. Where the court feels a care or supervision order may be appropriate it can order a local authority to carry out an investigation of the child's circumstances pursuant to s 27.

8.147 Although an application can be made by a local authority or authorised person for a care or supervision order, either as an application on its own or in other family proceedings (s 31), the court's inability to act on its own embodies the shift towards leaving responsibility for children with their parents and free from state interference.

8 Jurisdiction and procedure

8.148 By virtue of s 92 of the Act, the magistrates' court, county court and High Court all have concurrent jurisdiction in proceedings under the Act, and domestic proceedings in the magistrates' court are renamed "family proceedings".

8.149 The procedure applicable in relation to Children Act proceedings in all three courts is now almost uniform. Unlike some of the public law proceedings under the Act, the Children (Allocation of Proceedings) Order 1991 (SI 1991 1677), which details which proceedings are to be commenced in particular courts as well as the rules relating to transfer of proceedings between different courts, does not place any restriction on the court in which private law Children Act proceedings should be commenced. Thus an applicant and his or her legal adviser have a free choice (subject to any public funding or costs difficulties) as to where to commence an application for a s 8 order or a s 4 parental responsibility order, although any application for variation or discharge of an order under the Act should normally be made to the court which made the order (art 4). However, as noted below, case law now provides some guidance as to the most appropriate venue for certain types of cases.

8.150 In addition, the courts have power to transfer proceedings between the three jurisdictions (Sch 11, para 2 CA 1989) but the Order only provides for "upward and downward" transfers as between magistrates' and county courts and county courts and the High Court. Thus, the magistrates' court cannot transfer a case directly to the High Court, which itself is limited to a downward transfer to the county court. The order sets out the criteria to be taken into account by the court when considering any such transfer; a transfer may be effected only if it is in the best interests of the child. The CAAC and now the Family Law Advisory Board Children Act Sub-Committee have kept a close watch on procedure and some rule changes have been implemented. Some principles have emerged from case law, providing helpful guidance. In particular, the family proceedings court will not be the appropriate venue where there is an application to remove a child permanently from the jurisdiction (*Re L (a minor) (removal from jurisdiction)* [1993] Fam Law 280), nor is it appropriate where there were serious and difficult issues or evidence involving professional disagreements (*S v Oxfordshire County Council* [1993] Fam

Law 74), nor where there was to be a lengthy hearing (*L v Berkshire County Council* [1992] Fam Law 544), particularly if this involved hearings on non-consecutive days *(Essex County Council v L* [1993] Fam Law 458).

8.151 Amended court rules now provide details of the procedure to be followed in relation to applications under the Act, which have both changed and harmonised the procedure in all three jurisdictions. Part IV Family Proceedings Rules 1991 (SI 1991/1247) (FPR) contain the details of the procedure to be followed in the county court and High Court, and Part II of the Family Proceedings Courts (Children Act 1989) Rules (SI 1991/1395) (FPCR) set out the magistrates' courts procedure, which is broadly the same.

8.152 Proceedings are issued by completing the appropriate form. Simplified application forms and minor procedural amendments were introduced with effect from 3 January 1995. Where there are no family proceedings in existence, then applications for free-standing s 8 orders and parental responsibility orders are all made on Form C1. Where there are existing family proceedings, then the application is on Form C2. In the unmarried context, unless another party has already issued proceedings, or a separate issue has arisen within on-going proceedings, then the first application will be made on Form C1. There is now only one form per family, although in addition to the court giving a court reference number to the case, each child concerned in the application will be allocated a separate reference number which stays with that child for life. Form C1 is also used where leave to apply is required unless another party has already issued proceedings in respect of the child.

8.153 No affidavit evidence is required in any of the three jurisdictions but the application form requires fairly detailed information about the applicant, the child, the child's family and the respondent. Service on the respondent, giving notice of the hearing (provided by the court on Form C6), is required as specified in the rules and is now effected in all cases by the applicant, not by the court. It should be noted that in urgent cases applications for all s 8 orders may now be made *ex parte* (r 4.4(4) FPR 1991 and r 4(4) FPCR as amended and see *Re G* [1993] 1 FLR 910; *Re P* [1993] 1 FLR 915). Appendix 3 FPR and Sch 2 FPCR specify additional persons on whom the applicant is required to serve, or to whom the applicant must give, notice of the application (on Form C6A).

8.154 Any further evidence can be filed in the form of a statement which is signed and dated by the maker and contains a declaration by him or her that the contents of the statement are believed to be true and that it is understood that the statement may be placed before the court. This is the case in all three jurisdictions and no affidavit evidence is required in the county court or High Court in relation to Children Act proceedings. The respondent must file an acknowledgement of service to the application, within the period specified by the rules, on the appropriate form where there is one. In the case of s 8 proceedings, the period is fourteen days of service and the appropriate form is Form C7. An answer may (but need not now) be filed by the respondent and must be served at least two clear days prior to the hearing date.

8.155 The court then draws up a timetable and gives any necessary directions to ensure the timetable is adhered to. This will include a direction that service on the respondent be made at least 21 days prior to the hearing.

8.156 Where a person requires leave to apply for an order under the Act, a written request setting out the reasons for the application should be made to the court, and a draft of the appropriate substantive application form, with sufficient copies for service, should be filed. The court then considers whether or not to grant leave immediately; if so, the applicant is notified and the matter proceeds. If the court cannot grant leave immediately, it must fix a date for the hearing of the application and notify the applicant and other appropriate persons. The new uniformity of procedure throughout the family jurisdiction is a great advance and it is to be hoped that the further recommended rule changes will be acted upon in the near future.

9 Existing orders for custody and access and the transitional provisions

8.157 Orders for custody and access under the old law are preserved, although some modifications have been made to reconcile them with the new 1989 Act scheme. Whilst fewer and fewer old-style orders remain operative, some are still in existence. As has already been noted, parental rights orders made under the FLRA 1987 will be treated as if they were made under the 1989 Act, and will thus confer parental responsibility. Any unmarried father who has been awarded legal custody of his child will be deemed to have the benefit of a s 4 order and thus will acquire parental responsibility which cannot be terminated whilst the existing custody order continues in force (Sch 14, para 6 (4)). A person with access under an existing order may apply for a contact order, and such a person is broadly treated for the other purposes of the Act in the same way as a person with a contact order (see Sch 14, para 9) and thus, for example, may be named with consent in a family assistance order.

8.158 The making of a residence order in respect of a child who is the subject of an existing order discharges the existing order, and where any other type of s 8 order is made, the existing order remains in force subject to the s 8 order (para 11). Thus if a mother has been granted custody under the old provisions and the child's father subsequently applies for and is granted a contact order pursuant to s 8, then the mother's custody order will continue in force subject to the contact order.

8.159 However, if a residence order is granted to a grandmother, where previously orders had been granted giving custody to the mother and access to the father, the father's access order will be automatically discharged notwithstanding the grandmother's agreement to his continued contact with the child and he would therefore need to apply for a new-style contact order to preserve his right to see his child.

8.160 Generally, the court is given power to discharge an existing order (or part thereof) in any family proceedings where any question relating to the child's welfare arises, or on the application of any parent or guardian of the child or other person named in the existing order, or, with the leave of the court, the child him/herself. Where an application is opposed, then the court must have regard to the checklist of considerations set out in s 1(3).

10 Appeals

8.161 It is well established that the appeal courts will not interfere with the decisions of the court of first instance unless the reasoning can be shown to be plainly wrong (see *G v G (minors) (custody appeal)* [1985] FLR 894, HL). Appeal lies to the High Court from the magistrates' court against the making or refusal of any order (s 94(1)). Whether or not an appeal against a magistrates' court order will succeed will depend on whether reasons have been given and, if so, whether these can be shown to be plainly wrong. Where clear reasoning appears, the general principle of non-interference with the decision of those who had the benefit of hearing all the evidence at first hand equally applies.

8.162 With regard to the county court and High Court, appeal from a Circuit Judge/High Court Judge lies to the Court of Appeal. However, leave is not required where residence, education or welfare of a minor is concerned, nor where all physical contact has been refused (CPR 1998, PE52 and supplemented by Practice Direction – Appeals CPO 52 and *Re J (a minor) (residence)* [1994] 1 FLR 369). Note that in the case *Re W; Re A; Re B (change of name)* [2001] FAM 1 the Court of Appeal held that the test to be applied by the appellate court in children cases should be in accordance with the principles established in the case of *G v G (Minors) (Custody Appeal)* [1985] FLR 894.

8.163 Notice of Appeal must be filed and served within fourteen days of the decision, or such other time ordered by the judge and served not later than seven days after filing (CPR 1998, r 52.4).

11 Other useful information

8.164 Children Act case law is now available via the Court Service website at www.courtservice.gov.uk and in the reports of the Family Law Advisory Board Children Act Sub-Committee. The Lord Chancellor has also announced pilots of new Family Advice and Information Networks from October 2001 to enable people with family problems seeking legal advice to access a range of services through one single point of reference contracted by the Legal Services Commission, including some firms of solicitors. The National Association of Child Contact Centres (NACCC) provides a directory of centres in England and Wales where contact facilities can be made available to parents (see Appendix III).

Chapter 9

Financial provision for children

1 Introduction

9.01 Financial Provision for children continues to be dominated by the child support legislation which has been fundamentally amended yet again by the Child Support and Pensions Act 2000 (CSPSSA 2000). From 1 April 2002, when it is planned that the 2000 Act will be fully implemented for new cases, advisors will need to be aware of the two parallel systems of child support calculation for new and existing child claims. Much of the criticised child support terminology, for example the pejorative "absent parent", is also changed by the 2000 amendments and is already in use. The child support legislation transformed the approach necessary to child maintenance issues in both the married and unmarried contexts. Whilst the Child Support Act 1991 (CSA 1991), which came into force on 5 April 1993, did not repeal any of the legislation governing child maintenance, by virtue of s 8(3) CSA 1991, the courts have no power to decide periodical maintenance where the Child Support Agency (CSA) have jurisdiction. Child maintenance has therefore largely become an administrative rather than a judicial process. As will be developed below, the role of the courts in determining periodic child maintenance in both the married and unmarried contexts has been reduced to a small number of residual situations, and this remains unaffected by the amendments introduced by the Child Support Act 1995 (CSA 1995). The CSPSSA 2000 will further reduce the ability of parties to bypass the CSA by reaching enforceable agreements approved by the courts and will make knowledge of the CSA scheme imperative for all advisors. However, the courts retain jurisdiction in respect of all other aspects of financial provision, such as lump sum payments, settlements and transfer of property.

9.02 The current provisions for financial relief for children in unmarried families, other than child support maintenance as originally introduced by the FLRA 1987, are to be found in s 15 and Schedule 1 CA 1989. The 1987 reforms, which also abolished affiliation proceedings, brought the principles for financial relief for children of unmarried parents more into line with those found in the Matrimonial Causes Act 1973 (HCA 1973), which were and remain available on relationship breakdown to children of married parents only. Although significant differences remain, both the orders available and the criteria for making the orders under the Schedule can be seen to have descended from the MCA 1973.

9.03 Schedule 1 is not restricted to financial relief for children on the breakdown of unmarried relationships. However, given the continuation of the relevant provisions of the MCA 1973 in particular enabling orders for financial relief for children of married families to be made under more generous criteria, the schedule is mostly used by unmarried parents and is certainly of great importance to them, as it provides the only means for them to obtain final orders for financial provision for their children.

9.04 Applications for financial relief for children under Sch 1 can be made in their own right irrespective of whether any application for residence or contact orders are or have been before the court. However, as applications for financial provision come within the definition of "family proceedings" in the Act, a court can of its own motion make any s 8 order, or order a local authority to investigate a child's circumstances pursuant to s 27, during the course of the financial provision proceedings in the absence of any application.

9.05 Before the advent of the Child Support Acts, it was possible to deal with the issues of child maintenance and other financial provision for children as a global package which the court could assess using its powers under Sch 1 CA 1989. However, now, the issue of periodic child maintenance is, in most cases, both outside the jurisdiction of the court and effectively non-negotiable as between the parties. Certainly any agreements which are reached need to reflect the statutory child support levels if they are to be enduring, as discussed below, and the lack of encouragement for parties to make binding agreements runs counter to the very ethos of co-operation and mediation encouraged in other areas of family law governed by the CA 1989.

9.06 Thus the starting point where periodical maintenance for children of unmarried parents is sought must be to determine, firstly, whether the CSA has jurisdiction; and, secondly, what issues, if any, lie to be determined by the courts under Sch 1 CA 1989. In the unmarried context, where all the applications for financial provision can only be for the benefit of the child, the division of child support maintenance from other forms of financial provision makes the process of settling issues between the parties particularly fragmented and cumbersome. Although it is possible for parties not in receipt of welfare benefits to reach either voluntary or binding agreements about child maintenance, it is not possible to agree to oust the jurisdiction of the CSA. Thus, as will be developed further below, in most situations, any agreement could be superseded by a child support assessment, and would certainly be, should the parent with care become dependent on welfare benefits. In reaching any agreement, therefore, advisors need to provide contingencies for this turn of events, and parties must be carefully advised of the potential consequences.

9.07 The main changes are to be implemented, for the most part, in April 2002 for all new cases, and it is proposed to extend the new scheme to all existing cases with effect from April 2003. These are summarised in a check list at para.9.123.

2 Child support maintenance—The Child Support Acts 1991 and 1995 and the impetus for further reform in the Child Support, Pensions and Social Security Act 2000

9.08 The CSA 1991 passed through Parliament with all party support within a year of the initial government statement indicating that reform of child maintenance was to be considered. Its target was held out as being so-called "feckless fathers" who had abdicated financial responsibility for their children, leaving the state to support them. The White Paper *Children Come First* (1990, Cm 1264) followed, which made clear that the whole court-based discretionary child maintenance system, which it considered to be slow, fragmented, uncertain and ineffective, was to be changed. The fact that ex-husbands, already paying maintenance for their children were also to fall under its jurisdiction and would be subject to large maintenance increases was not, it seems, fully appreciated by many. After implementation, both the Act and the Child Support Agency responsible for it quickly attracted serious criticism. Much adverse publicity about the methods of assessments and an active and effective campaign for reform by those forced to pay much higher maintenance followed, once its impact on maintenance levels and the quality of life of second families began to be felt. This resulted in three House of Commons Select Committee reports criticising its operation and numerous subsequent minor and then more major amendments to the legislation. This process culminated in a further White Paper, *Improving Child Support*, (1995, Cm 2745) and then the CSA 1995.

9.09 The election of a Labour government in 1997, well aware of the deep-rooted dissatisfaction with child support by both mothers and fathers, prompted further review and legislation. Its Green Paper *Children First: A New Approach to Child Support* (Cm 3992) in 1998 followed by the White Paper, *A New Contract for Welfare: Children's Rights and Parents' Responsibilities* in 1999 (Cm 4349) set out its intentions and the proposals have now been enacted in the Child Support, Pensions and Social Security Act 2000 (CSPSSA 2000). It is hoped that the new much-simplified child support formula will address the three main problems identified in the 1999 White Paper –

- The complexity of the formula resulting in long delays in assessing liability and as stated by the latest report of the National Audit Office on the CSA "a significant risk of error inherent in the [current] assessment process." (1999/00, para 1.5).
- The fact that only a small proportion of children saw any financial gain following CSA involvement due to payment not being made in full.
- Children dependant on state benefit see no financial gain at all.

9.10 Whilst the antipathy of fathers, most often the non-resident parent following relationship breakdown, to the CSA is well documented, mothers too have had little satisfaction from it. As Baroness Hollis put it during the House of Lords debate on 17 April 2000:

" To the mothers, the CSA represents all hassle and no cash". (*Hansard* HL Deb, vol. 612, col. 461 17 April 2000).

9.11 Whilst the recommended new terminology has already been adopted by the CSA, and some of the strengthened enforcement procedures have also come into force, the main bulk of these latest reforms will be implemented in April 2002, with the existing case load being transferred over to the new formula in April 2003, if the new scheme proves successful. All of these reforms have been a response to the enormous and widespread dissatisfaction with the workings of the Child Support Agency and the perceived unfairness of legislation. It is hoped that the new formula will improve the accuracy of CSA maintenance calculations, which currently stands at only 67% a reduction despite attempts to improve accuracy from the 70.5% the year before (CSA Standards Committee Report, 2000/2001).

9.12 The CSA 1991 introduced both new procedures and a new vocabulary (defined for the most part in s 3) into the world of child maintenance and this has itself been subject to both criticism and now amendment (see Sch 11 to CSPSSA 2000). The Act applies only to "qualifying" children; the qualification being that one or both parents are "absent parents", renamed "non-resident parent" (NRP) by the 2000 Act. A "non-resident parent" is one who does not live in the same household with the child, where the child has his or her home with a "person with care". This person provides the day-to-day care for the child and, in the context of relationship breakdown, will usually be the other parent.

9.13 "Child support maintenance", "calculated" now rather than "assessed" in accordance with the child support legislation, must be paid by the child's non-resident parent(s) in respect of their qualifying child or children, and this is the only recognised way of discharging their duty to maintain their child (s 1(2)). The legislation focuses on "natural" or adopted children of non-resident parents. It does not in fact discriminate between married and unmarried parents, whose obligations to their children under the Act are identical, and is not concerned with stepchildren, save that they and other children residing with the non-resident parent may affect the amount of child support payable by the non-resident parent. Maintenance assessment (or now calculation) has, prior to implementation of the 2000 Act reforms, been based upon a prescribed formula, aimed at standardising assessment and minimising discretion. Its rigidity and complexity has attracted much criticism and pressure for reform resulted in rapid waves of changes to the governing regulations. The CSA 1995 further sought to address its problems and introduced the ability to apply for discretionary "departure directions", which in turn will be replaced by "variations" post-CSPSSA 2000 as discussed below. One aspect of the 2000 Act already in force is that the sum of child support maintenance payable is no longer reviewed every two years (s 24 CSPSSA 2000).

9.14 The CSA 1991 and 1995 are supplemented by a plethora of regulations and for a year at least, these will continue to be operated in tandem with the much simplified post-2000 Act scheme, which is itself in the process of being clarified by further delegated legislation. Anyone seeking to advise upon the accuracy of assessments or calculate liability under the current scheme needs to be in possession of all the statutory materials, as well as a calculator and an up-to-date list of benefit rates. All of these are available on the CSA website (see below). Many advisors have wisely invested in not only specialist texts on child support such as CPAG's

Child Support Handbook, but also dedicated computer software packages available for such calculations such as the highly acclaimed *Child's Pay*.

9.15 Special cases (indicated below) need particular attention. Further material including information leaflets for parents and employers published by the CSA, is available free through the Child Support Agency Enquiry Line (Tel: 08457 133 133 or e-mail contact on: csa-nel@new100.dss.gsi.gov.uk). Their most complete guide is now the *Decision-Maker's Guide* available through their website at http://www.dss.gov.uk/csa/. However, their publication *A Guide to Child Support Maintenance* (Publication Reference CSA 2008) aimed at advisors is also valuable and can be downloaded from the website.

9.16 There is also the Child Support Practitioners' Group to, *inter alia*, support and co-ordinate those giving advice on child support legislation and practice and a proposed new SFLA "Bulletin Board" initiative may be useful (contact for both is James Prirrie, The Family Law Consortium, 2 Henrietta Street, London WC2E 8PS). See also Wikeley's impressive series of articles in *Family Law*, [2000] 820 – 825 and 888 – 892, [2001]35 – 38 and 125 – 129 and Prirrie's excellent article "The CSA Update – August 2001" in *SFLA Review* (September 2001, p 12) which set out the differences between the new and the old schemes as well as in Prirrie's article (which is most recent), the practical issues for advisors to consider when advising on new cases prior to implementation.

9.17 Given the impending reforms, it is not proposed here to go through the current scheme of the child support legislation in great detail. However, given that it will continue to apply to existing cases until at least April 2003 and the ground rules of the scheme remain broadly the same, we begin with the scheme as it currently stands. Advisors should be aware that in the short term, there may be a great difference in the liability/payments in new cases depending on whether the assessment is made before or after 1 April 2002 and that there is the potential for negligence claims if the wrong or indeed no advice is given to clients. In the intervening period where clients have the choice of when or whether to approach the CSA, careful thought clearly needs to be given to the relative positions of maintenance calculations made before or after implementation. Thus the information currently required and applied in order to arrive at an assessment in straightforward cases is focused on first, but changes, which the new scheme introduces, are flagged. This is followed by a summary of the main tenets of the new scheme and its much-simplified formula. Attention will be drawn to special cases and possible departures/variations from the formula. Those requiring more detail of the current scheme are referred to the second edition of this book and/or to an up-to-date specialist text. Throughout, the relationship of the child support legislation with the courts will be considered as part of the discussion and its implications for unmarried parents on relationship breakdown are specifically noted.

9.18 A child support calculation is bound to have consequences for any other financial provision being sought for a child on relationship breakdown under Sch 1

CA 1989 and this calculation will often be the advisor's starting point. (All sections referred to below will relate to the CSA 1991 unless otherwise stated.)

(a) Preliminary issues

(i) Does the CSA or the court have jurisdiction?

9.19 Section 8(3) makes clear that where the CSA has jurisdiction, the general powers of the courts to make child maintenance orders are suspended, although they retain a residual jurisdiction in some circumstances. This remains the case under the new scheme, although, as discussed below, the protection from CSA intervention of orders made as written agreements and approved by the court in accordance with s 8(5) will, in future, be reduced to a 12-month period.

9.20 The general rule is that where one parent of a child (defined as for Child Benefit as under 16, or under 19 but in full time non-advanced education (s 55)) is "non-resident", the Child Support Agency (CSA), will have jurisdiction to make a child support assessment. Maintenance for children of former cohabitants will in most cases fall within this remit and thus the court will not normally decide their periodical maintenance. There are, however, two main situations in which the CSA has no jurisdiction to make an assessment:

- Firstly, where any one of the non-resident parent, the parent with care or the child is not "habitually resident" in the UK (s 44(1)). "Habitual residence" is not defined but is thought to take on the same meaning it bears in other legislation (eg s 5(2)(b) Domicile and Matrimonial Proceedings Act 1973)).
- Secondly where there is a written agreement or order for periodical maintenance which was made before the 5 April 1993 *and* the parent with care is not in receipt of prescribed welfare benefits (s 4(1) and s 7(10) CSA 1991).

9.21 In these situations, the court continues to have exclusive jurisdiction over child periodical maintenance and in the unmarried context will be governed by paras 1(2)(a) and (b), Sch 1 CA 1989, as discussed below. Rules 10.24–10.26 FPR 1991 are used by the court to determine whether the court or the CSA have jurisdiction with appeal to a district and then circuit judge.

9.22 Following the CSA 1995, s 8(3A) CSA 1991 gave back to the courts the power to vary pre-5 April 1993 orders or written agreements for periodical child maintenance where the parent with care is in receipt of state benefits but where no child support assessment has been made.

(ii) Supplemental role of the court

9.23 Where the CSA does have jurisdiction, there are also prescribed circumstances in which the court will be able to award periodical maintenance pursuant to paras 1(2)(a) and (b) to Sch 1 CA 1989 in addition to that payable through the CSA if the non-resident parent's income so permits. These are set out in ss 8(6)-(8). Firstly, top-up maintenance can be awarded where maximum child support is payable and the court thinks it is appropriate in the circumstances to award additional maintenance for the child. This obviously concerns those in high-income brackets only. Under the new scheme, a maximum level of child support will only become operable where the non-resident's net income exceeds £2,000 per week, and this is likely to further reduce the number of cases where a top-up maintenance will be awarded. Secondly, school fees or other educational expenses can be ordered to be paid as additional maintenance and, lastly, where the child is disabled further maintenance may be ordered to cover expenses arising as a result of that disability. In *C v F (disabled child: maintenance orders)* [1999] 1 FCR 39, it was held that the order could be made under the CA 1989 to extend beyond the child's 19th birthday even though there can never be child support liability beyond the age of 19. The CSPSSA 2000 does not change the position in relation to these last two categories and given that the level of child support payable under the new scheme seems likely to go down rather than up, more income may be available for such orders in appropriate cases.

(iii) Who can or must apply for child support maintenance?

9.24 Providing the CSA has jurisdiction (see above), a child support maintenance calculation may be triggered in one of two ways:

9.25 *Section 4 applications* Section 4 permits either the non-resident parent or the parent with care (but not the child) to voluntarily apply for a maintenance assessment in respect of a child. If an application is made the CSA is obliged to carry out a maintenance calculation. Thus, unless there is a court order or written agreement which pre-dates the coming in to force of the 1991 Act (in which case the CSA has no jurisdiction), or unless the written agreements order procedure has been followed (see discussion of this below) there is nothing to stop an application to the CSA for an assessment, whatever may have been agreed between the parents, as its jurisdiction cannot be ousted. A s 4 application can be withdrawn at any time before the assessment is made. Note, however, that where the parent with care is in receipt of a prescribed welfare benefit, a s 4 application is not possible (s 4(10)(b)).

9.26 *Section 6 applications* Currently, s 6 provides that where a person with care of the child is in receipt of prescribed benefits (currently, income support and income-based jobseeker's allowance) and regardless of whether or not there is an existing order or agreement for maintenance, they may be required to authorise the Agency to recover child support maintenance on their behalf. As discussed below, these coercive measures have been strengthened under the new scheme where the amended s 6 will allow the CSA to treat the parent with care as having applied for a maintenance calculation and take action to recover the sums payable (s 6(2) as amended). Thus, even where a couple make an agreement when the parent with care is not in receipt of benefits and both are content to hold to the agreement, they will lose control of the situation the moment the parent with care claims benefits as the CSA jurisdiction will be invoked and an application for child support will be forced upon them.

(iv) Effects of s 6 applications

9.27 In short, those on state benefits have no choice as to if and when they apply for an assessment, whereas those who are not, do. Failure on the part of a s 6 applicant to co-operate in making the application or in providing required information will normally result in a reduced benefit direction and here again the 2000 Act is introducing changes. Currently, the only means of avoiding a reduced benefit direction is where the CSA accepts that there are reasonable grounds for believing that such a requirement would subject them or any child living with them to a risk of suffering "harm or undue distress" (ss 6(2) and 46(3)). In effect this will remain the position, although the mechanism for arriving at this situation has been changed. Now, a parent with care can notify the CSA in writing that they do not wish to be treated as having made an application and they will not be (s 6(5) as amended). But, they must be warned that this will result in a reduced benefit direction unless they show that they or their child risk suffering "harm or undue distress" as a result of being so treated. This phrase is not defined in the Act, but potentially covers a wide range of situations. Much concern was focused on this aspect of the 1991 Act before it came into force. Case law has not yet emerged to help clarify this issue, although some Child Support Commissioners' decisions illustrate what may hold sway. Thus, where an application for child support would result in already fragile contact opportunities ceasing altogether for the child due, for example, to the hostility of the father's new partner, a risk of harm or undue distress was found (see CCS/1037/1995 and CCS/15109/1996).

9.28 However, whilst the House of Commons Social Security Select Committee in 1994 found that the CSA were dealing sensitively with this issue, the assessment of the risk of harm or undue distress was removed from the CSA in 1999 and is instead carried out in face-to-face interviews by the Benefits Agency when a parent with care makes a claim for benefit. According to the CSA Standards Committee Annual Report for 2000/2001 (available on the CSA website), the numbers of parents with care in receipt of benefits claiming be at such risk has reduced from 59% in April 1998 to 16% in March 2001. This may indicate that a harsher attitude to what constitutes a risk of "harm or undue distress" is emerging and will apply in to the post-2000 Act provisions containing the same phrase. Furthermore, it should be noted that a Child Support Commissioner's decision has confirmed that once a s 6 application is made under the pre-2000 Act legislation there is no right to withdraw it if it subsequently results in harm or undue distress being suffered (CCS/4725/95). It seems, however, that under the new scheme, a written request by a parent with care not to treat him/her as having applied for a maintenance under the amended s 6(5) at any stage prevents the CSA from both so treating the parent with care *and* from taking action to recover the maintenance from the non-resident parent. However, as noted below, whilst there is now an absolute right of veto, it comes at the price of a reduced benefit direction, unless harm or undue distress is proven under s 46 as amended. Thus whilst the 2000 Act has amended s 6, the new s 6(5) does not in practice improve the situation of parents with care reluctant to co-operate with the CSA.

9.29 Failure to give the CSA authority under s 6 or to co-operate in providing the necessary information (s 6(9)) where no undue harm or distress is accepted ultimately results in a "reduced benefit direction" (s 46). This originally involved 20% of the adult over 25 Income Support allowance being deducted from the parent with care's benefit for six months and then 10% for a further 12 months. With effect from October 1996, reg 36 Child Support (Maintenance Assessment Procedure) CS(MAP) Regs 1992 increased the penalty to 40% for a three-year period in the first instance, with the possibility of further penalty being imposed.

9.30 The reduced benefit direction must not be imposed where the child or parent with care is in receipt of a disability premium and in all other cases there is discretion as to whether to impose it. Here, as a discretion is being exercised, s 2 applies and the welfare of the child must be considered before it is imposed; this must be done quite separately from, and in addition to, the issue of whether there is a risk of harm or undue distress (para 1192 GAP Circular 2/2000). Under the new scheme, a reduced benefit direction will not only be imposed where a parent with care refuses "unreasonably" to be treated as having made an application or fails to provide sufficient information, but will also be imposed where the parent with care refuses to take a scientific test to help establish paternity (s 46(1)(c) CSA 1991 as amended and see ss 26–27A CSA 1991 as amended). The CSA Standards Committee Annual Report 2000/2001 also found that between April 1998 and April 2001 the number of reduced benefit directions imposed decreased from 19% to 3.5% of those cases where reduced benefit direction action was considered.

9.31 Importantly (it was thought), s 2 CSA 1991 provides that, wherever the CSA exercises discretion under the Act, regard must be had to the welfare of any child likely to be affected by the decision. However, the welfare of the child is not, of course the paramount or even the first consideration under the terms of this Act. Any alleged breach of s 2 must be challenged by way of judicial review (*R v Secretary of State for Social Security, ex p Biggin* [1995] 2 FCR 595, FD). In this case it was also found that s 2 did not affect the application and enforcement of the formula, which has left it with little role to play. Similarly, attempts to use human rights arguments to soften the implications of the legislation have so far met with failure. In *Logan v United Kingdom* (1996) 22 EHRR *CD* 178, a father who claimed he could not afford to have contact with his children because of high child support levels was held not to have had his Article 8 right to family life infringed because he had not shown he was unable to sustain contact. This may leave open a possible challenge in an even more extreme case, although the anticipated reduction in levels of maintenance payable following the reforms may narrow the opportunities for such a case. Appeals against reduced benefit directions lie to the child support appeal tribunal, which can substitute its own assessment (s20). Alternatively the revision procedure to the Secretary of State may be used in such cases (s 16(1A)(b)).

(b) The maintenance calculation process

9.32 This process is the same regardless of whether the application is made pursuant to s 4 or s 6 of the 1991 Act and little is to change following the reforms, although the method of calculation is to be greatly simplified and the level of maintenance payable is predicted, on average, to reduce.

9.33 Currently, the CS(MAP) Regs 1992 deal with the method of making applications. The CSA provide a maintenance application form free of charge and the application may be amended at any time before an assessment is made. An application will be effective where the application is properly completed. Once this is submitted, the Agency will give notice in writing to the non-resident parent and send him/her a maintenance enquiry form, which must be returned within 14 days. Maintenance becomes payable as of the date on which the enquiry statement is sent.

9.34 Where an assessment is applied for, the applicant must (subject to certain exceptions) provide the agency with information necessary for:

- the non-resident to be traced;
- the amount of child support payable to be calculated; and
- that amount to be recovered from the non-resident parent. (See s 4(4)–(8) and s 6(9)–(11)).

(i) Powers and duties of the CSA decision-makers

9.35 The pre-2000 Act s 11 requires CSA decision-makers (previously "officers") to gather information about the means of the parties and they have been given far-reaching powers to assist in collecting the necessary information. Section 14 and the Child Support (Information, Evidence and Disclosure) Regulations 1992 (SI 1992/1812) (CS(IED)R 1992) together with Sch 2 of the 1991 Act give them access to information held by the DSS, local authorities and the Inland Revenue for the purpose of tracing and assessing the means of non-resident parents, and ascertaining their habitual residence. Other information that can be required varies as between the different informants. These include the employer or former employer of either parent or carer, and officers of the court where there has been a maintenance order made in respect of the child. Information relating to a paternity dispute may be obtained from a relevant court.

9.36 Furthermore, s 15 gives inspectors wide powers to enter specified premises and to question people over 18, including employers. They may enter specified premises other than a dwelling house at reasonable times and may question the employer, employees or an occupier of the premises who must furnish the inspector with all information and documents "as the inspector may reasonably require". A person does not have to disclose information that may incriminate him/her or his/her spouse.

9.37 However, it is an offence punishable with a fine on scale 3 to intentionally delay or obstruct an inspector or refuse or neglect without reasonable excuse to answer questions or furnish information when required to do so. There is now a revised CSA leaflet *Advice for Employers* (available on the CSA website). The 2000 reforms increase the powers available to inspectors yet further (s 15(4A)) and introduce a new criminal offence for persons required to comply, of providing false information or documentation (s 14A). This applies to employers and accountants as well as both parents who either make a false statement or fail to provide information, with the latter being subject to a defence of "reasonable excuse". Both of these provisions were brought into force on 31 January 2001.

9.38 These powers do little to address the practical difficulties traditionally faced by the courts in extracting information from the self-employed, although the wider powers of search now extend to premises which are not exclusively residential and where it is believed a non-resident parent carries on a trade, business or profession. Nonetheless, it seems that this category of absent parent remains problematic for the CSA.

(ii) Delaying the final calculation – parentage disputes (s 26(1))

9.39 This has been amended by the 2000 Act and was implemented with effect from 31 January 2001. The changes are of particular significance to cohabitants where parentage is in dispute, as a new presumption of paternity has been introduced. It will be assumed, in future, that a man who is registered on a child's birth certificate as the father is the child's father and a child support maintenance calculation will not now be delayed by disputing paternity (s 26(2)(Case A2) as amended). Although previously, a paternity dispute, whereby the alleged father denies he is the father of the qualifying child, had the effect of suspending the assessment process until the issue of paternity was resolved (s 26(2)), this will not be the case where cohabitants have jointly registered the child's birth. It is suspected that this provision is likely to act as a deterrent to being named as the father on birth registration for many fathers pessimistic or cautious about the durability of their relationship with the mother.

9.40 Currently, unlike in other cases where there is insufficient evidence to proceed with the final maintenance calculation, there is no power to make an interim maintenance assessment pending the outcome of a parentage dispute (s 12). Thus, denial of parentage has been successfully used to delay the maintenance calculation and therefore was an obvious target for reform. In addition to extending a presumption of paternity to a man registered as the child's father, a presumption has also been extended to those who refuse to take a scientific test in order to determine paternity as well as those in respect of whom the test confirms paternity of the child (s 26(2)(Case A3)). Similarly, a presumption of parenthood is extended for child support purposes to deemed parents under ss 27 and 28 Human Fertilisation and Embryology Act 1990, where a child has been born as a result of infertility treatment to which they consented. This again ensures that a maintenance calculation will be made and financial liability designated rather than avoided as a result of a loophole.

9.41 The child support legislation still largely focuses on duties owed by "natural" parents to their children or those where the legal status of parenthood is attributed by law. Thus, adoptive parents and those deemed to be the legal parents by virtue of ss 27 and 28 Human Fertilisation and Embryology Act 1990 (HFEA 1990) come within the Act's definition of "parent" (s 54). However, whilst some of the gaps have been closed, denial of parenthood still prevents the CSA making a maintenance calculation unless the case falls within one of the specified and now expanded exceptions set out in s 26(2). These, in addition to the new presumptions outlined above, still include cases where the court has made a parental order under s 30 HFEA 1990, a declaration under s 56 Family Law Act 1986, affiliation orders, or a finding of paternity in any relevant proceedings for the purposes of s 12 Civil Evidence Act 1968, providing the child has not subsequently been adopted. The 2000 Act has also amended the provisions relating to declarations of parentage and inserts a new s 55A into the Family Law Act 1986 effectively replacing the current provisions contained in s 55(1)(a) of that Act. This was implemented on 1 April 2001 and aims to provide a single integrated mechanism for obtaining a declaration of parentage and replaces the dual mechanisms currently available under s 56 of the 1986 Act and s 27 of the CSA 1991. The new provision enables any person to apply for a declaration of status, not only a prospective parent and may be brought in the magistrates' court s well as the High Court and county court. It does not affect any proceedings pending at the date of implementation.

9.42 In situations not provided for in s 26, s 27 CSA 1991 provides that either the CSA or the parent with care (but not the non-resident parent) may (but need not) apply to the court for a declaration of parentage. If the child support calculation has not been made, then the process can go no further until the issue of parentage has been decided. If the calculation has been made prior to the denial, then it remains in force and the absent parent is powerless to challenge the issue under the Act and would have to apply for judicial review.

9.43 In paternity proceedings, refusal by the alleged father to submit to blood or DNA tests results in a strong inference that he is the father unless other cogent reasons for the refusal persuade the court otherwise (*Re A (a minor) (paternity: refusal of blood test)* [1994] 2 FLR 463, CA). The 2000 Act changes this into a statutory presumption as noted above (s 26(2)(Case A3)). Fees for the scientific tests are payable by the non-resident alleged parent but are refunded should the test prove negative. In the case of a mother refusing to submit herself and the child to blood tests, the Court of Appeal held in *Re H (a minor) (blood tests: parental rights)* [1997] Fam 89 that this was not of itself determinative of paternity. However, an adverse inference could be drawn and the welfare of the child was not paramount as every child had a right to know the truth about his/her parentage unless the child's welfare clearly required a different approach. This approach would appear to be consistent with Article 8 of the European Convention on Human Rights (see *Re T(Paternity: Blood Tests)* [2001] Fam Law 738.

9.44 In terms of child support liability, if paternity proceedings conclude that the alleged non-resident parent is not the father of the child, then no liability arises. If the opposite conclusion is reached, then liability is backdated to the date on which the maintenance enquiry form is sent.

(iii) Other delays – interim assessments

9.45 Obtaining all the information necessary to make a final assessment may take time, although it is hoped that the simplified new scheme will considerably speed up the whole calculation process.

9.46 Currently, Part III CS(MAP) Regs 1992 and s 12(1) and (1A), as amended, provide for the CSA to make interim maintenance assessments where it appears to the decision-maker that she/he does not have sufficient information to proceed with a full assessment. However, once the necessary information is available a final assessment must be substituted. Fourteen days' notice must be given of the intention to make an interim assessment and there are four categories of them (A-D) of which the general aim is to assess maintenance at a level higher than that of any final calculation. However, this incentive to co-operate has not proved a great success. Indeed, interim maintenance assessments (IMAs) have proved one of the greatest of the CSA fiascos and as Wickely ([2000] Fam Law 888 at p 890) notes.

> "In practice IMAs have been singularly ineffective, other than as a means of increasing the amount of arrears outstanding . . ..[A]round 90% of non-resident parents fail to comply".

9.47 Given the imminent repeal of the current s 12 CSA 1991, it is proposed now to consider only the new scheme. Readers are referred to the second edition of this book should they require full details of pre-2000 Act IMAs.

9.48 The new s 12 substituted by s 2 CSPSSA Act 2000 introduces in the place of IMAs "default" and "interim" rates. Where there is not sufficient information about the non-resident parent's income to make a decision, the default rate will apply. This is to be fixed to reflect a percentage of the average NRP's earnings dependant on the number of children for whom child support maintenance is payable. It is therefore anticipated that weekly default maintenance rates will be £30 where there is one child, £ 40 for two children and £50 for three or more (see Wickely, 2000, above). The element of penalty combined with the incentive to provide information quickly comes in the idea that when the final maintenance calculation is calculated and this proves to be lower than the default rate, any excess paid by the NRP is not repaid.

9.49 The interim rate, on the other hand, applies where a variation (which under the 2000 Act replace departure directions) has been made. Here the maintenance level will be set at that calculated under the normal maintenance calculation pending the outcome of the variation calculation. At this juncture, if the application is successful, the new rate will apply but again it seems there will be no retrospective adjustment in favour of the party who has been detrimentally affected.

9.50 In addition, there is also to be a new approach to voluntary maintenance payments which is currently not taken into account to reduce child support liability prior to the finalisation of the assessment, leading to no payments being made and (usually irrecoverable) arrears mounting. The new s 28J allows recognition of voluntary payments (normally to be made to the Agency rather than the parent with care) providing three requirements are met. First the application for child support maintenance (deemed or actual) must have been made. The CSA may direct that the payments should be made to the other parent or a third party, and regulations may provide that other payments although not payments in kind will be taken into account. The application must be pending and lastly the payment must have been made prior to notification of actual liability.

(iv) The current final maintenance calculation

9.51 Currently, when the CSA decision-maker has the information s/he needs, they must make the maintenance calculation in accordance with the complicated formula set out in Schedule 1 of the pre-2000 CSA 1991. The 1995 Act had left the formula broadly the same, although the 1994 and 1995 amendments generally aimed to reduce the non-resident parent's liability. Given that all financial provision advice needs to now begin with the non-resident parent's child support liability and courts may ask parties to provide this information (see *E v C (child maintenance)* [1996] 1 FLR 472), all practitioners need to be able to apply the formula. However the good news is that this is to be greatly simplified on the coming into force of the 2000 Act reforms and given it is entirely based upon the NRP's financial situation will greatly reduce the information required from clients. Nonetheless, the price paid for simplicity (and speed, the government hopes) is that the results will not necessarily be (and indeed are not attempting to be) fairer than those achieved under the current system. What is more, given that ability to avoid the CSA with certainty is now limited to a 12-month period, there is really now no place for practitioners to hide from getting to grips with CSA maintenance calculations.

9.52 In order to properly calculate child support maintenance under the current formula, over one hundred pieces of information are on average required and this is to be greatly reduced. It is now clear that the CSA are not wrong in disclosing information about the non-resident parent to the parent with care as this conforms with the requirements of natural justice (*Huxley c Child Support Comr* [2000] 1 FLR 898). Currently, and for clients whose maintenance was calculated prior to April 2002, the following information is needed:

- ages and income of the qualifying children;
- whether the parent with care is single;
- his/her gross income from all sources;
- his/her tax, national insurance and half any superannuation payments;
- his/her housing costs;
- travel to work costs;
- exactly the same information for the non-resident parent (NRP);

- whether there are any other children in that household and whether they are the NRP's children or not;
- the NRP's council tax liability;
- details of any partner's income;
- details where any child or children spend more than an average of two nights per week in the NRP's household;
- discrepancy between income and apparent affluent lifestyle of NRP;

9.53 AND, in relation to possible departure direction applications by NRP:

- travel costs incurred as a result of contact visits;
- details of any "clean-break" settlement or other financial provision order made prior to 5 April 1993;
- details of any long-term illness or disability affecting NRP or family; and
- details of pre-April 1993 debts incurred before they left and for the benefit of first family.

A calculator (or a computer software package) and an up-to-date list of welfare benefit rates are also essential.

(c) The current formula

9.54 The formula is dealt with in Sch 1 to the Act and the Child Support (Maintenance Assessment and Special Cases) CS(MASC) Regs 1992 and is based on income support rates. The original term "absent parent" is used for the "non-resident parent" in explaining the formula. It consists of four elements with each of these in turn requiring complex arithmetic calculation:

- the maintenance requirement;
- the assessable incomes of the NRP and the person with care;
- the deduction rate and basic and additional elements; and
- the protected income of the NRP.

9.55 When calculating these elements, advisors must consider whether provisions relating to special cases apply and following calculation whether an application for a departure direction would be appropriate.

(i) The maintenance requirement (MR)

9.56 MR = AG - CB.

MR = AG (aggregate of (i) IS rates for children (ii) personal allowance (over 25 rate) for the person with care reduced by 25% when youngest child reaches 11 and 50% at 14, (iii) family premium where child under 16 at appropriate rate) **LESS CB** (child benefit for each child).

(ii) Each parent's assessable income

9.57 Assessable income is net income (**N**) **LESS** exempt income (**E**). That of the absent parent is (**A**) and that of the parent with care is (**C**).

9.58 *Net income* Broadly, this is the income from all sources less income tax, national insurance and 50% of any contribution to an occupational pension scheme. Child benefit, personal injury damages, child maintenance for the child under assessment, income from capital to be used to provide a home following a divorce settlement are disregarded (see reg 7 and Schs 1 and 2 CS (MASC) Regs 1992).

9.59 *Exempt income* This is the calculation that has been most modified by the post-1993 amendments to assist the absent parent. It is defined in reg 9 CS (MASC) Regs 1992. Broadly, it comprises the weekly amount needed for essential expenses based on income support allowance for a single claimant over 25 and any dependent child, lone parent premium, care premium, family premium and disability premium where appropriate, allowable housing costs and the costs of any natural children for whom they are liable.

9.60 *Housing costs* A crucial element of exempt income is housing costs, which again have been the subject of reform. Housing costs are dealt with in regs 14–18 and Sch 3 CS (MASC) Regs 1992, as amended. All costs will not be accepted as a matter of course, but the following are included:

- mortgage interest and capital repayments but not arrears;
- linked capital payments such as endowment policy premiums or pension mortgage contributions;
- payments on loans for specified repairs and improvements (mainly repairs needed to maintain the fabric of the home and essential improvements such as the installation of a bathroom, lighting, damp proofing, heating, insulation and cooking facilities);
- rent, licence payments and mesne profits (less housing benefit) but **NOT** rent arrears;
- ground rent;
- payments under a co-ownership scheme;
- service charge (where payment is a condition of the right to occupy);
- site fees for a tent or caravan.

9.61 The absent parent or a member of their family must be directly liable for the housing costs and liability must not be to another member of the same household. The payment must be in respect of the provision of a home and if loans are taken out for another purpose, payments on them will not be eligible. Where housing costs are shared with a partner, they are no longer reduced, but only "reasonable housing costs" are allowed in full when calculating exempt income of the absent parent for whom there is a ceiling of the higher of either £80 per week of one half of net income. Costs exceeding this, will not be allowed, unless one of the following applies:

- there is a child in the family;
- housing benefit is being paid or has been applied for;

- the parent or partner are disabled;
- the absent parent is still in the former family home;
- the costs have been met for more than a year before the first assessment for child support maintenance;
- the costs breach the limit only because of rent or interest rate increases;
- the costs are high because of the unavailability of his/her share of the equity of the former family home still occupied by their former partner.

9.62 *Post-April 1995 adjustments to exempt income calculation* Travel to work costs where the straight-line distance between home and work exceeds 150 miles per week, now form part of exempt income (allowed at a rate of 10p per mile). More significantly, where there has been a pre-April 1993 "clean break" settlement, a weekly sum is currently imputed into the exempt income calculation to compensate for the loss of capital transferred (the "broad brush allowance"). This has been supplemented by the departure direction procedure (discussed below) which came into force on 2 December 1996. Schedule 3A of the CS (MASC) Regs 1992 now provides that where there has been a capital settlement made before 5 April 1993 and there is clear evidence of a transfer of land or other property made by court order or written agreement made by parents living apart, with the result that the whole of the value was given to the recipient and where it was not made expressly for the purpose only of compensating the parent with care for the loss of the right to apply for periodical payments, then a compensation allowance may be applied for. The value of the share transferred less any compensating payment made by the parent with care is therefore the starting point. Qualifying transfers between £5,000 and £9,999 result in £20 per week being added to exempt income, and will reduce the assessment by £10 per week. Transfers between £10,000 and £24,999 result in £40 per week exempt income allowance and those over £25,000 in £60 per week exempt income allowance. Given the great disparity between house prices in different regions of the country, it seems that the usefulness of this provision to absent parents may well depend on where and when the property was transferred, as the threshold is high relative to values of property in some areas of the country. The results of these calculations should be added to the absent parent's exempt income when calculating their assessable income.

(iii) The deduction rate and basic and additional elements

9.63 The next step is a comparison of the maintenance requirement with half the joint assessable incomes:

(A + C) x P (**P** is defined in regulations as (0.5))

9.64 Where this figure does not exceed the maintenance requirement (**MR**), the sum payable by the absent parent is **A x P, ie one half of the absent parent's assessable income** (subject since April 1995 to this sum not exceeding 30% of the absent parent's *net* income).

9.65 Where this figure exceeds **MR**, then further calculations are needed which in effect take account of the other parent's appropriate contribution. This is done by first calculating a basic element (**BE**) and an additional element (**AE**) which are added together to find the sum payable by the absent parent for the child. This final sum has to be compared with another formula which effectively provides a ceiling for the sum payable and the lower of these two sums is payable as the additional element, subject again to the general ceiling that no absent parent pays more than 30% of his/her net income. The calculations are as follows:

$$\mathbf{BE} = \mathbf{A} \times \mathbf{G} \times \mathbf{P} \text{ (where P = 0.5) and}$$

$$\mathbf{G} = \frac{\mathbf{MR}}{(\mathbf{A} + \mathbf{C}) \times \mathbf{P}}$$

$$\mathbf{AE} = (1 - \mathbf{G}) \times \mathbf{A} \times \mathbf{R}$$

where R is 0.25 where there are three or more children, 0.2 where there are two and 0.15 where there is only one child.

9.66 The result of the calculation of **AE** must be compared with the result of the alternative calculation of **maximum AE** by the following formula:

$$\mathbf{Z} \times \mathbf{Q} \times \frac{\mathbf{A}}{\mathbf{A+C}}$$

where Z (originally 3) is now 1.5 (reg 6(2) CS(MASC) Regs 1992) and Q is the total of income support allowances for the children plus the family premium multiplied by the number of children. If **maximum AE** is lower than the first **AE** calculation then the **maximum AE** applies. Otherwise, the first **AE** calculation applies. The appropriate **AE** is then added to the **BE** to arrive at the final maintenance assessment. All maintenance assessments are subject to their not reducing the absent parent to below their protected income and then to the 30% rule.

(iv) The protected income of the absent parent

9.67 The final calculation relates to the income below which the absent parent will not be allowed to fall. It results in a higher figure than that allowed as exempt income and includes allowances for a new spouse or cohabitant and any children whom the absent parent actually supports. Housing costs for protected income are the same as for exempt income. It is not available to those who withhold information and are consequently subject to an interim assessment (see *Huxley v Child Support Comr* (above)).

9.68 The calculation of protected income at the present time takes the following form:

9.69 ADD:

- adult personal allowance for over 25 if single or over 18 couple's allowance if the absent parent has a partner
- housing costs or I none the housing benefit non-dependant deduction

9.70 PLUS *any of the following as appropriate*

- personal allowance for each child in the family
- disabled child premium
- family premium
- lone parent premium or disability premium
- severe disability premium
- carer premium
- pensioner/enhanced pensioner/higher pensioner premium
- council tax less council tax benefit
- fees for residential accommodation
- high travel to work costs

9.71 PLUS

£30 (originally £8)

9.72 PLUS

Fifteen per cent (originally 10%) of the sum by which the disposable net income, defined (reg. 11(2)) as income from all sources of the absent parent's family, including a child and partner's income or maintenance and child benefit less maintenance payable under a court order for a child not eligible for child support maintenance exceeds the protected income level calculated so far.

9.73 Where the protected income exceeds the absent parent family's disposable net income the maintenance assessment will be reduced accordingly.

9.74 Finally, the assessment must again be checked to ensure it does not exceed 30% of the absent parent's net income (**N**). The lower of these two figures is then payable.

9.75 *Current minimum and maximum child support* Under the current formula, no NRP should pay more than 30% of their net income (as defined in the formula). The 30% rule is, however, subject to a minimum amount payable prescribed by reg 13 CS(MASC) Regs 1992. This is now twice 5% of the personal allowance of a single over 25 claimant:

ie for 2000/2001, $2 \times 5\% \times £53.00 = £5.30$

9.76 No maintenance calculation will be less than this amount unless the NRP falls into an exempt category. Non-resident parents on income support or income-based jobseeker's allowance will normally have this sum deducted from their benefit. Those exempt from paying the minimum are set out in reg 26 and include cases where the NRP has a child in his/her family, is a child, is in prison or is in receipt of certain sickness, incapacity, maternity or disability benefits specified in Sch 4

CS(MASC) Regs 1992. Those whose net income is less that £5.30 do not have to pay. As noted below, this minimum is set to reduce under the new scheme.

9.77 *Current special cases* Where parents are separated but share day-to-day care of a child and have a shared residence order or an absent parent has staying contact with a child for more than an average of two nights per week, this results in a reduction of the child support maintenance to take account of this (see reg 20 CS(MASC) Regulations 1992), although virtually all staying contact and shared residence will be taken into account under the new scheme. One parent, usually the parent who provides the lesser amount of care, is treated as absent. The logic of the adjustment to the formula in these situations is apparent albeit the number of days per week is somewhat arbitrary. This provision can also be seen to be potentially divisive for parents negotiating contact on relationship breakdown, a situation likely to worsen after the reforms as discussed below. Where the parent with care receives a direct benefit from the payment of child support, a desire by the absent parent for substantial staying contact or shared residence would reduce the child support payable and financial concerns could cloud the issues relating to residence and contact in contradiction of the welfare principle set out in the CA 1989.

9.78 Where a parent with care is looking after the children of more than one absent parent, adjustments are made to the formula to reflect this (reg 23). This is also the case where an absent parent has children cared for by more than one parent with care (reg 22).

9.79 Other special cases include where care is shared by a local authority and another person (reg 25), where both parents are absent and two non-parents are providing shared care (reg 24).

(v) Departure directions

9.80 These, as noted above, are to be replaced by "variations" as of April 2002 for new cases. Much of the non-resident parent outrage about child support was born of the sense of injustice felt by those who had made clean break settlements before the advent of child support. However, the common practice on divorce of trading capital for relief from substantial maintenance payments which had often resulted in parents with care becoming dependent on state benefits was perhaps one of the primary reasons for the introduction of the CSA 1991. In the divorce context there was statutory endorsement of the clean break principle (s 25A MCA 1973), although not of the common practice of trading child as opposed to spousal maintenance.

9.81 In *Smith v McInerney* [1994] 2 FLR 1077, FD the court was prepared to adjourn a father's property adjustment order where there had been a clean break separation agreement (which the court purported to uphold) under which a father had transferred his share in the family home to the mother in exchange for being released from maintaining the children, to see whether this should be used to indemnify him for substantial child support maintenance payments. However, the case of *Crozier v Crozier* [1994] 1 FLR 126 had shown the inability of the courts to rectify matters where there had been a consent order. Here, an absent parent, following a high child support assessment requiring payment of £29 per week, was refused leave to set aside a consent order under which he had transferred the whole of his share of the matrimonial home to his wife in return for nominal maintenance payable to the child in the sum of £4 per week. He and many others therefore felt aggrieved that little or no recognition was given to the disadvantage suffered by them in the clean break agreement. Absent parent pressure eventually prompted a response to the criticisms of the rigidity of the formula and an allowance in exempt income for the value of such a transfer as pre-figured in the White Paper *Improving Child Support* was introduced in April 1995. This broad-brush allowance (described above, (see para 9.62) has been supplemented by the discretionary departure direction procedure introduced by the 1995 Act.

9.82 As discussed below, the sum payable when calculated in accordance with the formula may be departed from in certain circumstances (see now s 28A-28I CSA 1991), and this procedure now provides an additional possible remedy to the rights of review and appeal. Cohabitants are less likely to have entered into pre-April 1993 clean break style agreements, not least because financial provision in the form of settlements and property transfer in unmarried families only became possible following implementation of the Family Law Reform Act 1987. The absence of any duty to provide maintenance for a former cohabitant is, of course, also significant. However, in contrast to the broad-brush measures, departure directions cover a wider range of possibilities and will be of as much interest in the cohabitation context as the matrimonial. Of particular importance is the ability of the parent with care as well as the absent parent to apply for a departure direction.

9.83 A departure direction can only be applied for after the assessment has been made and must be based on either the effect of the current assessment or a material change in circumstances since the current assessment (s 28A(2)). Applications may be made by either the absent parent or the parent with care and are to be screened through a preliminary assessment procedure whereby the Secretary of State may reject the application where it appears either that there are no grounds for a direction or that any revised assessment would result in a reduction of less than £1. At this point, the application may be treated as an application for a review under ss 17 or 19 CSA 1991.

9.84 The departure direction scheme was piloted in London and areas of South East England and is governed by the Child Support Departure Directions and Consequential Amendments Regulations 1996 (SI 1996/635) (CSDD Regs 1996). The new system does not replace the broad-brush allowances given to clean break absent parents and those with travel high costs (discussed above) and these must be applied first before arriving at the assessment from which departure is sought. Grounds for departure are now set out in Sch 4B CSA 1991 and include the following:

- the cost of travelling to work;
- the cost of maintaining contact with the child;

- costs attributable to the long-term illness or disability of the applicant or a dependant;
- debts incurred prior to separation for the joint benefit of the parents and/or the child;
- pre-April 1993 clean break orders where property transferred and less maintenance paid and this is not reflected in the assessment;
- pre-April 1993 clean break orders where property transferred but no reduction in maintenance ordered but child support assessment is inappropriately reduced due to high housing costs;
- pre-April 1993 financial commitments which it is impossible or unreasonable to withdraw from, where there was a court order or agreement in force at the time;
- costs of supporting a child who is not of that parent but is part of his family;
- where assets could produce income but do not;
- where a person's lifestyle is inconsistent with his claimed income; or
- where there are unreasonably high travel costs.

9.85 It can be seen that some circumstances would lead to an application by an absent parent and others to one by the parent with care. A direction will only be made if the application falls into one of the specified categories and it is just and equitable to make it, having regard to the financial circumstances of both parents and the welfare of the child (s 28F(2)). The general principles against which the application is decided are that:

- parents should be responsible for maintaining their children whenever they can afford to do so; and
- where a parent has more than one child, the obligation to maintain any one of them does not take precedence over the duty to maintain the others.

9.86 Section 28E(3) and reg 30 CSDD Regs 1996 go on to specify factors included and excluded from influencing the decision. Reasons for the decision must be given (s 28E(8)) and appeal is to a Child Support Appeal Tribunal (CSAT) (s 28H). The direction may apply for a fixed period of time or until a specified event (s 28G) and pending the application, a regular payment condition whereby the absent parent must pay the current assessment or some other specified reduced sum may be imposed (s 28C).

9.87 These are important and complex provisions which it is not feasible to detail here. Those advising on the possibility of such an application need careful study of the provisions and the regulations. An example of the possible context in which a parent with care may be able to apply for a departure direction is provided by the facts of the case of *Phillips v Peace* [1996] 2 FLR 230. A nil child support assessment was made in respect of a self-employed father who was drawing no salary from his company at the time of the mother's application but lived in a house worth £2.6 million and owned three cars valued at £190,000. It would seem that here, the father's lifestyle was inconsistent with his claimed income and a departure application would be most appropriate.

(vi) The New Child Support Scheme from April 2002

9.88 *Main changes to the Formula* The new simplified formula is found in Schedule 1 CSA 1991 as amended by the 2000 Act and bases calculations on percentages of net income which vary according to the number of children to be maintained. There are four rates:

9.89 *Basic rate* This is the normal or default rate whereby the non-resident parent (NRP) is liable to pay:

- 15% of his/her net weekly income where he has one qualifying child;
- 20% where s/he has two qualifying children; or
- 25% where s/he has three of more qualifying children.

Net income is defined in reg 1 the Child Support (Maintenance Calculations and Special Cases) Regulations 2001(SI 2001/155).

9.90 In a radical departure from the previous formula, the NRP's net income is taken to reduce by these same proportions where s/he has a child living in his new household, before the maintenance calculation is applied. Thus the social parenting role of (typically) the father in a reconstituted family is acknowledged for the first time, yet retains a slight preference for first families.

9.91 *Reduced Rate* Where a NRP's net weekly income is between £100 and £200 she/he is liable to pay a reduced rate of child support maintenance to be detailed in regulations. The intention is that the child support liability will increase in proportion to the amount by which the net income exceeds £100. The reduced rate must not be less than the flat rate (see below). This is governed by reg 3 the Child Support (Maintenance Calculations and Special Cases) Regulations 2001(SI 2001/155).

9.92 *Flat rate* The flat rate (initially £5 per week as compared with the current minimum under the present scheme of £5.30) will be payable in cases where the nil rate does not apply and the NRP has a net income of less than £100 per week or is in receipt of an increased range of prescribed benefits, pension or allowance (see reg 4 the Child Support (Maintenance Calculations and Special Cases) Regulations 2001(SI 2001/155)). If the NRP has a new partner who is also a NRP on benefit each partner's liability will be half the flat rate amount. This is a response to criticisms about the impact of the old minimum payment on the welfare of children in second families.

9.93 *Nil rate* This applies where a NRP has a net income of less than £5 per week or s/he falls into a prescribed category of persons, including students, children under 16 or, if on income support aged 16–17 and long-term hospital patients.

9.94 Maintenance calculations will be governed by the Child Support (Maintenance Calculation Procedure) Regulations 2001 (SI 2001/157) which will revoke, subject to transitional provisions, (and see also Child Support (Consequential Amendments and Transitional Provisions) Regulations 2001 (SI 2001/158)) the Child Support (Maintenance Assessment Procedure) Regulations 1992. Other of the

1992 Child Support Regulations including the Collection and Enforcement Regulations (SI 1992/1989) and the Information, Evidence and Disclosure Regulations (SI 1992/1812) have been amended rather than replaced.

9.95 *Shared Care and Approtionment* Where a child stays with the NRP for at least 52 nights per year, the maintenance payable will be reduced proportionately. Thus regular staying contact of once a week (but less than twice a week) results in a one-seventh reduction, two (but less than three) nights a week reduces it by two-sevenths. Between 156 and 174 nights a year (ie three but less than four nights per week) results in a three-sevenths reduction, and a reduction of one-half is made where staying contact amounts to at least 175 nights per year (plus £7 for each eligible child) (see Table in para 7 to Sch 1 CSA 1991 as amended). The Child Support (Maintenance Calculations and Special Cases) Regulations 2001(SI 2001/155), reg 7 deals with what amounts to shared care, but essentially where a child is in the NRP's care and stays overnight, this will be sufficient and the average staying contact over the previous 12 months will determine the appropriate apportionment. It should be noted that where the flat rate is payable because the NRP is on benefits then where there is staying contact of at least an average of 52 nights per year, their liability is reduced to nil. However, there is no apportionment where the flat rate of £5 is payable due to other reasons eg earnings of less than £100 per week. These new provisions could well result in increased hostility between parents on contact issues and certainly leave plenty of scope for dispute.

9.96 Where the NRP has more than one qualifying child by different mothers, then his child support liability is calculated and apportioned between the parents with care in proportion to the number of his children they care for.

9.97 *Income* Only the NRP's income is relevant and child support will be payable regardless of the parent with care's level of income. Although this is designed to meet criticisms of the old formula and increase administrative efficiency, it seems inevitable that it will result in perceived injustice in some (relatively rare but perhaps high profile) cases. For example, where the parent with care is on a far higher income than the non-resident parent, he or she must nonetheless pay the relevant percentage of their net income. Advisors should consider advising a client (likely to be a non-resident parent) to make an application before 1 April 2002 where this situation applies and the new formula will adversely affect them. Conversely, those acting for parents with care with high incomes may wish to bide their time! Whilst there is a cap on the maximum income to which the formula will apply, it is set at the very high level of £2,000 per week.

9.98 The information now required from the NRP to calculate net income is set out in Schedule 1 to the Child Support (Maintenance Calculations and Special Cases) Regulations 2001 (SI 2001/155). Most contentiously, the only deductions allowed from gross income are:

- Tax;
- National Insurance Contributions; and
- Approved pension contributions.

9.99 Most controversial is the omission of the taking into account of housing costs at any stage in the calculation and thus when taking instructions, it is only necessary to discover from the NRP plus details of their income and deductions mentioned above the following information:

(a) the number of qualifying children;
(b) the number of relevant other children;
(c) whether the non-resident parent receives a prescribed benefit, pension or allowance, including income support, income-based JSA or incapacity benefit;
(d) whether the non-resident parent's partner is in receipt of a prescribed benefit; and
(e) whether the non-resident parent is a student, a child him/herself, in prison.

9.100 *Variations from the new formula* These replace the current departure system (discussed below) but narrows the grounds and will be the exception rather than the rule, given the far more general approach in the new formula. They aim to meet cases such as where the lifestyle of the NRP does not reflect the declared income, or where their income is minimal but they have substantial capital (exceeding £65,000). In addition, where contact costs or other child-related expenses are high, where there are school fee payments or mortgage payments on the former family home, but only where this has been transferred completely to the parent with care. Sections 28F 28G CSA 1991 as amended together with the Child Support (Variations) Regulations 2001 (SI 2001/156) govern the new applications which retain much of the departure direction procedures. However, it is now possible to apply for a variation when the child support application is first made and does not have to be in writing unless particularly difficult issues are raised.

(d) Other issues

(i) Child maintenance bonus and child maintenance premium

9.101 The fact that child support maintenance has traditionally been deducted pound for pound from parent with care's income support confirmed to many that it was the Treasury's interests and not those of the children which dominated this legislation. However, where the person with care is in receipt of housing benefit, council tax benefit, family credit or disability working allowance but *not* income support or income-based jobseeker's allowance, the first £20 of child maintenance, including child support maintenance, is ignored in calculating their benefit entitlement. Calls to extend this disregard to income support have finally been listened to and the new scheme introduces the child maintenance premium in April 2002, which for the first time allows children dependant on state benefits to make a direct financial gain. As a consequence the old child maintenance bonus will be abolished. This currently allows those on income support or income-based jobseeker's allowance to accrue a credit of a maximum of £5 per week maintenance, up to a maximum of £1,000 which is payable upon them leaving benefit and taking up employment for sixteen hours per week or more.

9.102 The new premium to be introduced by regulations will allow parents with care on income support or income-based JSA to keep £10 per week (in total) of any maintenance paid. In effect this increases the benefit disregard, and it is predicted will only apply to new cases assessed under the new formula. The level of the premium is low and is not proposed to apply to each child, but only to each parent with care.

(ii) Arrears

9.103 This is another area of controversy, where much ground has been gained by the absent parent lobby and in respect of which the CSPSSA 2000 is both attempting to be realistic about what can be recovered yet fight back with tougher penalties and disincentives, including the loss of a driving licence.

9.104 Under the current scheme, fixed penalties were to replace the complex provisions on interest on late payments in 1997 (s 22 CSA 1995), however this provision was never brought into force and the original interest deterrent has remained nominally in place. Interest cannot be charged on arrears which accrued after 17 April 1995 (reg 4(1) Child Support (Arrears, Interest and Adjustment of Maintenance Assessments) Regulations 1992 (CS(AIAMA) Regs 1992) as amended). However, interest at 1% above base rate still accrues on arrears outstanding at that date providing an arrears notice has been served. Interest will stop running if an agreement to pay the arrears is entered into and adhered to and is not payable in other specified situations, such as where the arrears are due to a CSA error (see regs 3, 4 and 5 CS(AIAMA) Regs 1992). The CSA may decide not to collect more than six months' initial arrears arising before the assessment has been completed where there has been significant delay by the Agency and the absent parent gives a commitment to pay the liability and the six months' arrears. Currently, the parent with care is compensated by the government for any loss arising as a consequence. Where there are start up arrears, the rule limiting the sum payable to 30% of net income is varied to increase the maximum payable in maintenance and start-up arrears to 33%.

9.105 The 2000 Act is attempting a new regime. Section 41A of the CSA 1991, as amended, provides for a penalty system to replace the interest provisions, and such penalties which will be detailed in regulations, must not exceed 25% of the weekly child support payable. However, in contrast to previous approaches, the penalties are not to be automatically invoked on non-payers. Rather the defaulter can avoid the penalty if there is a good reason for non-payment (eg sickness) or if reasonable arrangements are made to pay the arrears. Any penalty that becomes payable will be payable to the CSA and not to the parent with care.

(iii) Collection and enforcement

9.106 One of the benefits of the child support system for parents with care is that the CSA will collect and enforce child support maintenance. Once an assessment has been made, the amount may (in s 4 cases) and will (in s 6 cases) be collected and enforced by the agency. The agency is also empowered by s 30 to collect other forms of maintenance, for example spousal maintenance if convenient, but does not yet do so. Its track record in chasing arrears is not good and the 2000 Act aims to provide new disincentives to non-payment to NRPs.

9.107 After the maintenance calculation has been made, a non-resident parent will be instructed how to make the payments, eg by standing order (see s 29). Otherwise, a deduction from earnings order can be made (s 31). Where there are arrears, the agency can apply for a liability order in the magistrates' court, although the court cannot question the assessment (s 33). This can be enforced by distress (s 35) or imprisonment (s 40) where there is wilful refusal or culpable neglect. In addition arrears can be enforced by a charging order on property or garnishee order on a bank account.

9.108 The case of *Department of Social Security v Butler* [1995] 1 WLR 1528, CA has revealed a gap in the CSA's enforcement armoury. An appeal against the refusal of a Mareva injunction to prevent disposal of assets up to the amount of outstanding child support maintenance arrears was rejected as it was held the High Court had no jurisdiction to grant interim relief where it had no substantive powers to enforce the right in respect of which the protection was sought.

9.109 Magistrates have now been given enhanced sanctions by the 2000 Act amendments and these are now in force. Whereas under s 40 the CSA can apply for a defaulting NRP to be committed to prison where they have been unable to recover maintenance through other means, resulting in a maximum of six weeks' imprisonment and where there has been "wilful refusal or culpable neglect", new ss 39A and 40B now also in such cases provide for the option of imposing a driving disqualification order for a maximum of two years. The order can be suspended, can be used to prevent the obtaining of a licence where none is held but must be revoked when the outstanding maintenance is paid in full. If payment has not been made by the end of the disqualification period, a further period can be imposed. The role of the magistrates' courts with regard to child support maintenance calculations is discussed below.

(iv) Revision, supercession and appeals

9.110 The revision and appeal process relating to child support cases were amended alongside social security appeals by the Social Security Act 1998 which inserted a new s 17 and Schedule 4C into the 1991 Act. These are now to be replaced following the 2000 Act. The basic principles under the current and post-2000 scheme is that the first line of appeal against a maintenance calculation is an internal CSA review now governed by s 16. Any decision, original or revised, may be superseded by a further decision of the CSA acting on behalf of the Secretary of State (s 17). Appeals are then available to the Child Support Appeal Tribunal by the parent with care or the non-resident parent (s 20). Appeals may then be made with leave on a question of law to the Child Support Commissioner (s 24) and from there to the Court of Appeal with leave (s 25).

(e) The role of the courts

9.111 Other than judicial review of the CSA's actions and the enforcement powers given to magistrates, the courts have no role in the child support assessment process. In *Secretary of State for Social Security v Shotton* [1996] 2 FLR 241, QBD it was confirmed that the magistrates' power to quash liability or deduction from earnings orders arose only on the technical grounds that either the orders were defective on the face of the order, or that the payments were not being deducted from "earnings" (see regs 8(1) and 9-11 CS(CE) Regs 1992). It was not for the court to declare an assessment defective as there was no jurisdiction and the review procedure established by the Act would have been followed. Judicial review and not an application to the magistrates' court was the correct procedure where a father wished to argue that the CSA had failed to have regard to the welfare of the children (s 2) when making a deduction from earnings order (*R v Secretary of State for Social Security, ex p Biggin* [1995] 2 FCR 595, FD). However, in *R v Secretary of State for Social Security, ex p Lloyd* [1995] 1 FLR 856, the Divisional Court rejected an absent parent's argument that in the light of the fact that attempts to recover child support would damage the relationship with the child, the CSA should have first made enquiries under s 6(2) CSA 1991.

9.112 Where a parent with care has a pre-April 1993 order, one theoretical possibility is that this should be revoked in order that a higher child support assessment can be made. However, in *B v M (Child Support: Revocation of Order)* [1994] 1 FLR 342, the county court judge refused to revoke the order to enable the mother to apply to the CSA despite the fact the child would have received far higher maintenance. It was stated that there would have to be particular circumstances which would make revocation in the child's best interests. Revocation is still therefore a possibility. However, an application for variation indicating what a child support assessment is likely to be would seem to be the best approach where some maintenance is being paid, and one in respect of which the court has jurisdiction even where the parent with care is dependent on benefit (s 8(3A)).

9.113 Interestingly, the child support legislation did not in principle fetter parental freedom to make enforceable maintenance agreements in new cases, although the 2000 Act goes much further towards this. Currently, it is still possible for the courts to approve agreements and consent orders for maintenance (see s 8(5)), with the caveat that they cannot oust the future jurisdiction of the CSA should the parent with care become dependent on benefits. Importantly, the 1995 amendments have given the courts jurisdiction to vary orders made in this way and to prevent the parent with care making a s 4 application (see ss 4(10) and 8(3A)). However, whilst this has proved popular with advisors, the protection from CSA jurisdiction is in future to be limited to a 12-month period.

9.114 The essential issue for advisors here is to ensure that careful advice is given to clients who choose to opt for an agreement and to be aware of the limitations and requirements of the Child Support (Written Agreements) Maintenance Order 1993 (SI 1993/620) (the Written Agreements Order), particularly as amended by the 2000 Act and consequent regulations.

(i) The Written Agreements Order

9.115 Currently, this enables a written agreement, whatever its date, to be converted into a court order under s 8(5) of the 1991 Act and then prevents an application to the Agency being made until either the order is amended by the Lord Chancellor, or the parent with care becomes dependent on benefits in which case s 6 will then apply. Section 2 of the CSPSSA 2000 inserts an amended s 4(10) into the 1991 Act enabling the CSA to accept child support applications from parents who have a court maintenance order which was made after the introduction of the new child support scheme. Thus the ability of parents to reach agreements about child maintenance outside which do not reflect child support maintenance rates can only be guaranteed for a period of 12 months from the making of the order, after which either parent can invoke the CSA process, regardless of whether or not the parent with care is in receipt of income support or income-based JSA (see now amended s 4(10)(aa) CSA 1991). The aim is to only allow parents to make private agreements at child support formula rates. However, this is not to be retrospective and written agreement orders in force in April 2002 when the changes will be implemented will remain effective. This has proved to be one of the most controversial aspects of the 2000 Act with the SFLA and the Family Bar Association opposing the changes, albeit to no avail.

9.116 Currently, the order still provides a possible means of enabling the parties to regulate their own settlements, unless and until such time as the parent with care becomes dependent on benefits. Thus, the jurisdiction of the agency may even now only be temporarily excluded by such an order. Whether a "clean break" style of agreement is appropriate will depend on the circumstances of the parties and the likelihood of the parent with care becoming dependent on the state. It must be said that the ability of parents in low to middle income brackets to achieve a clean break is almost impossible to do in the shadow of the CSA, and will become increasingly difficult post-2000 Act implementation. What is imperative is clear advice to both the parties about the ramifications of using this procedure and the possible repercussions should the Agency become involved, or either party apply to vary the agreement. Any agreed clean break settlement ought normally to protect the non-resident parent by permitting a review of the capital settlement should the agency's jurisdiction be exercised, as post-April 1993 clean break settlements do not give rise to grounds for a departure direction.

(ii) Conditions for making the order

9.117 The court can only make a written agreements order where there is a written agreement (not necessarily enforceable) providing for the making of maintenance payments to the child. The court may only make an order in substantially the same terms as the agreement, regardless of whether or not the court thinks the order is appropriate to the parties' needs and means. It cannot substitute an order it considers to be more appropriate and would have to refuse to make any order at all.

9.118 In *V v V (child maintenance)* [2001] 2 FLR 799, these constraints are illustrated. Here the parties were negotiating a global settlement in divorce proceedings. The mother sought yearly maintenance of £10,000 for each child, whereas the father offered £5,000. The judge agreed that the mother's figure was correct, but could only make an order by agreement for £5,000 and adjourned the case for submissions to be prepared on whether the father should make up the shortfall by means of lump sums payable to each child. The mother tried to salvage the situation by immediately applying for an upwards variation of the agreed maintenance order, but this was dismissed as there were not yet grounds for variation, and the court could not make any order which was not agreed between the parties. Interestingly, the Court of Appeal indicated that where the court finds its jurisdiction to make an appropriate order is blocked, as here, by withdrawal of consent, it should, following *Phillips v Peace* (above), seek to reflect the balance of the provision in another form of order. Accordingly substantial lump sums totalling £50,000 were ordered for the two children.

9.119 The agreement may be made at any time, although a consent order signed by both parties would normally be accepted as "a written agreement", but to reduce the ability for a party to renege at the door of the court it is wise for this to have been preceded by some other form of written agreement. In addition, the parties do not, it seems, necessarily have to positively consent to the order being made. However, where there is no concrete prior agreement and an objection to the proposed order, as in *V v V* (above), it is confirmed that the party is not estopped from disputing the court's jurisdiction to make an order without either consent or a written agreement and the court cannot make an order. The Lord Chancellor's Department indicated that these provisions were to be of a temporary nature and the further restriction on their ability to avoid the CSA scheme is a clear message that even where there is no dependency on state benefits, the government, as a matter of policy, do not want parents to agree child maintenance below CSA levels in exchange for greater capital security.

(iii) Advantages and disadvantages of the written agreements procedure

9.120 Until April 2002, parents can still enter into enforceable agreements for child maintenance with or without using the Written Agreements Order. However, use of this provision enables enforcement through the family courts, rather than having to sue separately on a maintenance deed and permits a return to the global approach to financial provision as the order may be made together with other orders in the parties' agreed package. The advantages of using the order are obvious for the non-resident parent as the level of child maintenance can be agreed at a lower rate than that provided for in the Act, although, as noted above, the Agency's jurisdiction is only ousted until the parent with care becomes dependent on benefit and in future can be ignored in favour of a child support application after just 12 months. The advantage for the parent with care is not in the amount of maintenance payable, but in the presumably compensatory capital settlement achieved which may, for example, avoid the need for a Mesher or Martin order or charge back to be made in relation to the family home. However, there are disincentives for the parent with care. In particular, they cannot take advantage of the enforcement and collection provisions in the 1991 Act but must personally pursue court enforcement procedures. Arrears under the order can be remitted in contrast with the provisions under the Act, although provision for interest on late payments could be built in. Unless they have agreed in the order not to, they are now able to apply to the court to vary the agreement (see ss 4(10) and 8(3A)), and it is of course possible to make provision for uprating maintenance in the agreement.

9.121 Generally, this procedure should only be used where the parties have been very carefully advised and where it is unlikely that the financial position of, particularly, the parent with care will change for the worse. It is probably most appropriate in high-income and capital cases. It is not appropriate where dependency on benefits is foreseen. Clean break style agreements are perhaps less likely in the context of cohabitation. But in a situation where the parties are agreed and it is appropriate for there to be a settlement or property transfer order as well as maintenance, or where there can only be a property transfer for the benefit of the child if child support maintenance is not payable, it is worthy of consideration. Where there has been some trading of capital for periodical maintenance, agreements must be carefully worded to permit a chargeback on property if and when the Agency assessment comes into force, in order to protect the non-resident parent's position. Implicit in this is a potential disadvantage for the parent with care, although it is one which they may be prepared to subject themselves in order to achieve a capital order. Any mortgagee would need to consent to a transfer on these terms in the usual way, and could also prove an obstacle to the parties achieving their agreed objectives.

(iv) Residual jurisdiction for the court

9.122 Finally, as indicated above, the courts will continue to have jurisdiction in respect of periodical maintenance payments for children not covered by the 1991 Act. The courts therefore retain exclusive jurisdiction where there are step-children, the child is over 19, or the non-resident parent, the person with care or the child is habitually resident outside the UK. Their supplemental jurisdiction to order maintenance in addition to child support maintenance in certain circumstances has been noted above (see para 9.23).

9.123 In the context of children of former cohabitants, applications for periodical maintenance where the court has exclusive or supplemental jurisdiction must be made under paras 1(2)(a) and (b) to Sch 1 CA 1989, which also governs other forms of financial provision for children on relationship breakdown. These provisions will now be considered together with the other orders available under the Schedule.

CHECKLIST OF MAIN CHANGES TO THE CHILD SUPPORT SCHEME INTRODUCED BY THE CHILD SUPPORT PENSIONS AND SOCIAL SECURITY ACT 2000.

- Change of terminology – absent parents become "non-resident parents", assessments become "calculations".
- Periodical reviews abolished (s 24 in force as of 28 July 2000).
- Reductions will be made for average weekly overnight contact stays by children.
- There will be a cut-off point for high earners but only at £2,000 per week net.
- Flat-rate payments of 15% of net weekly income for one child, 20% for two and 25% for three or more children with reduced rates for low earners replacing protected income but keeping a flat rate minimum of £5 per week unless there are more than 52 nights contact per year.
- NRP's income deemed to reduce by same percentages where any child(ren) living in new household.
- Simplification of net income calculation – all pension contributions deducted but all housing costs are to be ignored.
- PWC's income does not feature in the CSA maintenance calculation.
- Court approved agreements will not prevent CSA application – s 8(5) no longer a bar beyond an initial 12 month period from making an agreed order.
- Presumption of paternity where unmarried father named on birth certificate.
- Removal of departure directions and all discretion, although on an application for variation, some specific matters can be taken into account.
- Back to work bonus removed but child support premium provides some benefit for children.
- Increased powers for Child Support Inspectors and introduction of a new criminal offence for failure to provide or for false information – s 14A and note ss 39A, 40B and 41A introducing new penalties for wilful non-payment including disqualification from driving.

3 Orders for financial provision under Sch 1 CA 1989

9.124 All forms of financial provision for children of unmarried parents other than child support maintenance are contained in Sch 1 CA 1989. Both the orders available and the ways in which they can be used need now to be considered in the light of the small body of case law which has emerged.

9.125 All paragraph numbers cited in this section refer to Sch 1 CA 1989. Paragraph 1(2) lists the orders available as follows:

"(a) an order requiring either or both parents of a child—
   (i) to make to the applicant for the benefit of the child; or
   (ii) to make to the child himself, such periodical payments, for such term, as may be specified in the order;

(b) an order requiring either or both parents of a child—
    (i) to secure to the applicant for the benefit of the child; or
    (ii) to secure to the child himself, such periodical payments, for such term, as may be specified in the order;
(c) an order requiring either or both parents of a child—
    (i) to pay to the applicant for the benefit of the child; or
    (ii) to pay to the child himself, such lump sum as may be so specified;
(d) an order requiring a settlement to be made for the benefit of the child, and to the satisfaction of the court, of property—
    (i) to which either parent is entitled (either in possession or reversion); and
    (ii) which is specified in the order;
(e) an order requiring either or both parents of a child—
    (i) to transfer to the applicant for the benefit of the child; or
    (ii) to transfer to the child himself, such property to which the parent is entitled (either in possession or reversion) as may be specified in the order.''

9.126 In addition, para 2 of the Schedule provides for applications to be made by a person over 18 for periodical payments or a lump sum order, providing the applicant's parents are not living together in the same household and the applicant did not have the benefit of a periodical payments order in force when he or she reached the age of 16. Surprisingly, no specific reference is made excluding those children who have the benefit of a child support assessment at the age of 16 (see s 2(6)), although it would seem unlikely that an application for periodical payments in such circumstances would prove successful. In any event, as discussed on page 221, this is appropriate only where the person is or will be undergoing education or training, or where there are other special circumstances which justify the making of an order.

9.127 Paragraph 6 permits the variation or discharge, including the temporary suspension, of an order for secured or unsecured periodical payments. Interim orders for periodical payments and giving appropriate directions may be made pursuant to para 9. Post-CSA 1991, interim orders will only be made where the Agency have no jurisdiction, or where there is substantial wealth, clearly justifying "top-up" maintenance. On variation or discharge of an order under paras 1 or 2, the court has power at that stage to order the paying parent to pay a lump sum (para 5(3)).

9.128 Subject to s 8(3) CSA 1991, orders for periodical payments can be made for any appropriate amount as decided by the court having taken into account the matters set out in para 4. These factors (see para 9.141) must be considered in relation to any application made under paras 1 and 2 and are also referred to in relation to applications for variation and discharge. In practice, periodical payments will only now be made where either the CSA does not have jurisdiction or where the court's supplemental jurisdiction may be called upon pursuant to ss 8(6)–(8) CSA 1991. Where top-up maintenance is applied for under s 8(6), the applicant will first have to show that there has been a child support calculation and currently that the maximum additional element is payable (see para 9.66). From April 2002, they will have to show that the non-resident parent's income exceeds £2,000 per week or such other figure specified in para 10(3) to Sch 2 CSA 1991 as amended. They then have to satisfy the court that it is appropriate in all the circumstances for further maintenance to be paid by the non-resident parent. The dominating factors here would be the needs of the child and the means of the parents as compared with the size of the assessment. The court would then have to decide the additional sum to be paid in accordance with the criteria set out in para 4 CA 1989 (discussed below).

9.129 Section 8(7) enables the court to award additional educational expenses, regardless of whether there is a child support assessment in existence or not, for a child of 18 or under for the sole purpose of meeting the cost of the education or training being undertaken at an "educational establishment". This obviously covers school fees but is not limited to these and would cover all other expenses directly attributable to the education or training. Nor is it restricted to "recognised educational establishments". The criteria in para 4 would then be applied to the application. Where a child is disabled (defined in s 8(9)), additional periodical maintenance may be ordered to meet some or all the expenses directly attributable to the disability. Again, a child support assessment is not a pre-requisite, and the para 4 criteria would be applied where periodical maintenance for this purpose was made or secured under para 1(2)(a) or (b). As noted in *C v F (disabled child: maintenance orders)* (above) such an order can, unlike a child support maintenance calculation, extend beyond the child's 19th birthday.

9.130 Lump sum orders under paras 1 and 2 made in the magistrates' court are no longer subject to a ceiling of £1,000 but are now unlimited as they are in the county and High Courts. They may also be made in consideration of liabilities or expenses reasonably incurred before the making of the order in connection with the birth or in maintaining the child (para 5(1)). Thus if a court feels a lump sum should be made in respect of a child's future needs under para 1(2)(c), and in addition accepts that expenses have been incurred in maintaining the child prior to the application, this sum may be added to the former. This situation is most likely to arise where the parties have not been cohabiting and thus such earlier expenses have not been shared or met by the paying parent. In *Phillips v Peace* (above), a lump sum of some £24,500 was ordered to be paid by the father in respect of such expenses and to furnish a home for the child. More recently in *V v V (child maintenance)* (above), the Court of Appeal ordered lump sums of £21,000 and £29,000 for two children whose father would not agree to the level of periodic maintenance the court felt appropriate by means of a written agreement order. In *J v C (Child: Financial Provision)* [1999] 1 FLR 152, the child's parents separated when the mother was pregnant. Some two year's later the father won over a million pounds on the national lottery. The mother's application for a substantial lump sum to enable the child to be brought up in a manner which reflected the father's new-found wealth, including living in a four-bedroomed house and a car in which the child could be driven around, was granted by Hale J.

9.131 The court can also order the lump sum to be paid by instalments, and has power to vary such an order, to change the number of instalments or the amount payable in respect of any instalment and also the date on which any instalment is payable. The total amount of the lump sum cannot be varied (see sub-paras 5(5) and (6)). There is no limit on the number of applications for a lump sum that can be made and thus where circumstances change a further application is now possible in appropriate circumstances. Interestingly, in *Phillips v Peace* (above) the court felt unable to order a father with substantial capital assets to pay a lump sum by annual instalments in the sum the court would have assessed payable in periodical maintenance, to avoid the effects of the nil assessment by the CSA. It was considered inappropriate to exercise its jurisdiction in a way which deliberately avoided s 8(3) CSA 1991. However, the deliberate obstruction of the court's jurisdiction to make a consent order under the written agreements procedure in an appropriate sum entitled the court to make other substantial orders in *V v V (Child Maintenance)*.

9.132 The 1987 Act introduced for the first time, and Sch 1 preserves, the possibility of orders requiring the settlement or transfer of property for the benefit of a child of unmarried parents, as well as secured periodical payments. As indicated above, secured like unsecured periodical payments are, of course, now only available in situations permitted by the CSA 1991. Unsecured periodical maintenance payments and lump sum orders were available even in affiliation proceedings, albeit in more limited circumstances. Unlike lump sum payments only one application can be made for orders for settlements or transfers of property for the benefit of a child under sub-paras (d) and (e).

9.133 Settlement of property may require specialist advice, including advice on the tax implications, which is outside the scope of this book, although the possibility of settlement of the family home will be considered. Broadly, the same considerations apply as for children of married parents in divorce proceedings, subject to some significant differences apparent in the drafting of Sch 1 discussed below. Settlements will generally be appropriate where there are substantial assets available for the benefit of the child.

9.134 However, where property which was the family home is owned solely by one parent who is not to be the resident parent following breakdown, settlement of the property for the benefit of a child until the age of 18 or some other appropriate event, rather than transfer of the property to the resident parent for the benefit of the child which could lead to persons other than the child and the resident parent benefiting, is likely to be more appropriate. Settlements, on unmarried relationship breakdown where there is no duty to make provision for the resident parent, may be more frequently used in relation to families of less substantial means to establish an equivalent of the Mesher and Martin orders developed in the matrimonial jurisdiction. This may also be appropriate where both parents have contributed to the purchase of the home and both have legal and/or equitable interests in the property, but it is not possible to achieve a clean break, something which has, and will continue to, become increasingly difficult since the child support legislation increased the levels of periodic child maintenance payments.

9.135 Such case law as there is certainly favours settlements rather than outright transfers of property for the benefit of the child. In *A v A (financial provision)* [1994] 1 FLR 657, FD the father was enormously wealthy and a property had been bought as a home for the mother and child in the name of an off-shore company. However, the mother's application for outright transfer to her of the property for the benefit of the child was rejected and a settlement of the home for the benefit of the child on trust to terminate six months after she reached 18 or finished her full-time tertiary education was ordered instead. In *T v S (financial provision for children)* [1994] 2 FLR 883, FD a sum was ordered to be used to buy a small property to provide a home for the five children of former cohabitants and at first instance this was to be held on trust until the youngest child reached 21 and thereafter to be divided equally between the children. On appeal, the court varied the terms of the trust to secure the reversion for the father, as it was not appropriate either for the children to benefit as adults, or for the mother to be the recipient of an indirect windfall. Thus, the traditional reluctance of the courts in the matrimonial context to transfer capital assets directly to the child (see eg *Chamberlain v Chamberlain* [1974] 1 All ER 33, CA; *Kiely v Kiely* [1988] 1 FLR 248, CA) has been endorsed in the unmarried context, despite hopes that a different approach could be adopted, given the inability to adjust assets between the unmarried parents.

9.136 Some softening of this approach may be seen in the cases of *Phillips v Peace* and *V v V (child maintenance)* discussed above, where avoidance of child support obligations were legitimately compensated for by lump sum orders. In *T v S* (above) it was argued that the court's powers under Sch 1 CA 1989 should be construed widely, not narrowly, in the context of the new code. However, in both this case and in *A v A* (above) the court felt it could not ignore the "striking similarity" of the provisions with the MCA 1973 and felt constrained to make financial provision for children only "as dependants" unless there were special circumstances such as disability which justified a different approach. Thus, ironically, the reading of the Act in line with the matrimonial authorities which clearly indicate that, in most situations, financial provision for children should take the form of periodical payments during a child's dependency rather than a capital investment in his/her future, combined with the impact of the child support legislation have restricted the potential of transfer of property orders. The decisions make it clear that settlements of property which revert to the non-resident parent once the child reaches financial independence are the proper form of provision even in cases involving substantial assets. Thus in *J v C (child: financial provision)* (above), a case which usefully reviews all the authorities, it was ordered that £70,000 of the father's lottery winnings should be settled on trust to provide a house for the child, her mother and her two half-sisters to live in until the child reached 21 or six months after the end of her full-time education, whichever was the later. The property was to revert thereafter to the father, but subject to an option for the mother to buy at the open market price. Such a settlement offered some protection to the mother by allowing the trust to endure until the child reached 21, rather than just 18 and also provided an option to buy at the end of this period, although if she were unable to find the open market price at that stage, she would have to return to a humbler abode.

9.137 Transfers of property orders are possible, but at first sight unlikely on relationship breakdown of unmarried parents where it is the family home which is in dispute. However, the court has power to order the transfer of *any* property to which the parents are entitled, to either the applicant, who will usually be the other parent, for the benefit of the child; or to the child him/herself. "Property" includes both real and personal property and the court can order, for example, the transfer of stocks and shares. The transfer of property provision may therefore conceivably be used where there is an unresolved dispute relating to personal property vested jointly in the parents (such as shares or even a building society or bank account) which the court can order should be transferred to the resident parent for the benefit of the child.

9.138 Another potential use of Sch 1 transfer of property orders is in applications for a transfer of a rented tenancy. In *K v K (minors: property transfer)* [1992] 2 FLR 220, the Court of Appeal held that a transfer of property order for the benefit of a child pursuant to para 1(2)(e) was not limited to cases where a financial benefit was to be conferred on the child. Accordingly, a secure tenancy could be transferred in this way, although the court remitted the matter back to the county court for consideration of the implications of the father's lost potential "right to buy" discount. However, this remedy has been rather overtaken by the arguably superior transfer of tenancy order available to cohabitants on relationship breakdown introduced by s 53 and Sch 7 Family Law Act 1996, although itself subject to practical difficulties in some circumstances as discussed in Chapter 10.

9.139 A further point to note concerning Sch 1 CA 1989 applications was made in *J v J (a minor) (property transfer)* [1993] 2 FLR 56. Here it was confirmed that, as seemed apparent from the wording of the schedule, applications for transfer of property orders could not be made for the benefit of a child that was not the natural child of the parties, as orders could only be made in respect of a "parent".

9.140 As discussed below, the criteria to be applied by the courts when making these orders is, arguably, less generous to the child than those applied in orders made under the MCA 1973, although the case law has not sought to exploit this. The reader is first referred to the decision of *H v M* [1991] Fam Law 473, in which Waite J gives some guidance as to the appropriate procedure to be followed in resolving multi-faceted financial provision disputes concerning the unmarried family. As this case, which lasted some nineteen days, indicates, there is a clear need for a cohesive family jurisdiction to deal with family property disputes in the unmarried context. The provisions of Sch 1 CA 1989 which aimed to eradicate discrimination against the non-marital child (Law Com 118, para 6.2 and 6.3) by incorporating the possibility of capital orders into its scheme, provided this for those with children. Unfortunately, the effects of both the CSA 1991 and 1995 and also Sch 7 FLA 1996 combined with the unwillingness of the courts to distinguish capital orders for children in the unmarried context from the matrimonial line of authorities have been to once again fragment the available remedies and leave former cohabitants with a variety of possibilities, subject to differing procedures, rather than a global approach. This is very regrettable and makes the task of those advising in this field all the more difficult. It is to be hoped that the proposals for reform of cohabitation law put forward by the Law Society and SFLA (see Chapter 1) will ultimately lead to a new approach to the increasing number of disputes between cohabitants that the courts are statistically bound to be faced with in the future.

4 Criteria for making the orders

9.141 Paragraph 4(1) of Sch 1 directs the court on considerations to be taken into account in making, varying or discharging orders for financial provision for a child, prefaced by the indication that the court shall have regard to all the circumstances of the case. These considerations can be summarised as follows:

(a) the income, earning capacity, property and other financial resources which each parent has or is likely to have in the foreseeable future;
(b) the financial needs, obligations and responsibilities which each parent has or is likely to have in the foreseeable future;
(c) the financial needs of the child;
(d) the income, earning capacity (if any), property and other financial resources of the child;
(e) any physical or mental disability of the child;
(f) the manner in which the child was being, or was expected to be, educated or trained.

9.142 Where it is envisaged that an order is to be made against a non-parent (which means a step-parent in this context (see para 16(2)), then additional considerations apply (see para 4(2)). However, this is unlikely to affect the unmarried family directly, as marriage is the mechanism by which an adult becomes a stepparent.

9.143 The criteria can be seen to owe a great deal to s 25 MCA 1973, although important distinctions remain. Firstly, para 4 does not require the welfare of the child to be the "first consideration" as is specifically stated in s 25 MCA 1973. Although the court must take the child's welfare into account as a part of "all the circumstances of the case", this is not the first consideration, simply one of the factors to be taken into account. The general welfare principle does not apply to applications for financial provision as they do not concern the upbringing of the child (s 105(1) and see also *B v B (transfer of tenancy)* [1994] Fam Law 250).

9.144 Thus it is open to the court to give greater priority to, say, a father's difficult financial position than to the benefit to the child of remaining in a home which happens to be a property owned solely by the father. There is clearly scope for orders to be less generous than those made on divorce, partly of course because the court will not usually be dealing with a maintenance application for the resident parent, as there is no provision for the maintenance of cohabitants by each other. However, in *A v A* (above), Ward J stated at page 659H:

> "A purposive interpretation of the Act leads to the conclusion that the claims of children whose parents are unmarried should be dealt with in similar manner to the claims of children where the parents are or were married. I remain of that view, notwithstanding the fact that there are some differences between the Matrimonial Causes Act 1973 and Schedule 1 Children Act 1989."

9.145 This factor could in some circumstances benefit a child, as it will leave the departing parent with more disposable income than if he or she also had a duty to maintain the former partner. Given that another omission from the criteria is the standard of living of the family unit or of the child before the order, this approach is more helpful than unhelpful. Obviously, the family may never have lived as a unit, but where they have, this would seem to be a highly relevant factor which should be drawn to the court's attention as an important circumstance of the case. In any event, the financial position of the wealthy non-resident parent is likely to be very influential in terms of the award made. In *H v P (illegitimate child: capital provision)* [1993] Fam Law 515 (Wandsworth County Court), it was stated that the child was entitled to be brought up in circumstances which had some sort of relationship with the father's resources. In *A v A* (above), where the father was immensely wealthy, the court felt that the fact that the father had been paying large sums in maintenance "set some standard". Again in *J v C (child: financial provision)* (above) Hale J concluded that the child's standard of living should reflect that of her millionaire father.

9.146 Another distinction is that any future earning capacity the court feels either parent could reasonably be expected to take steps to acquire is not expressed to be a factor, in contrast with the MCA provisions. However, the financial needs and resources that either party is likely to have in the foreseeable future are express and fundamental criteria. It is significant that the resident parent's financial needs, as well as those of the child, form part of the express criteria. Obviously, care of the child will affect a resident parent's earning capacity, which raises the question of whether financial provision made under the Schedule could contain an element for the resident parent.

9.147 It was suggested in the first edition of this book that the *Haroutunian v Jennings* (1977) 1 FLR 62, FD approach, that maintenance for a child should include a proper sum towards the services rendered by the mother to that child should prevail. This has now been endorsed in *A v A* (above) with regard to periodical maintenance payments ordered under Sch 1. In this case, £20,000 per year maintenance, in addition to school fees and extras was ordered on this basis. Nonetheless, a settlement of the family home upon trust during the child's dependency with a right for the mother to occupy the home rent free to the exclusion of the father was preferred to the outright transfer of the home to the mother for the benefit of the child. The lack of occupation rent can be seen as some form of recognition of services rendered by the mother. Surprisingly, however, the court felt it immaterial that some of the periodical maintenance may in fact be used by the mother for the benefit of the child's half-sisters. Whilst it was thought that this approach may be restricted to the unusual facts of this case where the father led a precarious life and his residence outside the jurisdiction would prevent a claim under the I(PFD) Act 1975 in the event of his death, this attitude was echoed in the more recent case of *J v C* (above), although perhaps the fortuitous way in which the previously penniless father had won his fortune may have influenced the outcome. However, Hale J's judgment may mark a turning point in the way in which the courts deal with capital applications under Sch 1 CA 1989 and apply the relevant criteria. It was made it clear that the circumstances surrounding the child's birth and the poor quality of the parents' relationship (where the parties had never cohabited and the father had denied paternity which was subsequently confirmed) were not matters of great weight in this context. The child's welfare, whilst not paramount or the first consideration under Sch 1, must be one of the relevant circumstances to be taken into account when assessing whether and how to order financial provision. Where the father, as here, had sufficient resources for all of his children, the provision for this child should not be reduced because the mothers of his other children had not sought to make any claim on their behalf. Importantly, the concept of reasonable requirements was said to be as appropriate to considering the financial needs of a child as it would be in the case of a spouse. Such requirements clearly included the need for a carer and in turn the carer's needs (which here included the need to accommodate her other children) must be taken into account. Another important point made was that the fact that the father acquired his assets after relationship breakdown, was irrelevant and the child was entitled to be brought up in circumstances bearing some sort of relationship with the father's current resources. So lottery winners, beware!

9.148 Nonetheless, the lack of willingness by the courts to capitalise the contribution towards services rendered by the mother, combined now with the CSA 1991 and 1995, means that it will only be in cases where the absent parent is very wealthy, as in *A v A* (above) and *J v C* (above), that an element included in maintenance to recognise the carer's financial needs and services rendered will be visible. The child support formula itself does currently contain an element reflecting the carer's costs and thus thinking is consistent in this respect at least, although this will be lost following the 2000 Act implementation when the simpler percentage of net income is substituted. The lack of any statutory direction to achieve a "clean break" style settlement and the inability of the courts to make any express adjustment between the adult parties under the same legislation, in contrast to the position in the matrimonial context, makes it highly unlikely that the approach taken by the courts in Sch 1 cases to date will change in the absence of new legislation. In fact, post-*White v White* [2000] 2 FLR 981, the gulf between the settlements of the married as opposed to the cohabiting on relationship breakdown is set to widen.

9.149 However, although falling short of favouring outright transfers of the family home, as we have seen, there are now dicta to support a similar approach being taken as would be taken on divorce. This must be particularly the case where the parties have cohabited for a lengthy period of time and (in most cases) the mother's financial needs have been and will be affected by childcare, whether or not she is working. It seems clear from the developing case law that the courts are extremely reluctant to allow the resident parent to gain any capital windfall through the capital orders under the Sch (see *T v S* (above)), and rent free occupation of a home settled upon the child until s/he is no longer dependent plus regular child support payments may be the best a former cohabitant resident parent can hope for. As expected, the case law to date reinforces the view that adults seeking maximum protection on relationship breakdown should either marry, or at least enter into binding legal agreements relating to the ownership of their property where possible. It remains to be seen whether the Law Commission, when it reports in 2002, will recommend a more liberal approach to the redistribution of property on relationship breakdown in the cohabitation situation. For the moment cohabitants in England and Wales are not even able to claim for economic disadvantage they have suffered in their own right consequent upon the relationship as has been proposed should be the case in Scotland (Scottish Executive, 2000), and thus Sch 1 CA 1989 provides the only possibility of any redistribution of wealth following the breakdown of the relationship of opposite-sex cohabitants who have had children of the relationship.

5 Applicants and venue

9.150 Either parent or a guardian of a child, or any person in whose favour a residence order has been granted may apply for the financial provision set out in Sch 1, para 1 of the CA 1989. This is now subject, of course, to the child support legislation in the case of periodical payments, as discussed above. An application can be made to any of the three courts (magistrates', county or High Court) for order(s) requiring either or both parents to make periodical maintenance payments (para 1(2)(a)) or a lump sum (para 1(2)(b)) to the applicant for the benefit of the child or directly to the child. An application for any order under the schedule can be made by either parent, irrespective of whether the parents are living together at the time of the application, but periodical payments cease if the parents live together for more than six months. Applications can be made to the county court or High Court only where secured periodical payments under para 1(2)(c), settlement of property on, or transfer of property to or for the benefit of, the child is sought under paras 1(2)(c) and (d) respectively against either or both parents (Sch 1, para 1(1)).

9.151 In addition, when making, varying or discharging a residence order, the court may exercise any of its powers under Sch 1, even though no application has been made for financial provision for the child (Sch 1, para 1(6)) and thus the court can decide to look at the financial needs of the child at this stage of its own motion. The impact of this provision has been lessened by the child support legislation, although it is still possible for the court to order a lump sum. However, if the court is minded to do this it must ensure that it indicates its intention to the parties and has adequate findings of fact upon which to properly consider the criteria in para 4 to the Schedule (see *Re C* [1994] 2 FCR 1122, FD).

9.152 As was noted above, para 2 permits a person over 18 whose parents are not living together in the same household to apply for periodical payments and a lump sum order in special circumstances. The time limits and criteria for making such an application are discussed below.

9.153 Generally speaking, the greater the resources of the intended paying party, the more important it is to apply to the High Court or the county court rather than to the magistrates' court, which has limited powers, although the courts are able to transfer cases to other courts where appropriate. Where it is known at the outset that a small lump sum only can be obtained, then the magistrates' or county court will be most appropriate. Consideration should also be given to whether any other relief, such as an occupation order under the Part IV Family Law Act 1996, is to be sought which might make the county court the most appropriate forum. For, where there is a dispute as to the cohabitants' respective beneficial interests, the magistrates' court has no jurisdiction to make an occupation order.

9.154 Where either or both parents own a property and where there are contemplated concurrent proceedings relating to a dispute between the parents under s 14 of the Trusts of Land and Appointment of Trustees Act 1996 (TLATA 1996), which has replaced s 30 Law of Property Act 1925 (LPA 1925), it may be advantageous for both sets of proceedings to be consolidated. This might also be appropriate where there is an application under s 53 and Sch 7 FLA 1996 for a transfer of tenancy order. Consolidation enables the issues relating to the respective interests in the property and the financial provision appropriate for the child to be looked at in the round. This is the nearest unmarried parents can come to having their own financial situation and those of their children dealt with in the same manner as divorcing parents.

6 Time for applying and duration of orders

9.155 The court may exercise its powers to make any of the orders under the schedule at any time whilst the child is under the age of 18, although normally an order for periodical payments, whether or not secured, will not be made to extend beyond the child's seventeenth birthday. An extension beyond this is possible if it appears to the court that the child will continue beyond that time in full-time education or training (whether or not in gainful employment), or there are other special circumstances, such as a physical or mental handicap. Generally, though, there are no specific time limits in which an application for financial provision for the benefit of the child must be made, providing it is made before the child becomes of age. It should also be noted here that it is possible to apply for financial provision under the CA 1989 Sch 1 even though an old style affiliation order has been refused through lack of corroboration, if proof of paternity can be established through new techniques such as DNA testing (see *H v O* [1992] Fam Law 105, FD).

9.156 In para 2 there is provision for separate applications for periodical payments and/or lump sum orders by persons over 18 who remain in full-time education or training for a trade, profession or vocation, or where there are other special circumstances. However, this applies only where a periodical payments order (although not it seems a child support assessment), had not been in force immediately before the child reached the age of 16. This provision seems to apply where parents separate after the child is 18 or where for some reason there has not been a previous order. If it is known that a child is likely to require the order to continue, the child's parent can apply at any time before the child's eighteenth birthday for the order to be extended until his or her education or training is completed. On the other hand, where there was an order in force when the child reached 16 and which subsequently ceased, if the child later decides to return to full-time education or training after the age of 18, it is not possible for the 18-year-old then to apply under para 2 for further periodical maintenance. However, if such a decision is taken, or other special circumstances arise after the order has ceased but before the child's eighteenth birthday, an application may be made by the child to revive the order pursuant to para 6(5).

9.157 The court has power to make interim orders for periodical payments (para 9) in relation to any application under either para 1 or 2, and this order can be backdated to the date of the application. It can be an order on such terms and for such period as the court thinks fit. It will of course cease on the final disposition of the application.

9.158 Only one order can be made in relation to settlement or transfer of property to or for the benefit of the child. However, the number of applications for periodical payments, secured periodical payments and lump sum orders is not limited. All orders for periodical payments may be varied or discharged upon the application of the payer or the recipient (para 1(4)) and there is also provision for temporary suspension (para 6(2)). Once the child has reached 16, the child, as well as the parents, can apply for variation (para 6(4)).

9.159 An application for financial provision under the Schedule can be made by either parent irrespective of whether the parents are living together at the time of the application. However, an order for periodical maintenance payments, whether secured or unsecured, made in favour of a parent for the benefit of a child, ceases to have effect if the child's parents live together for a period longer than six months (para 3(4)).

9.160 In contrast, an order payable directly to a child does not cease to be payable in this situation and so, it is possible for an order to be made and to continue, despite the fact that the child's parents are cohabiting. All periodical maintenance payments are now treated as tax free in the hands of the recipient, but there is no tax relief for an unmarried parent making maintenance payments. It is not possible for Children's Tax Credit to be claimed by more than one parent in relation to a child where the care of the child is shared as discussed in Chapter 4.

9.161 Unsecured periodical payments made pursuant to para 1(2)(a) or 2(2)(a) cease automatically on the death of the paying party, notwithstanding anything in the order. Herein lies one of the advantages of secured periodical payments, but a child (and now also a cohabitant of two years' standing) would of course have the right to apply for provision pursuant to the Inheritance (Provision for Family and Dependants) Act 1975 as discussed in Chapter 5. Although secured periodical payments do not cease on death, it is open to the personal representatives of the deceased paying party to apply for variation or discharge, having regard to the same criteria as apply on making the order and the change in circumstances resulting from the death of the parent. Such an application must be made within six months of the taking out of a grant of probate or letters of administration, although leave may be given for a late application (para 7).

7 Alteration of maintenance agreements

9.162 Where parents have made a maintenance agreement in writing, whether before or after the commencement of the paragraph, which makes financial provision for a child, Sch 1, para 10 provides that the court has power to vary the agreement if it is satisfied either that it should be varied in the light of changed circumstances, or that the agreement does not contain proper financial arrangements for the child. As discussed above, the CSA 1991 and 1995 may render a maintenance agreement ineffective, particularly where the resident parent is in receipt of welfare benefits. It is also possible to have a written agreement approved by the court (see above para 9.115 ff), although this is likely to become of more limited value after the CSPSSA 2000 is fully implemented.

8 Enforcement of orders and preserving assets

9.163 Broadly, orders are enforceable in the same way as the equivalent financial orders made in matrimonial proceedings or in the magistrates' courts in the past, and are well documented in standard texts on family law.

9.164 However, one important distinction is the absence of any provision equivalent to s 37 MCA 1973, enabling one party to restrain the other party from disposing of their assets in order to defeat the financial provision claim or to set aside dispositions made with this intent. Where this situation arises, there is the procedural problem of ascertaining which judges of which court have jurisdiction to make interlocutory orders of this nature. It would seem that a High Court judge could be asked to exercise the inherent jurisdiction of the court to make an interlocutory order of this nature. Furthermore, in *Re W (injunction: jurisdiction)* noted at [1995] Fam Law 713, His Honour Judge Pugsley hearing an appeal from a district judge, held that there was jurisdiction under Sch 1 CA 1989 to issue an interlocutory injunction preventing a father dealing with money he had recently inherited. Whilst agreeing with the district judge that the case of *Shipman v Shipman* [1991] 1 FLR 250, where the inherent jurisdiction of the court had been invoked to grant an injunction to preserve assets in a matrimonial case, despite the husband having rebutted the presumption of intention under s 37(5) MCA 1973, was not authority for the proposition that the court had this jurisdiction, he found that reg 3(1) County Courts Remedies Regulations 1991, when read subject to reg 3(3), did provide authority. This was upon the basis that such an injunction could be made within family proceedings within the meaning of Matrimonial and Family Proceedings Act 1984, which, in the High Court is assigned exclusively to the Family Division, and CA 1989 proceedings were so assigned. His conclusion that this was the position was reinforced by his reading of *Rayden* at paras 2.10 and 28.9. For a comprehensive but pre-*Re W* discussion of these issues see Amos "Financial Injunctive Relief under the 1989 Act" [1994] Fam Law 445.

9.165 Finally, it should be noted here that there is no equivalent to s 24A MCA 1973 by means of which the court can order the sale of property in order to satisfy orders for secured periodical payments, lump sum orders, settlements or transfer of property orders made under Sch 1.

9 Procedure

9.166 Applications for financial provision for a child under Sch 1 CA 1989 are now governed by the procedure applicable to all Children Act proceedings. Part IV

Family Proceedings Rules 1991 (SI 1991/1247) (FPR) as amended contains the details of the procedure to be followed in the county court and High Court, and Part II of the Family Proceedings Courts (Children Act 1989) Rules 1991 (SI 1991/1395 (FPCR) as amended sets out the magistrates' court procedure, which is broadly the same. However, applications for transfer of property orders and settlement of property for the benefit of a child can be made to the county court or High Court only. Forms C1 and C10 need to be completed by the applicant; they require information relating to the applicant, the child, the child's parents, any other relevant proceedings or written agreements and the child's financial needs and resources. A statement of means form (C 10A) must also be completed by the applicant and served with the application form on the respondent. The respondent must file an acknowledgement of service on Form C 7, together with a statement of means form, within fourteen days. The first hearing will be a directions hearing, when matters such as discovery and the attendance of the parties at the hearing will be dealt with in accordance with the court rules. It should be noted that the new procedure for ancillary relief in divorce cases does not extend to claims brought under Sch 1 CA 1989.

10 Public funding and the statutory charge

9.167 Legal advice under the Legal Help/Help at Court level of funding by the LSC is available to those whose income and capital come within its prescribed financial limits.

9.168 Generally, a certificate of public funding (most commonly, legal representation), with its wider eligibility criteria, should be granted to those who are financially eligible to bring any of the applications under CA 1989 where merit can be shown. It would be rare for public funding to be refused on grounds of merit, certainly where residence and contact are in dispute, given the significance of the orders for those concerned, save that before a certificate can be applied for, consideration must be given to whether the case is suitable for mediation if a recognised mediator has initially investigated whether the other party is willing to attend a mediation meeting. How mediation on such issues will affect the same type of disputes in the unmarried as opposed to the married context remains to be seen. The child may now apply for public funding in his or her own right, and this may mean that such funding is more accessible to resolve disputes relating to financial provision within the unmarried family, as the means of residential parents will not be taken into account where the child is the sole applicant and thus, unquestionably, the assisted person. However, given the reluctance of the courts to pay substantial lump sums directly to the child, other than where payment of child support has been avoided, there may only be a theoretical advantage in proceeding in this way.

9.169 The caveat in this respect is of course the statutory charge which will apply to any property "recovered or preserved", to the extent of the legal costs incurred under the certificate, and the legal help. Any person applying for public funding must now be advised in writing by his or her solicitor of the effects of the statutory charge. The charge does not apply to periodical maintenance payments but it does apply to lump sum payments, although there is an exemption for the first £2,500 (reg 44 of the Community Legal Service (Financial) Regulations 2000 and which is set to increase to £3,000 in December 2001. Thus an applicant will always receive the first £2,500 of a lump sum order but the charge will apply to any amount over and above this. There is power to postpone enforcement of the charge in relation to a home or money recovered for purchase of a home, pursuant to reg 52CLS (Financial) Regulations 2000 regardless of whether the order is made under Sch 1 CA 1989 or s 14 TLATA 1996, providing the court order stipulates that the intention of the order is to provide a home. A suggested wording is found at para 5.29 (above). The effect of the charge should be borne in mind in negotiations, as must the duty to the Community Legal Servic fund. In particular, the decision in *Parkes v Legal Aid Board* [1996] 4 All ER 271, CA makes it clear that the charge applies to property where the sale is successfully deferred, even though the respective interests in the property are not in dispute. The right to exclusive possession (with a child) over a long period of years constituted property which had been preserved within the meaning of the then s 16(6) Legal Aid Act 1988 and thus the statutory charge applied. This is still good law.

9.170 Indeed, the advantage of property being settled on the child is that it may avoid the statutory charge. Although the child, who is the assisted party, has preserved the right of occupation, there is no beneficial interest in the child's favour to which the charge can attach and so the home escapes the charge. Nonetheless, this would not succeed in avoiding the charge if the parents are also disputing their respective beneficial interests in proceedings under s 14 TLATA 1996 where one or other of them is legally aided. Here the charge will attach to the preserved publicly funded partner's share to the extent of their legal costs but where this is used as a home, it may now be postponed as indicated above.

9.171 The orders that can be made in relation to the family home on relationship breakdown, pursuant to paras 1(2)(d) and (e) Sch 1, will be considered in Chapters 10 and 11.

Chapter 10

The family home on relationship breakdown: rented property

1 Introduction

10.01 On relationship breakdown jointly owned or shared property commonly becomes a focus for dispute, and it is at this time that many cohabitants belatedly regret not having made advance provision for such an eventuality. The family home, whether rented or purchased, is often both the couple's most valuable asset and the place where one or both of them wish to continue to live. Other jointly acquired property may also become an issue when parties are separating.

10.02 This chapter will attempt to identify and clarify the legal issues to be addressed in relation to rented homes; Chapter 11 concentrates on owner-occupied property. In Chapter 3, the various types of tenure of a family home were discussed. On breakdown, the first issue is to identify the tenure and consequent legal rights. Any advice to cohabitants on their housing position following breakdown is governed by the legal implications of their arrangements during cohabitation. Although the new transfer of tenancy provisions in the FLA 1996 have enhanced the remedies available on cohabitation breakdown, some difficulties have emerged. The distinctions between sole and joint tenancies, the history of the tenancy, the options exercised by cohabitants who have jointly purchased a property, the homelessness legislation and proposed reforms discussed in Chapters 3 and 7, are also still all relevant.

10.03 It is always wise to consider the possibility of mediation before litigation and this has become a requirement where a client is publicly funded. There are now many agencies offering professional mediation in relation to property disputes on relationship breakdown. Particularly in relation to property disputes, the cost of legal proceedings and, where appropriate, the effect of the Legal Services Commission's statutory charge, must be at the forefront of a practitioner's mind and makes the possibility of compromise an important avenue to explore, particularly since the decision in *Parkes v Legal Aid Board* [1996] 4 All ER 271, CA, as discussed in Chapter 11. It can indeed be one which a client may literally not be able to afford to ignore, although the statutory charge will not apply to rented accommodation which is recovered or preserved (see *Curling v Law Society* [1985] 1 All ER 705).

10.04 Until the implementation of Part IV Family Law Act 1996 in October 1997, the court did not always have power to intervene to resolve disputes between cohabitants relating to their rented family home. This was because Sch 1 Matrimonial Homes Act 1983 (MHA 1983) only applied to married couples and transfer of property orders under Sch 1 CA 1989 were only available where there were children of the relationship. In addition, the ability of even this remedy successfully to resolve the dispute depends upon the nature and terms of the tenancy. As indicated in the first edition of this book, this often meant that a separating cohabiting couple had either to reach an agreement or face total stalemate. The reforms foreshadowed in the Law Commission Report *Domestic Violence and Occupation of the Family* Home (1992, Law Com 207) and now contained in Sch 7 FLA 1996 provide a discretionary family law remedy on relationship breakdown for all heterosexual cohabitants whose family home was rented in the name of one or both of them, although some serious practical difficulties have emerged. Unlike the remedy contained in Sch 1 CA 1989, it is available in respect of all types of tenancy and regardless of whether or not there are children of the relationship, providing opposite-sex cohabitants without children a remedy in respect of rented accommodation for the first time. However, it is not a remedy available to same-sex cohabitants. As will be explored further below, there are specified matters to which the court in exercising its discretion must have regard (para 5 of Sch 7). The court also has power to award compensation to the transferring partner (para 10). A cohabitant may often now have the choice of whether to apply for a Sch 1 CA 1989 transfer of property order for the benefit of the child(ren) of the relationship or to apply for a transfer of tenancy order pursuant to Sch 7 FLA 1996. The appropriateness and relative advantages and disadvantages of these alternative procedures will be considered further below.

10.05 The provision of a family law remedy for cohabitants who lived together as husband and wife with regard to the rented family home arguably places them in a position of advantage as compared with both same-sex cohabitants living in rented accommodation and those cohabitants whose family home has been purchased by one or both of them. This last group, whilst not left in a position of stalemate, are not distinguished from other co-owners in dispute and, as discussed in the next chapter, family law considerations do not specifically apply to determining their shares of the family home. This matter is, however, currently still under review by the Law Commission.

10.06 The position of same-sex cohabitants in rented accommodation on relationship breakdown is unaffected by Sch 7 FLA 1996 and, consequently, their position with regard to achieving a final resolution as to the disposition of the rented home on relationship breakdown is governed by their ability to reach agreement subject to the vagaries of landlord and tenant law. Thus, although it may be possible for an occupation order to be obtained excluding a gay cohabiting partner from a rented family home as discussed in Chapter 8, a transfer of tenancy order is not an option, leaving joint tenant gay cohabitants in the unenviable and unjustifiable position of agreement or stalemate as will be outlined below.

2 Transfer of tenancy orders—Sch 7 FLA 1996

10.07 Although the focus of this text is on cohabitants, it should be noted here that this Schedule has affected the court's powers to transfer tenancies in the married as well as the unmarried context. It has repealed the MHA 1983 and introduced statutory criteria in accordance with which the court's discretion must be exercised, as well as a new power to order compensation. The power to transfer the tenancy in the married context arises wherever the court has power to make a property adjustment order under the Matrimonial Causes Act 1973 (ss 23A and 24). The criteria applied in the married context differ to some extent from those applicable to cohabitants on relationship breakdown; with the reassertion of the supremacy of the married state, not being a recommendation of the Law Commission, but one forced upon Parliament as a result of the Family Homes and Domestic Violence Bill débacle discussed in Chapter 7.

(a) Tenancies affected

10.08 On relationship breakdown, "relevant tenancies" may be transferred under Sch 7 and these are comprehensively defined in para 1 as including:

(a)   protected and statutory tenancies within the meaning of the Rent Act 1977;
(b)   statutory tenancies within the meaning of the Rent (Agriculture) Act 1976;
(c)   secure tenancies within the meaning of s 79 Housing Act 1985;
(d)   assured tenancies and assured agricultural occupancies within the meaning of Pt I Housing Act 1988. (This would also include assured shorthold tenancies as these are a form of assured tenancy (s 20(1) HA 1988) and statutory periodic tenancies arising after the expiry of a fixed-term assured or assured shorthold, which are deemed to be assured tenancies.); and
(e)   introductory tenancies within the meaning of Chapter I of Part V Housing Act 1996.

10.09 Thus, it can be seen that most rented family homes in the private, independent and public rented sectors can potentially be transferred on relationship breakdown, and the addition of introductory tenancies to the original list is welcome. However, only tenancies by virtue of which one or both partners of the cohabitation relationship are "entitled to occupy a dwelling-house" fall within the provision. Thus, at least one of a couple must be a tenant, but significantly the Court of Appeal have held in *Gay v Sheeran* [1999] 2 FLR 519 that a transfer of tenancy is *not* available to a cohabitant of a joint tenant who holds the home jointly with a third party. Here, Mr Sheeran and his original partner were granted a joint tenancy of a flat. When their relationship broke down his partner moved out and Ms Gay, his new partner moved in. However, a new joint tenancy was never granted, although the council were aware of the new position which was reflected in their council tax records. When their relationship subsequently broke down, Mr Sheeran moved out and Ms Gay continued to live in the home. The council, on discovering she was now the sole occupant of the flat, served her with notice to quit. Ms Gay successfully at first instance applied for an order under Sch 7 transferring Mr Sheeran's interest in the flat to her. The council's appeal to the Circuit Judge was granted, as was Ms

Gay's application for an occupation order under Part IV of the 1996 Act. Both parties then appealed to the Court of Appeal who decided that the power to make an occupation order had been properly used and was distinct from that of making a transfer of tenancy order. It was found that, in order to make a transfer of tenancy order under Sch 7, the wording of para 3(1) required Mr Sheeran to have entitlement to occupy either at the time of the application or of the order. It was not sufficient to have had such entitlement at the point at which the relationship broke down, although the provisions did not require the application to be made in any specified period after cohabitation ceased. Given Mr Sheeran's abandonment of the tenancy of the home, it was no longer a secure tenancy (s 81 Housing Act 1985), thus it was not a tenancy capable of transfer under the Schedule.

10.10 This is also a problem when a sole tenant abandons their cohabitant. Thus the only way of keeping the secure tenancy alive and capable of transfer in such a situation would be to immediately apply for an occupation order under s 36 FLA 1996 as, if granted, it allows the occupation of the non-tenant cohabitant to satisfy the 1985 Act occupancy condition of the secure tenancy. However, the Court of Appeal also made it clear that, whilst the statutory language of s 53 and Sch 7 FLA 1996 makes it apt to cover both the transfer by a sole tenant to their non-tenant cohabitant or by a joint tenant to their joint tenant, it is not appropriate to cover the transfer by a cohabitant who is a joint tenant with a third party to their non-tenant cohabiting party as that third party's interest in the tenancy cannot legitimately be transferred to create a joint tenancy between, as here, two strangers.

10.11 This decision is something of a body blow to these provisions as they affect cohabitants, although the finding would seem to apply equally to applications by non-tenant spouses where the tenancy of the home was held jointly by the other spouse and a third party. It has already been criticised for the interpretation given to the wording of paragraph 3 of the Schedule, requiring entitlement to be judged not at the point of breakdown but at the point of the application to or order by the court, by which time former partners (who are specifically entitled to use the provisions) would frequently be long gone from the home (see eg Coll, 'Gay v Sheeran: a Just result in the Circumstances' [2000] Fam Law 355). It is respectfully submitted that this interpretation is not compatible with what happens on relationship breakdown and is another example of the technical nature of the law which regulates disputes between cohabitants.

10.12 Giving the increasing incidence of "serial relationships" such as described in *Gay v Sheeran*, this decision underlines the need for couples to co-operate and to put matters in order on relationship breakdown if the home is to be preserved for either of them. If advice is sought, then where there is a sole tenancy and willingness to permit the non-tenant to remain, no-one should be advised to move out unless an occupation order can be obtained. Even then, whilst a s 36 occupation order, if granted, will, in essence, preserve a sole tenancy, it may not be granted in a case where the order is only needed to resolve the longer term housing rights rather than as an end in itself. As Gibson LJ indicated in *Gay v Sheeran*, the goal of a transfer order should be "a further purpose" of the occupation order. Where it is the sole purpose it risks not fulfilling the criteria under s 36(6)-(8) and may well not be granted. It is perhaps of interest to note that in the Housing (Scotland) Act 2001 (not yet implemented), the Scottish Parliament has greatly strengthened the position of people who occupy another person's public or independent sector tenancy as their home, permitting them to defend possession proceedings brought by the landlord and to have the right to apply to become a joint tenant of the property. There is however to date no provision equivalent to Sch 7 in Scotland.

10.13 Returning to the ambit of Sch 7, the term tenancy expressly includes sub-tenancies. However, a right of occupation by virtue of something other than a specified tenancy, such as a genuine licence to occupy premises (see *AG Securities v Vaughan* [1990] 1 AC 417), would not be subject to these provisions.

(b) When can a Part II order be made?

10.14 The orders for transferring different types of tenancy are contained in Part II of Sch 7 and are known as "Part II orders". It should firstly be noted that transfer is only possible of a tenancy of the family home in which cohabitants lived together as husband and wife (para 4(b)). If the parties never moved into the accommodation or never lived there together, it is not possible to use this provision. Given that in the married context a transfer of tenancy order is limited exclusively to the present or former matrimonial home (para 4(a)), thus theoretically, at least, permitting the transfer of more than one tenancy under the Schedule, the question is posed whether a tenancy of a rented second home could be transferred under the Schedule. The provision is not in relation to cohabitants specifically limited to a couple's principal home and it is arguable that a couple could live together as husband and wife in more than one property.

10.15 Secondly, the court's power to transfer the tenancy in the case of cohabitants/former cohabitants only arises *after* cohabitation "as husband and wife" has ceased. This is not to say that the parties will necessarily need to have separate addresses before an application is made, and indeed where the transfer of a sole tenancy is sought, this is likely following *Gay v Sheeran* (above) to prove fatal to the application unless a s 36 occupation order has been obtained in the non-tenant's favour. However, they will have to show that they are no longer living together as husband and wife. Despite its significance, "living together as husband and wife" goes undefined in the Act and thus the cessation of cohabitation, and indeed the requisite prior cohabitation, may in some circumstances be difficult to judge or to prove. What, for example, is the status of a couple whose work commitments require one of them to live and work away from home for a substantial part of the week? Are they living together as husband and wife?

10.16 In *Westminster City Council v Peart* (1991) 24 HLR 389, the Court of Appeal considered the meaning of the same phrase in the context of the Housing Act 1985, and concluded that the retention of accommodation elsewhere by one of the parties justified a finding that the parties were not living together as husband and wife, even though they had lived together in the same household. It is hoped that there will not be too rigid an interpretation put upon this phrase in the Family Law Act context, and that as common sense a view as possible will prevail, as was witnessed in *Re Watson*

(Deceased) [1999] 1 FLR 878 (see Chapter 5) and decided in the Inheritance (Provision for Families and Dependants) Act 1975 context which contains similar wording. With regard to cessation of cohabitation, although there is not here any statutory requirement of separate households, it may well be that this will be the interpretation put upon the phrase "ceased living together as husband and wife", which might then be construed with reference to the matrimonial authorities relating to the separate households test (see eg *Fuller v Fuller* [1973] 1 WLR 730, CA).

10.17   Thirdly, it must also be noted that it is only possible for the order to be made if the tenancy is in existence at the date of the application for a transfer (*Lewis v Lewis* [1985] AC 828). This may pose problems where the tenancy concerned is either vested in the sole name of the respondent or is a joint periodic assured or secure tenancy, as notice to quit by one joint tenant will validly determine the tenancy (*Hammersmith and Fulham London Borough Council v Monk* [1992] 1 AC 478, approving *Greenwich London Borough Council v McGrady* (1982) 81 LGR 288). Given the serious consequences of no tenancy being available for transfer, where it is feared that such action is a possibility, an application to transfer the tenancy should in all cases immediately be made and served on both the respondent and the landlord. In the case of a sole statutory tenancy under Rent Act 1977 or Rent (Agriculture) Act 1976, an occupation rights order pursuant to s 36(3)–(4) FLA 1996 (discussed above Chapter 7, page 129) to preserve the statutory tenancy must also be applied for by the non-tenant cohabitant. In the case of any other type of tenancy, an injunction pursuant to the Family Proceedings Rules, 1991 r 3.8(14), (which expressly incorporates r 3.6(9) empowering an injunction to be granted) restraining notice to quit being given in order to preserve the tenancy which is the subject of the dispute should be urgently considered. The injunction, which must relate to the preservation of the tenancy, should immediately be served upon the landlord (see *Bater v Greenwich London Borough Council* [1999] 2 FLR 993), although following the House of Lords decision in *Harrow London Borough Council v Johnstone* [1997] 1 All ER 929, it is still not clear whether or not a notice to quit served in breach of such an injunction is valid (see Arden, 'From Greenwich to Harrow: A Trip Down Memory Lane' [1997] 1 JHL 3 for a discussion of this). The decision in this case, reversing that of the Court of Appeal, seems to indicate that a notice to quit served by an excluded tenant when, known to the landlord, an occupation order was in force, will be valid unless a *Mareva*-style injunction requiring co-operation in preserving the tenancy is also obtained.

10.18   Another gap in the provisions relating to cohabitants arose in the case of *Gay v Sheeran* [1999] 2 FLR 519. Here, where the court was unable to transfer a secure tenancy to the cohabitant of a tenant who had held the tenant jointly with a third party and which had been abandoned by both joint tenants, an occupation order may be the only way to preserve the position of the cohabitant who wishes to remain in the home.

10.19   Finally, in contrast to the position of former spouses who have remarried (see para 13), it should be noted that there is no bar on applications being made by former cohabitants who have remarried or who have embarked upon another cohabitation relationship.

(c) Criteria for making orders

10.20 Following the Scottish example set in the Matrimonial Homes (Family Protection) (Scotland) Act 1981, the Law Commission recommended the introduction of statutory criteria for transfer of tenancy orders in both the married and unmarried contexts (see para 6.8 Law Com No 207). Thus, para 5 to Sch 7 directs the court to have regard to all the circumstances of the case including:

(a) the circumstances in which the tenancy was granted to, or acquired by the cohabitant(s);
(b) the matters relevant to the making of occupation orders; and
(c) the suitability of the parties as tenants.

10.21 Where "entitled" cohabitants are involved, these consist of the factors set out in s 33(6)(a)–(c) FLA 1996, namely:

- the housing needs and resources of the parties and any children;
- the financial resources of the parties; and
- the likely effect of the order or of no order on the health, safety and well being of the parties or any relevant child.

10.22 In the case of "non-entitled" cohabitants, those further matters set out in s 36(6)(e)–(h) must additionally be considered, namely:

- the nature of the relationship and the lack of commitment to marriage;
- the length of time they have cohabited;
- whether there are or have been any children for whom both parties have parental responsibility; and
- the length of time since the parties ceased living together.

10.23 In any application it seems clear that the circumstances surrounding the grant of the tenancy will normally be very influential and may outweigh in a court's view the other partner's greater housing needs. Unlike a transfer of property application under Sch 1 CA 1989, the aim of the transfer is not directly to benefit children of the relationship. However, the presence of children of the relationship may be very significant, as was acknowledged by the Law Commission (see para 6.9 Law Com No 207). Particularly where the original purpose of the tenancy was to provide a home for the parties and their children, the party with whom the children are to live may well be at an advantage even though the tenancy is not vested in their name. Generally speaking, however, the provision can be seen to be aimed at finding equity between the adult parties. Non-entitled cohabitants do, however, start from a position of disadvantage on any application for a transfer of tenancy order; and the shorter the period of cohabitation the more necessary it will be to establish greater need or vulnerability for an application to stand any chance of success. It is not uncommon for one cohabitant to have given up their secure accommodation in order to begin a cohabitation relationship and it should be noted that this is not a factor to which the court is specifically directed. Thus, the court's attention needs to be drawn to such a situation as one of the general circumstances of the case and any inducements or promises made to cement the cohabitation relationship in this way could be influential evidence. For a discussion of the county court case of *B v M*

[1999] FLP 19 March, where these criteria were weighed and the order made in favour of the original tenant who ran her florist business from the home rather than her alcoholic, unemployed former partner, see Woelke, "Transfer of Tenancies" [1999] Fam Law 72.

(d) Effect of transfer order

10.24 The nature of the orders in respect of different types of tenancy is set out in Part II to Schedule 7 (although it appears silent with regard to introductory tenancies).

10.25 In the case of protected, secure or assured tenancies, as well as assured agricultural occupancies, the court may by order direct that the respondent's estate or interest in the tenancy of the dwelling-house together with any rights attaching to it vest in the applicant without any further assurance (para 7(1)). Any obligations or liabilities under any covenants relating to the property arising after the date of the transfer are not enforceable against the respondent. Where the transferor cohabitant was a successor pursuant to the terms of the Housing Acts 1985 or 1988, then the transferee cohabitant is deemed to be that successor as of the date of the transfer, and effectively steps into the shoes of their former partner for these purposes.

10.26 With regard to statutory tenancies under the Rent Act 1977 and Rent (Agriculture) Act 1976, paras 8 and 9 provide that where an order is made, the court directs that the transferor is not entitled to occupy the family home from a specified date and that, from that time, the transferee cohabitant is deemed to be the statutory tenant. The transferee will acquire exactly the same status as their former partner and no succession of the statutory tenancy is deemed to have taken place for the purposes of determining further succession rights (see eg paras 5–7 Sch 1 RA 1977).

10.27 On making a Part II order, the court also has power to adjust liabilities and obligations in respect of the dwelling-house arising prior to transfer as between the parties and order that one party indemnify the other in respect of these (para 11). Thus, existing rent arrears could be apportioned, or an order could be made indemnifying one partner for rent they had paid but which was the responsibility of the other. Thus, advisors need to consider carefully what ancillary orders might be appropriate when an application is made. This power to make orders under para 11 are a separate and additional issue to the question of compensation under para 10, which will now be considered.

(e) Compensation orders

10.28 This is a provision introduced by para 10 of Sch 7 and recommended by the Law Commission in their report (Law Com No 207, paras 6.10-6.12). It embodies a principle which had already been incorporated into Scottish law (see s 13(9) and

(13) Matrimonial Homes (Family Protection) (Scotland) Act 1981) and one which it was observed by the Law Commission may be more appropriate in the cohabitation context than the married context, where there are obligations of mutual support (Law Com No 207, para 6.10). The sole object of the compensation is to compensate the transferor for the loss of the tenancy and, unlike in Scotland, consideration of the loss of the "right to buy" has not been specifically excluded. Given that it has been decided the loss of the right to buy may be taken into account on application for transfer of property orders under Sch 1 CA 1989 (see *K v K* (above)), this is likely to figure in the calculation of any compensation order made in respect of a secure tenancy. The Law Commission did not foresee compensation orders being made routinely, but did express the view that even where the tenancy had no real market value, it may be appropriate to grant compensation for provision of a deposit for a tenancy in the private sector or removal expenses (Law Com No 207, para 6.10). If the courts were prepared to adopt such an approach, it is submitted that quite large numbers of compensation orders could potentially be made. However, this has not to date proved to the case as the financial resources of the transferee cohabitant may make such an order inappropriate or unenforceable in many situations and this factor is often the determining one.

10.29 The court has power to make a compensation order payable by the transferee to the transferor cohabitant, wherever a Part II order is made. In exercising its discretion, para 10(4) provides that the court shall have regard to all the circumstances of the case including:

- the financial loss that would otherwise be suffered by the transferor as a result of the order;
- the financial needs and resources of the parties; and
- the financial obligations which the parties have, or are likely to have in the foreseeable future, including financial obligations to each other and to any relevant child.

10.30 The degree of long-term security of tenure (or lack thereof) offered by the tenancy is not a specific factor.

10.31 Paragraph 10(2) permits the court to defer payment of the compensation until a specified date or event, and also to allow payment of compensation by instalments. This power may be exercised by the court either on making the order or on the application of one of the parties "at any time before the sum whose payment is required by the order is paid in full" (para 10(3)(a)). The court also has power to vary the order up to this point in time (para 10(3)(b)). It therefore seems that an application for both variation of the original order and for delayed payment can be made after the date on which the payment has fallen due and, on applications made at this time, there is no presumption against delayed payment. However, there is a presumption against delayed payment, when an application is made at the time of making the compensation order. Here, deferred payment or payment by instalments may not be ordered by the court unless it appears that immediate payment of the sum required by the order would cause greater financial hardship to the transferee than that which would be caused to the transferor by delayed payment (para 10(5)). One situation where a deferred compensation order would certainly seem to be appropriate would be with regard to an order for the loss of the "right to buy" the property.

3 Transfer of tenancy order (Sch 7 FLA 1996) or transfer of property order (Sch 1 para 1(2)(e) CA 1989)?

10.32 The most obvious advantage of the new provision is that it provides a remedy for cohabitants where there are no children of the relationship, providing the home is not vested in the joint names of just one cohabitant and a third party. Schedule 1 CA 1989 does not even provide a remedy where children of one of the parties but not of the relationship have lived in the property with them (see *J v J (minors) (property transfer) (above)*). However, where there are children of a cohabitation relationship, there may be a choice between these two remedies. Having weighed the advantages and disadvantages of these alternatives, it seems quite clear that the 1996 Act overcomes the many practical difficulties (discussed in detail in the first edition of this book (see pages 191–195)) which exist in relation to Sch 1 property transfer orders, although other practical difficulties have arisen in relation to Sch 7 itself as identified in *Gay v Sheeran*. Given that the two remedies continue to co-exist, it is useful to make an assessment of the respective merits and difficulties pertaining to each of them.

(a) Situations where Sch 1 CA 1989 property transfer order might be used in respect of a tenancy

10.33 As will be considered below, the two classical difficulties that have arisen with regard to tenancy transfers under Sch 1 CA 1989 are, firstly, whether the tenancy in question is "property" and, if so, whether it is capable of being transferred, given that the Sch 1 order is not expressed to take effect "without further assurance" and requires a deed of assignment. These issues aside, the other important factor to consider is the difference in the criteria to which the court are referred when making the order. Unlike the provisions in the MCA 1973, the CA 1989 remedy, although only available for the benefit of a child of the relationship, does not make the child the "first" consideration and the welfare principle contained in s 1(1) CA 1989 does not apply to issues of financial provision. The criteria under Sch 1 contained in para 4 have been discussed in Chapter 9 and broadly comprise the income, earning capacity, needs, obligations and responsibilities of the parents; the financial needs and resources if any of the child; any disability of the child and the manner in which the child was intended to be educated or trained. In addition, all the circumstances of the case must be considered, although the court is not specifically directed to consider the duration or nature of the relationship nor the conduct of either party. The difference between the two sets of criteria contained in the 1989 and 1996 Acts do not immediately lead to any particular category of applicant being favoured more by one remedy than the other. The housing needs and resources of and the likely effect of an order on the "health, safety and well being" of any relevant child as well as the adults are also specific concerns of the 1996 Act. Difficulties with the assignability of some types of tenancy (discussed below) aside, it is perhaps possible that a more child-centred approach will prevail under the 1989 Act, to the extent that non-entitled applicants with children may in time be better advised to use the 1989 Act remedy.

10.34 Apart from this possible difference in judicial approach, there still may be situations where a Sch 1 property transfer order is the only order available to transfer a tenancy on relationship breakdown of former cohabitants. Where there are children of the relationship, but the parents have not lived together as husband and wife in the accommodation to which the tenancy refers, then the 1996 Act remedy is not available. Thus, if the tenancy relates to a second home in which the parties have not lived as husband and wife, or if parties have never moved into the accommodation together, or lived in it in separate households, a 1989 Act transfer of property order is likely to be the only possible remedy.

10.35 Although it is not thought that the courts are likely to make such an order, the 1989 Act remedy, unlike the 1996 provisions, provides the possibility of a transfer of the tenancy to a child under 18.

10.36 Finally, where the tenancy is assignable, or there is landlord co-operation with regard to assignment, a Sch 1 order does avoid the making of a compensation order as between the parties. However, the wording of the Sch 7 provisions in the 1996 Act enable the court to make orders of its own motion. Thus, if the court were persuaded by the respondent, or took the view itself that a transfer of tenancy order under Part II of Sch 7 rather than a property transfer order under the 1989 Act was appropriate, the court could decide to deal with the matter in this way. Once the Part II order has been made, then the question of compensation arises. Thus this method of attempting to avoid the issue of compensation is far from fool proof.

(b) Positive features of Sch 7 FLA 1996 as compared with Sch 1 CA 1989

10.37 Schedule 7 orders apply to all types of tenancy including statutory tenancies under the Rent Act 1977 and Rent (Agriculture) Act 1976 and, furthermore, the transfer of the tenancy takes place by virtue of the court order "without further assurance". Thus, the assignability of the tenancy is irrelevant to the application. In contrast, a problem which exists with Sch 1 property transfer orders is that whilst, with the exception of these statutory tenancies, most tenancies would be regarded as "property" (see *K v K* (above) and *Hale v Hale* [1975] 2 All ER 1090, CA), a deed of assignment is required to effect the transfer here, as the order to transfer is not expressed to take place "without further assurance". Thus, assignability of the tenancy and/or landlord co-operation is critical to giving effect to the order to transfer under Sch 1 CA 1989. Indeed, a court may be disinclined to grant a transfer of property order under Sch 1 in respect of a non-assignable tenancy where the landlord has not consented to the transfer in view of the risk that the transfer would be ineffective and all the parties concerned, including the children, would be rendered homeless. Given that there is an implied covenant against assignment in respect of all assured and assured shorthold tenancies unless expressly overridden; that Rent Act and Rent (Agriculture) Act statutory tenancies are not assignable; and that even secure tenancies are not strictly assignable as between cohabitants without landlord co-operation where a cohabitant has not lived with the tenant for twelve months (see s 91 HA 1985), the safest course of action is to use the 1996 Act remedy. However, this does then open up the possibility of an application for a compensation order which does not appear in the 1989 Act and were the 1989 Act provisions to be amended to enable transfers of tenancies to take place without further assurance then this amended remedy could be seen to be a more advantageous route if avoidance of a compensation order was an important factor. Nonetheless, this remains subject to the court's ability to decide the matter under Sch 7 of its own motion, and is consequently a strategy where success cannot be guaranteed. Once transferred under Sch 1, however, the issue of compensation becomes closed.

10.38 Although it remains to be seen exactly how the court will apply its power to make compensation orders, it certainly was not intended by the Law Commission that it would be greatly used, as discussed above. If this proves to be the case, then it seems likely that the unamended 1989 Act remedy will become little used in relation to tenancies. Although the criteria relating to the two orders are different, with the 1989 Act criteria being more child centred (see above page 234) and also requiring the order only be made for the benefit of a child, there does not seem to be any particular advantage to be gained from a non-tenant cohabitant seeking an order under the 1989 Act as opposed to the 1996 Act, unless the 1996 Act remedy were to be interpreted in such a way that property rights hold sway over the needs of the children. If this were to happen, then a resurgence of the use of the more specifically child-centred 1989 Act remedy for all its practical difficulties may take place. Given that Part VII Housing Act 1996 has reformed the law relating to homelessness to remove the direct route into secure housing, the consequences of preferring the property interests of the original tenant over the housing needs of the children in such applications are very serious, and probably, therefore, unlikely.

4 Procedure

10.39 Applications for transfer of tenancies under both the 1996 and 1989 Acts cannot be made to the magistrates' court and would normally be heard by the county court, although the High Court also has jurisdiction. In contrast to the divorce context, where currently decree nisi must be obtained before a property transfer application can be made, there is no reason to delay an application under either Act on unmarried relationship breakdown.

(a) 1996 Act applications (see Family Proceedings Rules 1991, rr 3.6, 3.8)

10.40 In relation to the 1996 Act application, notice must be served upon the landlord as defined in para 1, Sch 7 (para 14(1), Sch 7). The landlord has a right to be heard in all cases, although the court may make an order notwithstanding the landlord's objections. It should be borne in mind that whilst an application for transfer of a tenancy on relationship breakdown under Sch 7 cannot provide a ground for possession, it may provoke notice to quit being given by a landlord where no grounds are needed in the case of an assured shorthold tenancy. Advisors should therefore consider whether an application for an occupation order may be more appropriate in this situation, certainly in the first instance, as this could be undertaken without the need to serve the proceedings on the landlord. On the other hand, where a landlord agrees to the transfer, their written consent should be produced to the court on or before the hearing of any application or consent order.

10.41 Advisors should beware of suggesting consent orders where help in relation to rehousing is to be sought by the transferor cohabitant. Intentional homelessness remains a bar to the temporary rehousing duties currently found in Part VII Housing Act 1996 and will remain so following implementation of the Homelessness Bill 2001. Where agreement is reached in such a situation, it is vital that the order is made by the court, albeit at an unopposed hearing. Indeed, before advising a transferor cohabitant to sign a consent order, it is likely to be negligent not to have advised them that in doing so they are effectively rendering themselves intentionally homeless, unless they already have other "settled" accommodation (see Chapter 3).

(b) Sch 1 CA 1989 applications

10.42 Applications for transfer of property orders can be made to the county court or High Court only, by completing the appropriate forms introduced by the Family Proceedings Rules 1991 (Forms C1, C10 and C10A). Any additional evidence should be in the form of a dated and signed statement containing the appropriate declaration as to the maker's belief in its truth.

10.43 Although there is no requirement in the 1989 Act to seek the landlord's consent, where it will not prejudice the applicant and where there is an absolute or qualified covenant against assignment, the landlord's consent, subject to the court order being made, should be sought.

(c) Timing and preservation of the tenancy

10.44 As noted above, whichever application is being made, a problem arises where a respondent is a sole tenant (statutory, secure or assured) and has left the home. For as soon as the tenant cohabitant leaves and is no longer occupying the accommodation as his or her residence, the security of tenure falls and the tenancy ceases to exist. However, as noted above, it is enough for the tenancy to have been in existence at the time of the application rather than at the hearing date. In the House of Lords decision in *Lewis v Lewis* [1985] 2 All ER 449, it was held that the court had jurisdiction to transfer a statutory tenancy which was subsisting at the date of the application under the MHA 1983, despite its having been determined before the date of the hearing. This reasoning was followed by the Court of Appeal in the case of a secure tenancy in *Thompson v Elmbridge Borough Council* [1987] 1 WLR 1425. There is no reason why this cannot be extended to applications for property transfer orders between cohabitants for the benefit of a child and has been confirmed to be the case with respect to applications under Sch 7 FLA 1996 in *Gay v Sheeran* (above). It is clear that an application for a transfer of property order or transfer of tenancy order as appropriate in this situation must be lodged without delay to protect the remaining cohabitant's position and that a s 36 occupation order is the only other possibility where the sole tenant has abandoned the home.

10.45 In addition, where it is feared that a joint or sole tenant respondent may intend to determine the tenancy by notice to quit, which would leave the court without any property capable of transfer and the applicant homeless, an *ex parte* application for an order restraining the service of a notice to quit by the respondent pending the hearing should be urgently considered, and, where granted, served promptly upon the respondent and landlord (see FPR 1991, rr 3.6(9), 3.8(14). An application for emergency representation would be appropriate. For once the tenancy is determined, there can be no possibility of preserving the home. The possibility (or need in the case of a statutory tenancy) for an occupation rights order by a non-entitled cohabitant should also be urgently considered. Where it is not possible to preserve the tenancy, the applicant would be homeless, and in no way intentionally homeless. If they were also in priority need, for example because they had children residing with them the local housing authority would be obliged to secure accommodation in accordance with the provisions of Part VII HA 1996, which currently entails the provision of accommodation for a minimum of two years (see Chapter 3). It is only a valid notice to quit by one joint tenant that will act to terminate the tenancy as illustrated in *Hounslow London Borough Council v Pilling* (1993) 25 HLR 305. Here a cohabitant joint tenant who had been the victim of domestic violence gave notice to quit her joint tenancy "with immediate effect" at the request of the council who were to rehouse her. The Court of Appeal held that this did not operate to surrender the tenancy as it both failed to give the requisite contractual notice which the council could not waive in the absence of the concurrence of both tenants and also offended s 5 Protection from Eviction Act 1977.

10.46 Where one joint tenant does unilaterally give notice to quit on a periodic joint tenancy it was thought arguable that this amounted to a breach of trust towards the other tenant, for which the latter may be entitled to be compensated. However, in *Hammersmith and Fulham London Borough Council v Monk* (above), Lord Browne-Wilkinson doubted that this was the case and indicated that, even if it were, it did not invalidate the notice to quit. More recently, in *Crawley Borough Council v Ure* (1995) 27 HLR 524, the Court of Appeal rejected that such action in relation to a periodic secure tenancy could constitute a breach of trust due to lack of consultation with the other tenant pursuant to s 26(3) LPA 1925. This position, coupled with the reduced duties towards the homeless, makes it imperative that applications for transfer of tenancy orders are made without delay in all cases where there is jurisdiction.

10.47 Desertion by a sole tenant cohabitant who does not give the landlord notice may cause an insuperable problem pending the hearing of a transfer of tenancy application unless an occupation rights order is sought pursuant to s 36 FLA 1996 which, by virtue of s 36(13), extends the "matrimonial home rights" contained in s 30(3)–(6) to cohabitants and entitles the deserted cohabitant to make payment of rent and occupy as if they were their tenant partner for the period of the occupation order, which is a maximum of six months in the first instance and may be renewed for one further maximum period of six months only. Without this, the remaining partner has no right to pay the rent to the landlord, nor any occupation rights. Furthermore, if residence is a requirement of the continued subsistence of the tenancy, no application can be made under Sch 1 CA 1989 or Sch 7 FLA 1996. Attention is drawn to the need to resolve the substantive application under Sch 7 FLA 1996 or Sch 1 CA 1989 within the period for which the court granted the occupation order.

(d) Enforcement of orders for compensation

10.48 Compensation orders are not subject to any special enforcement procedure and thus may only be enforced in the same way as any other debt. They are not "maintenance" and thus cannot be enforced by judgment summons (see Sch 8 Administration of Justice Act 1970).

5 Limits to the FLA 1996 reforms

10.49 As noted above, the transfer of tenancy provisions contained in Part IV FLA 1996 are a welcome improvement and have removed an anomaly which had left childless joint tenant cohabitants without any form of remedy on relationship breakdown in relation to disputes about the family home. In addition, the legislation has removed some of the difficulties associated with the Sch 1 CA 1989 provisions, but has itself been exposed by the decision in *Gay v Sheeran* (see above) as being unable to preserve a non-tenant cohabitant's home where the tenancy was originally granted to one of the cohabitants jointly with a third party. It is also of little use where the tenancy is abandoned by a sole tenant cohabitant who may at best obtain a s 36 occupation order, no matter how long he or she may have lived in the home. Furthermore, these reforms deliberately left same-sex cohabitants – who have been excluded by s 62(1) FLA 1996 from falling within the definition of "cohabitant" under the Act, and now by the House of Lords as well as the Court of Appeal from inclusion within the definition of those "living together as husband and wife" (see *Fitzpatrick v Sterling Housing Association* Ltd [1999] 4 All ER 705, HL) and Harrogate *Borough Council v Simpson* [1986] 2 FLR 91, CA) – in a very unsatisfactory position. For even if they can reach agreement as to what should happen to the family home on relationship breakdown, they may not be able to implement the agreement; and where there is no agreement, there may be no mechanism for resolving the dispute. Although same sex cohabitants may now apply for non-molestation orders as they fall within the definition of "associated persons" (see s 62(3)-(6) FLA 1996), and if they are entitled applicants (but not otherwise) may apply for an occupation order pursuant to s 33, which may be made for an indefinite period, may even succeed to a Rent Act tenancy on death (*Fitzpatrick v Sterling Lousing Association Ltd* (above)) the Sch 7 transfer of tenancy provisions do not extend to same-sex cohabitants, leaving joint tenants without any or any satisfactory final remedy.

6 The rented family home and same-sex cohabitants

10.50 Effectively, on relationship breakdown, same-sex cohabitants have two options in relation to the rented family home. Either they are dependent on the general law of landlord and tenant in order to establish their occupation rights or implement any agreement; or, if the applicant seeking to remain in the family home is an "entitled" applicant (ie they are a sole or joint tenant of the family home), and only in that situation, can they seek to obtain an occupation order pursuant to s 33 FLA 1996. This last alternative has been discussed in Chapter 7. The likely difficulty with it is that although orders can be made excluding a partner indefinitely (s 33(10)), and this may pose no problem when a non-tenant violent partner is excluded, a joint tenant partner who has not been violent and whose needs equate with those of the tenant seeking to remain under the order is unlikely to be excluded for any length of time if at all, leaving the cohabitants with no remedy other than agreement as to how to continue to live under the same roof or as to which of them is to go. Even then the assignability of the tenancy is critical to whether or not a final solution can be achieved.

10.51 The various possibilities will be considered in outline in the context of the nature of the tenancy and whether or not there is agreement. Even if there is agreement, only where a tenancy is capable of assignment can a straightforward resolution of the situation be guaranteed. Whether or not a tenancy is assignable depends on the terms of the tenancy agreement and the security of tenure afforded by the type of tenancy in question.

10.52 It is to be regretted that same-sex cohabitants have not been afforded the Sch 7 transfer of tenancy remedy, on relationship breakdown. Having gone so far as to extend occupation orders to entitled associated persons, it is unsatisfactory that they are then left without any final means of resolution of their dispute.

7 Joint tenancies—the general position

10.53 Any form of joint tenancy gives each joint tenant the right to occupy the accommodation let, and renders each jointly and severally liable to pay the rent regardless of whether or not in occupation. These factors raise obvious problems on breakdown of a relationship, even where there is broad agreement as to who should remain in the home. One partner will wish to remain in occupation without the other partner exercising the right to occupy, and the departing partner will not want to remain liable to the landlord for the rent in the event of non-payment by the former partner.

10.54 Overcoming these problems may depend on the assignability of the tenancy. Where the joint tenancy permits assignment, there is little difficulty if the parties agree a solution. Where there is agreement, but the tenancy cannot be assigned, perhaps the best protection that can be achieved is for the parties to enter into a deed of indemnity. The remaining partner will agree to indemnify the departing partner against any liability in respect of the rent, the departing partner agreeing in turn not to exercise his or her rights of occupation. In this way, the landlord does not have to know that one partner has left and the remaining partner remains a tenant. However, notwithstanding the indemnity, the departing partner will still be liable to the landlord for the rent in the event of non-payment. Also, it is not clear whether the courts would uphold an agreement to suspend legal rights of occupation. As shall be seen, where there is no agreement, one joint tenant may unilaterally terminate a periodic tenancy regardless of whether or not the former partner wishes to remain, with varying effects on the remaining partner.

8 Rent Act tenancies

(a) Joint contractual tenancies (excluding protected shortholds)

10.55 Where the parties agree who should continue to occupy the home, the situation is relatively simple. If there is no covenant against assignment or where there is a qualified covenant but the landlord consents, (and consent should not be unreasonably withheld – s 19 Landlord and Tenant Act 1927), the departing partner can assign his or her interest in the joint tenancy to the former partner, who will then become the sole contractual tenant. Assignment should be in writing, in the form of a deed, witnessed in the normal way to comply with s 52 LPA 1925.

10.56 Where assignment is not possible and there is a periodic tenancy, the departing partner can serve notice to quit on the landlord. Providing the notice is in the form required by the agreement and complies with s 5 Protection from Eviction Act 1977, giving a minimum of four weeks notice in writing, it operates to determine the contractual tenancy in accordance with the decision in *Hammersmith and Fulham London Borough Council v Monk* (above) unless the tenancy agreement expressly provides otherwise. However, in contrast to the periodic secure or periodic assured tenant's position, it does not operate to terminate the remaining partner's right of occupation. Instead the latter becomes the statutory tenant of the premises, providing he or she continues to occupy the home as his/her only or principal residence (see *Lloyd v Sadler* [1978] 2 All ER 529). At the same time, the notice determines the departing partner's liability to pay the rent and, of course, the right to occupy. The remaining partner will only be the statutory, and not the contractual, tenant of the premises, which can have certain disadvantages.

10.57 A fixed-term tenancy cannot be surrendered by one joint tenant alone, but only by all the joint tenants acting together (*Leek and Moorlands Building Society* *v Clark* [1952] 2 All ER 492, CA) and thus effective assignment to the remaining joint tenant is dependent upon the terms of the tenancy permitting assignment.

10.58 Where the parties do not agree, or where the departing partner has deserted the remaining partner, there are various options. Where one partner has left the premises, the remaining periodic joint tenant can himself or herself give notice to quit to the landlord, and providing he/she then continues in occupation of the home, the remaining partner becomes the sole statutory tenant of the premises. By this action the departing partner loses the right to occupy and liability to pay rent, but the remaining partner unfortunately thereby gives the landlord a discretionary ground for possession under Case 5 of Sch 5, Part I Rent Act 1977. The landlord would have to prove not only that the remaining partner gave notice to quit, but also that it is reasonable to make a possession order (s 98(1)). Given that Rent Act tenancies are generally unattractive to landlords, they may be keen to attempt to obtain possession in such a situation and advisors must warn of the possible consequences of a tenant's notice.

(b) Joint statutory tenancies

10.59 In this situation, where there is agreement as to who should remain, no problem arises. Both joint statutory tenants have occupation rights, but once the departing tenant ceases to occupy the premises as his or her residence and abandons any intention to return, then that person ceases to be a statutory tenant and ceases to have rights of occupation (see s 2(1)(a) Rent Act 1977). A notification by either tenant to the landlord that one but not both of them has ceased to reside in the premises should ensure that the liability of the departing partner to pay rent ceases, and falls solely on the remaining partner, who becomes the sole statutory tenant of the home and whose occupation rights are unaffected.

10.60 However, should both joint statutory tenants wish to remain in occupation, then no mechanism exists to resolve the dispute, other than the possibility of an occupation order pursuant to s 33 FLA 1996.

(c) Sole contractual Rent Act tenancies

10.61 Whether a non-tenant cohabitant, whom the parties agree should stay, can lawfully remain in occupation depends on the terms of the tenancy agreement. Note that here there is no possibility of an occupation order remedy as the non-tenant same-sex cohabitant will not be an "entitled" applicant. There is no difficulty where the tenancy agreement does not contain a covenant against assignment, as a deed of assignment in the proper form will be effective to transfer the tenancy. An oral tenancy where no notice to quit has been served will remain contractual and will therefore usually be assignable.

10.62 Where there is a covenant against assignment, even if the sole tenant wishes his or her former partner to remain in occupation, this may not be possible. If the tenant, after departure, having made a *de facto* assignment of the tenancy, were to continue to pay the rent to the landlord, this would constitute breach of the tenancy agreement and give the landlord grounds for possession. However, if the landlord, with knowledge of the facts, continues to accept the rent, then it is arguable that he has waived the breach and accepted the cohabitant as a new tenant although after 15 January 1989 the new tenancy will be assured, not Rent Act protected. If at any point the landlord serves notice to quit, then, unless it can be argued that a new tenancy has been granted, on expiry, the contractual tenancy comes to an end. A statutory tenancy arises only if the tenant occupies the home as his/her only or principal residence or can show they have not relinquished possession despite a temporary absence and there is a definite intention to return. The longer the tenant is away, the less likely it is that such an argument will be convincing.

10.63 Once there is a statutory rather than a contractual tenancy, neither the absent tenant nor the non-tenant partner remaining in the property has a defence to possession proceedings. If a landlord is approached for consent to a new tenancy, the likely outcome is at best an offer of an assured shorthold tenancy, which will give security for a minimum six months, but is thereafter determinable by the landlord without need for grounds for possession other than the expiry of the initial fixed term and compliance with the statutory procedures.

10.64 Where there is a dispute between the parties, if the cohabitant who is the sole tenant wishes to remain, then their former partner has no right to remain and can be forced to leave by means of possession proceedings, as they are no more than a licensee with no occupation rights once these have been revoked.

(d) Sole statutory tenancies

10.65 Statutory tenancies are a personal right and cannot be assigned unless the landlord consents and is a party to the deed of assignment (see para 13, Sch 1 Rent Act 1977). Given the protection and rent restriction which a Rent Act tenancy affords, the landlord's consent is most unlikely to be forthcoming.

9 Tenancies governed by the Housing Act 1988

10.66 Assured tenancies will be found most commonly in the independent sector, and will be granted mainly by housing associations. Although they can be granted in the private sector, most private sector landlords prefer assured shorthold tenancies which afford tenants very little security, although during the initial fixed-term period are treated as fixed-term assured tenancies with regard to assignability. Schedule 2 HA 1996 now makes all tenancies granted on or after 1997 assured shorthold unless the landlord expressly states it as assured.

(a) Joint assured tenancies

10.67 On breakdown, the joint tenants each retain the right to occupy, and remain jointly and severally liable to pay rent; as each same-sex cohabitant will be "entitled" in this situation, the possibility of a s 33 occupation order can be considered.

10.68 In the case of a fixed-term tenancy, assignment is permitted where the terms of the tenancy agreement do not prohibit it. Thus if there is agreement between the cohabitants and assignment is possible, the situation is simple. All that is required is a deed of assignment in proper form.

10.69 However, in the case of periodic tenancies, regardless of whether they are periodic from the outset or are statutory periodic tenancies which arise on expiry of the fixed term, a covenant against assignment without the landlord's express consent is implied by s 15 Housing Act 1988 (HA 1988) (unless, in the case of an expressly periodic tenancy, the agreement provides otherwise, or a premium is payable on the grant or renewal of the tenancy). The statutory proviso that consent cannot unreasonably be withheld is specifically excluded. Thus, in direct contrast to the Rent Act position, an oral periodic assured tenancy where nothing at all is said about assignment, is unassignable without the landlord's express consent. This is also the case with statutory periodic tenancies arising after the expiry of the fixed term, even though the original fixed-term tenancy permitted assignment. The only way to achieve certainty is therefore to obtain the landlord's consent. Whether or not this is forthcoming is entirely within the landlord's discretion.

10.70 Again, in contrast to the Rent Act position, a notice to quit given by one of two joint tenants will bind all, and thus bring a periodic assured tenancy to an end (*Hammersmith and Fulham London Borough Council v Monk* (above)). No statutory tenancy arises by operation of law as in the Rent Act situation, and accordingly the landlord will be entitled to possession. However, it seems that a notice to quit by one joint tenant will not operate to determine a fixed-term assured tenancy (see s 5(2)(b) and s 45(2) HA 1988 which, read together, confirm the common law rule that it requires all the joint tenants to determine the fixed-term tenancy).

10.71 Where one cohabitant deserts a joint tenant partner, the tenancy remains an assured joint tenancy, as s 1(1)(b) HA 1988 requires that just one of the joint tenants occupies the premises as his only or principal home to qualify for protection. A landlord may agree to accept a notice to quit from the deserted joint tenant and to grant him or her a new sole assured tenancy. Given that otherwise the remaining joint tenant continues to be vulnerable to their former partner determining the tenancy without their knowledge, this is a possibility worth exploring.

(b) Sole assured tenancies

10.72 Assignability of a sole assured tenancy depends on the landlord's express consent, and where the non-tenant wishes to remain in occupation, the landlord must be approached.

10.73 Residence by the tenant is required to continue security. Thus, once the sole tenant leaves, the protection afforded by the Act falls, as the tenant's leaving must amount to a "surrender or other action" by the tenant which brings the tenancy to an end (s 5(1)(b) HA 1988). The landlord, on discovery of the situation, can obtain possession. Alternatively, the landlord may be prepared to grant the remaining partner a new tenancy, quite possibly, in the private sector, at an increased rent.

10.74 Once a notice to quit is served by the tenant, then again the tenancy is surrendered and there can be no defence to possession proceedings. Acceptance of rent from the remaining partner, who has no right to pay the rent may constitute evidence that a new tenancy has been granted, which in turn may assist the remaining partner's position.

(c) Assured shorthold

10.75 Assured shortholds are the most popular form of private sector tenancy, as on the expiry of the initial fixed term of a minimum of six months, a landlord can obtain possession without now even needing to comply with the statutory notice provisions and needs no ground for possession (see ss 19A and 21 HA 1988). In this situation, other than the protection afforded for the initial fixed term, neither the tenant nor a non-tenant wishing to remain has any security of tenure, although a departing tenant remains liable for the rent. Only an indemnity to pay the rent and any legal costs incurred by the departing tenant as a result of the partner's continued occupation can assist the position between the parties, but there is no protection from ultimate eviction by the landlord.

10 Secure tenancies

10.76 A local authority tenant will usually have a periodic secure tenancy, now governed by the Housing Act 1985. Housing association tenancies granted before 15 January 1989 will also be secure tenancies, but those granted after this date will be assured tenancies and are subject to the provisions of HA 1988 as described above.

(a) Joint secure tenancies

10.77 As with all other types of joint tenancy, secure joint tenancies confer rights of occupation and liability to pay the rent on both joint tenants. Again, security of tenure is preserved if just one of the joint tenants occupies the premises as his or her residence. Thus, where a joint tenant is deserted, he or she continues to have security and the right to remain.

10.78 However, where a partner who has left the accommodation, serves a notice to quit upon the local authority, it will terminate the periodic tenancy even though the partner wishes to remain: *Hammersmith and Fulham London Borough Council v Monk* (above). Thus a deserted joint tenant partner is in a vulnerable position. A remaining partner, having obtained the local authority's promise subsequently to grant a new tenancy, can himself or herself give notice to quit, but again the new tenancy is purely at the discretion of the landlord.

10.79 The only other option is to persuade the outgoing partner or the landlord to agree to an assignment or new tenancy before a notice is served. Advisors should be aware of the remaining partner's vulnerability and take preventative action where possible. It is thought that an injunction restraining the deserting partner from determining the tenancy may be possible. Alternatively, a s 33-occupation order excluding the deserting partner and allowing the remaining partner to enter and remain in the premises may have the desired effect, but problems of service on the deserting partner may arise. Arguably, if the local authority were given notice of the occupation or restraining order, this may persuade it to grant a new tenancy if a notice to quit were served in breach of either order. Once the notice has been served, all that can be done is to ask the council to grant the remaining partner a new tenancy—again a matter entirely within its discretion. Ironically, a cohabitant who would be entitled to succeed to the tenancy on death may have no right to remain in the property if deserted.

10.79A Where there is agreement, it had been thought that a the secure tenancy could be assigned to the remaining joint tenant cohabitant regardless of whether or not they were capable of being a statutory successor. Section 92 HA 1985 permits assignments to a person who would have succeeded to the tenancy on death, which, by operation of law, although not by inclusion in the list of statutory successors, includes a joint tenant, and security of tenure would be retained. This would then count as one succession on death, as discussed in Chapter 3 (see para ??). However, it is now clear that a secure joint tenancy cannot be assigned by one joint tenant to the other where the other would not be a statutory successor, such as an assignment to a same-sex former cohabitant. Assignment is only possible where the assignee joint tenant also falls within the statutory list of qualified successors set out in s 113 which defines "members of the family" who are permitted to succeed under s 87. In *Burton v Camden London Borough Council* [2000] 2 WLR 427 the House of Lords found (by a majority, with Millett LJ dissenting) that a deed of release by one joint tenant in favour of her friend, the other joint tenant who had moved elsewhere amounted to an assignment of the tenancy. This was held to be ineffective where the remaining joint tenant could not have succeeded to the tenancy as a member of the tenant's family, even though she would succeed as a surviving joint tenant on death. It is feared that an indemnity (as suggested above) may share a similar fate if challenged, which would often arise where the remaining same-sex cohabitant wished to claim housing benefit in the place of their former partner who had vacated the home. However, such a cohabitant would remain a secure joint tenant of the home. An assignment of this nature can still be achieved as between opposite-sex cohabitants who have lived together for at least 12 months, or in other cases where the local authority agree. In *Burton*, the local authority were not willing to agree to the arrangement as it would have left a single person occupying three-bedroomed accommodation; a drain on resources to which the House of Lords appeared sympathetic. Both parties would need to notifythe local authority, who may have a form for the purpose, although there is no reason why the assignment should not be achieved by means of a deed executed in accordance with s 52 LPA 1925 as long as any agreement by the local authority is annexed.

(b) Sole secure tenancies

10.80 Sole secure tenancies can be assigned between cohabitants by agreement, where permitted by the terms of the tenancy, but security of tenure will be retained only if, immediately before the assignment, the remaining partner could have succeeded to the tenancy on the death of the outgoing tenant partner. Thus, same-sex cohabitants who are not joint tenants cannot effect assignment of a secure tenancy, nor can they succeed on death as illustrated by *Harrogate Borough Council v Simpson* (above), although following *Fitzpatrick v Sterling Housing Association* (above) they can now succeed to a Rent Act tenancy as a member of the tenant cohabitant's family (but not as his or her cohabitant/spouse).

10.81 As discussed in Chapter 3 in the context of succession to tenancies on death, although a heterosexual cohabitant does not qualify as a "spouse" (in contrast to the wording in HA 1988 relating to assured tenancies), he or she comes within the definition of "a member of the tenant's family", but must satisfy the twelve-month residence qualification. In *Peabody Donation Fund Governors v Higgins* [1983] 1 WLR 1091, it was held that such an assignment was permissible even though the tenancy agreement contained an absolute covenant against assignment. Unfortunately, this provision does not permit assignment to a non-tenant cohabitant of the same sex, who cannot be regarded as a member of the tenant's family. The benefits of a joint tenancy in this situation are more than apparent.

10.82 It may be of assistance to see the respective legal positions of married, opposite- and same-sex cohabitants with regard to the rented family home set out in table form.

Cohabitants and the Rented Family Home

Married cohabitants	Opposite-sex cohabitants	Same-sex cohabitants
Automatic statutory occupation rights for non-tenant under s30 Family Law Act 1996	No automatic statutory occupation rights for non-tenant- s36 occupation order possible	No statutory occupation rights or occupation orders available to non-tenant
Non-tenant spouse succeeds on death to assured periodic tenancy	If living as husband and wife, succeed on death to assured periodic tenancy	Following *Fitzpatrick*, cannot live as husband and wife, no succession to assured periodic tenancy

Married cohabitants	Opposite-sex cohabitants	Same-sex cohabitants
Non-tenant spouse Succeeds on death to Rent Act protected tenancy	If living as husband and wife, non-tenant succeeds on death to Rent Act protected tenancy	Following *Fitzpatrick,* cannot live as husband and wife, no succession to Rent Act protected tenancy Can succeed as 'member of family' after 2 years cohabitation to less protected assured tenancy
Succeed on death to secure tenancy	Succeed as 'member of tenant's family' if lived with them as husband/wife for 12 months	Following *Harrogate Borough Council v Simpson* and *Fitzpatrick,* no succession to secure tenancy
Discretionary transfer of tenancy on breakdown – FLA 1996	Discretionary transfer of tenancy on breakdown - –FLA 1996	No transfer of tenancy on breakdown

10.83 CHECKLIST FOR DISPUTES CONCERNING THE RENTED FAMILY HOME

- Identify the tenant or tenants and the nature of the tenancy (secure, assured, assured shorthold, contractual or statutory Rent Act protected), asking for and examining any relevant documentation, such as written tenancy agreement, correspondence, notices served, rent book.

- Urgently consider whether an occupation order is appropriate where there is a sole tenancy or joint periodic tenancy which could be determined by the other partner or where there is a statutory tenancy which will cease to exist if not occupied by the tenant.

- Urgently consider whether, where in addition to or instead of an occupation order, other steps should be taken to preserve the tenancy pending hearing of transfer of tenancy application such as obtaining an injunction pursuant to FPR 1991, rr. 3.6(9), 3.8(14) restraining notice to quit being served.

- Where application for tenancy transfer is to be made/resisted under Sch 7 FLA 1996, take full statement of all relevant matters specified, including a history of the tenancy and of the cohabitation relationship, details of any relevant children, the relative suitability of the parties as tenants, their relative housing and financial needs and resources.

- Consider whether ancillary orders under para 11 to Sch 7 adjusting liabilities and obligations, eg in respect of rent arrears, are appropriate.

- Consider whether compensation could be sought or payable.

- Ensure applications and orders are served on landlord where appropriate.

Chapter 11

The home on relationship breakdown: owner-occupied property and other arrangements

1 Introduction

11.01 In contrast to the position of cohabitants in relation to the rented family home, where legislation (albeit imperfect) has recently been enacted, the legal position on relationship breakdown of cohabitants whose family home has been purchased by one or both of them is still currently under scrutiny by the Law Commission. Whilst both the Law Society's Family Law Committee and the Solicitors' Family Law Association (SFLA) have independently in the last two years both published their own proposals for reform of the cohabitation law, the Law Commission's long-awaited consultation on the reform of the law relating to shared ownership of property or "homesharing" is not now likely to be published until at least Spring 2002. Furthermore, it is widely predicted that the 10 minute rule Relationship (Civil Registration) Bill currently before Parliament will not be passed. Thus we are very unlikely to see the introduction of a partnership registration scheme to regulate cohabitants and their property in the near future. Therefore, unless and until the Law Commission publishes its proposals, and any recommendations it makes following the consultation process are, acted upon by Parliament, resolution of disputes between cohabitant co-owners on relationship breakdown remains very much a matter of property law rather than family law. This means that similar disputes concerning family assets including the owner-occupied family home are treated very differently by the law, depending on whether the family concerned is married or unmarried. What is more, given that recent legislative intervention has favoured drawing sharper distinctions between the treatment of married and unmarried couples in the context of domestic violence and occupation of the family home, accentuation upon a tiered regulation of family life privileging marriage may be extended rather than reversed in any proposals put forward by the Law Commission. Thus, reform may not mean mirroring the progressive approach of equating cohabitation with marriage in this sphere now found in other Commonwealth jurisdictions such as Canada and Australia.

11.02 There have, however, been significant reforms to the law of property as well as developments in the case law which affect how the courts deal with disputes relating to the owner-occupied family home arising between cohabitants on relationship breakdown. For the future, the Land Registration Bill 2001, currently before Parliament, will abolish Charge Certificates and unregistered land, radically change the caution and notice procedures and promote electronic conveyancing. The Trusts of Land and Appointment of Trustees Act 1996 (TLATA 1996), which came into force on 1 January 1997, has acted upon the reforms put forward by the Law Commission in their report *Transfer of Land: Trusts of Land* (Law Com No. 181 (1989)). It has abolished settled land for the future and effectively existing and future, express and implied trusts for sale as well. Both categories have been replaced by the by now familiar "trust of land", itself modelled on the old-style trust for sale. The fiction of the doctrine of conversion was also abolished (s 3). These reforms provided a new conveyancing regime for co-owners, who were given new powers as trustees (ss 6 and 7) and rights of occupation (s 12).

11.03 Of greatest significance in the context of this chapter was the repeal of s 30 Law of Property Act 1925, which gave the courts jurisdiction to order the immediate or postponed sale of beneficially jointly owned land held under a trust for sale. This has been replaced by s 14 TLATA 1996, which gives the court wider powers than to order or not order sale. Any trustee or beneficiary under a trust of land or any secured creditor of a beneficiary may apply to the court under s 14 for any such order as the court thinks fit relating to the exercise by the trustees of any of their functions or for a declaration as to the nature or extent of a person's interest in the property subject to the trust. This obviously gives the court a broader range of options for resolving disputes. Section 15 directs the court to statutory criteria relevant to determining applications which include the welfare of any child occupying the property, which is another innovation. The impact of these reforms on resolution of co-ownership disputes by the courts will be dealt with in more detail below. For present purposes it is sufficient to note that where, on breakdown of a cohabitation relationship, the preferable options of negotiation and agreement have failed, the courts have gained arguably enhanced powers to resolve litigated disputes between co-owner cohabitants.

11.04 Although the statutory basis for resolving disputes has changed, the determination of beneficial ownership of property is still governed by the law of trusts and this will remain the case after enactment of the Land Registration Bill 2001. Thus, although the court may have greater discretion as to what remedy to offer, and can, for example, postpone sale but order that an excluded co-owner be paid an occupation rent by an occupying co-owner, determination of their respective beneficial interests is still governed by the doctrines of express, implied, constructive and resulting trusts.

11.05 Thus, if there is a cohabitation contract in the form of a deed, dealing with beneficial ownership of the home and the division of property on breakdown, the courts will probably give effect to it, as discussed in Chapter 1. If there is a declaration of trust, either in the conveyance or in a separate document executed as a deed, setting out the beneficial interests, the courts will, in the absence of fraud or mistake, treat this as conclusive. With the possible exception of cases where there are children of the relationship, there will be little reason for the parties to go to court, as their interests will have been clearly defined. As home ownership continues to be an attractive option, financial considerations make it expedient for cohabiting couples to pool their resources and buy jointly; and legal advisors have a critical role to play in establishing at the outset a couple's intentions when they purchase the property and ensuring that the title deeds clearly reflect this. Not to do so is clearly negligent (see *Walker v Hall*, *Springette v Defoe* and *Taylor and Harman v Warner* discussed below). Whilst it is difficult for couples and their legal advisors to foresee every eventuality, it is perfectly possible for declarations of trust to establish beneficial interests contingent upon the size of future contributions to a mortgage, as well as to reflect unequal contributions to the capital deposit, requiring only arithmetical calculations to be made on breakdown to realise each party's share. Cohabitation contracts can also set out proposed agreements for the division of property on separation, and for the effect on the beneficial interests in the property of temporary inability of either party to contribute to the mortgage due. An example of a cohabitation contract can be found in Appendix I.

11.06 Where there is a declaration of trust or binding agreement relating to the beneficial ownership of the home, this does not of course prevent an application being made, where there are children, for a transfer of property order for the benefit of a child under para 1(2)(e), Sch 1 CA 1989. The jurisdiction of the court to order transfer of property cannot be ousted, but the property capable of transfer can at least be made readily identifiable by virtue of an express agreement between the parties and will save the court having to establish the interests for itself.

11.07 Where there is no conclusive express declaration of trust or cohabitation agreement relating to the cohabitants' beneficial interests, the rights of the respective parties on breakdown depend in the first instance on the legal and equitable ownership of the family home as established by the title deeds. However, these are subject to any resulting or constructive trusts, or claim to equitable proprietary estoppel, which a court deems to have been created by the parties in relation to the property. Thus where the parties have lived in a property of which the legal and equitable estate is on the face of it vested in the sole name of one of them, this is not necessarily conclusive. Conversely, unequal contributions to a property vested in joint names of the parties without further declaration as to their respective interests, may lead to a conclusive presumption that the property is beneficially owned in equal shares, although the most recent case law moves away from this position as discussed below. The rights of third parties, particularly mortgagees, are also likely to be significant on breakdown and steps to be taken in this regard must also be considered. The co-operation of the mortgagee is, of course, critical where there is a negative equity situation and a sale is sought.

11.08 However, the first task on breakdown is to establish the legal ownership of the family home. Secondly, any steps necessary to protect the client's interest in that property should be identified.

2 Establishing legal ownership

11.09 Most clients are aware of the details of ownership of the family home, but this is not always the case. Where the title is registered, a Land Registry search of any title, to discover the registered proprietor, can now be made by virtue of the provisions of the Land Registration Act 1988. If the title number is not known the search should be combined with an index map search. Indeed following the anticipated passing and implementation of the Land Registration Bill 2001 (LRB 2001), the Land Registry is to become the only source of information about a title, as charge certificates will be abolished and land certificates will be reduced to a short certificate of ownership not containing any details of the title.

11.10 If the mortgagee is known, it can, at present, be approached for details of ownership, or for the deeds, upon the usual undertaking as to safe custody and return, although the symbolic depositing of deeds with the mortgagee is no longer always a requirement, and will become completely redundant after the implementation of the provisions of the LRB 2001. Refusal to release the deeds would normally indicate either that the client is not a legal owner of the property, or that they have been released for another purpose. It is (and will remain so) usually a good idea to inform the mortgagee of a dispute between co-owners and to obtain its undertaking to give notice to the legal adviser before issuing any possession proceedings if there are mortgage arrears. Where the property is leasehold, enquiries should be made about any arrears of ground rent or service charges, and advice must be given in relation to the risk of forfeiture for non-payment.

11.11 The next stage will depend on whether or not the client cohabitant is a legal owner. Joint owners will be jointly and severally liable for payment of mortgage instalments and of ground rent and service charge due under a jointly owned lease, and it may be possible to claim JSA income support, or increased JSA income support, to cover these payments where the estranged co-owner is failing to do so. The property cannot be sold without the co-owner's consent or an order from the court. Beneficial joint tenants may also need to sever the joint tenancy, and another urgent enquiry will relate to the need to revise any Will that has been made.

11.12 Where the title documents reveal that the client's partner is the sole legal owner of the home, the client does not have the automatic protection of matrimonial home rights: rights of occupation of the matrimonial home afforded to spouses under s 30 FLA 1996. If this is the case, thought should be given to whether an occupation order under s 36 FLA 1996 should be applied for. This will, if granted, give a personal right of occupation and not one which may be protected by registration

11.13 If in actual occupation of the home, the absent partner is unlikely to be able to sell the property without the occupying partner's agreement. In the case of registered land, the occupying partner will have an overriding interest, which will bind a purchaser, but this cannot be protected by placing a caution on the register. However, it is for a purchaser to make enquiries of overriding interests (see *William & Glyn's Bank v Boland* (Chapter 3 above)). The LRB 2001 preserves actual occupation as an overriding interest but abolishes cautions. These are to be replaced with a system of consensual and non-consensual notices, one of which must be served on the registered proprietor. (Whilst not of direct relevance to cohabitants, it is perhaps of interest to note that notice of proposed registration of matrimonial homes rights is already, with effect from May 2001, given to registered proprietors as a matter of practice as it was feared that previous Land Registry practice was not Human Rights Act compliant (see [2001] *Fam Law* 414.)

11.14 Currently, in the case of unregistered land a person in actual occupation is in a more precarious situation, as it is not possible to register any land charge protecting occupation, yet only a purchaser with actual or constructive knowledge of the occupation will be bound. In *Caunce v Caunce* [1969] 1 WLR 286, occupation itself did not fix a purchaser with constructive notice of a wife's occupation and it seems that this would extend to other occupants. Actual occupation has been interpreted quite broadly. In *Kingsnorth Finance Ltd v Tizard* [1986] 1 WLR 783, a wife who no longer slept at the matrimonial home but attended every day to look after the children and had left many of her belongings there was held to be in actual occupation. In *Abbey National Building Society v Cann* [1991] 1 AC 56 at page 93, it was stated that what amounted to occupation was a question of fact but that the concept involved "some degree of permanence and continuity". Following implementation of the LRB 2001 reforms (which will greatly accelerate the disappearance of unregistered land and lead to its virtual demise (see Cooke, "The 2001 Land Registration Bill" [2001] *Fam Law* 753*),* whilst actual occupation will remain an overriding interest, it will not bind a purchaser unless the occupation is apparent on reasonable inspection of the property. Thus it will be in the interests of the proprietor to hide the existence of their cohabitant's actual occupation of the property and place non-owner cohabitants in a weakened position, although any interest they subsequently can be shown to have in the property would still be enforceable as against the proprietor who will normally then be in receipt of the proceeds of sale.

11.15 However, the cohabitant will have no claim against the home unless he or she can show some form of equitable interest under a resulting or constructive trust or due to the equitable doctrine of proprietary estoppel. Where a beneficial interest under a trust, including a resulting or constructive trust, can be shown, then s 12 TLATA 1996 now gives a right of occupation, as opposed to a mere interest in the proceeds of sale as was previously the case. Thus, although s 13 TLATA 1996 gives trustees the new right to restrict occupation by a beneficiary, these powers may not be exercised to oust any beneficiary already in occupation by virtue of s 12 or otherwise. Thus, where an informal trust has arisen between cohabitants in relation to the family home occupied by them both, the non-owning cohabitant will have both a right of occupation and protection from being excluded by use of the s 13 power. In practice, where there is a beneficial interest of a party who is no longer in actual occupation and the land is unregistered, it is usually advisable to issue proceedings under s 41 Trustee Act 1925 for the appointment of another trustee if the legal owner refuses to do so. Proceedings under s 14 TLATA 1996 can follow where appropriate.

11.16 As noted above, any trustee or beneficiary under a trust of land or any secured creditor of a beneficiary may apply to the court under s 14 for any such order as the court thinks fit relating to the exercise by the trustees of any of their functions or declaring the nature or extent of a person's interest in the property subject to the trust. Thus, where the extent of a cohabitant's beneficial interest is in dispute, either because they are not a legal owner or because no express trust was declared at the point of acquisition, this is the mechanism for ascertaining it. The court has far wider powers on such applications than was the case under s 30 LPA 1925. It is still possible to apply for an order for sale, where this cannot be agreed, and the new powers are also wide enough to include an order preventing sale or exercise of other powers by trustees. In addition, orders that a beneficiary occupying the property pay an occupation rent to a beneficiary out of occupation are within the court's powers, in contrast to the position under the old law. In making orders under s 14 (other than where the application is made by a trustee in bankruptcy, which is governed by s 335A Insolvency Act 1986), the court must have regard to the matters set out in s 15, which may be summarised as:

- the intentions of the person who created the trust;

- the purposes for which the property subject to the trust is held;

- the welfare of any minor who occupies or might reasonably be expected to occupy the property as their home; and

- the interests of any secured creditor of any beneficiary.

11.17 It is, however, clear from the wording of the section that this list is not exhaustive and other relevant factors may be taken into account where appropriate. The introduction of these criteria, although broadly reflecting the case law developed under s 30 LPA 1925 to discover the "collateral purpose" of the trust, can be seen to be particularly helpful in the family law context. Furthermore, the specified criteria which include the intentions of those creating the trust and the original purpose of the trust, which may often be to provide a family home, as well as an express direction to consider the welfare of any minor child who resides or may in the future reside in the property, arguably provide greater opportunity for a family law based approach to prevail. Nevertheless, there is no guidance on the relative priority that the court is to give to these factors. Thus if, as may often be the case, the interests of a secured creditor conflicts with the welfare of a child living in the property, whose interest will prevail? The Law Commission concluded that there was much of value in the existing case law under s 30 (Law Com No. 181, para 12.9) and in the case of *Re Citro (A Bankrupt)* [1991] Ch 142, the court took the view that the interests of the creditors should prevail, at least in a bankruptcy situation.

11.18 Some case law has now developed under the 1996 Act which appears to limit the availability of a "family home defence" against creditors seeking to repossess. In *Bank of Ireland Home Mortgages Ltd v Bell* noted at [2001] Fam Law 714, the Court of Appeal considered the impact of the new statutory criteria in s 15 of the 1996 Act. Here, it was held that the trial judge, who had refused to order the sale of the home, had failed to give due weight to the creditor's interest, had erred in referring to the property as a "family home" when the husband's departure had put an end to the purpose for which the property had been purchased. Furthermore, he had given undue weight to the occupation of a son who was almost 18 and the poor health of the wife. However, in *Mortgage Corporation v Shaire* [2000] 1 FLR 973, it was acknowledged that s 15 had changed the law and allows the court greater flexibility as to how to exercise its discretion on an application for sale. Whereas under the old law, there was no distinction between cases where the sale was sought by the trustee in bankruptcy and those where a mortgagee or chargee wished to sell, with the wishes of those wanting sale prevailing, s 15(4) indicated that a different approach applied in bankruptcy cases. The legislature intended to tip the balance somewhat more in favour of families and against banks and other chargees. Consequently on such an application for sale, the old authorities under s 30 had to be treated with caution.

11.19 Whenever s 14 proceedings are issued, a caution or land charge on the basis of a pending land action should immediately be lodged; this will give any purchaser actual notice of the non-owner's beneficial interest, achieving indirectly that which cannot be done directly. Where the land is registered, a beneficial interest can be protected as a minor interest by way of caution, restriction or notice and this should be done without delay where the non-legal owner is not in occupation. Any prospective purchaser on notice of the claim is unlikely to complete the purchase at least until the proceedings have been concluded. Under the LRB 2001, the mechanisms for protecting third party rights against a registered title will be simplified. All minor interests currently protected by caution or notice will be protected by a "notice on the register" and will no longer be known as minor interests. However, restrictions which flag a limitation in the registered proprietor's powers to dispose of the property will remain.

11.20 As will be seen, the courts have vacillated in their preparedness to use the law of trusts to intervene in disputes between former cohabitants relating to the family home. Recent decisions have unfortunately not added much clarity to the law in this area and the need for reform continues to be very apparent when the inconsistencies within the case law are examined (see below para 11.66 ff). Yet it is still fair to say that a non-owner cohabitant who does not have hard evidence of having made a monetary contribution to the purchase of a property has no guarantee of having earned an equitable interest in the property, no matter how long the period of cohabitation. The case law reveals that much depends on the individual circumstances and motivation for the arrangements between the parties. Legal advisors will therefore need, at an early stage, a comprehensive proof of evidence giving the history of the relationship; the stated intentions and contributions in money or money's worth of the parties; when the property was purchased or improved; and the cohabitants' periods of residence therein.

3 Joint legal ownership

11.21 Joint owners must hold a property as joint tenants of the legal estate, but as either joint tenants or tenants in common in equity. Normally, the conveyance or transfer contains a declaration of the beneficial interests. A declaration may be made subsequently or in a separate document providing it complies with the requirements of s 53 LPA 1925. In the absence of fraud or mistake, an express declaration by joint legal owners as to their respective beneficial interests in the property will be conclusive (see *Pettitt v Pettitt* [1970] AC 777; *Goodman v Gallant* [1986] 1 All ER 311). Normally, the beneficial interests will crystallise on purchase of the property in accordance with the express declaration and notwithstanding the actual contributions to the purchase price and can be altered only by proof of a subsequent express declaration or agreement. As indicated earlier, however, it is possible for a declaration to specifically provide that the parties' respective interests will crystallise at a later date and be calculated in accordance with stated criteria.

11.22 A joint owner must apply under s 14 TLATA 1996 for an order for sale, an order restraining sale, and/or a declaration as to the nature and extent of the beneficial interests in the family home where there is a dispute. There is unlimited county court jurisdiction for all s 14 claims. Proceedings are commenced in the county court by way of Part 8 claim form with supporting signed statement setting out the grounds for the application. Despite the court's wider powers under s 14 in the context of co-ownership disputes between cohabitants or former cohabitants, the court's role is likely to involve determining the respective beneficial interests of the parties in the home where these have not been clearly expressed or are subject to challenge. It must then decide, in accordance with the statutory criteria contained in s 15 (above), whether the home should be sold or prevented from being sold and the conditions upon which any order should be executed.

11.23 The starting point will be how the property is expressed to be held in the title documents. Following the implementation of TLATA 1996, conveyancing practice is likely to improve so that co-owners will be asked to express the purpose of the trust for land when they purchase. Thus, it should be becoming increasingly common for the fact that the property is the family home to be expressed in the conveyance or transfer, and this will be of great importance in any s 14 proceedings, as discussed below. Where there is an express declaration (which may be in writing or oral (see *Lloyds Bank PLC v Rosset* [1991] 1 AC 107, HL (below) and should in practice now be made or referred to on the Land Registry Transfer form as discussed in Chapter 3), the position is relatively straightforward. Where there is no declaration, the joint legal ownership will usually raise a strong presumption that the parties were each intended to be beneficially entitled, unless the property was put into joint names by mistake or for a completely different purpose (see for example *Thames Guaranty Ltd v Campell* [1985] QB 210).

11.24 Normally the court will look to the parties' contributions to establish their intention regarding their respective beneficial interests at the date of purchase (see for example the Court of Appeal decisions of *Bernard v Josephs* [1982] Ch 391 and *Walker v Hall* [1984] FLR 126). However, following the decision in *Huntingford v Hobbs* [1993] 1 FLR 736, it is highly inadvisable to rely upon a declaration on a registered land transfer that the survivor of joint purchasers can or cannot give a valid receipt for moneys arising on sale, to prove the existence of a beneficial joint tenancy or tenancy in common as appropriate. In this case, the Court of Appeal took the view that although the standard form declaration that the survivor could give a valid receipt was consistent with the existence of a beneficial joint tenancy, it was not a declaration of trust to this effect and would have been equally consistent with the parties holding the property on trust for a third party.

11.25 This contrasts with the earlier case of *Re Gorman* [1990] 2 FLR 284, CA, where a declaration that the transferees were "entitled to the land for their own benefit" and that the survivor could give a valid receipt for capital money arising on the disposition of the land, was held sufficient to constitute a declaration of a beneficial joint tenancy. Note, however, that in *Roy v Roy* [1996] 1 FLR 541, the Court of Appeal went so far as to give effect to an unsigned declaration of trust contained in a transfer indicating that the purchasers held as joint tenants in law and in equity. In practice and for the future, the Land Registration Rules in 1997 (see SI 1997/3037 rr 19 and 98) now require a statement on the Land Registry Transfer Form TR2 as to whether the property is held by the purchasers as joint tenants, tenants in common in equal shares or tenants in common in other specified shares, which should avoid uncertainty as to beneficial ownership.

11.26 Where it is clear that both co-owners are beneficially entitled, but the extent and nature of their respective interests is uncertain, the court will look at all the evidence available, including evidence of their intentions, to determine the nature and extent of the respective beneficial interests, before making a declaration under s 14 TLATA 1996. In so doing, the same principles will be applied as in the situation where the legal estate is vested in one person but the beneficial interests are shared as discussed below. These principles have also recently been most usefully summarised by Neuberger J in the case of *Mortgage Corpn v Shaire* [2000] 1 FLR 973, where the beneficial ownership of cohabitants who were the registered joint proprietors of a home who had failed to make any declaration as to their respective beneficial interests fell to be determined.

4 Joint tenants in equity

11.27 A declaration that co-owners hold property as beneficial joint tenants has the effect of attributing to each of them an identical interest in the whole of the land until the joint tenancy is severed. If the property is sold, that interest is transferred to the proceeds of sale and each joint owner will take one half. Severance of the joint tenancy can be effected by either joint tenant giving written notice to the other pursuant to s 36(2) LPA 1925 and they will then hold as beneficial tenants in common in equal shares, notwithstanding their actual contributions to the property, unless the original declaration specified that unequal shares would arise on severance (*Goodman v Gallant*, above). It should be noted that acting in a way inconsistent with a joint tenancy may also sever it without notice being served, as in *Ahmed v Kendrick* [1988] 2 FLR 22, which involved the unilateral sale of the property; and *Re Draper's Conveyance, Niham v Porter* [1969] 1 Ch 486, where the issuing of proceedings under s 30 LPA 1925 was deemed to be sufficient.

11.28 Another important effect of a beneficial joint tenancy is the right of survivorship whereby on the death of one joint tenant, the deceased's share of the property passes automatically to the surviving joint tenant. This contrasts with the position of beneficial tenants in common where the interest of the joint owner passes with his or her estate and not necessarily to the co-owner. In unregistered land, there will always be a declaration of the beneficial interest in the conveyance, and legal advisors must make enquiries, and give advice to their clients about the effect of a beneficial joint tenancy before completion of the transaction. Not to do so is negligent (*Walker v Hall* [1984] FLR 126) in both the registered and unregistered land context. Another case where the role of legal advisors has been held to be even more arduous is *Taylor and Harman v Warner* discussed at (1988) L Soc Gaz, vol 85, No 25, p 26. A woman entering her second marriage bought a farm with her new husband and she provided most of the purchase price. The property was put into joint names and, being registered, there was no express declaration of the beneficial interests, but the transfer did contain a declaration that the survivor of the joint purchasers could give a valid receipt for the property. When the woman died, her children by her first marriage believed her share of the farm would come to them under her will, but instead it passed to the husband by the right of survivorship. Warner J held that the solicitor who had explained the effect of joint tenancies and tenancies in common on purchase was negligent in that he had a duty to address his mind and the client's mind, to the source of the purchase money, and should have stressed that the joint tenancy would effectively disinherit the children.

11.29 Thus, cohabitants who have purchased as beneficial joint tenants where there is an express declaration, are entitled to the net proceeds of sale in equal shares. Difficulties arise where there is no declaration or no sufficient declaration of trust, as in a *Huntingford v Hobbs* (above) situation. In *Bernard v Josephs* (above) property was transferred jointly to cohabitants without any reference to the beneficial ownership. On relationship breakdown it was held that there was no automatic presumption that the parties held the property in equal shares, but the court decided it should look at the evidence to see whether it supported an intention of the parties to hold the property other than in equal shares. In that case, broadly equal contributions showed an intention to hold the property in equal shares.

11.30 The case law is to the effect that practitioners should make sure that clear advice is given concerning the implications of a beneficial joint tenancy and that instructions are followed. Clear advice at this stage will avoid both a finding of negligence, and, perhaps, a dispute between co-owners on subsequent breakdown of their relationship, where only in limited circumstances will it be possible to avoid the effects of an express declaration. Indeed, it is arguable that, in the cohabitation context, it is almost never appropriate for co-owners to create an equitable joint tenancy without providing for the shares that are to arise on severance or at least the mechanism by which such shares are to be calculated. Where clear instructions are given to create an equitable joint tenancy, the practitioner must ensure that both clients understand that this will result in them sharing the equity equally, however much their situation and contributions change. This advice is best given in writing to each of the co-owners and consideration should be given as to whether they should be separately advised.

11.31 When consulted on breakdown, the effect of severance of the joint tenancy must be explored and explained immediately. It may be that a declaration has been made providing for the property to be held on severance as tenants in common in unequal shares; this was specifically regarded as a possibility in *Goodman v Gallant* (above). Usually, severance will be appropriate, as it will mean that the right of survivorship will cease to apply, which will accord with the wishes of most (but not all) clients on breakdown. However, although the shares of the property will no longer pass automatically to the co-owner on death, conversely, in the absence of a Will in favour of the co-owner, his or her share of the home will also devolve elsewhere.

11.32 Instructions should also be taken with regard to the need for new Wills.

5 Tenants in common in equity

11.33 Although the legal estate must be held by co-owners as joint tenants, the beneficial interests may be held as tenants in common. The effect of this is that the co-owners each have a specified share in the equity, usually determined at the date of purchase. Such share does not pass automatically to the co-owner on death, but instead devolves to the beneficiaries of the estate. Thus, if a co-owner who holds as tenant in common wishes to leave his or her share of the home to his/her cohabitant on death, it is necessary to make a Will to that effect, as the cohabitant would not benefit on intestacy.

11.34 A tenancy in common is particularly appropriate where there have been unequal contributions to the purchase price and where the joint owners wish to preserve their interests in the property in unequal shares, although a tenancy in common can, if required, specify that the shares are held equally. A situation where parties must be advised particularly carefully about a declaration of trust and the quantification of their beneficial interest is where a property is purchased under the "right to buy" scheme. In the cohabitation context, it is common to find one partner's contribution to be capital mainly in the form of a substantial discount awarded by virtue of their having been a local authority tenant for some years, and the other co-owner's contribution taking the form of some or all of the mortgagable income. This was the situation in *Springette v Defoe* [1992] 2 FLR 388, where solicitors were roundly criticised by the Court of Appeal for having transferred the property to the couple jointly without even having taken any instructions in relation to their beneficial interests, let alone having advised them to make a declaration of trust. This is undoubtedly a breach of a solicitor's professional duty to their client. In this case the court used resulting trust principles to establish the parties' respective interests in the property in accordance with their capital and mortgage contributions. Furthermore, a solicitor who, in a conveyance, declares a beneficial tenancy in common but does not go on to specify the shares is negligent (*Walker v Hall*, above). Once a declaration as to the beneficial interests has been made, it is again conclusive, in the absence of fraud, mistake or a subsequent express agreement.

11.35 Thus, if cohabitants on purchase declare that they hold the property beneficially as tenants in common in shares of three quarters to one quarter, on breakdown of the relationship when the property is sold, the net proceeds of sale will be divided in these proportions. If, before breakdown of the relationship, one partner has paid for or undertaken improvements to the property, in the absence of express agreement to the contrary, this does not alter the beneficial interests in the property and the proceeds of sale will still be divided according to the original ratio, although there may be some scope for a claim for compensation for expenses incurred (see *Re Pavlou (a bankrupt)* [1993] 1 WLR 1046). It is therefore necessary to advise joint purchasers to consider making a fresh declaration of trust if future contributions render their original agreement unfair. Alternatively a clause could, and arguably should, be inserted in the original declaration providing for this and other contingencies such as revised contributions to any joint mortgage. Recent case law has recognised that, in practice, where there is no express agreement but a clear intention to share a property beneficially, the real intention of the parties (certainly in the married context) is not to quantify their respective interests on acquisition, but to wait and see what contributions, direct and indirect, have been made, and determine their beneficial shares at the end of the mortgage term or on disposition of the property (see *Passee v Passee* [1988] 1 FLR 263 and *Midland Bank plc v Cooke* [1996] 1 FCR 442). It is submitted that such an approach is often mirrored in the cohabitation context. However, given that the pooling of resources on this basis is perhaps not so readily recognised as between cohabitants, particularly in terms of indirect contributions to a household being translated into beneficial ownership of the family home (see *Burns v Burns* [1984] Ch 317, below), a declaration of trust recognising the true flexibility of the agreement between the parties and setting out the ground rules that are agreed for establishing each partner's share of the equity is all the more essential and should be entered into, if true effect is to be given to these common intentions.

6 Fraud or mistake

11.36 An express declaration as to the beneficial ownership is conclusive in the absence of fraud or mistake. If it was induced by fraud, it will be set aside. If it was entered into as a result of a mistake in that it fails to reflect the parties' common intentions, rectification may be sought, although this will not be granted where it would prejudice a *bona fide* purchaser for value who was not on notice of the mistake. In *City of London Building Society v Flegg* [1988] AC 54, HL, it was held that an express declaration by purchasers that they held as beneficial joint tenants was not conclusive where their parents had contributed to the purchase price with the intention that they should retain a beneficial interest.

7 Quantification of shares on breakdown

11.37 Whether co-owners hold the home as joint tenants or tenants in common in equity, once the appropriate share due to each has been established, an arithmetical calculation is necessary to translate this into the correct share of the proceeds of sale. It may well be that on breakdown the property is not actually sold, but rather one co-owner buys the former partner and co-owner's share, but the principles remain the same. Whether or not the property is sold, it is still necessary to establish the correct method of quantifying the share in cash terms. Where there is no mortgage, the calculation is often simple. The net proceeds of sale are the sale price, less the costs incidental to the sale such as estate agents' fees and legal costs. The balance is then divided in accordance with the established shares of the equity. Alternatively, it is possible to divide the gross proceeds of sale between the co-owners in the agreed ratio, each paying towards the incidental costs in the same proportions out of their share of the proceeds of sale. In fact the same figure will be arrived at, but as a matter of practice, the net proceeds of sale are usually taken as the total equity available for distribution and the courts have tended to follow this method.

11.38 Where the property is subject to a mortgage the situation may be less straightforward. As Sparkes (1991) has highlighted in relation to establishing beneficial ownership in the absence of an express declaration, there has been no specific investigation by the courts of the correct method of quantifying interests arising from contributions by way of mortgage, despite the frequency with which properties are purchased in this way. Should the proportions arrived at be assessed in relation to the net equity after the outstanding mortgage as well as costs incidental to the sale have been deducted from the proceeds of sale? Or should they be assessed in relation to the gross proceeds of sale and the mortgage redemption figure be deducted proportionately from each party's share? Where a separate declaration of trust or a cohabitation contract has been entered into, that document should provide the answer.

11.39 Where there is only a simple declaration of beneficial ownership in the conveyance, the situation may not be clear, particularly if one party has contributed mainly to the deposit and the other chiefly by capital borrowed on mortgage. Where each party has contributed consistent proportions to both the capital and mortgage repayments, then either method of calculation will achieve the same result, as was the case in *Bernard v Josephs* (above). However, this is not the case where the proportions contributed to capital and mortgage are not consistent, and the most anomalous situation is where these proportionate contributions are inverted.

11.40 There seems to be no single correct approach, as much will depend on whether or not the parties contributed to the deposit and/or mortgage equally, with the result that legal advisors need to press for the method which is most advantageous to their client, or that which can be recommended as the fairest in all the circumstances. Where one party has contributed by way of capital and the other by way of mortgage, assessment of the shares from the net, rather than the gross, proceeds of sale can produce inequitable results. In this situation, it is fairer to deduct the shares from the gross proceeds of sale and to deduct the mortgage solely from the share of the party whose contribution was by way of mortgage.

11.41 Where there is an endowment mortgage payments of interest only will have been made to the mortgagee, with premiums being paid under a policy which guarantees to repay the capital borrowed under the mortgage at the end of the term, or on death. On breakdown, the sum needed to redeem the mortgage will be greater than the policy will then provide, although there will usually be a surrender value of a joint endowment policy which needs to be taken into account. It may be possible for each party to transfer the accrued benefits to new policies in sole names, or the policy may be surrendered. Where the mortgage is in joint names and the parties have contributed to both the payment of interest to the mortgagee and to the endowment policy premiums, the surrender value should normally be divided in accordance with the contributions to the policy. It should perhaps be noted here that there is now a second-hand market for endowment policies which were taken out at least ten years ago. This can sometimes boost the proceeds to be divided between cohabitants and may be of particular assistance in a negative equity situation.

11.42 The date for valuation of the shares and calculation of the sums due out of the proceeds of sale presents another problem. Where there is an express trust the shares will be valued at the date of acquisition of the property, but following breakdown the date on which the sum to be paid over is calculated, should be the date of realisation, that is, the date of sale or deemed sale, and not the date of separation. This was established in *Turton v Turton* [1988] Ch 542. When house prices are the subject of rapid increases, or indeed decreases, the date of calculation of the shares in the proceeds of sale can make an enormous difference and this should be borne in mind when negotiations take place or valuations are agreed.

11.43 In view of this approach, both parties may be expected to contribute to the cost of repairs, improvements and mortgage repayments until sale. Where one party has failed to contribute after separation, the sums payable will be adjusted to reflect it, and this process is known as equitable accounting. In *Bernard v Josephs* (above), equitable accounting was employed to make a fair adjustment in the light of contributions after the date of separation. In that case one half of the mortgage repayments was held to be a fair monetary allowance. Furthermore, in some situations, it has been held where one co-owner is involuntarily no longer in occupation of the home and the former partner thereby has the sole benefit of occupation of the property but is making the whole of the mortgage repayments, that these payments are balanced by an "occupation rent payable to the absent co-owner. This was also considered in *Bernard v Josephs* (per Kerr LJ). Given that s 13 TLATA 1996 specifically gives trustees the power to make a beneficiary in occupation make compensation payments to an excluded beneficiary, an occupation rent provision could undoubtedly be attached to any order made in proceedings under s 14 TLATA 1996 (which enables the court to make any order in relation to any of the functions of the trustees) certainly pending sale of the property. Similarly, where an occupation order is obtained pursuant to ss 33 or 36 FLA 1996, an order that an occupation rent be paid is also a possibility by virtue of s 40(1)(b) of that Act.

11.44 As Sparkes (see above) details, case law is inconsistent as to whether this principle should apply to a co-owner who has left his or her partner (see *Cracknell v Cracknell* [1971] P 356; *Eves v Eves* [1975] 1 WLR 1338 and *Dennis v McDonald* [1981] 1 WLR 810). It seems where a co-owner continues to have the right of occupation and has left voluntarily, occupation rent is not appropriate (*Jones v*

Jones [1977] 1 WLR 438). Interest, but not capital payments, under a mortgage were held to be paid as equivalent to occupation rent in *Suttill v Graham* [1977] 1 WLR 819. Unfortunately, the opportunity to fully consider the conflicting existing authorities was missed in the most recent decision of *Re Pavlou (A Bankrupt)* [1993] 2 FLR 751. This case did make it clear that co-owners must account to each other for any increase in value of the property brought about by expenditure of just one of them after separation, and thus payment for improvements or capital payments on mortgage instalments which reduce the mortgage debt and increase the equity must be credited to the party who made the payments. The position relating to payment of mortgage interest and its relationship to whether this equates with the payment of an occupational rent is less clear. The starting point is that a co-owner is entitled to occupy the property and if he or she chooses not to do so this should not affect their rights and liabilities. Thus, ostensibly, they remain liable for half the interest and capital payments on a joint mortgage, but conversely could return to the home at any point. If, on the other hand, they were excluded by the other co-owner, it would normally be equitable that they should be entitled to an occupation rent, often assessed in practice as half the mortgage interest payments. This places great importance on the issue of whether or not a party was excluded. In contrast to *Suttill v Graham* (above), the court in *Re Pavlou* seemed to favour a broad examination of the parties' conduct premised upon the starting point that no occupation rent will normally be payable. However, it was also stated that the ultimate test is what is fair and equitable and thus, arguably, a co-owner who has voluntarily left and would be welcomed back to the family home would be unlikely to be awarded an occupation rent.

11.45 If the approach in *Turton v Turton* (above) is followed, and the respective interests are valued at the date of realisation, adverse effects of house price increases or decreases will be minimised for both parties. This will not avoid the need for equitable accounting in relation to events following separation even though the actual valuation of the shares will not take place until realisation. Issues of payment of subsequent mortgage instalments, or improvements and occupation rent, remain relevant and need to be assessed to determine the actual sum payable on realisation.

8 Sole legal ownership

11.46 It is where the home is owned by one partner alone that the most difficulty on the breakdown of relationships between cohabitants arises, and it is here that the non-owner partner must rely on the law of trusts or the doctrine of proprietary estoppel if they are to establish any equitable interest in the home. For a recent and very useful summary of the principles used by the courts to ascertain the respective beneficial interests of two persons who are living in a house together see the judgment of Neuberger J *Mortgage Corpn v Shaire* [2000] 1 FLR 973.

11.47 Where a property is purchased in the sole name of one partner during the currency of the relationship, or where one partner moves into a property which was purchased by the other previously, on breakdown of the relationship, the non-owner partner is in a vulnerable position.

11.48 No rights of occupation accrue to a non-owner cohabitant unless they can either establish a beneficial interest under an express trust or more usually a resulting, implied or constructive trust as recognised by s 53(2) LPA 1925, in which case s 12 TLATA 1996 grants them occupation rights; or alternatively following the introduction of Part IV FLA 1996, they obtain a s 36 occupation order. If granted, the latter would obviously afford them protection from exclusion for up to six months in the first instance and could be renewed only once for a further six-month period maximum. This option should now be considered in all cases where exclusion is a possibility, as the FLA 1996 remedy is not premised upon the need for a violent situation to exist before such an order is made and it may offer a vital emergency remedy pending collation of evidence needed for s 14 TLATA 1996 proceedings. Particularly where prevention from exclusion alone is sought, the nature of the cohabitation relationship has been fairly long-term and stable and particularly where there are children, it seems likely that the courts will be prepared to preserve occupation of the family home in this way, pending final resolution of other issues between the parties. Where s 14 TLATA 1996 proceedings are to be issued with a view to establishing a beneficial interest in the property, and there is strong *prima facie* evidence of the existence of a resulting or constructive trust, it may be possible to secure occupation for the non-legal owner cohabitant by obtaining an interlocutory order or an undertaking from the legal owner cohabitant preventing them excluding their partner or former partner. The strategy adopted will depend on the quality of the evidence to hand, the nature of the cohabitation relationship and the existence of any relevant children, the availability of public funding for either course of action where appropriate and consideration of the effects of the statutory charge.

11.49 In terms of establishing beneficial ownership, there must either be an express trust or evidence sufficient to convince the court that a resulting or constructive trust has been created. Once again recent case law has arguably caused further confusion in relation to the principles applied to resulting trusts. Indeed, a partial return to the flexibility and uncertainty of the Lord Denning era is thought by some to have occurred, as discussed below.

(a) Express trusts

11.50 If on purchasing or moving to a property, the sole legal owner makes a valid express declaration of trust that he or she holds the property beneficially for himself or herself and for their partner, then the parties' respective shares on breakdown of the relationship will be determined in accordance with that express declaration, which will be conclusive as has already been discussed in the context of joint legal owners. For the declaration to be valid, it must conform to the requirements of s 53(1)(b) LPA 1925, but any written agreement will be evidence of the parties' intentions at the date of acquisition and may be of great significance where a party is attempting to show a common intention as to the beneficial ownership of the property.

(b) Resulting, implied and constructive trusts

11.51 Case law is still in the process of clarifying the distinctions between the effects of the above types of trust, which, in contrast to express trusts, arise without being evidenced in writing. It seems that these trusts break down into two rather than three categories and although the term "implied trust" has on occasions been used, it is necessary to explain and distinguish between resulting and constructive trusts. It is perhaps crucial to note here that there are two important stages in ascertaining the effects of both resulting and constructive trusts. Firstly, the court has to establish through the finding of a common intention (presumed, actual or imputed) that a non-legal owner does have a beneficial interest; and secondly, it must go on to quantify that interest (see generally Wragg, "Constructive Trusts and the Unmarried Couple" [1996] Fam Law 484). It is in this second stage of quantification that we have witnessed a recent shift in the approach of the Court of Appeal, beginning with the case of *Midland Bank plc v Cooke* (above), as will be considered below.

(i) Resulting trusts

11.52 Traditionally a resulting trust gives effect to the parties' presumed common intention at the date the property was acquired. It will arise where a non legal owner contributes in money or money's worth to the purchase of the property which will be held on trust in shares relative to their contributions. Equity presumes that where two parties contribute to the purchase that they intend to share the property beneficially in proportion to their contributions, although such a presumption can be rebutted by proof that the contribution was intended as a loan, a gift or rent. The presumption of advancement applies to gifts by a husband to a wife or by a fiancée (although not by gifts made in the reverse direction). It may therefore apply to heterosexual cohabitants who were engaged to be married at the time the property was purchased in the sole name of the man, however, and this may override the presumption of a resulting trust.

11.53 In *Sekhon v Alissa* [1989] 2 FLR 94, Ch D, the presumption of a resulting trust had not been rebutted where a mother had contributed £22,500 to her daughter's purchase of a house as there was no evidence that it was intended as a gift or a loan. Another example is *Richards v Dove* [1974] 1 All ER 888, Ch D, where a woman's contribution to a deposit was held to have been intended as a loan.

11.54 Application of the resulting trust principle can be seen in *Springette v Defoe* (above). Here middle-aged cohabitants purchased the council flat of which the woman had been a tenant for some eleven years. Her contribution, comprising her right to buy discount, some capital and half the mortgage liability amounted to 75% of the total purchase price, whereas the man's contribution which was in effect his share of the mortgage liability alone, amounted to 25%. In the absence of any other communicated common intention that the proceeds of sale should be divided differently, their respective shares were assessed at 75% and 25% in accordance with their contributions on resulting trust principles.

11.55 Similarly, in *Tinsley v Milligan* [1994] 1 AC 340, resulting trust principles were applied to the shares of a house jointly paid for but placed in the sole name of one of them by gay cohabitants intending to run a bed and breakfast business. Despite the fact that the property was placed in the sole name of Ms Tinsley with the illegal motive of enabling Ms Milligan to claim means-tested welfare benefits, this did not prevent the House of Lords from holding that she was entitled to a share of the equity proportionate to her direct contributions to the purchase price by virtue of a resulting trust and did not have to rely upon the illegal purpose to establish her claim.

11.56 Where the contribution has been made in money, and providing resulting trust principles are applied to quantification, and not constructive trust principles based on an actual or imputed common intention to share the property in different proportions to those derived from the monetary contributions (as happened in *Midland Bank plc v Cooke*), the valuation of the respective shares is relatively simple. However, the problem of quantification where there are disproportionate contributions to the capital and mortgage with which a purchase was effected, as discussed above, may also feature here.

11.57 Further difficulties arise where it is alleged that the contribution was made in money's worth rather than money. The courts themselves can be seen to have blurred the distinction between resulting and constructive trusts in that in some cases actual physical work by a non-owner partner which has improved the property has been held to give rise to a resulting trust, whilst in others it has been considered only as conduct relevant to establishing whether or not the requisite intention for a constructive trust was present. The case law is considered below.

(ii) Constructive trusts

11.58 Constructive trusts similarly depend on a common intention; although here the common intention is not *presumed* but may be the actual or imputed common intention of the parties. Establishing a common intention is only the first stage in identifying a constructive trust, as further elements are also required to be present for the court to find that a constructive trust has arisen.

11.59 A clear exposition on the first stage of identifying constructive trusts is found in the judgment of Mustill LJ in the Court of Appeal decision of *Grant v Edwards* [1986] Ch 638 at page 652. He set out four situations on acquisition (or later in appropriate circumstances) which could give rise to a common intention constructive trust, providing the non-owner claimant subsequently conducted himself or herself in a manner which was both to his/her detriment and referable to the promise of common intention established on acquisition:

> "(a) An express bargain whereby the proprietor promises the claimant an interest in the property in return for an explicit undertaking of the claimant to act in a certain way.
> (b) An express but incomplete bargain whereby the proprietor promises the claimant an interest in the property, on the basis that the claimant will do something in return. The parties do not themselves make explicit what the claimant is to do. The court therefore has

to complete the bargain for them by means of implication, when it comes to decide whether the proprietor's promise has been matched by conduct falling within whatever undertaking the claimant must be taken to have given *sub silento*.

(c) An explicit promise by the proprietor that the claimant will have an interest in the property unaccompanied by any express or tacit agreement as to a *quid pro quo*.

(d) A common intention not made explicit to the effect that the claimant will have an interest in the property, if she subsequently acts in a particular way."

11.60 In situations (a), (b) and (d), once the non-legal owner acts in a way which is to his or her detriment and is referable to the legal owner's promise, in that it can be explained only by a belief that they had a beneficial interest in the property, the bargain is complete and a beneficial interest is established. The court must then go on to quantify the non legal owner's share of the equity. In situation (c), the position is still not clear, although in *Gissing v Gissing* [1971] AC 886, Diplock LJ stated *obiter* that if this category of claimant had acted to his/her detriment in reliance on such a promise, a beneficial interest would thereby be conferred.

11.61 In *Lloyds Bank plc v Rosset* [1991] 1 AC 107, HL (discussed below) Lord Bridge drew attention to a critical distinction between an express common intention based on evidence of express discussions between the parties, and an inferred common intention based on conduct. In the former situation, he stated:

". . . it will only be necessary for the partner asserting a claim to a beneficial interest against the partner entitled to the legal estate to show that he or she acted to his or her detriment or significantly altered his or her position in reliance on the agreement in order to give rise to a constructive trust or proprietary estoppel."

In the latter situation, he went on:

". . . direct contributions to the purchase price by the partner who is not the legal owner, whether initially or by payment of mortgage instalments, will readily justify the inference necessary to the creation of a constructive trust. But as I read the authorities, it is at least extremely doubtful whether anything less will do."

11.62 This strict approach to the first stage of establishing a common intention to share the beneficial interests and thereby evidence the existence of a constructive trust is still good law. However the issue of what, if anything else, may amount to direct contributions has again resurfaced following the recent and controversial Family Division decision of *Le Foe v Le Foe and Woolwich plc; Woolwich plc v Le Foe and Le Foe* [2001] 2 FLR 970 (discussed below). Here the court managed to gloss over the need for a direct financial contribution to the purchase price in order to establish a common intention constructive trust, and is already subject to criticism (see comment by Professor Bailey Harris at [2001] Fam Law 740). However, whereas it had been thought that this last category (where there has been a direct contribution) may in any event fall within the definition of a presumed resulting trust by virtue of a monetary contribution on acquisition of the property, unless the presumption can be rebutted, a series of Court of Appeal decisions culminating in *Midland Bank plc v Cooke* [1995] 2 FLR 915 and *Drake v Whip* [1996] 1 FLR 826 have introduced a second stage in which a broad brush approach may be taken to *quantification* of the beneficial interests under a constructive trust. This new two-stage approach has been followed in subsequent cases, and thus quantification of interests in accordance with resulting trust principles seem to have become limited to situations where there is evidence of an express agreement so to do, as discussed further below.

11.63 The application of the principles established in *Rosset* governing the first stage of establishing a common intention can be well illustrated by the case of *Hammond v Mitchell* [1991] 1 WLR 1127. Here cohabitants who had lived together for eleven years and had two children were in dispute relating to assets including a property in England which had been the family home and a property in Spain, both of which had been purchased in the sole name of Mr Hammond. In relation to the English property, the court accepted Ms Mitchell's account of two conversations as evidence of an express agreement that the property should be shared beneficially and that agreement was held to apply to various extensions they had built on the property and additional adjacent land they subsequently purchased. It was accepted that Mr Hammond had claimed the house had been put in his name for tax reasons and told her not to worry as when they were married it would be half Ms Mitchell's. He had also assured her that he would always look after her and their son. Her detrimental acts relying on this agreement took the form of her "contribution as mother/helper/unpaid assistant and at times financial supporter to the family prosperity" and entitled her to a half share in the equity of the English property in the court's view. In relation to the Spanish property, however, there were no express discussions as to shared beneficial ownership and again no direct financial contributions had been made by her. She thus attempted to show that by reason of the parties' whole course of dealing an intention to share beneficial ownership became apparent. However, the court found that:

> "Useful at times though her activities may have been in Spain, . . . Miss Mitchell's activities generally fell a long way short of justifying any inference of intended proprietary interest." (per Waite J at page 1138)

11.64 A common intention to share the beneficial ownership without a written declaration of trust, and in the absence of any detrimental conduct or contribution to the purchase price, will not be enough to give a non-legal owner a beneficial interest, as was the case in *Midland Bank plc v Dobson* [1986] 1 FLR 171, CA.

11 65 Apart from common intention or a promise by the legal owner, the relevant factors needed to establish shared beneficial ownership comprise acts which are detrimental to the claimant, although there are no set rules about the nature and degree of detriment required; and a causal link between the common intention or promise and the detrimental act. It is felt that the best way to assess the impact of these additional requirements is to attempt a review in summary of the case law. Factors relevant to establishing common intention will also be considered, although it should be recognised that there are issues yet to be comprehensively defined by the courts.

(c) The case law

(i) Common intention

11.66 In the case of *Cooke v Head* [1972] 1 WLR 518, the Court of Appeal, headed by Lord Denning, agreed unanimously that Ms Cooke was entitled to a beneficial interest amounting to one third of the proceeds of sale. The facts of the case were that the parties who, it was accepted, had an intention to marry, purchased a plot of land in Mr Head's sole name. Ms Cooke then assisted him in building a bungalow on the land which was intended to be the family home. She assisted him by way of hard physical labour, which impressed the court as work over and above that which was expected of a wife, and she assisted in the mortgage repayments which were made from their pooled resources. Before the parties moved into the property the relationship broke down and Ms Cooke claimed a beneficial interest. Lord Denning asserted, without attempting to clarify the distinction between the different types of trust, ". . . Whenever two parties by their joint efforts acquire property for their joint benefit, the courts may impose or impute a constructive or resulting trust."

11.67 In this case there was an express common intention which gave rise either to a presumed resulting trust consequent upon Ms Cooke's contribution to the acquisition of the property in both money and money's worth, or a constructive trust whereby the beneficial interest was established by Ms Cooke's acting to her detriment, as evidenced by her labour and monetary contribution on the basis of the common intention.

11.68 This case can be directly contrasted with the more recent Court of Appeal decision in *Thomas v Fuller-Brown* [1988] 1 FLR 237. Here, the parties lived together in a house purchased in the sole name of the woman without any financial contribution from the man claimant whom she supported. However, she subsequently obtained an improvement grant and she agreed that the man, who was unemployed but skilled in building work, should carry out the necessary repair and improvement works in return for her providing him with accommodation and his keep plus "pocket money". The work involved was of a substantial nature but shortly after it was completed the relationship broke down. The Court of Appeal upheld the trial judge's decision that on the facts the only reasonable inference was not that the parties intended joint beneficial ownership. On the contrary, it was accepted that she had never led him to believe that he would acquire an interest in the property and accordingly he remained no more than her licensee. The woman's explanation of the arrangement was preferred and neither a resulting nor a constructive trust was imputed. These two cases also illustrate the difficulty of establishing an indirect contribution to the acquisition of a property.

11.69 The Court of Appeal decisions of *Eves v Eves* [1975] 1 WLR 1338 and *Grant v Edwards* (above) can also be contrasted with *Thomas v Fuller-Brown*. In both these cases, the women cohabitants were misled by their partners about why the family home had not been purchased in joint names. In *Eves*, the man told her that she was too young to appear on the title of the property which was not true. She subsequently carried out repair works and improvements to the house to prepare it for joint occupation but then the relationship broke down. The court unanimously held that she was entitled to a quarter of the equity, but Lord Denning differed in his reasoning from the other two members of the court. He felt that the court had power to impose a constructive trust regardless of the presence or absence of a common intention to share the beneficial ownership. However, the majority of the court considered that the woman's work on the property could be explained only by a common intention that she had a beneficial interest in the property. Her conduct evidenced both the common intention and her contribution in money's worth and thus the property was held on a resulting trust.

11.70 More recent cases, with the possible exception of the complex and questionable case of *Le Foe v Le Foe and Woolwich plc; Woolwich plc v Le Foe and Le Foe* [2001] 2 FLR 970 discussed further below, have not adopted Lord Denning's approach of imposing a trust which will produce an equitable result. Although, as will be seen, following a return to a more orthodox trust law approach in order to determine common intention for the purpose of deciding whether or not a constructive trust exists (the first stage), a broad-brush approach with regard to the quantification of the actual beneficial interests in a second stage has emerged in recent decisions, as noted above. As shall be seen, this in practice means that although the first stage is still governed by the strict trust law approach set out by Lord Bridge in *Lloyds Bank v Rosset* (below), any beneficial co-owner who gets over this hurdle is, following *Midland Bank plc v Cooke, Mortgage Corpn v Shaire* and *Drake v Whip* (discussed below), now afforded greater flexibility in the matters which the courts are prepared to take into account in determining the extent of their share.

11.71 In *Grant v Edwards* the parties lived together and had a child. The man purchased a property in the name of himself and his brother (whom it was accepted, had no beneficial interest in the property). The man told his partner that the reason the property was not bought in their joint names was to avoid complications in relation to the matrimonial proceedings in which she was involved at that time. The court held that this ostensible reason raised the clear inference of a common intention that the woman should have an interest in the house. She subsequently contributed to the household and mortgage expenses in a substantial way, and without such a contribution the man could not have afforded to purchase the house. Accordingly, she had acted to her detriment in an appropriate way and a constructive trust was found to exist under which she was beneficially entitled to a half interest in the property. It is questionable whether the deceptions in both *Eves* and *Grant v Edwards* could realistically be evidence of a common intention to share beneficial ownership. Indeed, the men in both cases were attempting to avoid beneficial joint ownership. Their conduct, particularly in the light of the subsequent detrimental acts of their partners, was clearly inequitable and justified the court's intervention. It is submitted that the courts are in this type of situation readier to follow Lord Denning's approach.

11.72 However, a common intention is not always easy to establish. In *Howard v Jones* [1989] Fam Law 231, a man who was cohabiting with a woman purchased a property in his sole name whilst they continued to live in rented accommodation.

She maintained that her payment for most of the household expenses enabled the man to purchase the property but the Court of Appeal found that she had no beneficial interest as she had failed to establish any common intention. In *Windeler v Whitehall* [1990] 2 FLR 505, Ch D, Millet J held that a woman cohabitant who had contributed nothing to the acquisition of the property but had lived with the defendant for six years, during which period she did not work and was supported by the man, could not establish a common intention that she was to have a beneficial interest by virtue of the man's having previously left the property to her in his Will. There was no evidence that she had been led to believe that whatever happened she would inherit the property, or that she did believe this. The Court of Appeal decision in *Ivin v Blake* [1995] 1 FLR 70 seems to go as far as to say that in the absence of any express agreement or assurance from the legal owner, indirect contributions such as a daughter working unpaid in her mother's business in order to buy a family home, can never found an intention to share a property beneficially; only direct contributions will do.

11.73 Obviously, direct financial contributions are one means by which it is possible to establish a common intention through conduct. In both *Midland Bank plc v Cooke* (above) and *McHardy v Warren* [1994] 2 FLR 338, a joint wedding present of a small deposit paid on the matrimonial home by a parent was sufficient to establish a common intention to share the property beneficially. Furthermore, in *Halifax Building Society v Brown* [1996] 1 FLR 103, even a loan by a parent to a couple to pay the deposit on their home was found to be sufficient to establish common intention by the couple to share it beneficially.

11.74 The recent first instance case of *Le Foe* purports to extend the conduct which can give rise to a common intention beyond direct contributions, but only an appeal confirming this decision will progress the law in this direction, leaving the current state of the law somewhat uncertain. The facts of the case were complicated and the creditor's application for an order for sale of the matrimonial home and the wife's application for ancillary relief under the Matrimonial Causes Act 1973 were heard together. The husband and wife were respectively approaching and in their 70s and had separated after 40 years of marriage. The matrimonial home had been purchased in the husband's sole name in 1971 financed out of the sale of some of the husband's assets and a mortgage. The wife worked but the husband earned between 80 and 90% of their combined income, out of which he paid the mortgage and other outgoings. The wife met their day to day expenses. The home was remortgaged to pay off debts and further arrears arose. In 1995, the wife used some of an inheritance from her mother to pay off one mortgage and pay the arrears on the other, with the balance being invested in a business from which the profits were used to meet mortgage repayments. In 1999, the husband, who intended to leave the wife for a younger woman, made various false declarations to obtain a further mortgage from the Woolwich for £750,000 without the wife's knowledge or consent, in order to strip the matrimonial home (valued at £1.5 million) of most of its equity. He repaid the existing mortgage and purchased another property with the balance of the Woolwich loan and a second mortgage in excess of £1 million. He then left the wife who applied for ancillary relief in judicial separation proceedings.

The Woolwich applied for an order for sale of the matrimonial home and a money judgment against the husband. Of greatest relevance to cohabitants was the fact that the court held that the wife was entitled to a 50% beneficial interest in the home under a constructive trust, despite the fact that she had not made any direct contributions to the purchase price. She had however preserved the equity in the home by her actions some 25 years later between 1995 and 1999, when she applied her inheritance and business profits to the repayment of the mortgage arrears, interest and future repayments. The mortgages to which these debts applied, however, had not been taken out to purchase the property but subsequently to pay off debts and provide living expenses and may not therefore be seen to constitute orthodox direct contributions within the meaning of *Rosset*. Thus, if endorsed by the Court of Appeal, this case may have paved the way for an extended notion of "direct contributions" or conduct sufficient to found a common intention constructive trust, although, as noted above, academic commentators to date have proved pessimistic about such a prospect.

(ii) Detriment and contributions

11.75 The cases cited above in relation to common intention can similarly be used to illustrate what the courts have considered to be a sufficiently detrimental act by the non-owner, and there is some overlap between the issues. It should be noted here that where the common intention found by the court is based upon *express discussions* that the beneficial ownership should be shared (as in *Hammond v Mitchell*, above), a lower level of detriment is required by the legal non-owner to complete the constructive trust than in other cases. Here contributions to the welfare of the family would seem to be sufficient (see *Stokes v Anderson* [1991] 1 FLR 391, at page 400 per Nourse LJ and *Grant v Edwards* (above per Browne Wilkinson V-C at page 658).

11.76 Direct or indirect contributions can also be seen to be a detrimental act by the non-owner in some circumstances and detriment referable to the common intention or promise is indispensable where there are indirect rather than direct contributions.

11.77 Thus in *Eves v Eves* and *Cooke v Head* physical labour in building or improving the home was considered both a detrimental act and a direct contribution in money's worth to the properties. However, in *Thomas v Fuller-Brown* the same type of hard physical work was not a sufficient contribution and was not considered detrimental given that the claimant was receiving his keep and some pocket money.

11.78 The detriment must always relate to the common intention and not to any other purpose. In *Lloyds Bank plc v Rosset*, the matrimonial home was purchased in the husband's sole name because of the terms of the trust under which he was entitled to the money which he used to purchase the property. Unbeknown to his wife, a mortgage on the property was taken out to fund renovation works. The wife, who was an interior designer, supervised the building works, worked extremely hard in assisting the progress of the renovation works, but the husband paid for the materials and workmen. It was accepted that there was a common intention that the property was to be occupied by the parties and their daughter as the matrimonial home, but no express common intention was found that the wife was to have any beneficial interest in it. The court therefore had to look at the wife's contributions to the property to see whether this evidenced a resulting or constructive trust in her favour. There were no direct monetary contributions, only her decoration work and supervision of the renovation works, but these were adjudged to be *de minimus* relative to the overall cost of the property and the works. Lord Bridge said:

> "Mrs Rossett was anxious to have the property ready for Christmas. In these circumstances, it would seem the most natural thing in the world for any wife, in the absence of her husband abroad, to spend all the time she could spare and to employ any skills she may have, such as the ability to decorate a room, in doing all she could to accelerate progress of the work, quite irrespective of any expectation she might have of enjoying a beneficial interest in the property. The judge's view that some of this work was work 'on which she could not have reasonably expected to embark unless she was to have an interest in the house' seems to me ... to be quite untenable ... On any view, the monetary value of Mrs Rossett's work expressed as a contribution to a property at a cost of £70,000 must have been so trifling to be *de minimus*."

11.79 This illustrates the far greater difficulty there is in evidencing a common intention to share beneficial ownership where there have been no express discussions and the non-legal owner has made no direct contributions to the purchase price. In *Le Foe*, this same position, where there had been no express discussions and arguably no direct contributions to the purchase price might have been expected to prove fatal to Mrs Le Foe's claim to be the beneficiary of a constructive trust, despite having applied a substantial amount of her inheritance to protecting the home from the creditors. The decision in *Midland Bank plc v Cooke* (in contrast to the robust approach taken in *Le Foe*) did nothing to ameliorate the non-legal owner's position in this context. Indeed, it widened the gulf in terms of effect between those who make small but nonetheless direct contributions to a property, and those whose contributions are or are interpreted as being to the welfare of the family alone. For the latter group the impact of the decisions in *Rosset* and *Burns v Burns* (below) have not been mollified, although the approach in *Le Foe* if endorsed by the Court of Appeal does contain such potential. In *Rosset,* the court felt that Mrs Rosset's work was not a sufficiently substantial detrimental act, and may not in any event have been referable to the belief in having a beneficial share. Rather, it was no more than the fulfilment of natural wifely duties. Perhaps in such a situation a cohabitant would have fared better than a wife, although the leading decision of *Burns v Burns* [1984] 1 All ER 244 involving cohabitants makes it clear that it is not sufficient to look after children and run the family home to establish the common intention necessary to earn an interest in the property.

11.80 Lord Denning's broad-brush approach, in which he allowed a contribution to the household by means of domestic services to be taken into account in assessing the parties' respective beneficial shares in much the same way as happens on divorce, was specifically rejected in *Burns*. Lord May provides a useful summary of his assessment of the various situations where a beneficial interest can be identified, despite one partner's being the sole legal owner. A contribution to the initial deposit will on resulting trust principles give rise to a beneficial interest for the non-owner, and this share will be increased by subsequent contributions to mortgage repayments. Similarly if, having contributed to the deposit, the non-owner partner meets other household expenses without which the legal owner would be unable, or find it more difficult, to pay the mortgage, this also increases the non-owner's share. Thus, a contribution by indirect means in addition to a direct contribution was recognised as a possibility. It is this idea which has been expanded upon by the more liberal approach taken to the quantification of beneficial interests in the decision in *Midland Bank plc v Cooke*, as discussed below.

11.81 Both in *Burns* and in *Gissing* the court recognised that as a matter of convenience, one partner's salary may be used to meet the mortgage repayments and the other salary to meet other household expenses, with the intention that both parties would thereby be entitled to share in the property to the extent that their overall contributions, whether direct or indirect, merited. However, these contributions must be made with the intention of assisting in the purchase of the property and not for any other purpose. If they are made with a view to sharing day-to-day expenses only, this will not be considered a sufficient indirect contribution as they lack referability to the intention to acquire an interest in the property (see Lord Diplock in *Gissing*). It is vital to establish referability or, as in both these cases, the non-owner will fail to establish any beneficial interest in the property, despite having devoted many years to looking after the home and family. Where there are indirect contributions through household expenses, without any contribution to the initial deposit, an interest may be acquired if the non-owner's contribution were essential to enable the legal owner to meet the mortgage repayments, although the position has not been made clear (see *Hazell v Hazell* [1972] 1 WLR 301). Again, it seems that such indirect contributions can produce a beneficial interest only if they were made with the intention of assisting in the acquisition of the property in any event. In *Burns* the couple had lived together for nineteen years and had two children of whom the woman was the primary carer. The family home had been purchased in the man's sole name after they had been cohabiting for two years without any contribution from the woman to the deposit or mortgage. She later went out to work and her earnings were used for general household expenses but were not crucial to the man's ability to pay the mortgage. The court held that she had no beneficial interest in the property as no common intention or direct or indirect contribution to the acquisition of the property could be found on the facts. Had the parties been married, the result would have been different indeed, and this case is a dramatic illustration of the disadvantage to which a non-owner cohabitant can be put and in respect of which reform of the law is still awaited.

11.82 Where one partner moves into a property already purchased by the other, it is possible, providing there is sufficient evidence, for the non-owner cohabitant to earn a beneficial interest in the property. It seems that evidence of a complete recasting of the financial arrangements of the parties, disclosing direct or indirect contributions to the mortgage or, say, improvement works, accompanied by a referable intention that the non-owner would acquire an interest would be necessary; this was discussed in *Gissing*, where a change in intention was specifically canvassed as a possibility.

11.83 Thus, in this first stage of establishing a common intention to share beneficial ownership, the authorities lean towards an onerous interpretation of the nature and/or degree of the contribution and detrimental acts needed to acquire a beneficial interest in a property in the absence of either a common intention proven by express discussions or inequitable behaviour by the legal owner of the property such as inspires the court to step in and infer a common intention. However, a liberalisation in approach can be seen in the recent case law relating to the second stage of quantification.

9 The second stage

(a) Quantification of beneficial interests under constructive trusts

11.84 The decision in *Midland Bank plc v Cooke* has increased the significance of the second stage quantification process through which the size of the beneficial interests under a constructive trust is determined. In so doing, it has arguably moved closer to the flexibility of approach advocated by Lord Denning. Not, it must be emphasised, with respect to the first stage, where common intention and detriment must still be evidenced in accordance with the principles set out above; but in the second stage context of quantification of the beneficial interests. Here, where no express agreement has been made as to the proportions in which the parties share in the property, the courts have seemingly gained the ability to cast the net much more widely in terms of the factors they may take in to account in determining the appropriate shares. This change comes through clearly in the recent case on *Mortgage Cororpation v Shaire* (above). Most surprisingly, and perhaps most difficult to reconcile with earlier authorities such as *Springette v Defoe* (above), is the rejection of the resulting trust principles where a direct contribution to the purchase price is found to have been made.

11.85 In *Midland Bank plc v Cooke*, the family home had been purchased in Mr Cooke's sole name in 1971 and was purchased for £8,500 by means of a mortgage of £6,450, and a wedding gift from his parents of £1,100, with the balance of £950 contributed from the husband's savings. Aside from any share of the wedding gift deposit, Mrs Cooke's contribution lay in her using her earnings to meet household bills, and carrying out work in decorating and improving the property in a minor way. Subsequently, the property was transferred into the parties' joint names when the mortgage was increased with Mrs Cooke's consent and agreement to postpone her interest in the property to that of the bank in order to cover Mr Cooke's business overdraft. In defending possession proceedings brought by the mortgagee, Mrs Cooke's consent to the increased mortgage was found by the court at first instance to have been obtained through her husband's undue influence; they also found that by virtue of her direct contribution to the purchase price in the shape of her half-share of parents'-in-law wedding gift, she was and always had been a joint owner with an overriding interest in the property which took priority over the bank's claims. At first instance, her share of the property was assessed on resulting trust principles in proportion to her original contribution of £550 as a percentage of the total purchase price of £8,500, giving her 6.74% of the current value. However, her appeal to the Court of the Appeal resulted in her being awarded a 50% share.

11.86 The Court of Appeal's reasoning for this was considered innovatory, and took an approach which had before been limited to cases where the constructive trust arose by virtue of an excuse as to why joint ownership of the property was not possible followed by detrimental acts (see *Eves v Eves, Grant v Edwards* and *Hammond v Mitchell,* discussed above). In their view, however, once a beneficial interest was established by means of a direct financial contribution to the purchase price of the property, the court was not limited to quantifying that interest in proportion to the extent of that contribution, but was under a duty (per Waite LJ at page 926):

> "to undertake a survey of the whole course of dealing between the parties relevant to their ownership and occupation of the property and their sharing of its burdens and advantages. That scrutiny will not confine itself to the limited range of acts of direct contribution of the sort that are needed to found a beneficial interest in the first place. It will take into consideration all conduct which throws light on the question what shares are intended."

11.87 The court went on to find that despite express evidence from Mr and Mrs Cooke that at the time of the purchase there had been no discussion as to how the property was to be owned beneficially, there was an inferred agreement that the beneficial interests should be shared equally. The reasoning for this was based upon Lord Diplock's speech in *Gissing v Gissing* (above) that where there was no express agreement, the court should:

> "do its best to discover from the conduct of the spouses whether any inference can reasonably be drawn as to the probable common understanding about the amount of the share of the contributing spouse" (at pages 908–909)

or, failing this, should resort to the equitable maxim that "equality is equity". This approach permits contributions other than direct contributions to be taken into account in the quantification process.

11.88 Lord Diplock also envisaged that some married couples, whilst having an understanding that the wife has a beneficial interest in the home, defer its quantification to a later date to be assessed in accordance with "what would be fair, having regard to the total contributions, direct or indirect, which each spouse had made by that date". In the view of the Court of Appeal, the Cookes' marriage was based on equal contributions in all matters. As Waite LJ comments (at page 576):

> "One could hardly have a clearer example of a couple who had agreed to share everything equally: the profits of his business while it prospered, and the risks of indebtedness suffered through its failure; the upbringing of their children; the rewards of her own career as a teacher; and, most relevantly, a home into which he had put his savings and to which she was to give over the years the benefit of the maintenance and improvement contribution. When to all that there is added the fact (still an important one) that this was a couple who had chosen to introduce into their relationship the additional commitment which marriage involves, the conclusion becomes inescapable that their presumed intention was to share the beneficial interest in the property in equal shares."

11.89 Effectively, the court was prepared to impute an agreement as to quantification of the parties' shares where there was none by taking account of the parties' dealings with each other as a whole. It distinguished the approach to quantification in *Springette v Defoe (above)*, where the court had not been prepared to look behind the parties' direct contributions in the absence of any communicated intention to share in any way other than in proportion to the purchase price, on the facts. That case, in their view, involved a middle-aged cohabiting couple whose dealings were more akin to commercial partnership. The court did not accept that the absence of express agreement precluded inference of presumed agreement other than that of a resulting trust.

11.90 The problem with the approach in *Midland Bank plc v Cooke* is that it leaves the quantification process in a state of great uncertainty as it is not entirely clear when the courts will apply the resulting trust approach found in *Springette v Defoe*, and when they will adopt the flexible *Midland Bank plc v Cooke* approach. Where there are express discussions as to how the beneficial interests are to be held under a constructive trust, then presumably these will prevail as in *Huntingford v Hobbs* (above) and *Savill v Goodall* [1994] 1 FCR 325. On the other hand, where, as in most cases under a constructive trust, there have been no express discussions of the proportions of the beneficial interests, then the recent cases are moving towards the flexible approach to quantification. In *Drake v Whip* [1996] 1 FLR 826, cohabitants purchased a barn in the sole name of the man in 1988 with a view to converting it into a shared residence. No declaration of trust was made although Ms Drake contributed £38,000, 19.4% of the original purchase price plus conversion costs totalling £195,790, with Mr Whip contributing the balance. They each contributed their labour in the proportions 70% to Mr Whip and 30% to Ms Drake. She also provided the food and household expenditure out of her salary. By 1992, after Mr Whip had formed another relationship, they were living separately in the barn and subsequently Ms Drake moved out, seeking a declaration as to their respective beneficial interests. At first instance, resulting trust principles applied, and she was found to be entitled to a share of 19.4%. On appeal, this was increased to one third, on the basis that the trust had incorrectly been characterised as a resulting as opposed to a constructive trust. Once the existence of a constructive trust was established, then the broad-brush approach to quantum of the shares with reference to the parties' whole course of conduct could be taken. Here, their intention to set up a joint home, their labour contributions, the existence and financing of a joint bank account and Ms Drake's contributions to household expenses and housekeeping were taken into account and her share was assessed at one third.

11.91 Similarly in *Mortgage Cororpation v Shaire* [2000] 1 FLR 973, Mrs Shaire and her ex husband transferred the former matrimonial home (which they owned in equal shares) to Mrs Shaire and her cohabitant Mr Fox, following the breakdown of the marriage, subject to a mortgage, although no declaration was made as to the cohabitants' respective beneficial interests. Mrs Shaire worked part time but Mr Fox paid the mortgage and household expenses. Unbeknown to Mrs Shaire, Mr Fox forged her signature to secure further substantial sums by way of mortgage secured on the family home occupied by the cohabitants and Mrs Shaire's son. Following

Mr Fox's death, the new mortgagee sought possession and Mrs Shaire's interest in the home fell to be determined under a constructive trust and was assessed in the light of their contributions and subsequent conduct as 75% of the equity despite having made no direct contributions in excess of 50%, with the mortgagee's interest being enforceable in the circumstances only against Mr Fox's share.

11.92 Although the ability to gain some credit for what can broadly be termed contributions to the welfare of the family through domestic labour is to welcomed on one level, the new approach to quantification throws up some practical difficulties. Why, for instance why, was Mrs Cooke awarded a half-share, whereas Ms Drake's share was limited to one third? Ms Drake's direct financial contribution was far greater than that of Mrs Cooke, and her labour contribution to the barn conversion was not negligible. This, coupled with her payment of household bills and undertaking of domestic work, could arguably have resulted in her being awarded a larger share. How exactly did Mrs Shaire increase her half share of the home which she had "earned" during her marriage to Mr Shaire, to 75% when Mr Fox had assumed total financial responsibility for all the outgoings? In *Le Foe*, even accepting that a constructive trust had been established, on what basis was Mrs Le Foe's beneficial interest assessed at 50%? Unfortunately, the method of calculation is not clear. Did the fact that in *Drake v Whip* the parties had not given each other the special commitment of marriage, considered important in *Cooke*, make the equality is equity maxim less likely to be resorted to? If so, why did this approach not prevail in *Mortgage Corpn v Shaire*? Is the involvement of a mortgagee seeking to foreclose on a family home a factor which in practice is likely to enhance the size of the interest being quantified?

11.93 Reform of the law in this area is keenly awaited and a comprehensive checklist of factors to be weighed in the equation in such cases would hopefully provide greater clarity and consistency in approach. Pending legislative reform, we are left with an unsatisfactory two-stage and two-tier approach to the establishment and determination of beneficial interests under a constructive trust. In the first stage, in the absence of express discussions, the court will only impute a common intention to share beneficial ownership from direct or indirect *financial* contributions followed by acts of detriment referable to the common intention in accordance with *Rosset*. Following *Le Foe*, there is some doubt as to exactly what will and will not constitute a direct contribution. The degree of detriment seems to be greater for those relying upon indirect financial contributions than for those relying upon express discussions or direct financial contributions, so that contributions to the welfare of the family will not suffice as detriment in the former category but will in the latter categories, providing two tiers within the first stage. Such contributions to welfare of the family alone are certainly not in the first stage regarded as evidence of a common intention to share the property beneficially and are not even universally accepted as evidence of detriment. Thus recent developments in the case law have not helped the cohabitant in the *Burns v Burns* situation, although clarification of the implications of the first instance decision of *Le Foe* are keenly awaited.

11.94 Yet in the second stage, once through the narrow gateway, having established common intention, and providing there is no express agreement as to the proportion of the beneficial interests, the court looks at the whole course of dealings between the parties and may impute an agreement from this as to their respective beneficial interests. Here, contributions to welfare of the family assume far greater significance and can greatly enhance a cohabitant's share beyond that which would be presumed on resulting trust principles, as seen in *Cooke*. Yet why should such contributions be valid evidence of an imputed common intention as to the size a couple's shares in the second stage but not of their intention to share beneficially in the first? The distinction seems artificial, certainly in terms of its effect. For it widens the gulf between those who are arguably deserving, such as Mrs Burns, yet fail to get through the gateway to the second stage, receiving nothing; and those, such as Mrs Cooke, who by virtue of an imputed, small but direct financial contribution pass through the gateway and are then deemed to have evidenced by conduct very similar to that exhibited by Mrs Burns, an agreement that she owned a half-share in the family home.

11.95 The only further possibility to explore for a cohabitant in Mrs Burns' position if, unlike her, there were still minor children of the relationship, would be the provisions relating to transfer and settlement of property orders for the benefit of the child in para 1(2) of Sch 1 CA 1989, considered further below.

10 Proprietary estoppel

11.96 Another principle under which beneficial interests can be established by non-legal owners is that of proprietary estoppel. The crucial distinction between this doctrine and that of the constructive trust has been identified by Hayton ("Equitable Rights of Cohabitees" (1990) 54 The Conveyancer 370). He asserts that the common intention constructive trust requires a bilateral understanding or agreement that if the non-owner acts in a particular and detrimental way, they will obtain a fair share in the family home. To succeed in a claim for proprietary estoppel, however, there need be only unilateral conduct by the legal owner which leads the partner to believe that he or she has an equitable interest in the home. Should that partner subsequently act to his or her detriment in reliance upon that conduct, it then becomes unconscionable for the legal owner to insist upon total ownership of the property. The court then intervenes to prevent the unconscionable conduct affecting the non-owner detrimentally. It will not necessarily perfect the gift, but rather decide what is the minimum equity to do justice. The non-owner will not necessarily obtain a realisable interest in the proceeds of sale of the property but may be deemed to be entitled to a personal right of occupation only until the children are eighteen, or an equitable life interest.

11.97 In fact, it can be argued that there is a good deal of overlap between the situations in which these two doctrines apply, and from a practical point of view it may well be appropriate to use both lines of argument in the alternative where the facts warrant such an approach. In *Grant v Edwards* (above), Sir Nicholas

Browne-Wilkinson remarked that in other cases of that kind, useful guidance might in the future be obtained from the principles underlying the law of proprietary estoppel which are closely akin to the constructive trust approach laid down in *Gissing v Gissing* (above). He went on to say that although the two principles had developed separately without cross fertilisation, they rest on the same foundation and have on all other matters reached the same conclusion.

11.98 The doctrine is of greatest use where it is not clear whether or not the non-owner would have done the detrimental acts relied upon in the absence of a common intention that a beneficial interest had been acquired, rather than for other reasons, such as mutual love and affection, not specifically referable to the house. In contrast to the constructive trust approach, the doctrine of proprietary estoppel does not require the detrimental acts to be specifically referable in this way, although reliance on the inducement must be shown. However, once there is evidence of an inducement and some detrimental act, the burden then falls on the legal owner to show that the non-owner did not do the act in reliance upon the inducement.

11.99 In *Pascoe v Turner* [1979] 1 WLR 431, CA, a woman who relied on the man's assurance given after breakdown of the relationship that "the house and everything in it is yours" to the extent of spending a large proportion of her capital on the property successfully defended possession proceedings later brought by the man. The Court of Appeal found that although there was insufficient evidence to justify a trust, the man was estopped from revoking his imperfect gift of the house to the woman. The court then ordered that the gift be perfected by the transfer of the house to the woman.

11.100 A more restrictive approach was taken in the later case of *Coombes v Smith* [1986] 1 WLR 808, Ch D. Here, a woman who found herself pregnant by her lover, left her husband and job and moved into a property owned by her lover. He never moved in to live with her but she was assured by him that he would always look after her. She failed to establish proprietary estoppel on the grounds that the assurance did not lead her to believe she was acquiring an interest in the property and she had not acted to her detriment in leaving her husband and job and having the baby. This can be seen to be an ungenerous approach to the definition of "detriment" which illustrates the precarious nature of relying solely upon this doctrine.

11.101 In *Greasley v Cooke* [1980] 1 WLR 1306, although a proprietary estoppel was established, it was held to give rise only to a right to occupy the property rent free for life and not to the right for the property to be transferred to the non-owner as in *Pascoe v Turner* (above). Where proved, the nature of the remedy is at the court's discretion and may therefore result in an award of monetary compensation.

11.102 A more liberal approach to establishing proprietary estoppel is demonstrated in *Wayling v Jones* [1995] 2 FLR 1029. Same-sex cohabitants had lived together for some sixteen years when Mr Jones died. During that period they had changed residence several times and throughout Mr Wayling assisted Mr Jones in his business ventures, by helping him run his cafe and then acting as his companion and chauffeur and assisting in his hotel businesses. In return, the plaintiff received just pocket money coupled with a promise made by Mr Jones that he would leave him the business and update his Will to ensure he was left the currently owned hotel. However, he failed to do this and all the plaintiff inherited on Mr Jones's death was a car and some furniture. On the plaintiff's claim based on proprietary estoppel, it was found that the promises were made by the deceased, that Mr Wayling had believed that he would inherit the property and that he had suffered detriment in not having been paid a proper wage for his work as a consequence. On appeal it was also held that the promises relied on did not have to be the sole inducement for Wayling's conduct and that once it had been established that promises had been made and there was conduct from which inducement could be inferred, the burden shifted to the defendant to prove that the plaintiff had not relied on the promises. Despite arguably conflicting evidence of the plaintiff as to whether he would have undertaken or continued his role without the inducement, this burden had not been discharged. Wayling was awarded the net proceeds of sale of the hotel amounting to some £70,000 as recompense for his detriment.

11.103 The most recent case of *Gillett v Holt* [2000] 2 FLR 266 did not involve cohabitants. Here the owner of a farm persuaded the appellant to live and work on the farm in the expectation that he would inherit the business on his death. The Court of Appeal held that it was not conscionable for the owner to repudiate these assurances and the appellant had an enforceable claim to an interest in the farm founded on proprietary estoppel. In the cohabitation context, it may be more difficult to establish proprietary estoppel where other reasons such as love and affection may account for the detrimental acts undertaken.

11 Alternative occupation rights

11.104 A non-owner cohabitant will at the very least have a bare licence to occupy the home of the partner. However, such a licence amounts to little more than permission to occupy the home, and is determinable upon reasonable notice. On breakdown of the relationship, the licence will usually be revoked, and in the absence of any defence to possession proceedings by virtue of any of the matters discussed in this chapter, the licensee will have to leave. However, in some cases, even if it is not possible to establish a beneficial interest or use the doctrine of proprietary estoppel, it may be possible to show an alternative right of occupation.

(a) Contractual licences

11.105 Although it is usually not possible for a cohabitant to show that he or she was the tenant of the partner, there have been cases where a contractual licence to occupy has been established. Most notable is the case of *Tanner v Tanner* [1975] 1 WLR 1346. Here, the woman gave up her rent controlled flat and moved into a property owned by the father of her two children, although the parties never cohabited. The Court of Appeal held that giving up her flat and looking after the children amounted to good consideration for an inferred contractual licence that she should be allowed to occupy the property until the children left school. However, this remedy has not been liked by the courts in more recent cases. In *Coombes v Smith*, discussed above in relation to proprietary estoppel, the court specifically rejected the argument that a licence had been created in not dissimilar circumstances, in that the woman's acts of leaving her husband and moving into the property did not amount to sufficient consideration.

(b) Licence by estoppel

11.106 Where the legal owner induces in the partner a belief that he or she has a right to long term occupation of the property rather than a beneficial interest in it, then a licence by estoppel rather than proprietary estoppel will arise, whereby the court will hold that the legal owner is estopped from denying that right of occupation. This argument succeeded in *Greasley v Cooke* (above) where the woman who had originally come to live with the man as his housekeeper but subsequently lived with him as his wife had been led to believe, following breakdown of the relationship, that she could continue to live in the property for as long as she wished. As the successors in title were unable to prove that she had not acted to her detriment in reliance on the inducement, and had indeed continued to care for a member of the family who was ill without any payment, the court took the view that they were estopped from denying that she had such a right of occupation.

(c) Occupation pursuant to a life interest in possession

11.107 The decision in *Tanner v Tanner* (above) specifically avoided a finding that the woman's right of occupation amounted to an exclusive irrevocable licence to occupy land which would have made her the tenant for life under the Settled Land Act 1925. However, in *Ungurian v Lesnoff* [1990] Ch 206 where insufficient evidence to infer a beneficial interest under a constructive trust existed, a tenancy for life under the Settled Land Act 1925 was found to have been created. In this case the woman who was a Polish academic, gave up her career and the valuable tenancy of her flat in Poland. She came with her sons to live in a property in London purchased by the man in his sole name for joint occupation by them and her children. His children, who were being educated in England, were also to live there from time to time. He purchased the property and she and her sons did some repair and renovation work to the property. It was found that she undertook the work not on the basis of a common intention that he had bought the house for her, but on the understanding that she had the right to reside there and that there was a common intention to provide her with a secure home. The judge stated:

> "I do not think that full effect would be given to the common intention by inferring no more than an irrevocable licence to occupy the house. I think the legal consequences that flow from the intention to be imputed to the parties was that Mr Ungurian held the house on trust to permit Mrs Lesnoff to reside in it during her life unless she consented to the sale and another property purchased for her in substitution."

11.108 The consequences of this finding were that she was the tenant for life with the power to sell and have the benefit of the proceeds of sale during her life. Following implementation of the TLATA 1996, it is no longer possible to create strict settlements either expressly or impliedly. Thus, should a court in the future find that successive interests have been created under a trust of land in a similar situation, the beneficiary of the life interest could and ought to be advised to apply to the court to order the reversioner trustee to delegate their management functions under s 14 to the beneficiary in possession. The court would have to consider the application in accordance with the s 15 criteria and is able and likely to consent upon conditions which would limit the otherwise absolute power of the beneficiary in possession.

11.109 In this case, given the man's promise was not found to constitute any beneficial share in the property, it was still open to the court to find a licence by estoppel or a contractual licence since there was consideration in that the woman had given up her nationality, home and career in Poland. The abolition of strict settlements, combined with the fact that this approach seems to have been confined to the unusual facts of this case, probably mean that a similar case would in future be decided using estoppel principles, rather than an imputed life interest.

12 Transfer and settlement of property orders for children

11.110 As was discussed in relation to tenancies and in Chapter 9, para 1(2)(e) of Sch 1 to the CA 1989 enables the court to order the transfer of property between parents for the benefit of the child. Any beneficial interest in the home, or any other property owned by one parent, may be transferred either to the child or to the other parent for the benefit of the child. This opens up the possibility of the court's effectively ordering the transfer of the home to the residential parent. Paragraph 1(2)(d) empowers the court to order the settlement of property owned by one parent for the benefit of the child.

11.111 In both cases, only one such order can be made against a parent in respect of the same child. The criteria set out in para 4 of Sch 1 discussed above in Chapter 9, identify the factors to be taken into account by the court. However, courts have been reluctant to transfer property to children directly in matrimonial cases (see *Chamberlain v Chamberlain* [1974] 1 All ER 33) and this reluctance has been extended to the Sch 1 CA 1989 provisions as discussed in Chapter 9. In *A v A (financial provision)* [1994] 1 FLR 657, FD, an application by the woman cohabitant for an outright transfer of the family home for the benefit of the child was rejected in favour of a settlement for the benefit of the child until six months after the child's eighteenth birthday or completion of her tertiary education. In *T v S (financial provision for children)* [1994] 2 FLR 883, FD, it was specifically argued that the court's powers under Sch 1 should be widely construed to urge a different approach to capital orders in favour of children to that decided in the matrimonial context. However, the striking similarity of the provisions with those of the MCA 1973 was interpreted as preventing a different approach. Here, an order made on the mother's application which had at first instance provided that the property to be purchased with a lump sum for the benefit of the children was to be held on trust until the youngest reached 21 and thereafter revert to the father, not be divided equally between the children as had been ordered at first instance.

11.112 Similarly, in *J v C (Child: Financial Provision)* [1999] 1 FLR 152, whilst a substantial property was placed at the disposal of the child, her mother and half-siblings until she was 21, the property reverted to the father at that point in time, subject to an option in favour of the mother to purchase at open market value. In *Hammond v Mitchell* (above), capital provision for children of an unmarried couple was deemed inappropriate and only periodical maintenance payments were ordered in favour of the children, although lump sums in favour of children have been willingly used to compensate for failure to meet child support obligations (see eg *Phillips v Peace* [1996] 2 FLR 230 and *V v V* (Child maintenance) [2001] 2 FLR 799) as noted in Chapter 9.

11.113 Thus, case law to date seems to indicate a definite reluctance to use the court's powers more liberally or substantially differently to the matrimonial context. Yet where a child's parents are unmarried, there may be no other means through which to adjust property rights as between parents and it may have been thought appropriate in some instances to effect some redistribution by virtue of the Sch 1 orders for the benefit of the child. However, the courts have shied away from developing different principles in relation to capital orders in the unmarried context, other than to compensate for non-payment of child support. They are clearly opposed to the resident cohabitant obtaining what was described in *T v S* as an "indirect windfall" through the reversion of the matrimonial home vesting in the children, and given the lack of duty for cohabitants to maintain each other, unless a beneficial interest exists or can be established on constructive trust principles, a resident cohabitant applying under Sch 1 CA 1989, even in a case involving substantial assets is likely only to acquire a right of occupation in the family home until the youngest child reaches the age of majority or completes their tertiary education. Nonetheless, Sch 1 remains an important means by which to preserve a home for the child during their minority and the courts have at least been willing to achieve Mesher and Martin style orders to this end, albeit with the consequent insecurity for the resident parent, usually the mother, on the youngest child reaching their majority. For an example of how to draft a trust deed providing a home for a child following an application under Sch1 CA 1989, see Spon-Smith, "Provsion of a Home under Children Act 1989, Sch 1 – A Suggested Trust Deed" [1999] *Fam Law* 763.

11.114 It should also be noted that there is in any event no power in the schedule to order the sale of the property. Where, as often will be the case, the property is jointly owned or the non-legal owner claims a beneficial interest in it, it will be appropriate to combine any application under Sch 1 CA 1989 for a transfer or settlement of property order with an application for a declaration as to the beneficial interests, or an order for or restraining sale under s 14 TLATA 1996. All such applications may be heard by the county court. This is as near as it is possible to get to achieving a family law based consideration by the courts of a property dispute between cohabitants. The case of *Hammond v Mitchell* (above) gives guidance as to how multifarious claims incidental upon unmarried family breakdown should be dealt with procedurally. All possible issues, including financial provision for the children, should be raised at the earliest stage so that the appropriate forum and procedure, leading to the quickest and most effective outcome, can be decided. Waite J made it clear that discovery orders should be made at an early stage and strictly enforced and the emphasis accorded by the law to express discussions required that those discussions should be pleaded in the greatest detail and, in the Family Division, this involved detailed evidence in the claimant's initial statement filed with the Part 8 claim form (s 14 TLATA 1996) or the applicant's forms C2/C10 (Sch 1 CA 1989).

11.115 Transfer and settlement of property orders extend to any property owned by a parent in possession or reversion and therefore, as discussed in Chapter 9, are not limited to use in respect of the family home.

13 Public funding

11.116 As in the matrimonial context, any advice given to cohabitants concerning a dispute relating to the family home must include information about both costs, and where appropriate, the availability of public funding, the consequences of the requirement to pay a contribution and the LSC statutory charge under s 10(7) Access to Justice Act 1999.

11.117 In relation to proceedings under s 14 TLATA 1996, brought to establish the beneficial interests in the family home, there is power for the Legal Services Commission (LSC) to postpone enforcement of the charge where property recovered or preserved is to be used as a home for the assisted person or their dependants (reg 52, Community Legal Service (Financial) Regulations 2000). Similarly, where a sum of money is recovered under such proceedings for the purpose of purchasing a home in accordance with the order or agreement, the charge may also be deferred providing the property is bought within a year of the order or agreement and in both cases, the Commission has power to agree to the purchase of a substitute property to which the charge will be transferred (reg 52). Postponement is always at the discretion of the LSC and is dependent upon the property concerned offering sufficient security for the sum charged.

11.118 The court order must also make it clear that the property or sum awarded is to provide a home for the assisted person or their dependants and it is critical that advisors ensure that this wording is included in the wording of the order or agreement. For an example see the wording suggested above in Chapter 5 at para 5.29. Simple interest on the charge accrues at the rate prescribed (currently 8%) on the charge as of the date of registration and an assisted person may at any time make repayments in respect of the charge which will be applied first to the outstanding interest (see reg 52(3)). Where an order is made under Sch 1 CA 1989 to a publicly-funded party, the charge will not attach to the first £2,500 (to be increased to £3,000 in December 2001) of any award, but only to the balance, if appropriate.

However, in the context of proceedings under s 14 TLATA, the exemption of the first £2,500 (or in future £3,000) of the charge does not apply (see reg 44).

11.119 The Court of Appeal decision in the case of *Parkes v Legal Aid Board* [1996] 4 All ER 271 also makes it clear that where, as in this case, an order for sale is successfully resisted under s 14 TLATA 1996; even though the extent of the beneficial interests were not in dispute, as there had been a recovery of the exclusive right to possession which had previously been a shared right, this would bring the property within s 10(7) Access to Justice Act 1999 and the property would be subject to the statutory charge to the extent of the costs incurred under the certificate of public funding.

11.120 In proceedings under Sch 1 CA 1989, a child is able to apply for a legal aid certificate in their own name or alternatively the resident parent may apply, where they seek orders for the benefit of the child. If a court orders that the former family home, where the interests of the parents in the property are agreed or have been decided, be settled on the child or children, then, as the child has only recovered an interest in possession in a property of which he or she is not an owner, the statutory charge would seem to be avoided. Care must always be taken not to deliberately evade the charge and good reason must be provided for making payment in an order direct to a child, particularly if the order is made by consent. Section 10(7) of the Access to Justice Act 1999 states that where the dispute or proceedings result in a payment to someone other than the funded client, such as a dependant child or a creditor but where the payment is for the benefit of the client (eg to repay a debt on behalf of the funded client) then the charge will still arise on that payment. Wherever a publicly funded co-owner acquires through proceedings an exclusive right of occupation for a substantial period, this may mean that the statutory charge applies and could in theory at least apply to long-term occupation orders granted in respect of an owner occupied property under Part IV FLA 1996, where the successful applicant has a beneficial interest in the family home.

11.121 These developments underline the need for a full consideration of the public funding implications, which must be discussed with and communicated to the client at every stage and seriously taken into account when considering the possibility of settlement. It should be noted that where an agreement is reached in consequence of Legal Help advice, the statutory charge does not arise where the property is the client's main or only dwelling which may be significant where preservation of the home by agreement is a real possibility and the client is eligible for Legal Help advice.

14 Negative equity and mortgage arrears

11.122 Cohabitants facing relationship breakdown today may face the added problem of dealing with negative equity and/or mortgage arrears. Given that co-owners are jointly and severally liable for a mortgage debt, it may often be difficult to get a mortgagee's consent to a transfer of property order in a negative equity situation. The attitude of mortgagees to this problem varies. However, where the repayment record is good and there is sufficient income or income support available to meet repayment of the interest element, it should be possible to negotiate the desired outcome. Borrowers who have taken out a mortgage on or after 2 October 1995 are now subject to a thirty-nine-week delay before income support will be paid to meet mortgage interest repayments and insurance may not be available. For an instructive article about the effect on a deserted partner's ability to claim mortgage interest as income support, see Wikeley, "Income Support, Mortgage Interest and the Concept of abandonment" [2001] *Fam Law* 672. Particularly where the property market remains depressed, however, there is little for a lender to gain in forcing a sale in adverse conditions if the interest on the repayments is being made. Where a sale is the only option in a negative equity situation on relationship breakdown, it is generally financially advisable for the borrowers to take urgent action to sell the home themselves, as they are likely to obtain a higher purchase price than the mortgagee selling in possession and where no other option is possible both parties, should agree to limit the damage to each of them. However, consent of the mortgagee to the sale is needed in a negative equity situation or the sellers will not be able to redeem the mortgage and secure the release of the charge on completion of the sale. If the mortgagee refuses, then the borrowers can apply to the court to order sale pursuant to s 91 LPA 1925 to enable the court to direct sale on terms that the court considers appropriate (see *Palk v Mortgage Services Funding plc* [1993] Ch 330, CA). Such proceedings must be issued in the High Court where the total mortgage debt exceeds £30,000.

11.123 One important factor to bear in mind, however, is that a sale by the co-owners prior to a possession order may make them intentionally homeless if they are in priority need and not eligible for assistance as a homeless person (discussed below). Tentative enquiries can be made to the local housing authority as to how they view homeless applicants in this situation. The 1996 Code of Guidance on Parts VI and VII of the Housing Act 1996 provided that genuine inability to keep up with the mortgage repayments even after payment of benefit and for whom no further financial help was available should not be regarded as intentionally homeless, although their ability to pay the mortgage when the commitment was taken on was to be examined (para 15.6). The new draft Code of Guidance (DLTR, December 2000) again suggests that a lenient view may be taken where arrears arise due to ignorance of the availability of welfare benefits (see para. 13.7). A misrepresentation of the applicants financial position when the mortgage was taken out may make them intentionally homeless and ineligible for accommodation under the homelessness legislation and the sale or loss of the home due to wilful refusal to pay rent or mortgage repayments will be a deliberate omission warranting a finding of intentional homelessness, although not if payment would leave them without the means to provide for the ordinary necessities of life (see *R v Hillingdon London Borough Council, ex p Tinn* (1988) 20 HLR 305, QBD).

11.124 Another matter to consider in a negative equity situation where there is an endowment mortgage of at least ten years standing, is for the couple to switch to an ordinary repayment mortgage and for the life policy to be sold to a specialist broker for a price much higher than the surrender value. The proceeds can then be applied to discharge or reduce the negative equity.

11.125 Where there are arrears and possession proceedings, suspension of any possession order should be made where it can be shown that the mortgagor will pay off the arrears and be able to pay the repayments after a "reasonable period" (see s 36 Administration of Justice Acts 1970 and 1973 (AJA 1970 and 1973)). In *Cheltenham and Gloucester Building Society v Norgan* [1996] 1 All ER 449, CA, in assessing a reasonable period the whole of the remaining period should be taken into account. Where, as is often the case with second mortgages, the loan is under £15,000 and governed by the Consumer Credit Act 1974, time orders under s 129 Act are available "if it appears to the court just" to make one in respect of any sum owed to the lender at a rate which is reasonable taking into account the debtor's financial position. This is an easier hurdle to overcome than the AJA 1970 and 1973 test and the provision enables both further time to pay and the rescheduling of payments beyond the original term of the loan. It is also possible for the debtor under the 1974 Act to apply for the order without awaiting proceedings being issued by the lender.

11.126 Finally, the possibility of a mortgage rescue scheme can be explored. These are operated by many mortgagees and some local authorities and involve a housing association buying the property and enabling the current occupier to remain either as a tenant or under a shared ownership scheme. This may be particularly useful where one cohabitant and the children wish to remain in the home, but cannot afford to take on the mortgage debts. The availability of the schemes is patchy and initiative needs to be taken to see whether the mortgagee concerned or local authority for that area do operate such a scheme.

11.127 Following sale, legal co-owners will remain jointly and severally liable for the balance of the mortgage debt not met out of the sale proceeds and, if there have been possession proceedings, then a money judgment may also have been obtained. Although the mortgagee can in theory seek to enforce the whole of the debt against either of the co-owners, an agreement as between the former cohabitants as to how this should be borne should be considered on relationship breakdown. Where there has been an agreement as to the proportions in which the mortgage repayments were made, then the debt would be shared between them in these same proportions.

15 Homelessness

11.128 If it has not been possible to preserve the home, the final remedy to explore where there are children or a vulnerable cohabitant who are now homeless, is the duty under Housing Act 1996 Part VII to secure accommodation for those who are eligible for assistance homeless, in priority need and not intentionally homeless. Unfortunately, the provisions of the 1996 Act have reduced the duty to secure accommodation to a minimum period of two years, although the Homelessness Bill 2001 currently before Parliament is set to reverse this position as discussed in Chapter 3. Thus, homelessness is not currently a direct route into settled accommodation and consideration should be given to clients applying to go onto the housing register pursuant to s 163 HA 1996. There was some indication to the White Paper *Our Future Homes* (Cm 2901) that the register would be used to give priority to conventional married families and those who have delayed having children due to inadequate housing in the allocation of social housing. However, no such evidence of direct discrimination is found in the Code of Guidance and the most recently revised draft of the Code (DLTR, December 2000) definitely rejects such an approach. Anyone accepted as homeless under the statutory criteria will be automatically put on the register and must be given 'reasonable preference' although the register is set to be abolished under the Housing Bill 2001.

11.129 The relevant provisions of Part VII of the 1996 Act and the Code have already been considered in detail in Chapter 3. Where there are children or the homeless cohabitant is vulnerable within the meaning of the s 189 Housing Act 1996, there is likely to be a priority need. Where it has not proved possible to obtain long term relief from the court, as a result of which the vulnerable cohabitant or family become homeless unintentionally, the local authority would owe them a duty to secure them accommodation for the minimum two-year period in accordance with s 193 HA 1996. Where there are children who can reasonably be expected to reside with the applicant, there is always priority need for homelessness purposes. The local authority then has a duty to secure accommodation for the partner with whom the children are to remain.

11.130 An interesting issue is the likely reaction of local authorities asked to house cohabitants in priority need to the availability of enhanced remedies for cohabitants to secure occupation of the home. Where a cohabitant's former partner is likely to be in priority need themselves, due to their vulnerability or dependant children residing with them, then this should ensure that a cohabitant is not put under pressure to use their other legal remedies. However, the ability to apply for occupation orders where there is not a violent situation, and where the interests of the child have been given increased prominence, may make authorities more inclined to advise potentially homeless applicants to apply for occupation orders in the first instance and subsequently use their legal rights to secure long-term occupation of the home. Whether or not refusal to do so would amount to intentional homelessness would depend on the facts of the case but remains a possibility. It is certainly possible that authorities would expect cohabitants to use s 14 TLATA 1996 or the transfer of tenancy remedy in respect of the family home (Sch 7 FLA 1996) or perhaps even the settlement and transfer of property orders available under Sch 1 CA 1989 for the benefit of any child of the relationship. Refusal to do so once advised of this possibility, certainly without clear reasons, could arguably amount to failure to do something which has resulted in homelessness and provide a basis for an intentional homelessness finding. Certainly, if there is an agreement between cohabitants that the one of them with priority need should leave to attempt to gain accommodation under the homelessness legislation, this may fall foul of s 191(3) HA 1996, although to do so it must have been reasonable for them to continue to occupy the accommodation.

11.131 Indeed, the current lack of permanent housing available through the homelessness route makes these remedies more attractive than homelessness on relationship breakdown in many cases, although the balance may alter after the 2001 Bill is implemented. However, in the context of relationship breakdown, there may be clear reasons why it is not reasonable to continue to occupy accommodation and s 177 HA 1996 provides that actual or threatened domestic violence where those threats are likely to be carried out by an "associated person" will ensure that continued occupation would not be reasonable. This again is more clearly recognised in both the 2001 Bill and the most recent Draft Code of Guidance (DLTR, 2001).

11.132 It is to be stressed that in cases where there is no right of occupation of the family home by the cohabitant in priority need and they have left and become homeless, temporary accommodation should be provided pending enquiries (s 188 HA 1996) and subsequently at the very least pending the outcome of any court proceedings taken to obtain either an occupation order or an appropriate longer term remedy.

11.133 Finally, where a cohabitant who is not in priority need becomes homeless on relationship breakdown, they are entitled to advice and assistance from the local authority in obtaining accommodation (s 192) and may be able to place themselves on the housing register. The position of this group is again enhanced under the provisions of the 2001 Bill, as discussed in Chapter 3.

16 Personal property

11.134 With the advent of the "share-owning democracy", an increase in the number of disputes between cohabitants in relation to their personal property such as savings and shares is becoming more common. Essentially the rules relating to the division of personal property of cohabitants on relationship breakdown are the same as for real property. The law of trusts can be used where the property is of sufficient value and it is alleged a non-legal owner is beneficially entitled to a share of the property. Indeed this was vividly illustrated in the interesting recent case of *Rowe v Prance* [1999] 2 FLR 787. Here Mr Prance, a married man, had a relationship with another woman, Ms Rowe, over a 14-year period, promising to leave and divorce his wife but never doing so. However, when the matrimonial home was sold, the couple found a boat which was purchased in the Mr Prance's sole name with a view to the couple living together on it an fulfilling their plan to sail the world. Ms Rowe, who had found the boat to purchase, was told it was registered in the man's name alone because she did not have an Ocean Master's Certificate. In reliance on his representations to this effect, she gave up her rented home, placed her furniture in storage and began living on the boat which the man referred to as "ours". Eventually, Ms Rowe realised that he was not coming to live with her and demanded her share of the boat. The court, accepting her evidence, held that Mr Prance had constituted himself an express trustee of the boat as no writing was required in the personal property context. Consequently they had no need to find a constructive trust and applying the equitable maxim "equality is equity" confirmed Ms Rowe held a half share in the boat.

11.135 Generally, anything owned before the relationship or purchased by one of the cohabitants during the relationship remains the property of that partner. Gifts remain the property of the donee. It seems that joint bank or building society accounts held by cohabitants and intended to be a common pool of funds will be deemed to be held as joint tenants in equity, regardless of any disproportion in the relative contributions, in the same way as is presumed in the case of a married couple (see *Bernard v Josephs* (above) and *Jones v Maynard* [1951] Ch 572). Severance of that joint tenancy by giving written notice to the other will result in the creation of a tenancy in common in equal shares of those monies. If the common pool presumption can be rebutted, by an express or implied contrary intention, then the funds will be held on resulting trust for the contributors in shares proportionate to their contributions. If there is a cohabitation contract or other written declaration which deals with the ownership of such funds this is likely to be conclusive.

11.136 Share ownership in joint names entails considerations similar to those relating to real property and discussed in relation to the family home. It seems that resulting trust principles are most appropriate here in the absence of any express declaration to the contrary.

11.137 As a matter of practical importance, it is always essential to alert the bank or building society of a dispute and, if appropriate, to alter the drawing arrangements to prevent the funds being drawn by the other party. Any dispute concerning personal property which is litigated by a legally aided client will again be subject of the legal aid statutory charge. Transfer and settlement of property orders can be sought where there are children as discussed above.

11.138 In terms of jurisdiction relating to personal property disputes, the general equitable jurisdiction given under s 23 County Courts Act 1984 enables applications for a declaration of trust in relation to personal property up to a current value of £30,000 to be heard in the county court, with claims relating to property of greater value needing to be made in the High Court. Where chattels owned in undivided shares, are concerned, s 188 LPA 1925 permits an application for an order as to the appropriate division to be made by the court. Again, the county court has jurisdiction up to a value of £30,000 and thereafter applications should be made to the High Court.

11.139 In all cases concerning cohabitants' personal property, consideration should be given to whether such applications should be joined together with applications for financial relief under Sch 1 CA 1989 and in relation to the family home under s 14 TLATA 1996 or Sch 7 FLA 1996, as suggested to be appropriate to avoid proliferation of time-consuming proceedings in *Hammond v Mitchell* (above).

17 Proceedings under the Married Women's Property Act 1882 and the Matrimonial Proceedings and Property Act 1970

11.140 It is easy to overlook the possibility of proceedings under these two Acts when advising heterosexual cohabitants, as they are likely to be relevant in a minority of cases only. However, an application can be made under s 17 of the 1882 Act for a declaration as to the ownership of disputed property where the parties had an agreement to marry. The application must be made within three years of the termination of the agreement and may be particularly useful in relation to personal property since the proceedings are considered family proceedings in respect of which the first £2,500 of property recovered or preserved is exempt from the statutory charge where the litigant is legally aided. Section 37 of the 1970 Act provides that where a spouse (which includes a partner in couples with an agreement to marry) makes a substantial contribution in money or money's worth to the improvement of property that person is entitled to a beneficial share. This avoids the need to prove common intention under a resulting trust and may therefore be advantageous.

PRACTITIONERS' CHECKLIST ON COHABITANT CO-OWNERSHIP DISPUTES

11.141

- Establish legal ownership of the family home and the rights of any third parties, including the mortgagee.
- Gather detailed evidence as to equitable ownership and look to what the intention was at the date of purchase and subsequently, including:
    - documentary evidence (eg title documents, written agreements);
    - correspondence, declarations of trust;
    - evidence as to express discussions between the parties;
    - detrimental acts by the non-legal owner;
    - the history of the relationship and the whole course of dealing between the parties during the period of ownership;
    - direct and indirect contributions made to the purchase price;
    - direct and necessary indirect contributions to the mortgage repayments;
    - details of who carried out improvements to the property and on what basis.
- Consider whether there is an express trust or whether resulting or common intention constructive trust case law is appropriate to establish the parties' respective interests remembering the different approaches to stages 1 and 2.
- Consider issues relating to proprietary estoppel.
- Quantify the share claimed, and consider the date of valuation and whether equitable accounting will be appropriate.

- Notify and liaise with the mortgagee where appropriate.

- Enquire whether the cohabitants are engaged to be married.

- Consider whether conciliation or mediation would be appropriate.

- Consider whether an occupation order and/or injunction restraining disposition of the assets pending the hearing should be applied for.

- Consider the statutory provisions available and most applicable in relation to determining the shares in and disposition of the family home and other assets.

- Consider whether other provisions relating to chattels, personal property and financial provision for children are relevant and ensure that all proceedings are consolidated to enable the issues to be heard together in an appropriate jurisdiction.

- Consider the impact of costs, public funding and the statutory charge.

Framework cohabitation agreement

(FOR OWNER OCCUPIERS)

This Cohabitation Agreement is made this   day of   20

BETWEEN

(*insert name*) of (*insert address*) (hereinafter called "X") of the one part

and

(*insert name*) of (*insert address*).(hereinafter called "Y") of the other part

WHEREAS:

(1) The parties [are cohabiting] [intend to cohabit]

(2) The parties wish to enter into an agreement regulating their rights and obligations towards each other and [any children of the relationship and] in relation to their family home and other property

(3) The parties intend this agreement to be legally binding upon them [for a period of (*insert no.*) years] and have each [taken] [been advised to take] independent legal advice as to the effect of this agreement [and a certificate signed by each legal advisor on the effect of this agreement is annexed]

(4) Full and frank disclosure has been made by each party to the other of the material facts relating to their respective financial circumstances [and a statement of each party's assets, income and liabilities is set out in Schedule 1 hereto]

(5)(a) The parties presently have [no][*insert number*] child[ren] of their relationship, who is[are] [a] minor[s][, namely]:--

(*set out names, dates of birth, and details of parental responsibility*)

AND/OR

(b) X has [number] child[ren] by a previous relationship, [who is[are] [a] minor[s]]

(*set out names, dates of birth, and details of parental responsibility*)

AND/OR

(c)   Y has [*insert number*] child[ren] by a previous relationship, who is[are] [a] minor[s]

(*set out names, dates of birth, and details of parental responsibility*)

The Family Home—Legal Title
(6) The parties are presently living at [*insert address*] ("the family home") which is a [free][lease]hold property purchased in the [sole][joint] name[s] of [*insert name(s)*]

OR

(6) The parties (*or name of one of them as appropriate*) intend[s] to purchase as [their joint residence][the joint residence of the parties] a [free][lease]hold property at [*address*]("the family home") in the [joint] [sole] name[s] of [*insert name(s)*]

The Family Home—Beneficial Ownership
(7) The parties [intend to enter][have entered] into a deed of trust [dated (*insert date*)] which reflects their express common intention [to share][not to share] the beneficial interest in the family home as set out below. Furthermore they shall enter into a new deed of trust in respect of any other family home they may acquire in the future for their residence. [In default of any such deed of trust and subject to any contrary intention expressly included in the Conveyance, Transfer, Lease or Assignment or in any variation of or substitute for this agreement made between the parties, any replacement family home bought by the parties hereto shall be held in the same proportions as set out herein.]

IT IS HEREBY AGREED

(*Choose appropriate option from following possibilities*)

Sole beneficial ownership
1. That the family home [has been][will be] purchased in the sole name of [*name*] and irrespective of any direct or indirect contributions made towards the purchase price, mortgage repayments, maintenance or improvement of the home made by [*name of non-owning party*] he/she [has not and] will not acquire any beneficial interest in the family home.

(*In this situation, independent legal advice for both parties and particularly the non-owner is imperative.*)

OR

Equitable joint tenancy [converting to equitable tenancy in common]
1. That the beneficial interests of the parties in the family home are held as joint tenants in equity [unless and until severance of the joint tenancy occurs, whereupon

they shall hold as tenants in common in equity in the shares specified below.] (*In this case one of the following clauses relating to beneficial tenancies in common as may be appropriate from instructions should follow.*)

AND/OR

Equitable tenancy in common in fixed shares
1(a). That irrespective of their direct or indirect contributions made towards the purchase price, mortgage and mortgage-related repayments, maintenance or improvement of the family home made by either party, their beneficial interests in the property are held as tenants in common in equity in the following shares calculated with reference to the [net proceeds of sale as at the date of sale or transfer defined as (*insert definition agreed, eg the gross sale price less, sum required to redeem mortgage, estate agent's fees, legal expenses incurred in the sale*)] *or* [gross proceeds of sale as at the date of sale or transfer, with each party undertaking to redeem their share of the mortgage, estate agent's fees and legal expenses in the same proportion (*or specify other proportions agreed*)]:

X (*insert percentage*) and Y (*insert percentage*)

OR

Equitable tenancy in common in floating shares proportionate to direct contributions to the purchase of the family home
1(a). That their beneficial interests are held as tenants in common in equity in shares proportionate to their respective direct contributions towards the purchase of the family home calculated in the first instance as a percentage of the [gross] proceeds of sale as at the date of sale or transfer (*define or adapt if legal or estate agency expenses are to be deducted prior to calculation of proportions*) [but subject to each party redeeming their share of the mortgage redemption figure as at that date, to be calculated in the same proportions as their agreed contributions to the mortgage instalments [and linked endowment policy premiums] set out in clause 2, and subject also to account being taken of any lump sum capital repayment of the mortgage in accordance with clause 3].

1(b). For the avoidance of doubt, direct contributions to the purchase of the family home include (*specify as appropriate and indicate whether it is intended the list should be exhaustive:*)

[capital contributions (including right to buy/acquire or other discount) to the purchase price] (*where the home was originally the home of just one partner, the value of their unencumbered share at the outset of cohabitation could be inserted as their capital contribution*).

[lump sum repayment of mortgage capital pursuant to clause 3]

[payment of mortgage instalments] [pursuant to clause 2]

[payment of endowment policy premiums linked to mortgage] [pursuant to clause 2]

(*Consideration should be given and instructions taken as to whether the following should be specifically included or excluded and the position clarified in the agreement.*)

[AND DO NOT INCLUDE]

[contributions to the cost of repairs and/or improvements to the family home]

[legal expenses incurred on purchase and/or sale of the home]

1(c). A statement of the direct contributions made by each of the parties at the date hereof is set out in Schedule 2 hereto.

General note: The effect of this option is to create an express resulting trust which crystallises at the date of sale or transfer of the property at which point the beneficial interests can be calculated. Parties will need to ensure that records and receipts are kept of all contributions and this is a possible disadvantage of such a clause. Note also that the clause is looking at the contributions themselves and not at the effect of the contributions on any change in value of the property, which may be appropriate especially in respect of payment for improvements. If this is required, this should be made clear. Floating share calculations are of necessity complicated and to some extent cumbersome as will be seen. However, the advantage is that this is a method which may well commend itself to parties as being as fair as possible, both when entering into the agreement and on relationship breakdown. Thought needs to be given, however, to the position of a party who cannot make contributions due to changed circumstances. Do the parties want this to reduce that party's beneficial interest? Is this fair? In a situation where the inability to pay is triggered by child care undertaken on behalf of both parties, parties may wish to protect the beneficial interest of that party. See clause 10(b) below

Method of calculation:

The proportionate shares of each partner are calculated by determining the separate proportion of each partner for each relevant heading (eg capital contributions and mortgage) as a percentage of the combined contributions made by both parties under that heading and adding the percentages calculated for each partner for each heading together to arrive at their total proportion of the gross proceeds of sale from which their respective agreed proportions of the mortgage redemption figure should be deducted. The aim of using the gross proceeds of sale rather than the net proceeds of sale is to ensure that any increase or decrease in value is passed on on sale in proportion to the contributions originally made to the purchase price either by way of capital or mortgage.

A simple illustration may assist:

Assuming X and Y bought a property 10 years ago for £100,000 with a mortgage advance of £75,000 and have agreed to sell it for £120,000 on relationship breakdown, with a mortgage redemption figure of £65,000 in respect of an ordinary repayment mortgage:

Capital contributions on purchase were:

X – £10,000 (ie 10,000/100,000 = 10%)

Y – £15,000 (ie 15,000/100,000 = 15%)

Mortgage contribution arrangements in respect of repayment of the advance of £75,000

X – 75% of the mortgage (ie (75% × £75,000) ÷ (£100,000) = 56.25%

Y – 25% of the mortgage (ie (25% × £75,000) ÷ (£100,000) = 18.75%

Total shares subject to mortgage

X – 10% + 56.25% = 66.25%

Y – 15% + 18.75% = 33.75%

Mortgage redemption liability

X – (75% × £65,000) = £48,750

Y – (25% x £65,000) = £16,250

Thus Total share of gross proceeds of sale (£120,000) but subject to mortgage redemption liability (£65,000) is:

X – (66.25% × £120,000) – £48,750 = £30,750

Y – (33.75% × £120,000) – £16,250 = £24,750

(subject to payment of expenses related to the sale in the proportion agreed).

In a negative equity situation the calculation would result in a negative share for one or both parties. Although it would not effect the joint and several liability of joint mortgagors to the mortgagee, it would indicate the agreed proportions in which the resultant debt to the mortgagee should be paid.

If felt appropriate, the commentary on the method of calculation of the shares set out above could be included in the clause and a step by step guide to calculation could be detailed in a schedule by means of a formulaic example. This approach has been adopted in the Schedule to the Declaration of Trust below see page 305.

For a discussion of a net proceeds of sale calculation in respect of floating shares see Lush, 1993, pages 32–42.

Contributions to mortgage, mortgage related payments and other outgoings in respect of the family home

2(1). The mortgage repayments [and mortgage-related endowment policy premiums] shall be paid by (*insert name of paying party*) alone.

OR

2(1). [Subject to clause 10(b) below,] (*This should be inserted where the parties have agreed floating shares and a reduction in contributions to the mortgage during a period of child care suggested in clause 10(b).*) the parties shall contribute to the mortgage repayments [and mortgage-related endowment policy premiums] in the following proportions:--

X (*insert percentage*)

Y (*insert percentage*).

OR

2(1). The parties shall contribute to the mortgage repayments [and mortgage-related endowment policy premiums] in proportions to be agreed from time to time between the parties [and [subject to clause 10(b) below] their respective beneficial interests in the family home shall be calculated by reference to the payments actually made by each party].

Failure to pay

[2(2). If, other than [by agreement in writing,] [or][by virtue of one party having reduced their income in order to undertake child care of a child or children of the [parties] [family] [or] [by virtue of any practical arrangement whereby one party undertakes instead to make a greater contribution than agreed to the payment of other outgoings [or debts] in respect of the family home on behalf of] [both parties][the other party], one party fails to make his/her agreed contributions to the mortgage repayments [and mortgage-related endowment policy premiums], the calculation of the respective shares of the parties attributable to mortgage-related contributions [shall be adjusted to reflect the actual payments made] *OR* [shall not be thereby affected] [but in the event that these repayments are made in full or in part by the other party, unless otherwise agreed, such payments shall be treated as a loan to the party in default (*insert any terms with regard to interest*) by the other party. It is further agreed that on sale or transfer of the family home any sums outstanding in respect of such a loan be deducted from the defaulting party's share of the net proceeds of sale (*define here if not previously defined*) and paid to the other party without prejudice to their right to recover any further balance of the loan debt]. (*Carefully consider instructions on the various options and delete as appropriate. Note this will not affect each party's joint and several liability to the mortgagee.*)

Capital lump sum mortgage repayments

3. In the event that either party makes a capital payment in discharge or part discharge of any mortgage secured on the family home, that party's beneficial interest in the home shall be adjusted to reflect such a payment. [Calculation of the adjusted share shall be made as a percentage of the value of the family home at the date of the capital payment, which if not agreed between the parties shall be determined by an independent valuer appointed jointly by the parties or in default by a valuer to be appointed by the President of the Royal Institution of Chartered Surveyors (RICS).] [A note of such variation shall be endorsed hereon in accordance with clause 12 hereof.]

Improvements and Repairs

4(a). Unless previously agreed between the parties, improvements which may change the value of the family home shall not be undertaken. [Where such an agreement is reached, the parties' respective contributions to the cost of the improvements will be in the proportions agreed between them (*or specify the proportions here if appropriate*) and any necessary adjustments to their respective shares in the family home [which will reflect the change in value of the home] shall be calculated with reference to the value of the home at the date the work is commenced (*or insert other date if considered more appropriate*)] [as agreed by the parties or as determined by an independent valuer appointed jointly by the parties or in default by a valuer to be appointed by the President of the RICS]. A note of such variation shall be endorsed hereon in accordance with clause 12 hereof.]

4(b). Repairs to the property which are reasonable and necessary shall be paid for in the proportions

X (*insert contribution*)% and

Y (*insert contribution*) %,

save that any major repairs exceeding the cost of (*insert agreed threshold*) shall not be undertaken unless at least 2 (*or insert agreed number*) independent estimates have been obtained. Any other repairs shall not be undertaken without the prior agreement of the parties.

Non-monetary contributions

5. Unless previously agreed in writing and noted as a variation in accordance with clause 12, non-monetary contributions to the property shall not affect the parties' beneficial interests in the family home. [Nothing in this clause shall affect the agreement reached in clause 10(b) hereof.] (*Clause 10(b) considers changed contributions where one party gives up work to care for children and it is agreed that this will not affect the parties' beneficial interests.*)

Outgoings

6. Payment of [the ground rent and service charge due under the Lease of the family home],[building insurance premiums][contents insurance premiums] [all household bills including council tax, water rates, other utility bills (*define and/or add to these as appropriate, eg telephone, television rental and licence, food, joint holidays, decorating costs, minor repair costs etc.*) shall be made by the parties in the proportions

X (*insert contribution*) %

Y (*insert contribution*) %.

(*Note: Generally where parties are sharing the beneficial interest in the home, contributions to items relating to any lease or insurance of the property are likely to be made in the same proportions as those in which the beneficial interests are held. All parties will need to decide how the living expenses should be shared. There is no reason (other than lack of simplicity) why parties should not agree to pay bills in proportions specified by individual item. If this is decided, a schedule annexed to the agreement may be most appropriate.*)

Personal property and contents of the family home

7(a). All personal effects intended for the personal use of one party acquired prior to this agreement (*or specify other date such as when cohabitation began as appropriate*), or subsequently belong to that party and shall remain their separate property regardless of who acquired them or how they were acquired. (*This is aimed at items such as clothing, jewellery, personal computers etc. which may have been purchased, inherited or given as gifts. Any exceptions such as a family heirloom of the other party should be detailed and examples of items included may be specified or included in a Schedule.*)

7(b). All other personal property acquired by X prior to this agreement (*or specify other date such as when cohabitation began as appropriate*), whether by gift, inheritance or purchase [and listed in Schedule (*insert appropriate number*)] shall also remain the property of X, even though intended for the joint use of the parties during their period of cohabitation. (*This may include furniture, motor car, rugs, kitchen equipment etc. Provision for the running costs of a car could be set out here if appropriate.*)

7(c). All other personal property acquired by Y prior to this agreement (*or specify other date such as when cohabitation began as appropriate*), whether by gift, inheritance or purchase [and listed in Schedule (*insert appropriate number*)] shall also remain the property of Y, even though intended for the joint use of the parties during their period of cohabitation. (*This may include furniture, motor car, rugs, kitchen equipment etc. Provision for the running costs of a car could be set out here if appropriate.*)

Jointly acquired contents or other property and property acquired on credit

8. All property acquired after the date of this agreement (*or specify other date such as when cohabitation began inserted in clause 7*) and during the period of cohabitation, for the joint use and/or benefit of the parties in their home (including furniture, household or garden equipment) shall be owned jointly and in equal shares (*or specify shares agreed*) by the parties regardless of which of the parties acquired them, SAVE THAT any items acquired by one party by means of any loan, credit agreement or arrangement (other than a credit or charge card in the name of one party on which the other party is a second cardholder) shall [until such time as the full debt has been repaid] be owned solely by the party liable under such a loan, credit agreement or arrangement who shall retain sole liability for all repayments in respect of the credit obtained. Where items are acquired jointly on credit, by means of a joint bank loan, overdraft, joint credit or charge card (including a second cardholder arrangement), or other joint credit facility (other than a loan secured on the family home), these shall be jointly owned in equal shares (*or specify as appropriate*) and the parties shall be jointly responsible for making all the repayments in equal shares (*or specify as appropriate*).

(*Note: If loans are or may be taken from friends or relatives on an informal basis, it may be appropriate to except these from the above clause and make provision in a separate clause indicating where responsibility for repayment lies.*)

Bank and Building Society Accounts

9(a). Any Bank or Building Society Account or other capital asset (not previously referred to in this agreement) in the sole name of either party shall remain the sole property of that party.

9(b). Any Bank or Building Society Account or other capital asset (not previously referred to in this agreement) vested in the joint names of the parties shall belong to the parties in the proportions

(*insert percentage*) to X and

(*insert percentage*) to Y

notwithstanding the proportions of their respective actual contributions made to the account or to acquisition of the asset.

Children/Child Care

[10(a). The parties agree that they will share responsibility for the care of their children.] [This includes their intention to enter into a parental responsibility agreement in respect of any children of the relationship and to share in the costs of the birth of any child.] [Where both parties are working, they will take turns in staying at home with the children if they are ill or on holiday and no other child care arrangements can be made or are appropriate.]

AND/OR

[10(b). If [whilst the parties are cohabiting] one party [gives up work] [reduces their hours of work] to care for the children of the relationship, the other party will pay them [50% (*or specify percentage or figure as appropriate*) of their disposable income (*insert definition*)] until the youngest child [attends nursery/primary school] [reaches the age of 5 (*or specify other age agreed*)]. [During this period, the party undertaking the child care [shall continue to make their contributions to the mortgage and other outgoings previously referred to] [shall make reduced contributions to the mortgage and other outgoings namely (*either specify the new contributions if these can be agreed or in most cases indicate that these will be reduced in proportion to the carer's new share of the family's joint gross income, or as agreed between the parties*). Nothing in this clause will act to proportionately reduce the beneficial interest in the family home of the party undertaking the childcare.] (*This aims to protect the beneficial interest of the partner undertaking child care where the parties have agreed to the floating share method of calculation. Cross reference needs to be made to this clause in other relevant clauses.*)

[10(c). Any child support or maintenance received for the benefit of a child(ren) of one of the parties from a previous relationship shall be used for the benefit of [that][those] child(ren).]

Review

11. The parties agree to review this agreement every two years (*or specify other appropriate period*) and whenever there is a major change in their financial or personal circumstances including but not limited to the birth of a child, serious illness or injury, loss of employment, significant reduction or increase in either party's income or capital, with the intention of considering whether any variation of the agreement should be undertaken.

Variation

12. Any variation of this agreement shall be in writing and executed by both parties in the form of a deed. The variation shall be noted and endorsed upon each party's copy of this agreement.

Termination

13. This Agreement will be terminated on the happening of any of the following events;

i) The death of either party

ii) The parties marrying each other

iii) Mutual agreement of the parties that cohabitation shall cease whereupon the Separation Provisions set out below shall apply

iv) The expiry of (*insert number*) month[s] notice in writing by one party to the other that they wish to cease cohabiting and terminate the agreement whereupon the Separation Provisions set out below shall apply

v) The voluntary abandonment of the family home by one party for a period of (*insert number*) weeks, whereupon the Separation Provisions set out below shall apply.

[vi) The expiry of the agreement at the end of the agreed period of (*insert no. of years referred to in recital*) where one or both parties do not wish to renew the agreement. (*This will only be appropriate where the agreement is expressed to have a fixed duration.*).]

The Separation Provisions

The family home

14(a). As soon as possible on termination, each party should notify the other in writing whether or not they wish to remain in occupation of the family home [and, if not previously severed, will serve notice severing the joint tenancy in equity of the family home]. An independent open-market valuation of the property will be obtained by a valuer agreed by the parties or in default appointed by the President of the RICS. If only one party wishes to remain, they will be given a period of (*insert number*) months from the date of termination of the agreement in which to complete the purchase of the other party's share of the family home, calculated on the basis of the independent valuation and in accordance with the provisions of this agreement.

14(b). If both parties wish to remain, preference shall be given [to the party with whom the children of the relationship will reside] [the party in whom the legal title is vested] [the party who is in a position to complete the first purchase of the other party's interest as evidenced by a mortgage offer and or cleared funds sufficient for this purpose].

14(c). If neither party wishes to remain in the home, or if the party wishing to remain fails to complete within the specified period, the home shall be sold for the best price obtainable as agreed between the parties or in default of agreement certified by [the jointly instructed Selling Agent] [an independent valuer appointed by the President of the RICS].

Mortgage related payments by occupier

15. Pending sale of the family home, [the mortgage repayments [and mortgage related endowment policy premiums] shall [be made wholly by the party in occupation in satisfaction of any claim for an occupation rent] [shall continue to be paid by the parties in the proportions set out in clause 2 hereof] *and/or* [where one party has excluded the other party from the family home against their will and

without reasonable cause, the party remaining in occupation shall pay to the other party an occupation rent of a sum to be agreed or advised by an independent valuer].

(*Which option is appropriate will depend on who has made the major capital and mortgage contributions to the property and the reasons for the other party leaving the property.*)

Other outgoings

16. The parties agree to notify the relevant authorities and utility companies of the date on which cohabitation ceased and remain liable for their share of the outgoings up until that date. Thereafter, [the party in occupation shall make payment of all the outgoings specified in clauses 4(b) and 6] [the parties shall continue to make payments [in the same proportions] [in the following proportions (*specify proportions agreed*)] [in proportions which reflect the parties' ability to pay] pending sale of the home.

Bank and Building Society accounts, other capital assets, credit cards etc.

17. On termination of the agreement, other than by reason of death of one of the parties, the parties agree:--

i. to notify the banks and building societies concerned and close all accounts held in their joint names, destroying all cheques and cheque cards, cancelling standing orders and dividing the credit balances equally (*or state proportions*) between them or remaining liable in respect of any overdraft in the same proportions with each party being responsible for repayment and interest and charges on their allocated share of the debt and keeping the other party indemnified against the consequences of failure so to do.

ii. to notify all credit and charge card companies where the parties are joint or first and second cardholders, cancelling and destroying all relevant credit and charge cards and allocating responsibility for the debts at the point of closure in accordance with which of them is to retain the goods thereby purchased or enjoyed the benefit of the services thereby obtained, with each party being responsible for repayment and interest on their allocated share of the debt and keeping the other party indemnified against the consequences of failure so to do.

Other capital assets

iii. that any other capital asset jointly owned by the parties will be sold and divided between the parties equally (*or state appropriate proportions*) with incidental sale costs being borne in the same proportions. (*Where there is an endowment mortgage, consideration can be given to whether the endowment policy is to be surrendered on breakdown and the sum obtained divided or whether it may be possible to sell or transfer it to one of the parties. A clause could indicate that the parties agree to consider the options available.*)

Personal property and jointly owned property
18. On termination of this agreement, it is agreed that:

i. all personal effects, chattels and other property solely owned by one of the parties in accordance with the terms of this agreement will be retained by that party and any party not remaining in the family home will remove all their personal effects on or before sale or transfer of the property.

ii. all jointly owned property will be divided [equally (*or state appropriate proportions*)] by agreement between the parties. In default of agreement as to division of the goods, [all jointly owned items] [those jointly owned items which both parties wish to retain] will be sold, and the proceeds divided [equally (*or state appropriate proportions*)] between them.

Mediation/Arbitration
19. In case of any dispute arising concerning the terms of this agreement, the parties agree that the dispute will be referred to (*insert name or organisation*) who will act as a [mediator][arbitrator] between the parties [without prejudice to either party's right to apply to the court for resolution of the dispute] [whose decision shall be binding upon both parties].

Maintenance and children
20. On termination of this agreement, [neither party shall be under any obligation to maintain the other.] [X will pay Y (*insert figure and amend order of parties as appropriate*) per month for (*specify fixed period if appropriate*).] [Where one party has reduced their income in order to undertake child care responsibilities any payments being made in accordance with clause 10(b) shall continue to be paid save that child support payments being made in respect of the child(ren) may be made in satisfaction or partial satisfaction of this clause (*or indicate any other agreement which the parties wish to insert*).]

21. On termination of the agreement, the children shall live with (X or Y *or specify how children will divide their time*) who shall ensure that they have regular contact with the other party and their family. Neither party shall change the child(ren)'s surname without the consent of the other party. (*This is of course subject to any orders made by the court.*)

22. This agreement shall be interpreted in accordance with the law of England and Wales. Any provision found by the Court to be illegal, invalid or unenforceable may be severed from the agreement and the remaining provisions shall continue to have full force and effect.

Signed as a deed by X

in the presence of

Signed as a deed by Y

in the presence of

Schedule 1

Insert statement of the parties' respective assets, income and liabilities (See Recital 4)

Schedule 2

Insert statement of the parties' respective direct contributions at the date of the agreement (See clause 1(b)).

Note that additional Schedules may have been referred to in clauses 6 & 7, and the footnote to clause 1(b) (method of calculation).

Appendix II

Declaration of trust for co-owners of freehold Property with deferred tenancy in common and subject to ordinary repayment mortgage

THIS DECLARATION OF TRUST is made this   day of   20
BETWEEN (*insert name*) of (*insert address*) (X) and
(*insert name*) of (*insert address*) (Y), hereinafter jointly called "the co-owners"

IT IS HEREBY AGREED AND DECLARED THAT:--

1. By a [conveyance][transfer] dated (*insert date*) and made between (*insert seller's name*) of the one part and the co-owners of the other part, the freehold property known as (*insert address of the family home*) [and registered at HM Land Registry under Title Number (*insert number*)] (hereinafter called "the Family Home") was for a purchase price of £(*insert purchase price*) [conveyed][transferred] to the co-owners in fee simple TO HOLD as joint tenants in equity until severance of the equitable joint tenancy, whereupon they shall hold as tenants in common in equity in the shares specified in clause 5 below.

2. The co-owners purchased the Family Home to provide a joint home for themselves [and their children] (*Add details where the children are not all the children of the relationship*)]. (*Note that this makes clear the purpose of the trust which may be important in the context of the Trusts of Land and Appointment of Trustees Act 1996*). [The co-owners have entered into a Cohabitation Agreement dated (*insert date*) governing their occupation of the Family Home]. (*Where a Cohabitation Agreement is being entered into, the clauses governing the beneficial interests in the Family Home may be referred to or repeated in the declaration of trust. Advisors should ensure that the two documents are not inconsistent as regards the beneficial interests in the family home or indicate which is to prevail.*)

3. The Family Home has been purchased with the aid of a mortgage advance of £(*insert sum of advance*) from (*insert name of mortgagee*) plus capital contributions made by [each of the co-owners] (*or specify which co-owner if only one*) to the Total Purchase Price in the proportions referred to in Schedule 1 hereto.

4. The mortgage is an ordinary repayment mortgage and [subject to any agreed adjustment of contributions consequent upon reduction of a co-owner's income due to child care responsibilities and set out in the cohabitation agreement (*the relevant clause should be referred to or a similar clause added here where there is no cohabitation agreement*)] the co-owners covenant with each other to contribute

349

[equally][in the following proportions] to the mortgage repayments [and upon sale or transfer of the Family Home, to redeem the mortgage in those same proportions *(This should be used where the calculations of the shares are based upon the gross proceeds of sale and the co-owners' agree to redeem their share of the mortgage redemption figure)*]:-

[X *(insert proportion)*% and Y *(insert proportion)*%]

Fixed shares

5. Upon severance of the equitable joint tenancy and thereafter, the co-owners shall HOLD the Family Home as tenants in common in equity in [equal shares]

OR

[the shares specified below calculated with reference to the net proceeds of sale defined as *(insert definition agreed, eg the gross sale price less, sum required to redeem mortgage, estate agents fees, legal expenses incurred in the sale)*]:—

X *(insert percentage)* and
Y *(insert percentage)*]

regardless of the contributions actually made towards the purchase price, mortgage repayments and other outgoings.

OR

Floating shares

5(a). Upon severance of the equitable joint tenancy and thereafter, the co-owners shall [subject to clause 6 below] HOLD the Family Home as tenants in common in equity in shares calculated by ascertaining in the first instance their respective proportions of direct contributions towards the purchase of the family home expressed as a percentage of the [gross] proceeds of sale *(define or adapt if legal or estate agency expenses are to be deducted prior to calculation of proportions)* but subject to deducting from each party's respective proportions, their individual mortgage redemption liability required to redeem their share of the mortgage redemption figure to be calculated in accordance with clause 4 as at the date of sale or transfer of the family home. The method of calculation of the co-owners' respective beneficial interests is set out in Schedule 1 hereto.

5(b). For the avoidance of doubt, direct contributions to the purchase of the family home include *(specify as appropriate and indicate whether it is intended the list should be exhaustive)*:—
[capital contributions (including right to buy/acquire or other discount, incidental purchase costs) to the total purchase price]
[payment of mortgage instalments in accordance with clause 4 hereof]
[legal expenses incurred on purchase of the home]

[AND DO NOT INCLUDE]
[contributions to the cost of repairs and/or improvements to the family home]

Failure to pay mortgage repayments

6. If, other than [by agreement of the co-owners in writing,] [by operation of the Separation Provisions of the Cohabitation Agreement made between the co-owners and dated (*insert date*)] [or] [by virtue of one of the co-owners having reduced their income in order to undertake child care on behalf of them both] [or] [by virtue of any practical arrangement whereby one co-owner undertakes instead to make a greater contribution than agreed to the payment of other outgoings [or debts] in respect of the family home on behalf of] [both co-owners][the other co-owner], one of them ("the co-owner in default") fails to make his/her agreed contributions to the mortgage repayments, it is hereby agreed that the calculation of the respective beneficial shares of the co-owner in default in the family home [shall not be thereby affected] *or* [shall be affected in so far as the consequent increased indebtedness to the mortgagee shall be added to the proportion of the mortgage redemption figure to be debited from the co-owner in default on sale or transfer of the Family home. Any payment towards this debt made by the other co-owner to the mortgagee, unless otherwise agreed, shall be treated as a loan to the co-owner in default (*insert any terms with regard to interest*), which it is agreed may at the date of the sale or transfer be deducted from the co-owner in default's beneficial interest in the Family Home in so far as it has not been repaid and without prejudice to the other co-owner's right to recover any further balance of the loan debt.] (*This last option assumes instructions have been given that other than in specified situations, any default by one co-owner of the mortgage repayments is to remain that co-owner's debt and that any additional repayments made are to be treated as a loan to the co-owner in default.*)

General Note: Carefully consider instructions on the issue of failure to pay and cross refer to any Cohabitation Agreement executed by the co-owners. Other relevant clauses included in the draft cohabitation agreement (above) can be inserted instead in the declaration in the same form where no cohabitation agreement is to be executed. In particular clauses in relation to sharing of outgoings, procedure and effect of payment of repairs and improvements, non-monetary contributions, lump sum repayment of mortgage.)

Signed as a deed by X
in the presence of

Signed as a deed by Y
in the presence of

Schedule 1

Method of calculation of shares of co-owners following severance of the equitable joint tenancy

1. Calculate the Total Purchase Price:
> **ADD**
>> Purchase Price +
>> Legal Costs and Disbursements
>> **TOTAL PURCHASE PRICE**

2. Calculate capital contribution of each co-owner
> **ADD**
>> Capital paid by X +
>> Right to buy discount etc. +
>> Contribution to Legal Costs made by X
>> **X'S TOTAL CAPITAL CONTRIBUTION**

> **Divide** this by the TOTAL PURCHASE PRICE:
>> $$\frac{\text{X'S TOTAL CAPITAL CONTRIBUTION}}{\text{TOTAL PURCHASE PRICE}} = \textbf{X's capital share\%}$$

> **Repeat in relation to Y:**
>> $$\frac{\text{Y'S TOTAL CAPITAL CONTRIBUTION}}{\text{TOTAL PURCHASE PRICE}} = \textbf{Y's capital share\%}$$

3. Calculate the mortgage share of each co-owner
$$\frac{\text{Total mortgage advance} \times (\% \text{ payable by X in clause 4})}{\text{TOTAL PURCHASE PRICE}} = \textbf{X's mortgage share\%}$$

$$\frac{\text{Total mortgage advance} \times (\% \text{ payable by Y in clause 4})}{\text{TOTAL PURCHASE PRICE}} = \textbf{Y's mortgage share\%}$$

4. Calculate each co-owner's total share of the purchase price:
> **ADD**
>> X's capital share +
>> X's mortgage share
>> **X's total share %**

Then:
> **Repeat in relation to Y**

5. Calculate each co-owner's liability in respect of redemption of the mortgage
Multiply mortgage redemption figure **by** % payable by X in clause 4

Then:
> **Repeat in relation to Y**

6. Calculate final share of each co-owner on sale
Multiply
X's total share % **by** Gross Proceeds of Sale and **DEDUCT** X's redemption liability
> **Repeat in relation to Y**

Appendix III

List of Useful Addresses, Telephone Numbers and Websites

Child Support

Child Support Practitioners' Group
Contact James Prirrie,
Family Law Consortium
2 Henrietta Street
LONDON WC2E 8PS

Domestic Violence

Criminal Injuries Compensation Authority
Tay House,
300 Bath Street,
Glasgow G2 4GR
Tel: 0141 331 2287
Website: www.cica.gov.uk

REFUGE 24–Hour Domestic Violence Helpline
Tel:0990 995443

Women's Aid Federation, England
PO Box 391
Bristol BS99 7WS

Women's Aid National Domestic Violence
Helpline 0845 702 3468

Welsh Women's Aid, Cardiff
Tel: 029 2039 0874

Housing and Homelessness

Shelter
88 Old Street,
London, EC1 9HU
Tel: 020 7253 0202
Website: http://www.shelter.org.uk

Shelter Cymru
25 Walter Road
Swansea SA1 5NN
Tel: 01792 469400

Counselling and Mediation

Afro-Carribbean Family Mediation Service
Mrs Myrtle Kirton: Director
Suite 83
Eurolink Business Centre
49 Effra Road
London SW2 1BZ
Tel: 0207 733 0637
Fax: 0207 733 0637
Emergency tel: 0207 737 2366
Telephone helpline: 0207 738 6090

Family Mediators Association
1 Wyvil Court
Wyvil Road
London SW8 2TG
Tel: 020 7881 9400

Family Mediation Wales
66 Lower dock Street
Newport
South Wales NP20 1 EF
Tel: 01633 263065
Fax: 01633 222743
National Family Mediation
9 Tavistock Place
London WC1H 9SN
Tel: 020–7383 5993
Website: http://www.nfm.u-net.com/

RELATE
Herbert Gray College
Little Church Street
Rugby CV21 3AP

Tel: 01788 573241

UK College of Family Mediators
24–32 Stephenson Way,
London NW1 2HX
Tel: 020 7391 9162 / 9158
Website: http://www.ukcfm.co.uk/

PIPPIN (Parents in Partnership – Parent Infant Network)
Dr Mel Parr:
Director'Derwood'
Todds GreenStevenage
Herts SG1 2JE
Tel: 01438 748478/ 01992 471355
Fax: 01438 748182/ 01992 444579

General

Solicitors' Family Law Association
PO Box 302
Orpington BR6 8QX
Tel: 01698 850227
Website: HYPERLINK http://www.sfla.org.uk www.sfla.org.uk

National Association of Child Contact Centres
Minerva House
Spaniel row
Nottingham NG1 6EP
Tel: 0115 948 4557
Fax: 0115 941 5519
E-mail: contact:naccc.org.uk
Website: www.naccc.org.uk

Websites

CAFCASS (Children and Families Court Advisory and Support Service) – http://www.cafcass.gov.uk/

Child Support Agency – http://www.dss.gov.uk/csa/

Court Service – http://www.courtservice.gov.uk

Criminal Injuries Compensation Authority – http://www.cica.gov.uk

Department of London Transport and the Regions (Housing) – http:// HYPERLINK http://www.housing.dltr.gov.uk www.housing.dltr.gov.uk

Department of Work and Pensions (Formerly the Department of social security) – http://www.dss.gov.uk

Home Office – http:// HYPERLINK http://www.homeoffice.gov.uk www.homeoffice.gov.uk

Inland Revenue – http://inlandrevenue.gov.uk

Law Society – http://www.lawsociety.org.uk

Legal Services Commission – http:// HYPERLINK http://www.legalservices.gov.uk www.legalservices.gov.uk

London Partnerships Register — http://www.london.gov.uk/mayor/partnerships

Lord Chancellor's Department – http://www.lcd.gov.uk

National Assembly for Wales – http://www.wales.gov.uk

National Family and Parent Institute – http://www.nfpi.org

Scottish Executive – http://www.scottish.executive.gov.uk

Solicitors' Family Law Association (SFLA) – http://www.sfla.org.uk

The Stationery Office (for all UK legislation) – http:// HYPERLINK http:// www.hmso.gov.uk www.hmso.gov.uk

Bibliography

Amos, "Financial Injuctive Relief under the 1989 Act" [1994] *Fam Law* 445

Arden, "From to Greenwich to Harrow: A Trip down Memory Lane"[1997] 1 *JHL* 3

Arden and Hunder, *Homelessness and Allocations: A Guide to the Housing Act 1996 Parts VI and VII*, Legal Action Group, 1997

Bailey-Harris, Barron and Pearce, "Settlement Culture and the Use of the "no Order" Principle under the Children Act 1989" (1999) *CFLQ* 11:53

Barlow, *Living Together: A Guide to the Law*, Fourmat, 1992

Barlow, *Cohabitants and the Law*, 2nd edition, Butterworths, 1997

Barton and Douglas, *Law and Parenthood*, Butterworths, 1995

Barlow and Duncan, "New Labour's Communitarianism, Supporting Families and the "Rationality Mistake: Part II [2000] (22) (2) *JSWFL* 130 – 143.

Barton, *Cohabitation Contracts*, Gower, 1985

Berkowits, "The Family and the Rent Acts: Reflections on Law and Policy" [1982] *Journal of Social Welfare Law* 83–100

Bird, *Child Maintenance*, Family Law,

Bissett-Johnson, "Parents and Children – A Scottish White Paper on Family Law" [2000] IFL 155

Bond, *Simon's Taxes*, Butterworths (looseleaf encyclopaedia)

Burrows, "A Child's Understanding" [1994] Fam Law 579

Burrows (gen ed), *Butterworths Family Law Guide*, Butterworths, 1997

Burrows, *Legal Aid and the Family Lawyer* [2000] *Fam Law* 834

Butler *et al*, "The Children Act 1989 and the Unmarried Father" (1993) 5 JCL 157 and [1993] *Fam Law* 90

Children Act Advisory Committee, Annual Reports, Lord Chancellors' Department 1993/4 and 1994/5

Children Act Advisory Committee, Final Report, 1997

Children Act Advisory Committee, *Handbook of Best Practice in Children Act Cases*, 1997

Conway, "Shared Residence Orders" [1996] *Fam Law* 435

Cooke, "The 2001 Land Registration Bill" [2001] *Fam Law 753*

CPAG, *Child Support Handbook*, 4th edn, 2000/2001

CPAG, *Welfare Benefits Handbook,* 2000/2001

Cretney and Masson, *Principles of Family Law* 6th edn, Sweet and Maxwell, 1997

Crisell, "Injunctions v Bail Conditions", [1995] *Fam Law* 85

Daniel, "Spouses, Cohabitees, Their Home and Lenders" [1990] *Fam Law* 445–447

Department of the Environment, *Access to Local Authority and Housing Association Tenancies*, January 1994

Department of the Environment, Code of Guidance on Parts VI and VII of the Housing Act 1996, December 1996

Department of the Environment, *Our Future Homes* (Cm 2901), 1995

DETR, *Quality and Choice: A Decent Home for All*, 2000

DLTR, Draft Code of Guidance on Allocations and Homelessness, December 2000

Eekelaar, *Do Parents Have a Duty to Consult?* (1988) *LQR* 337

Family Law Advisory Board, *Report to the Lord Chancellor on the Question of Parental Contact in Cases where there is Domestic* Violence, The Stationery Office, April 2000

Gouriet, "Cohabitation Update" [2000] *Fam Law* 210)

Grace, *Policing Domestic Violence in the 1990s*, HMSO, 1995

Hayton, "Equitable Rights of Cohabitees" (1990) 54 *The Conveyancer* 370–387

Herring, *Family Law*, Longman, 2001

Hoggett, Pearl, Cooke and Bates, *The Family, Law and Society*, 4th edn, Butterworths, 1996

Home Office, *Supporting Families*, Home Office, 1998

Home Office, *A Choice By Right* Home Office, 2000a

Home Office, *Multi-Agency Guidance for Addressing Domestic Violence,* Home Office, 2000a

Home Office, *Domestic Violence: Break the Chain*, Home Office, 2000a

Horton, *Family Homes and Domestic Violence: The New Legislation*, FT Law and Tax, 1996

Humphries, "Occupation Orders Revisited" [2001] *Fam Law* 542

Jackson, "People who live together should put their affairs in order" [1990] *Fam Law* 439–441

Kaganas and Day Sclater, "Contact and Domestic Violence – The Winds of Change?" [2000] *Fam Law* 630

Kenny and Kenny, *The Trusts of Land and the Appointment of Trustees Act 1996*, Sweet and Maxwell, 1997

Law Commission, *Distribution on Intestacy* (Law Com No. 1 187), 1989

Law Commission, *Family Law Review of Child Law Guardianship and Custody* (Law Com No. 172), HMSO, 1988

Law Commission, *Fourteenth Annual Report, 1978–1979* (Law Comm No. 97), HMSO, 1979

Law Commission, *Reform of the Grounds of Divorce; the Field of Choice* (Cmnd 3132), HMSO, 1966

Law Commission, *Transfer of Land: Trusts of Law* (Law Com. No. 181), 1989

Law commission, *Claims for Wrongful Death,* (Law Com. No. 263), 1999

Law Society, *Cohabitation – Proposals for Reform of the Law*, 1999

McRae, *Cohabiting Mothers: Changing Marriage and Motherhood*, Policy Studies Institute, 1993

Maidment, "The Law's Response to Marital Violence in England and the USA" (1977) 26 *International and Comparative Law Quarterly* 403–444

Maidment, *Parental Responsibility: Is There a Duty to Consult?* [2001] *Fam Law* 518

Miers, *State Compensation for Criminal Injuries*, Blackstone Press, 1997

Mirless-Black, Home Office Research Study 191: *Domestic Violence*, 1999

Mostyn, *Child's Pay*, 2nd edn, Sweet and Maxwell, 1996

National Inter-Agency Working Party, *Domestic Violence*, Victim Support, 1992

Office of National Statistics, *Social Trends 27*, The Stationery Office, 1997

Office of Natinal Statistics, *Social Trends 30*, The Stationary Office, 2000

Oliver, "Why do people live together" [1982] *Journal of Social Welfare Law*, 209–222

Pahl, "Police Response to Battered Women" [1982] *Journal of Social Welfare Law* 337–343

Pahl (ed), *Private Violence and Public Policy. The Needs of Battered Women and the Response of Public Services*, Routledge, 1985

Parker and Eaton, "Opposing Contact", [1994] *Fam Law* 636

Pickford, *Fathers, Marriage and the Law*, Family Policy Studies Centre, 1999

Pizzey, *Scream Quietly or the Neighbours will hear*, Penguin Books, 1974

Rodgers, *Private Sector Housing Law*, Butterworths, 1995

Ross. "The Implications of White v White for Inheritance Act claims" [2000] *Fam Law* 547–550 and 619–623

Sawyer, "The competence of children to participate in family proceedings" [1995] CFLQ 7(4) 180

Scottish Executive White Paper, *Improving Scottish Family Law*, 2000

Scottish Law Commission, *Report on Family Law* (Scot Law Com No. 135), 1992

Scottish Law Commission, *The Effects of Cohabitation in Private Law*, Discussion Paper No. 86, 1990

Sharp, "Paternity Testing – Time to update the law" [2000] *Fam Law* 560, Smart and Stevens, Cohabitation Breakdown, Family Policy Studies Centre, 2000

Solicitors Family Law Association, *Fairness for Families – Proposals for Reform of the Law on Cohabitation*, SFLA, 2000

Solicitors Family Law Association, *Guide to Good Practice for Solicitors Acting For Children* SFLA, 1999

Sparkes, "The Quantification of Beneficial Interests: Problems arising from Deposits, Mortgage Advances and Mortgage Instalments" (1991) 11 Oxford Journal of Legal Studies 39–62

Spon-Smith, "Provsion of a Home under Children Act 1989, Sch 1 – A Suggested Trust Deed" [1999] Fam Law 763.

Treitel, *The Law of Contract*, 9th edn, Stevens, 1995

Vine, "Is the paramountcy principle compatible with Article 8? [2000] *Fam Law* 826

Weitzman, *The Marriage Contract: Couples, Lovers and the Law*, Free Press (New York), 1981

White *et al*, *The Children Act in Practice*, 2nd edn, Butterworths, 1995

White Paper, *Adoption: The Future* (Cm 2288), 1993

White Paper, *Children Come First* (Cm 1264), 1990

White Paper, *Improving Child Support* (Cm 2745), 1995

White Paper, *A New Contract for Welfare: Children's Rights and Parents' Responsibilities* (Cm 4349), 1999

Wikeley, "Income Support, Mortgage Interest and the Concept of abandonment" [2001] Fam Law 672

Wikeley, *Child Support: the New Scheme Parts I-IV* [2000] Fam Law 820 – 825 & 888 – 892, & *Family Law* [2001] 35 – 38 & 125 – 129

Wikeley, "Income Support, Mortgage Interest and the Concept of abandonment" [2001] Fam Law 672

Woelke, "Transfer of Tenancies" [1999] Fam Law 72.

Wood, Lush and Bishop, *Cohabitation: Law, Practice and Precedents*, Family Law, 2001

Wragg, "Constructive Trusts and the Unmarried Couple" [1996] Fam Law 484

Index